Reflections on Human Potential

BRIDGING THE PERSON-CENTERED
APPROACH AND
POSITIVE PSYCHOLOGY

Edited by
Brian E. Levitt

PCCS BOOKS
Ross-on-Wye

First published in 2008

PCCS BOOKS Ltd
2 Cropper Row
Alton Road
Ross-on-Wye
Herefordshire
HR9 5LA
UK
Tel +44 (0)1989 763 900
www.pccs-books.co.uk

This collection: © Brian E. Levitt, 2008

Preface © B.E. Levitt, 2008; Introduction, © S. Joseph & T.G. Patterson, 2008;
Chapter 1 © C.R. Rogers, 2008; Chapter 2 © J. Bozarth & B.T. Brodley, 2008;
Chapter 3 © T. Merry, 2008; Chapter 4 © B.E. Levitt, 2008;
Chapter 5 © K. Tudor, 2008; Chapter 6 © P.F. Schmid, 2008;
Chapter 7 © J. Bozarth and C.-C. Wang, 2008;
Chapter 8 © J.H.D. Cornelius-White & J. Kriz, 2008;
Chapter 9 © A. Zucconi, 2008; Chapter 10 © C. Wolter-Gustafson, 2008;
Chapter 11 © K. Tudor, 2008; Chapter 12 © A.C. Bohart, 2008;
Chapter 13 © E. Freire et al., 2008; Chapter 14 © J.A. Mejia, 2008;
Chapter 15 © K.A. Moon, 2008; Chapter 16 © N. Nera, 2008;
Chapter 17 © G. Prouty, 2008; Chapter 18 © B.E. Levitt, 2008.

All rights reserved.
No part of this publication may be reproduced, stored in a retrieval system, transmitted or utilised in any form by any means, electronic, mechanical, photocopying or recording or otherwise without permission in writing from the publishers.
The authors have asserted their rights to be identified as the authors of this work in accordance with the Copyright, Designs and Patents Act 1988.

**Reflections on Human Potential:
Bridging the person-centered approach and positive psychology**

A CIP catalogue record for this book is available from the British Library

ISBN 978 1 898059 96 7

Cover design by Old Dog Graphics
Printed by Athenæum Press, Gateshead, UK

For Noel,
my love always.
Thank you for sharing this journey so fully all these years.

For Barbara,
my mentor and friend.
Your voice will be with me always.

ACKNOWLEDGEMENTS

On a number of levels, this book was a greater challenge than my previous one. In seeing it through, one person was always there for me. That person is my husband and partner in life, Noel Nera. He has my deepest gratitude for his constant and unconditional support, as well his appreciation for what this work and these ideas mean to me.

Two other authors in this volume, Kathy Moon and Carol Wolter-Gustafson, provided enormous validation and support at various points along the way, helping me not to give up on this project. They, too, have my gratitude.

Special acknowledgment goes to my mother, who introduced me to the joys of reading, and my father, who introduced me to the joys of language—precious gifts that have brought me a life filled with wonder. Working with my father in his translation of Javier Armenta Mejia's chapter on sexual diversity was an unexpected and unforgettable gift.

My thanks go to my publishers, Pete Sanders and Maggie Taylor-Sanders, and the team at PCCS Books (Sandy, Jill, Heather, Di, Sue and Helen). They continue to support me in making whatever I visualize become a reality. Stephen Joseph inspired me to expand my earlier ideas for this project, and to build bridges beyond the person-centered community. My thanks go to him also.

Acknowledgment must go to Nebraska Press for allowing me to reproduce Carl Rogers' 1963 classic paper on the actualizing tendency here. Of course, thanks to Jerold Bozarth and Barbara Brodley for allowing their 1991 paper on the actualizing tendency to be a part of this project. Barbara was my mentor and friend. She died as I was nearing completion of this book. Typically generous in her correspondence over the years, Barbara once sent me an email that said simply, 'publish.' I know she would have enjoyed seeing this book in print.

Special thanks again to BAPCA (British Association for the Person-Centred Approach) for permitting Tony Merry's 2003 paper on the actualizing tendency to appear here. Tony was planning to write a paper on the actualizing tendency for my previous book, *Embracing Non-Directivity*, but he died before completing it. He expressed such enthusiasm over being a part of that project. It is only fitting that his paper on the conundrum of the actualizing tendency appear in this follow-up project, grouped with Rogers' 1963 'motives' paper and Bozarth and Brodley's 1991 'functional concept' paper. Tony published my first paper, and will always have my gratitude for taking my voice seriously and supporting my writing.

My admiration goes to each of the authors in this volume—all that is special in these pages is due to them. It is an honor to find myself among them. And of course, my gratitude goes to you, the reader. These words can only come alive with you.

CONTENTS

PREFACE   i

INTRODUCTION

   The Actualising Tendency: A meta-theoretical perspective for positive   1
   psychology   *Stephen Joseph and Thomas G. Patterson*

SECTION I   HISTORICAL CONTEXT: THE ACTUALIZING TENDENCY IN
                PERSON-CENTERED THEORY

1   The Actualizing Tendency in Relation to 'Motives' and to Consciousness   17
    (Nebraska Symposium, 1963)   *Carl R. Rogers*

2   Actualization: A functional concept in client-centered therapy (1991)   33
    Jerold D. Bozarth and Barbara Temaner Brodley

3   The Actualisation Conundrum (2003)   *Tony Merry*   46

SECTION II   CONTEMPORARY EXPLORATIONS OF HUMAN POTENTIAL IN
                 PERSON-CENTERED THEORY

4   The Myth of the Actualizing Tendency: The actualizing tendency concept   56
    as a guiding story   *Brian E. Levitt*

5   Verbal Being: From being human to human being   *Keith Tudor*   68

6   A Personalizing Tendency: Dialogical and therapeutic consequences of   84
    the actualizing tendency axiom   *Peter F. Schmid*

7   The 'Unitary Actualizing Tendency' and Congruence in Client-Centered   102
    Theory   *Jerold D. Bozarth and Chun-Chuan Wang*

8   The Formative Tendency: Person-centered systems theory,   116
    interdependence and human potential   *Jeffrey H.D. Cornelius-White*
    and Jürgen Kriz

SECTION III HEALTH AND HUMAN POTENTIAL

9 From Illness to Health, Well-Being and Empowerment: The person-centered paradigm shift from patient to client *Alberto Zucconi* 131

10 Non-dualism and Non-directivity: A person-centered concept of health and the fully functioning person *Carol Wolter-Gustafson* 147

11 Psychological Health: Autonomy and homonamy *Keith Tudor* 161

12 How Clients Self-Heal in Psychotherapy *Arthur C. Bohart* 175

SECTION IV MARGINALIZED POPULATIONS AND HUMAN POTENTIAL

13 Resilience and the Self-Righting Power of Development: Observations of impoverished Brazilian children in person-centered play therapy *Elizabeth Freire and associates* 187

14 Psychotherapy and Sexual Diversity: A person-centered approach *Javier Armenta Mejia* 195

SECTION V PERSONAL ACCOUNTS OF HUMAN POTENTIAL: THE PERSONAL AS THEORETICAL

15 An Essay on Children, Evil and the Actualizing Tendency *Kathryn A. Moon* 203

16 Conditions of Worth and an Artist's Journey *Noel Nera* 215

17 The Actualization of the Existential Self in Human Dying *Garry Prouty* 223

AFTERWORD

18 Beyond Fiefdoms *Brian E. Levitt* 227

Contributors 236

Index 239

PREFACE

Concepts as rich and layered as non-directivity and the actualizing tendency cannot possibly be captured by a simple definition, a few key phrases, or a single voice. The idea behind *Embracing Non-directivity* (the companion volume that preceded this book) was to present a multitude of perspectives on non-directivity, with the hope that this would flesh out the concept more fully for the reader in a way that one single voice never could. I have the same hope for *Reflections on Human Potential* in relation to the actualizing tendency—that bringing together varied perspectives on the actualizing tendency may bring a fuller understanding of this rich concept. I have the additional hope that this book will help build bridges beyond the person-centered community. In particular, this book is an attempt to build some bridges to the promising new discipline of positive psychology.

Joseph and Patterson begin our exploration by presenting the actualizing tendency concept as a theoretical construct that can inform positive psychology. They also reveal a rich vein of research in self-direction theory that supports the person-centered approach. Joseph and Patterson's introduction is followed by three essential historical papers on the actualizing tendency in the person-centered literature. The first is Rogers' seminal paper on the actualizing tendency, published originally in 1963. It is a critical paper in understanding person-centered theory as organismic. Bozarth and Brodley's 1991 paper on the actualizing tendency as a functional concept is one of the clearest pieces in the person-centered literature with respect to explaining the actualizing tendency and its place in person-centered practice. Rounding out this set of papers is Merry's 2003 paper on what he calls the conundrum of the actualizing tendency. This paper, in resolving an apparent contradiction in person-centered theory, elaborates on the significance of person-centered theory as organismic.

Building on a rich base of person-centered literature, five contemporary views in relation to the actualizing tendency are offered. In my chapter I explore the theoretical concept of the actualizing tendency as a guiding story that can inform values and behaviors. Tudor, in his paper, presses for an understanding of *the tendency to actualize*—an important shift in perspective from understanding the actualizing tendency as a noun. Schmid expands on the relational element of human potential, providing an essential perspective on the actualizing tendency. Bozarth and Wang provide a unifying perspective that brings together a number of important ideas in person-centered theory in understanding the actualizing tendency as it relates to therapist and client congruence. Cornelius-White and Kriz then go beyond the actualizing tendency to explore the broader concept of the formative tendency in relation to systems theory.

The next section is comprised of four papers that focus on health and the central role of the person. Zucconi outlines the dramatic paradigm shift that Rogers brought about with respect to models of illness and health—a shift that is captured in the simple yet profound change in language from the use of the word patient to the word client. Wolter-Gustafson issues a challenge to psychologists to catch up with other disciplines and to move beyond outmoded and dualistic frames of thinking. She asks us to consider the tremendous implications of a non-dualist organismic perspective, as offered by the person-centered approach. Tudor also offers a non-dualist perspective on illness and health with a call for dis-alienation and a recognition of the importance of the interdependence of the individual and the environment. Providing yet another essential perspective, Bohart examines the idea of clients as self-healers—an idea with far-reaching implications for an understanding of health, human potential, and helping relationships.

The person-centered approach has always been about the incredible potential of the individual. Rogers and others came to understand that this approach has political implications. These implications are reflected in the next section of this book, which offers two papers that focus on human potential in marginalized populations. Freire and her co-authors focus on a particularly vulnerable population, impoverished children, and highlight the ever-present potential for human change, as well as the political implications of the person-centered approach. Mejia's paper on sexual diversity and the person-centered approach helps us to understand just how profoundly political and liberating this approach can be.

We conclude our exploration of human potential with three very different personal accounts. Moon reflects on her own life, from the time she was a child to the present, and also on her experiences with children in group therapy, producing an essential contribution to the person-centered literature—it is a paper that is already close to my heart. Nera shares his journey as an artist, reflecting on conditions of worth and their impact on his development. His paper is uniquely theory-free, in the traditional sense, offering a deeply personal perspective on his own life. Prouty offers reflections on death and human potential through his own personal observations and the observations of his dying friend's wife and granddaughter. He highlights how facing the ultimate existential struggle can be a reflection of human potential, taking person-centered theory on actualization a step further.

Finally, I offer an afterword that attempts to synthesize my understanding of the implications of the collection of voices in this book. I have lived with these chapters in various ways for the better part of three years. They have each worked their way into my thoughts and my heart, leaving me a different person than when I began this journey. As such, I also attempt to share something of that impact and how it has become a part of the way I understand myself and my values in relationship to others and the field of psychology. I hope you will also discover the continually unfolding gifts these authors can bring when you take the time to encounter them.

Brian Levitt
Oakville
Winter 2008

Introduction

THE ACTUALISING TENDENCY: A META-THEORETICAL PERSPECTIVE FOR POSITIVE PSYCHOLOGY

STEPHEN JOSEPH AND THOMAS G. PATTERSON

Abstract

The positive psychology movement has gained in momentum over the last few years to become a major influence in mainstream psychology. Positive psychologists argue that for too long mainstream psychology has been overly concerned with distress and dysfunction at the expense of well-being and optimal functioning. Person-centred psychologists would agree with this shift in emphasis because they have always been concerned simultaneously with both the negative and the positive sides of human experience. Thus, there is now an unprecedented opportunity for person-centred psychologists to re-engage with mainstream research and discussion. In particular, the person-centred approach is able to offer an alternative paradigm based on the fundamental assumption that people are intrinsically motivated towards optimal functioning. In this chapter, which builds on our recent paper in the *Journal of Humanistic Psychology* (Patterson and Joseph, 2006), we will discuss the interface between person-centred psychology and positive psychology, with the ambition that these two psychologies be drawn closer together. First, we will provide a brief overview of positive psychology and person-centred personality theory, showing how person-centred theory offers a meta-theoretical approach to positive psychology that stands in contrast to the illness ideology, and that is consistent with calls by positive psychologists to develop alternative conceptions to the medical model. Second, we will show how the empirical evidence in positive psychology is supportive of person-centred theory.

POSITIVE PSYCHOLOGY AND PERSON-CENTRED THEORY

Positive psychology was formally launched by Martin Seligman in his presidential address to the American Psychological Association (Seligman, 1999). Much interest in the topic of positive psychology followed; for example, the publication of a a special issue of the journal *American Psychologist* (Seligman and Csikszentmihalyi, 2000), and of the British Psychological Society journal, *The Psychologist* (Linley, Joseph and Boniwell, 2003). For too long, positive psychologists claim, mainstream psychology has been concerned with distress and dysfunction at the expense of well-being and optimal functioning.

Correspondence concerning this introduction should be addressed to: Stephen Joseph, School of Sociology and Social Policy, University of Nottingham, Nottingham NG7 2RD, UK. Email: <stephen.joseph@nottingham.ac.uk>.

This is a stance that will be instantly recognisable by person-centred psychologists whose focus has always been on the fully functioning person and understanding people from the stance of thwarted potential, rather than from an illness ideology. Thus, there is much in common between positive psychology and person-centred psychology, but this rapprochement has largely gone unnoticed by the positive psychology movement principally because of the stereotype that counselling and psychotherapy are concerned with distress and dysfunction, and by the person-centred community because of their marginalisation from mainstream practice and research. One of the topics in positive psychology has been the re-evaluation of our understanding of human nature and the search for alternative conceptions of well-being and ill-being to the medical model, and it is here that we think the person-centred approach has most to offer.

PERSON-CENTRED PERSONALITY THEORY

According to person-centred theory, the human organism, in common with all living organisms, is born with an innate motivational drive, the *actualising tendency*. Rogers (1959) defined the actualising tendency as:

> [T]he inherent tendency of the organism to develop all its capacities in ways which serve to maintain or enhance the organism ... [This tendency involves] development toward autonomy and away from heteronomy, or control by external forces. (p. 196)

Under favourable social-environmental conditions, Rogers (1959) proposed that the individual's self-concept actualises in accordance with their *organismic valuing process* (OVP). The OVP refers to the evaluation of experiences in a manner that is consistent with one's intrinsic needs:

> [T]he human infant is seen as having an inherent motivational system (which he shares in common with all living things) and a regulatory system (the valuing process) which by its 'feedback' keeps the organism 'on the beam' of satisfying his motivational needs. (Rogers, 1959: 222)

Rogers (1957a) coined the term *fully functioning person* to describe an ideal of autonomous psychological functioning that occurs when self-actualisation is organismically congruent. The conceptualisation of the fully functioning person necessarily presupposes that such individuals have first been able to satisfy their most fundamental needs, as proposed by Maslow (1970). Although the term 'fully functioning' might seem dated to some, it essentially captures the characteristics of well-being and optimal functioning which are now the interest of positive psychologists.

Rogers (1963, 1964) proposed that the attitudes and behaviours of more fully functioning individuals are consistent with certain internally generated *value directions*. The value directions include moving toward increasingly socialised goals, where sensitivity to others and acceptance of others is positively valued, and where deep relationships are also valued positively; and moving in the direction of greater openness to experience, where the person comes to value an openness to all of his inner and outer experience (Rogers, 1964: 166).

However, in contrast, under unfavourable social-environmental conditions, the actualisation of the self-concept becomes discrepant from organismic experiencing causing a conflict, a state of *incongruence*:

> If self and experience are incongruent, then the general tendency to actualize the organism may work at cross purposes with the subsystem of that motive, the tendency to actualize the self ... The state is one of tension and internal confusion, since in some respects the individual's behavior will be regulated by the actualizing tendency, and in other respects by the self-actualizing tendency, thus producing discordant or incomprehensible behaviors. (Rogers, 1959: 197–203)

Thus, self-actualisation does not necessarily refer to the realisation of optimal psychological functioning (as it does in other humanistic writings), and Rogers (1959) is clear that conflict between self-actualisation and the actualising tendency is the usual state of affairs (see, Ford, 1991). Rogers (1959) further proposes that the actualising tendency is more usually usurped and thwarted by an unfavourable social environment characterised by *conditions of worth*. Conditions of worth refer to those attitudes, beliefs and values that are introjected by the individual from his or her social interactions, and which stem from the need of the developing infant for positive regard from significant others in his or her social environment. When the infant receives positive regard that is *conditional*, then he or she learns to evaluate experiences according to whether or not they satisfy the externally imposed conditions. As the child develops, the conditions of worth are introjected, acting as an internalised social other, and replacing organismic valuing as the principle governing the individual's attitudes and behaviour.

In this way, person-centred theory can be seen to adopt a position that, rather than naïvely asserting that people always behave in a positive and constructive way, recognises that the usual response to unfavourable social-environmental conditions is for the actualisation of the self to become incongruent with the individual's organismic experiencing, leading to development of the self in a direction that is discrepant with the *intrinsic* motivation toward positive and constructive functioning (Ford, 1991). As the individual becomes estranged from his or her organismic needs, there is a loss of trust in the person's own *internal* judgements, and an increasing tendency to defer to the external judgement of others, while defensive processes of distortion and denial of organismic experiencing act as potential sources of vulnerability to psychopathology (Rogers, 1959).

The aim of client-centred therapy is to create facilitative social-environmental conditions, within the context of a therapeutic relationship, that will enable the client to evaluate experiences organismically rather than in accordance with his or her conditions of worth (Rogers, 1957b, 1959). Rogers proposed six *necessary and sufficient* relationship conditions that characterise the social-environment that promotes therapeutic change—

the *core* conditions being empathy, congruence (genuineness) and unconditional positive regard (acceptance).

POSITIVE PSYCHOLOGY VERSUS THE MEDICAL MODEL

Thus, person-centred personality theory offers an alternative positive psychological paradigm to the medical model. Experiences of distress and dysfunction are not viewed as clinically separate disorders, but as expressions of thwarted potential as the organism self-actualises incongruently to its actualising tendency (see Joseph and Worsley, 2005). Such an approach resonates with recent work in positive psychology in which the illness ideology has come under question (Joseph and Linley, 2006a, 2006b).

In their groundbreaking critical analysis of the philosophical origins of clinical psychology, and their subsequent development of what they describe as an agenda for 'positive clinical psychology', Maddux, Snyder, and Lopez (2004) argued that clinical psychology is defined by its illness ideology. Maddux et al. (2004) reject these implicit medical-model assumptions and instead present the assumptions of what they describe as a positive clinical psychology:

Assumption 1: Positive clinical psychology is concerned with everyday problems in living as much as it is with the more extreme variants of everyday functioning, that we might refer to as psychopathology. Positive clinical psychology is also as much concerned with understanding and enhancing subjective well-being and effective functioning as it is with alleviating subjective distress and maladaptive functioning.

Assumption 2: Psychopathology, clinical problems, and clinical populations, differ *only in degree*, rather than in kind, from normal problems in living, non-clinical problems and non-clinical populations: they are considered to be related entities falling somewhere on a *continuum* of human functioning. This *dimensional model* suggests a focus on health and fulfilment as much as on illness and distress, since they are related constructs that can be defined by the same psychological theories. Within this dimensional model, normality and abnormality, wellness and illness, and effective and ineffective psychological functioning lie along a *continuum* of human functioning. They are not separate and distinct entities, rather they are considered extreme variants of normal psychological phenomena.

Assumption 3: Psychological disorders are *not* analogous to biological or medical diseases. Rather, they are reflective of problems in the person's interactions with his or her environment, and not only and simply of problems within the person himself or herself. Further, these problems in living are not construed as being located within an individual, but rather are construed as being located within the interactions between an individual, other people, and the larger culture. This demands a closer inspection of the much more complex interplay of psychological, social and cultural factors that bear on an individual's psychological health.

Assumption 4: Following on from these three former assumptions, the role of the positive clinical psychologist is to identify human strengths and promote mental health as assets which buffer against weakness and mental illness. The people who seek this assistance are clients or students, not patients. The professionals providing these approaches may be teachers, counsellors, consultants, coaches, or even social activists, and not just clinicians or doctors. The strategies and techniques they use are educational, relational, social, and political, not medical interventions. Further, the facilities providing this assistance may be centres, schools, or resorts, and not clinics or hospitals.

Maddux et al. call for positive psychology to develop a new vision. It is evident that person-centred psychology can offer a new vision for positive psychological practice whose ultimate purpose would be in line with the aspiration expressed by Sanders (2005), to 'plan and organise a future where to be frightened, confused and overwhelmed is not considered to be an "illness"' (p. 38).

CONVERGENCE BETWEEN PERSON-CENTRED THEORY, SELF-DETERMINATION THEORY AND POSITIVE PSYCHOLOGY

A number of meta-theoretical hypotheses arise from person-centred theory as outlined above. These will now be briefly summarised in order to set the context for our examination of both the theoretical and the empirical support for person-centred theory provided by recent developments in positive psychology.

Hypothesis 1. It is hypothesised that the human organism is born with an innate need to actualise, which he or she responds to by a process of organismic valuing.

Hypothesis 2. It is hypothesised that the presence of certain social-environmental conditions will result in an organismically congruent process of self-actualisation that will be positively associated with psychological well-being.

Hypothesis 3. It is further hypothesised that this process of change will result in certain specifiable outcomes, which will be positively associated with healthy psychological functioning.

Hypothesis 4. It is hypothesised that experiences of conditional regard from significant others will lead to displacement of the individual's organismic valuing process and the introjection of conditions of worth, with negative consequences for psychological well-being.

Hypothesis 5. Finally, it is hypothesised that more fully functioning individuals will share common, universal, and specifiable internally generated *value directions*.

Although the person-centred approach has received little attention within mainstream psychology over recent years, the idea human beings have an inherent tendency toward growth, development, and optimal functioning has become a focus for theory and research within the new movement of positive psychology. In particular, self-determination theory (SDT) is a more contemporary organismic theory of human motivation and personality functioning that also emphasises the central role of the individual's inner resources for personality development and behavioural self-regulation (see Deci and Ryan, 1985, 1991, 1995, 2000, 2002; Ryan and Deci, 2000, 2002). In accord with person-centred theory, SDT views the person as an active growth-oriented organism, attempting to actualise his or her potentialities within the environment he or she functions in. The organismic tendency toward actualisation is seen as one pole of a *dialectical interface*; the other pole being the social environment which can either be facilitating or inhibiting of the person's synthesising tendency (Ryan and Deci, 2002). SDT therefore provides the same meta-theoretical perspective as person-centred personality theory:

> The first is that human beings are inherently proactive, that they have the potential to act on and master both the inner forces (viz., their drives and emotions) and the external (i.e., environmental) forces they encounter, rather than being passively controlled by those forces ....
>
> Second, human beings, as self-organizing systems, have an inherent tendency toward growth, development, and integrated functioning ....
>
> The third important philosophical assumption is that, although activity and optimal development are inherent to the human organism, these do not happen automatically. For people to actualize their inherent nature and potentials—that is, to be optimally active and to develop effectively—they require nutrients from the social environment. To the extent that they are denied the necessary support and nourishment by chaotic, controlling, or rejecting environments, there will be negative consequences for their activity and development. (Deci and Vansteenkiste, 2004: 23–4)

These are the same meta-theoretical elements that constitute the person-centred personality theory of Carl Rogers (1959). The parallels between the two theories are shown with clarity in Barrett-Lennard's (1998) summary of person-centred meta-theoretical assumptions:

> *The organism functions as an organized whole, responding to its own, moving perceptual field.* The perceptual field is its reality ... This thought is in accord with viewing the organism as a purposeful open system, in particularly active interchange with its environment ... Through its behaviour, *the human organism interacts with perceived 'outer' and 'inner' reality in the service of the actualizing tendency.* ... Under certain conditions ... the organism develops strong inhibitory tendencies and 'defensive' patterns that block the flow of some classes of experiential data, impair and restrict the organismic valuing process, and imply a lowering of integration. ... The self-concept is a pivotal region of the organism's perceptual field, and a major influence in guiding behaviour. (pp. 75–6)

As well as theoretical convergence at the meta-theoretical level, there is also much theoretical convergence at the sub-theory level, although this is obscured by the different terminology of SDT and person-centred theory. As we discuss these points of terminological convergence in our previous paper, as well as the empirical evidence supporting self-determination theory (see Patterson and Joseph, 2006), we will only briefly summarise here the empirical evidence derived from the self-determination theory and positive psychology literature for each of the five meta-theoretical hypotheses that arise from person-centred theory.

Hypothesis 1. It is hypothesised that the human organism is born with an innate need to actualise which he or she responds to by a process of organismic valuing.

Empirical evidence supporting the existence of a growth-oriented organismic valuing process (OVP) comes from research by Sheldon, Arndt and Houser-Marko (2003). These investigators studied how people changed their goal pursuits over three different time periods (ranging from twenty minutes to six weeks). Based on the rationale that a tendency to move goal pursuits toward goal choices that are more beneficial for self and others would provide evidence for the existence of an OVP, the results showed that participants demonstrated relatively greater ratings shifts toward goals that were more likely to be beneficial to both their own well-being and that of others. Other research found that, in terms of the longitudinal effects of self-concordant goal selection, individuals who chose more *self-concordant* goals (i.e., intrinsically motivated choices which represent the individual's implicit interests and values), put more sustained effort into those goals, thus enabling them to better attain their goals. Goal attainment in turn is associated with stronger feelings of autonomy, competence and relatedness, which lead to greater well-being. Furthermore, these processes were illustrated in an integrated path model supported by causal modelling procedures (Sheldon and Elliot, 1999). These findings provide evidence supportive of the hypothesis that individuals who act concordantly with their organismic valuing process experience positive psychological growth and well-being (see also Sheldon, 2002).

Hypothesis 2. It is hypothesised that the presence of core social-environmental conditions will result in an organismically congruent process of self-actualisation that will be positively associated with psychological well-being.

Support for the predicted beneficial effects of the person-centred *core* relationship conditions is provided by research demonstrating that the provision of choice, acknowledgement of feelings, and opportunities for self-direction enhance intrinsic motivation because they give the individual a greater sense of autonomy (Deci and Ryan, 1985). A meta-analysis of research on tangible rewards (Deci, Koestner and Ryan, 1999), found that all expected tangible rewards made contingent on task performance undermine intrinsic motivation. In addition to the findings for tangible rewards, the research demonstrated that threats, deadlines, directives, pressured evaluations, and imposed goals all reduce intrinsic motivation, because, as with tangible rewards, these are all conducive to an external perceived locus of causality. These findings are in line with the person-centred assertion that certain conditions in the therapy relationship such as the communication of accurate empathy and unconditional positive regard to the client, are more likely to be therapeutically beneficial than the use of directive techniques.

Hypothesis 3. It is hypothesised that the process of change, which is most often observed in the context of therapy, will result in certain specifiable outcomes, which will be positively associated with healthy psychological functioning.

Person-centred theory asserts that the key indicators of successful therapy are increased congruence, increased openness to experience, and reduced defensiveness (Rogers, 1959). While research investigating the processes and outcomes of client-centred therapy is documented elsewhere (see Barrett-Lennard, 1998; Bozarth, Zimring and Tausch, 2002) we restrict ourselves here to a consideration of evidence relating Rogers' hypothesised positive therapeutic outcomes to healthy psychological functioning.

Increased congruence

The relationship between congruence and well-being is supported by evidence from empirical research by Koestner, Bernieri and Holt (1992). These researchers designed an experiment to investigate the relationship between the individual's autonomy and integration in personality. Participants were divided into an autonomy orientation group and a control orientation group. It was hypothesised that *autonomy* participants would demonstrate greater consistency or integration than *control* participants across three aspects of personality. Comparing participant scores on a free-choice behavioural measure and on a self-report-of-interest measure of intrinsic motivation, the first study found that more autonomous individuals showed greater integration between behaviours and feelings than non-autonomous individuals. A second study showed that autonomy was associated with greater congruence between self-report and action. Taken together, these findings suggest that more autonomous individuals show greater congruence between feelings and behaviours and are more fully integrated individuals. These findings fit with the person-centred assertion that more autonomously functioning, self-actualising individuals more accurately symbolise their organismic experiencing, and therefore show greater integration of feelings and behaviours.

Increased openness to experience

Openness to experience has been conceptualised by Rogers as *the polar opposite of defensiveness* and perhaps the most important outcome of therapeutic change (Rogers, 1957a, 1959, 1961). An overview of self-determination theory research findings regarding openness to experience is provided by Hodgins and Knee (2002). Of relevance to the person-centred hypothesis of therapeutic outcomes is evidence from research by Knee and Zuckerman (1996), indicating that increased openness to experience is positively associated with autonomous functioning. This study examined whether autonomy and control orientations are moderators of self-serving bias (a defensive attributional tendency in which people take more responsibility for success than for failure), and found that only participants who were high in autonomy orientation showed no self-serving bias, making fewer self-enhancing attributions for success and fewer defensive attributions for failure. These findings provide support for the person-centred proposal that self-directing individuals will show greater openness to experience, while also indicating that such individuals will tend to show a more accurate and less defensive perception of experience.

The above findings are complemented by research by Hodgins, Koestner and Duncan (1996), who examined naturally occurring interpersonal behaviour between students and their parents over a three-week period, while also investigating all student interpersonal relationships over a seven-day period. In terms of student–parent interactions, the study found that autonomy predicted experiencing greater pleasantness, higher self-honesty and other-honesty, and higher self-esteem than participants scoring high on control orientation. A similar pattern of findings occurred in the one-week study of all of the students' interpersonal relationships, suggesting that autonomy orientation is associated with greater openness in social experience, as predicted by both SDT and person-centred theory.

Reduced defensiveness

Reduced defensiveness refers to the ability to respond to experience in a non-threatened way due to perceiving no threat to self from one's experiencing (Rogers, 1959, 1964). In a study of people's behaviour in terms of accepting responsibility and apologising for their actions after wrongdoing, Hodgins, Liebeskind and Schwarz (1996) found that autonomy orientation was related to a higher number of apologies and greater complexity of apologies in participants, while control and impersonal orientations predicted less apology (i.e., greater defensiveness). Similarly, Knee and Zuckerman (1998) found that individuals who are high in autonomy and low in control engage in less defensive coping strategies and exhibit less self-handicapping behaviours. Taken together, these findings suggest that self-directing individuals exhibit lower use of defensive coping strategies, consistent with the predictions of person-centred theory.

Hypothesis 4. It is hypothesised that experiences of conditional regard from significant others will lead to displacement of the individual's organismic valuing process and the introjection of conditions of worth, with negative consequences for psychological well-being.

Evidence demonstrating that conditional regard from significant others leads to the introjection of conditions of worth comes from a study of students by Assor, Roth and Deci (2004), which found that participants' perceptions of the use of conditional regard by their parents was associated with introjected internalisation of behavioural regulations, feeling resentful toward parents, perceived parental disapproval, and fluctuations in self-esteem. This study provides evidence in support of the person-centred assertion that parental conditional regard leads to internalisation of conditions of worth which then act as determinants of the individual's behaviour. Assor and colleagues' findings are consistent with those from a study by Kasser, Ryan, Zax and Sameroff (1995), showing that teenagers who embrace materialism (an extrinsically motivated behaviour) have grown up in environments characterised by an absence of parental warmth and excessive parental control.

An early indication of the detrimental impact of introjected conditions of worth on autonomy was provided by SDT research into the social and environmental factors that facilitate or undermine intrinsic motivation (see Deci and Ryan, 1985). *Ego-involvement* experiments set out to induce a self-esteem contingent (ego-involved) condition versus a task-involved condition in two groups of participants carrying out an inherently interesting activity. In one such study, Ryan (1982) demonstrated that participants induced to become competitively *ego-involved* in achievement tasks where they would be contingently evaluative of themselves, showed a decrease in intrinsic motivation compared to control subjects. Ryan's preliminary findings are supported by a meta-analysis of experimental studies which confirmed that being ego-involved while performing tasks is associated with a decrease in intrinsic motivation (Rawsthorne and Elliot, 1999). This observation is important because it lends support to the person-centred proposal that actions contingent upon conditions of worth (ego-involved) will be more constrained and will displace the OVP, whereas more organismically congruent actions (task-involved) will result in more autonomous, intrinsically motivated functioning.

A negative association between internalised conditions of worth and psychological well-being is indicated by findings from a second study by Assor, Roth and Deci (2004). Investigating mothers' perceptions of their own parents' use of conditional regard, the study found that subjectively estimated parental conditional regard predicted poorer psychological well-being as well as adherence to more controlling parenting attitudes in the participants themselves, providing evidence that parental conditional regard has negative consequences for psychological well-being. Furthermore, findings from studies of intrinsic versus extrinsic life aspirations strongly indicate that aspirations reflecting extrinsic goals such as financial success, appearance, and social recognition are associated with psychological ill-being (see Kasser, 2004), including lower levels of vitality, self-actualization and positive affect, but higher levels of depression, anxiety and narcissism (Kasser and Ryan, 1996), and lower self-esteem, more television consumption, greater drug use and lower quality of relationships with friends and romantic partners (Kasser and Ryan, 2001).

Hypothesis 5. It is hypothesised that more fully functioning individuals will share common, universal, and specifiable internally generated value directions.

As previously mentioned, person-centred theory hypothesises that individuals who are engaged in an organismically congruent process of self-actualisation will share common, universal and specifiable value directions (Rogers, 1963, 1964), which are internally generated. Here, we will restrict ourselves to a consideration of just one of Rogers' specified value directions: valuing sensitivity to others, acceptance of others and deep relationships (Rogers, 1964).

Valuing sensitivity to others, acceptance of others, and deep relationships
Empirical evidence supports the hypothesis that intrinsically motivated individuals will move in a direction of increasing relatedness with others. According to SDT, we have a basic need for *relatedness*, defined as the urge to be in relationship with others, to care for

others, and to be cared for by others (Deci and Ryan, 1991). Similarly, according to person-centred theory, the self-actualising individual is one who values sensitivity to others, acceptance of others, and deep relationships (Rogers, 1957a, 1961, 1964). Evidence supporting the hypothesis that this value direction emerges in those people who actualise in line with their OVP comes from research by Sheldon and Kasser (1995), who found that people with extrinsically oriented goals were less empathic, while those with an intrinsic goal orientation were more empathic, and were also more likely to help friends experiencing problems. Further evidence of the association between source of motivation for behaviour and experience of relatedness comes from research by Kasser and Ryan (2001) which examined the quality of participants' relationships with friends and lovers, through measuring both length of relationship and other relationship variables including trust, acceptance, and jealousy. Results showed positive correlations between the quality of relationship and the importance participants placed on intrinsic goals. A corresponding negative correlation was demonstrated between quality of relationship and the importance given to extrinsic goals, suggesting that people are more likely to place greater value on their relationships when they are more intrinsically motivated, as is the case in more fully functioning individuals.

PERSON-CENTRED POSITIVE PSYCHOLOGY IN PRACTICE

As we have seen, Carl Rogers' person-centred personality theory suggests that the path to psychological well-being involves following innate guidance mechanisms, and research in self-determination theory and positive psychology shows an empirical base consistent with person-centred theory. Although not necessarily using the term 'person-centred', the fundamental meta-theoretical assumption of a tendency towards actualisation is now being picked up by the new generation of positive psychologists. This comes at a time when it is becoming increasingly common to question the medical-model view that has come to permeate clinical psychology (e.g., Maddux, Snyder and Lopez, 2004), and there have been calls within the positive psychology movement to re-evaluate our fundamental assumptions (Joseph and Linley, 2006a; 2006b).

What we have been describing throughout this chapter is how the person-centred meta-theoretical approach is identical to that of self-determination theory, and thus how both theoretical systems can complement each other. As well as theoretical complementarity, we have attempted to show that empirical literature testing aspects of SDT can be examined from the perspective of person-centred theory. A fuller discussion of this literature is available in Patterson and Joseph (2006). While person-centred theory stands to benefit from the substantial body of essentially supportive research findings from SDT, one area where SDT might usefully benefit from person-centred theory and practice is in the application of SDT to psychotherapy. Discussing potential future applied directions for SDT, Deci and Ryan point to the need for research into psychotherapy, identifying a need 'to provide a clear and comprehensive analysis of the processes of psychotherapeutic change' as an important future agenda

(Deci and Ryan, 2002: 439). Rogers (1959) has emphasised that the person-centred theory of therapy is an *if–then* theory: If the *necessary and sufficient* social-environmental conditions are present within the context of the therapeutic relationship (the essential *nutrients* for therapeutic change), then certain process changes and outcomes would occur. Empirical studies have consistently supported the person-centred assertion regarding the importance of the necessary and sufficient relationship conditions in achieving psychotherapeutic change (Barrett-Lennard, 1998; Bozarth, 1998; Bozarth, Zimring and Tausch, 2002; Rogers, 1959; Rogers and Dymond, 1954; Truax and Mitchell, 1971). Recently, the American Psychological Association Division 29 Task Force on Empirically Supported Therapy Relationships found that empathy, positive regard and congruence/genuineness were all either *demonstrably effective* or *promising and probably effective* in terms of successful therapeutic outcome (Ackerman, Benjamin, Beutler et al., 2001; Cornelius-White, 2002).

Finally, we suggest that the person-centred account of the necessary and sufficient relationship conditions provides a convincing framework that SDT researchers could utilise in attempting to identify and explain the 'how' of healthy goal striving. Person-centred theory identifies key social-environmental relationship conditions that promote organismically congruent self-actualisation—relationship conditions that facilitate psychotherapeutic change away from a direction that is discordant with intrinsic motivation, and toward the pursuit of more internally congruent goals and aspirations.

Person-centred theory can benefit from the theoretical insights of self-determination theory, and self-determination theorists can learn from the fifty years of practice-based research about application. Similar arguments to these have also recently been put forward by Vansteenkiste and Sheldon (2006) who compare SDT with motivational interviewing (MI), suggesting that the applied approach of MI and the theoretical approach of SDT might be fruitfully married.

CONCLUSION

As person-centred practitioners we base our work on the meta-theoretical assumption that people have an intrinsic motivation toward optimal functioning. Rogers (1959) provides the meta-theoretical foundation for the person-centred movement and the client-centred approach to coaching, counselling, and psychotherapy. As we have seen, the crux of the theory is the assumption that human beings have an inherent tendency toward growth, development, and optimal functioning. In reviewing the empirical evidence from positive psychology and self-determination theory, it is shown that there is considerable extant research consistent with and supportive of person-centred theory. This seam of research activity has developed in isolation from the person-centred community. A common criticism of the person-centred approach is its lack of research support, but as we have seen this can be countered with reference to this other related literature. We have shown that at the meta-theoretical level, person-centred theory and self-determination theory provide similar perspectives, and thus the empirical evidence testing aspects of self-determination theory is equally supportive of the account of personality development, psychological functioning, and the process of therapeutic growth, as hypothesised within person-centred theory. This is an important convergence to document because too often we hear critics of the person-centred approach claim that it lacks empirical evidence. Certainly, there is limited evidence from within the person-centred movement, but when we take into account the hugely impressive body of literature developed over the years by personality and social psychologists interested in self-determination theory we can see that the criticisms of person-centred theory as lacking in evidence are largely unfounded. This is an observation that will be of theoretical interest and practical relevance to those who specialise in person-centred therapies, helping them make their case for the person-centred approach as empirically based. Furthermore, our observations on person-centred meta-theoretical assumptions also promise to be of interest to positive psychologists.

This chapter provides an overview of the interface between person-centred psychology and positive psychology. As already mentioned, for too long the person-centred community has allowed itself to become marginalised from mainstream psychological discussion and practice. This has led to the position that person-centred psychology is not well represented in the academic psychology curriculum, receives limited attention in postgraduate training courses in applied psychology, and has become almost invisible within funded health services and established guidelines for the treatment of psychological problems. The advent of the positive psychology movement has provided an opportunity to re-engage with the wider academic and clinical community, to put the ideas of person-centred psychology under empirical scrutiny, and to communicate with mainstream audiences in psychology. We think that person-centred academics and practitioners need to write for mainstream journals, to develop theoretical approaches that stand the scrutiny of the international academic community, to continue to engage with research, and to seek rapprochement with positive psychology.

REFERENCES

Ackerman SJ, Benjamin LS, Beutler LE, Gelso CJ, Goldfried MR, Hill C et al. (2001) Empirically supported therapy relationships: Conclusions and recommendations of the Division 29 Task Force. *Psychotherapy, 38*, 495–7.

Assor A, Roth G, & Deci EL (2004) The emotional costs of parents' conditional regard: A self-determination theory analysis. *Journal of Personality, 72*, 47–88.

Barrett-Lennard GT (1998) *Carl Rogers' Helping System: Journey and substance.* London: Sage.

Bozarth JD (1998) *Person-Centered Therapy: A revolutionary paradigm.* Ross-on-Wye: PCCS Books.

Bozarth JD, Zimring FM & Tausch R (2002) Client-centered therapy: Evolution of a revolution. In D Cain & J Seeman (Eds) *Handbook of Humanistic Psychotherapy: Research and practice.* Washington, DC: American Psychological Association, pp. 147–88.

Cornelius-White JHD (2002) The phoenix of empirically supported therapy relationships: The overlooked person-centered basis. *Psychotherapy: Theory Research/Practice/Training, 39* (3), 219–22.

Deci EL, Koestner R & Ryan RM (1999) A meta-analytic review of experiments examining the effects of extrinsic rewards on intrinsic motivation. *Psychological Bulletin, 125*, 627–68.

Deci EL & Ryan RM (1985) *Intrinsic Motivation and Self-Determination in Human Behavior*. New York: Plenum.

Deci EL & Ryan RM (1991) A motivational approach to self: Integration in personality. In R Dienstbier (Ed) *Nebraska Symposium on Motivation. Vol. 38: Perspectives on motivation*. Lincoln, NE: University of Nebraska Press, pp. 237–88.

Deci EL & Ryan RM (1995) Human agency: The basis for true self-esteem. In MH Kernis (Ed) *Efficacy, Agency, and Self-Esteem*. New York: Plenum, pp. 31–50.

Deci EL & Ryan RM (2000) The 'what' and 'why' of goal pursuits: Human needs and the self-determination of behavior: *Psychological Inquiry, 11*, 227–68.

Deci EL & Ryan RM (2002) Self-determination research: Reflections and future directions. In EL Deci & RM Ryan (Eds) *Handbook of Self-Determination Research*. Rochester, NY: University of Rochester Press, pp. 431–41.

Deci EL & Vansteenkiste M (2004) Self-determination theory and basic need satisfaction: Understanding human development in positive psychology. *Ricerchedi di psicologia: Special issue in positive psychology, 27*, 23–40.

Ford JG (1991) Rogerian self-actualization: A clarification of meaning. *Journal of Humanistic Psychology, 31*, 101–11.

Hodgins HS & Knee R (2002) The integrating self and conscious experience. In EL Deci & RM Ryan (Eds) *Handbook of Self-Determination Research*. Rochester, NY: University of Rochester Press, pp. 87–100.

Hodgins HS, Koestner R & Duncan N (1996) On the compatibility of autonomy and relatedness. *Personality and Social Psychology Bulletin, 22*, 227–37.

Hodgins HS, Liebeskind E & Schwartz W (1996) Getting out of hot water: Facework in social predicaments. *Journal of Personality and Social Psychology, 71*, 300–14.

Joseph S (2003) Why the client knows best. *The Psychologist, 16*, 304–7.

Joseph S & Linley PA (2006a) *Positive Therapy: A meta-theory for positive psychological practice*. London: Routledge.

Joseph S & Linley PA (2006b) Positive psychology versus the medical model. *American Psychologist, 61*, 332–3.

Joseph S & Worsley R (2005) (Eds) *Person-Centred Psychopathology: A positive psychology of mental health*. Ross-on-Wye: PCCS Books.

Kasser T (2004) The good life or the goods life? Positive psychology and personal well-being in the culture of consumption. In PA Linley & S Joseph (Eds) *Positive Psychology in Practice*. Hoboken, NJ: Wiley, pp. 55–67.

Kasser T & Ryan RM (1996) Further examining the American dream: Differential correlates of intrinsic and extrinsic goals. *Personality and Social Psychology Bulletin, 22*, 280–7.

Kasser T & Ryan RM (2001) Be careful what you wish for: Optimal functioning and the relative attainment of intrinsic and extrinsic goals. In P Schmuck & KM Sheldon (Eds) *Life Goals and Well-being*. Gottingen: Hogrefe and Huber, pp. 116–31.

Kasser T, Ryan RM, Zax M & Sameroff AJ (1995) The relations of maternal and social environments to late adolescents' materialistic and prosocial values. *Developmental Psychology, 31*, 907–14.

Knee CR & Zuckerman M (1996) Causality orientations and the disappearance of the self-serving bias. *Journal of Research in Personality, 32*, 115–30.

Knee CR & Zuckerman M (1998) A nondefensive personality: Autonomy and control as moderators of defensive coping and self-handicapping. *Journal of Research in Personality, 32,* 115–30.

Koestner R, Bernieri F & Holt K (1992) Self-determination and consistency between attitudes, traits and behaviours. *Personality and Social Psychology Bulletin, 18,* 52–9.

Linley PA, Joseph S & Boniwell I (Eds) (2003) In a positive light. *The Psychologist, 16,* 126. (Special issue on positive psychology).

Maddux JE, Snyder CR & Lopez SJ (2004) Toward a positive clinical psychology: Deconstructing the illness ideology and constructing an ideology of human strengths and potential. In PA Linley & S Joseph (Eds) *Positive Psychology in Practice.* Hoboken, NJ: Wiley, pp. 320–34.

Maslow AH (1970) *Motivation and Personality* (2nd edn). New York: Harper and Row.

Patterson TG & Joseph S (2006) Person-centered personality theory: Support from self-determination theory and positive psychology. *Journal of Humanistic Psychology, 47,* 117–39.

Rawsthorne LJ & Elliot AJ (1999) Achievement goals and intrinsic motivation: A meta-analytic review. *Personality and Social Psychology Review, 3,* 326–44.

Rogers CR (1951) *Client-Centered Therapy: Its current practice, implications and theory.* Boston: Houghton Mifflin.

Rogers CR (1957a) A therapist's view of the good life. *The Humanist, 17,* 291–300.

Rogers CR (1957b) The necessary and sufficient conditions of therapeutic personality change. *Journal of Consulting Psychology, 21,* 95–103.

Rogers CR (1959) A theory of therapy, personality, and interpersonal relationships as developed in the client-centered framework. In S Koch (Ed) *Psychology: A study of a science. Vol. 3: Formulations of the person and the social context.* New York: McGraw-Hill, pp. 184–256.

Rogers CR (1961) *On Becoming a Person.* Boston: Houghton Mifflin.

Rogers CR (1963) The actualizing tendency in relation to 'motives' and to consciousness. In MR Jones (Ed) *Nebraska Symposium on Motivation,* Vol. 11. Lincoln, NE: University of Nebraska Press, pp. 1–24.

Rogers CR (1964) Toward a modern approach to values: The valuing approach in the mature person. *Journal of Abnormal and Social Psychology, 68,* 160–7.

Rogers CR & Dymond RF (Eds) (1954) *Psychotherapy and Personality change.* Chicago: University of Chicago Press.

Ryan RM (1982) Control and information in the intrapersonal sphere: An extension of cognitive evaluation theory. *Journal of Personality and Social Psychology, 43,* 450–61.

Ryan RM & Deci EL (2000) Self-determination theory and the facilitation of intrinsic motivation, social development and well-being. *American Psychologist, 55,* 68–78.

Ryan RM & Deci EL (2002) An overview of self-determination theory: An organismic dialectical perspective. In EL Deci & RM Ryan (Eds) *Handbook of Self-Determination Research.* Rochester, NY: University of Rochester Press, pp. 3–33.

Sanders P (2005) Principled and strategic opposition to the medicalisation of distress and all of its apparatus. In S Joseph & R Worsley (Eds) *Person-Centred Psychopathology: A positive psychology of mental health.* Ross-on-Wye: PCCS Books, pp. 21–42.

Seligman MEP (1999) The president's address. *American Psychologist, 54,* 559–62.

Seligman MEP & Csikszentmihalyi M (2000) Positive psychology: An introduction. *American Psychologist, 55,* 5–14.

Sheldon KM (2002) The self-concordance model of healthy goal striving: When personal goals correctly represent the person. In EL Deci & RM Ryan (Eds) *Handbook of Self-Determination Research*. Rochester, NY: University of Rochester Press, pp. 65–86.

Sheldon KM, Arndt J & Houser-Marko L (2003) In search of the organismic valuing process: The human tendency to move toward beneficial goal choices. *Journal of Personality*, 71, 835–86.

Sheldon KM & Elliot AJ (1999) Goal striving, need satisfaction, and longitudinal well-being: The self-concordance model. *Journal of Personality and Social Psychology*, 76, 482–97.

Sheldon KM & Kasser T (1995) Coherence and congruence: Two aspects of personality integration. *Journal of Personality and Social Psychology*, 68, 531–43.

Sheldon, KM & Kasser T (2001) Goals, congruence, and positive well-being: New empirical support for humanistic theories. *Journal of Humanistic Psychology*, 41 (1), 30–50.

Truax CB & Mitchell KM (1971) Research on certain therapist interpersonal skills in relation to process and outcome. In AE Bergin & SL Garfield (Eds) *Handbook of Psychotherapy and Behaviour Change*. New York: Wiley, pp. 299–344.

Vansteenkiste M & Sheldon KM (2006) There's nothing more practical than a good theory: Integrating motivational interviewing and self-determination theory. *British Journal of Clinical Psychology*, 45, 63–82.

Chapter 1

THE ACTUALIZING TENDENCY IN RELATION TO 'MOTIVES' AND TO CONSCIOUSNESS

Carl R. Rogers

THE ACTUALIZING TENDENCY

This paper, in its later sections, contains many ideas and beliefs which are at this point tentative and uncertain in me. They may therefore be the most profitable for discussion and clarification. This first section, however, presents a conviction which has grown stronger in me over the years. I should like to introduce it by telling of an experience, very remote from psychology, which made a strong impression on me.

During a vacation weekend some months ago I was standing on a headland overlooking one of the rugged coves which dot the coastline of northern California. Several large rock outcroppings were at the mouth of the cove, and these received the full force of the great Pacific combers which, beating upon them, broke into mountains of spray before surging into the cliff-lined shore. As I watched the waves breaking over these large rocks in the distance, I noticed with surprise what appeared to be tiny palm trees on the rocks, no more than two or three feet high, taking the pounding of the breakers. Through my binoculars I saw that these were some type of seaweed, with a slender 'trunk' topped off with a head of leaves. As one examined a specimen in the intervals between the waves it seemed clear that this fragile, erect, top-heavy plant would be utterly crushed and broken by the next breaker. When the wave crunched down upon it, the trunk bent almost flat, the leaves were whipped into a straight line by the torrent of the water, yet the moment the wave had passed, here was the plant again, erect, tough, resilient. It seemed incredible that it was able to take this incessant pounding hour after hour, day and night, week after week, perhaps, for all I know, year after year, and all the time nourishing itself, extending its domain, reproducing itself; in short, maintaining and enhancing itself in this process which, in our shorthand, we call growth. Here in this palm-like seaweed was the tenacity of life, the forward thrust of life, the ability to push into an incredibly hostile environment and not only to hold its own, but to adapt, develop, become itself.

Now I am very well aware that we can, as we say, 'explain' many aspects of this phenomenon. Thus we can explain that the weed grows on top of the rock rather than

---

Reprinted from the 1963 NEBRASKA SYMPOSIUM ON MOTIVATION by permission of the University of Nebraska Press. Copyright © 1963 by the University of Nebraska Press. Copyright © renewed 1991 by the University of Nebraska Press.

on the protected side, because it is phototropic. We can even attempt some biochemical explanations of phototropism. We can say that the plant grows where it does because there is an ecological niche which it fills, and that if *this* plant had not developed to fill this niche, the process of evolution would have favored some other organism which would gradually have developed much these same characteristics. I am aware that we can now begin to explain why this plant assumes the form it does, and why if it is damaged in some storm, it will repair itself in a way consistent with its own basic species-form. This will all come about because the DNA molecule, as long as it is a part of, and is interacting with, a living cell, carries within it, like a program for guiding a computer, instructions to each emergent cell as to the form and function it will assume in order to make the whole a functioning organism.

Such knowledge *explains* nothing, in any fundamental sense. Yet it *is* very valuable as a part of the continuing differentiation, the finer description, the more accurate picture of functional relationships, which our curiosity demands, and which gives us at least a deeper respect for and understanding of the complexities of life.

But my reason for telling this story is to call attention to a more general characteristic. Whether we are speaking of this sea plant or an oak tree, of an earthworm or a great night-flying moth, of an ape or a man, we will do well, I believe, to recognize that life is an active process, not a passive one. Whether the stimulus arises from within or without, whether the environment is favorable or unfavorable, the behaviors of an organism can be counted on to be in the direction of maintaining, enhancing, and reproducing itself. This is the very nature of the process we call life. Speaking of the totality of these reactions within an organism Bertalanffy says: 'We find that all parts and processes are so ordered that they guarantee the maintenance, construction, restitution, and reproduction of organic systems' (Bertalanffy, 1960: 13). When we speak in any basic way of what 'motivates' the behavior of organisms, it is this directional tendency, it seems to me, which is fundamental. This tendency is operative at all times, in all organisms. Indeed, it is only the presence or absence of this total directional process which enables us to tell whether a given organism is alive or dead.

It was considerations of this kind which led me to formulate the actualizing tendency as the motivational construct in my own theory of personality and therapy (Rogers, 1959). I was influenced in my thinking by the work of Goldstein, Maslow, Angyal, and others. I wrote of the actualizing tendency as involving 'development toward the differentiation of organs and functions, expansion and enhancement through reproduction. It is development toward autonomy and away from heteronomy, or control by external forces' (Rogers, 1959: 196).

Although it was ten years ago that I worked out this formulation (there was a long lag before publication), I have found no reason to change this basic notion of the process underlying all behaviors. Indeed, there seems to have been an increasing degree of support for a conception of the organism as an active directional initiator. The 'empty organism' school of thought, with nothing intervening between stimulus and response, is on the decline.

Only after attempting to formulate my own theory did I become aware of some of the work in biology which supported the concept of the actualizing tendency. One example, replicated with different species, is the work of Driesch with sea urchins many years ago, quoted by Bertalanffy (1960: 5). He learned how to tease apart the two cells which are formed after the first division of the fertilized egg. Had they been left to develop normally it is clear that each of these two cells would have grown into a portion of a sea urchin larva, the contributions of both being needed to form a whole creature. So it seems equally obvious that when the two cells are skillfully separated, each, if it grows, will simply develop into some portion of a sea urchin. But this is overlooking the directional and actualizing tendency characteristic of all organic growth. It is found that each cell, if it can be kept alive, now develops into a whole sea urchin larva—a bit smaller than usual, but normal and complete.

I am sure that I choose this example because it seems so closely analogous to my experience of dealing with individuals in psychotherapy. Here, too, the most impressive fact about the individual human being seems to be his directional tendency toward wholeness, toward actualization of his potentialities. I have not found psychotherapy effective when I have tried to create in another individual something which is not there, but I have found that if I can provide the conditions which make for growth, then this positive directional tendency brings about constructive results. The scientist with the divided sea urchin egg is in the same situation. He cannot cause the cell to develop in one way or another, he cannot (at least as yet) shape or control the DNA molecule, but if he focuses his skill on providing the conditions which permit the cell to survive and grow, then the tendency for growth and the direction of growth will be evident, and will come from within the organism. I cannot think of a better analogy for psychotherapy where, if I can supply a psychological amniotic fluid, forward movement of a constructive sort will occur.

Support for the concept of an actualizing tendency comes at times from surprising quarters, as in the simple but unusual experiments of Dember, Earl, and Paradise, which show that rats prefer an environment involving more complex stimuli over an environment involving less complex stimuli. It seems striking that even the lowly laboratory rat, within the range of complexity that he can appreciate, prefers a more richly stimulating setting to a more impoverished one. The authors' theory states, and is thus far confirmed, that 'a shift in preference, if it occurs, will be unidirectional, toward stimuli of greater complexity' (Dember, Earl, and Paradise, 1957: 517).

Better known are the increasing number of studies having to do with exploratory behavior, curiosity, play—the spontaneous tendency of the organism to seek stimulation, to produce a difference in the stimulus field (Berlyne, 1960; Harlow, 1953, are examples). This concept has become well accepted during the past decade.

The work in the field of sensory deprivation underscores even more strongly the fact that tension reduction or the absence of stimulation is a far cry from being the desired state of the organism. Freud (1953: 63) could not have been more wrong in his postulate that 'the nervous system is … an apparatus which would even, if this were feasible, maintain itself in an altogether unstimulated condition.' On the contrary, when deprived of external stimuli, the human organism produces a flood of internal stimuli sometimes of the most bizarre sort. As Goldstein (1947: 141) points out, 'The tendency to discharge any tension whatsoever is a characteristic expression of a defective organism, of disease.'

Much of the material summarized by White (1959) in his excellent article on motivation adds up to the point I too have been making, namely, that the organism is an active initiator and exhibits a directional tendency. He puts this in very appealing terms when he says, 'Even when its primary needs are satisfied and its homeostatic chores are done, an organism is alive, active, and up to something' (White, 1959: 315).

As a consequence of these and other developments in psychological and biological research, I feel considerably more secure than I did a decade ago in calling attention to the significance of those directions in the human organism which account for its maintenance and enhancement.

I would like to add one comment which may be clarifying. Sometimes this tendency is spoken of as if it involved the development of all of the potentialities of the organism. This is clearly not true. The organism does not, as Leeper has pointed out, tend toward developing its capacity for nausea, nor does it actualize its potentiality for self-destruction, nor its ability to bear pain. Only under unusual or perverse circumstances do these potentialities become actualized. It is clear that the actualizing tendency is selective and directional, a constructive tendency if you will.

Thus, to me it is meaningful to say that the substratum of all motivation is the organismic tendency toward fulfillment. This tendency may express itself in the widest range of behaviors, and in response to a very wide variety of needs. Maslow's hierarchy of needs manages to catch something of the fact that certain wants of a basic sort must be at least partially met before other needs become urgent. Consequently, the tendency of the organism to actualize itself may at one moment lead to the seeking of food or sexual satisfaction, and yet unless these needs are overpoweringly great, even these satisfactions will be sought in ways which enhance rather than diminish self-esteem. And other fulfillments will also be sought in the transactions with the environment—the need for exploration, for producing change in the environment, for play, for self-exploration when that is perceived as an avenue to actualization—all of these and many other behaviors are basically 'motivated' by the actualizing tendency.

We are, in short, dealing with an organism which is always motivated, is always 'up to something,' always seeking. So I would reaffirm, perhaps even more strongly after the passage of *a* decade, my belief that there is one central source of energy in the human organism; that it is a function of the whole organism rather than of some portion of it; and that it is perhaps best conceptualized as a tendency toward fulfillment, toward actualization, toward the maintenance and enhancement of the organism.

WHO NEEDS 'MOTIVES'?

At this point, however, I should like to introduce an idea which, if it has gained some limited acceptance during recent years, is still far from being acceptable to most psychologists. I can introduce it by posing this question. Given the motivational substratum of the actualizing tendency, is anything added to our theories by postulating more specific motivational constructs? How helpful has it been in the past and how helpful is it likely to be in the future to specify and try to give meaning to a variety of special motives? I am not arguing that these differing types of seeking do not take place. Men do seek food, and they do tend toward increasing their competence in dealing with the environment, and most people wish to increase their self-esteem, but I am not at all sure that there is any profit to thinking of a hunger motive, a competence motive, or a self-esteem motive. Are these heuristic concepts? Do they lead to significant discovery? Are they provocative of effective research? Obviously I am dubious.

As I endeavor to discover what constitutes science in its truest sense, it seems to me clear that science has not made progress by positing forces, attractions, repulsions, causes, and the like, to explain *why* things happen. As we all know, there are very few answers to the question 'why.' But science has progressed and found itself on more fruitful paths when it restricts itself to the question of 'how' things happen. When the theory was offered that nature abhors a vacuum, and that this explained *why* air rushes in to fill any vacuum or partial vacuum, this led to little effective research. But when science began to describe, in empirical terms, the functional relationships which hold between a partial vacuum and the atmospheric pressure outside the container, significant results accrued, and the question as to whether nature feels this particular abhorrence was forgotten. Or, as Galileo so forcefully demonstrated, when we cease trying to formulate the reasons as to *why* a stone falls, and concentrate on the exact description of its rate of fall per second, and the degree of its acceleration, then these exact descriptions of functional relationships open up whole new fields of investigation and are incredibly fruitful of further knowledge. One of the by-products is a loss of interest in *why* the stone falls.

In the same vein, I doubt if psychologists make progress in their science so long as their basic theory focuses on the formulation that man seeks food *because* he has a hunger motive or drive; that he interacts in an exploratory and manipulative manner with his environment *because* he has a competence motive; that he seeks achievement *because* he has a mastery drive or a need for achievement. Even in the area that has seemed so clear to so many, the concept of a sexual motive has not been too helpful in unraveling the vastly complex variables which determine sexual behavior even in animals—the genetic, physiological, environmental, maturational, social, perceptual, and other elements which enter in. As Beach (1955: 409) has pointed out in regard to instincts, such concepts of specific energy sources lead to oversimplified theories and even to an insistence upon theories rather than upon observation. His proposal regarding the improvement of the situation regarding instincts bears consideration in regard to motives.

The analysis that is needed involves two types of approach. One rests upon determination of the relationships existing between genes and behavior. The other consists of studying the development of various behavior patterns in the individual, and determining the number and kinds of factors that normally control the final form of the response.

When these methods have been applied to the various types of behavior which today are called 'instinctive,' the concept of instinct will disappear, to be replaced by scientifically valid and useful explanations.

In much the same fashion I believe that when we have developed and tested hypotheses as to the conditions which are necessary and sufficient antecedents to certain behaviors, when we understand the complex variables which underlie various expressions of the actualizing tendency of the organism, then the concept of specific motives will disappear.

AN ILLUSTRATION

The point I am making could be illustrated from many areas of psychology but you will not be surprised if I speak of it from the area of my own work. I would like to sketch briefly a chain of experiences in theory and research regarding the therapeutic relationship, and endeavor to relate these experiences to what I have been saying about motivational constructs.

In a lifetime of professional effort I have been fascinated by the process of change which sometimes occurs in human beings in the therapeutic relationship when it is, as we say, 'successful.' Individual clients in such a relationship could be described in very general and theoretical terms as moving in the direction of actualization of their potentialities, moving away from rigidity and toward flexibility, moving toward more process living, moving toward autonomy, and the like. In more specific and empirical terms we know that they change in their observed behaviors, exhibiting more socially mature behavior, that they change in the way in which they perceive themselves, that they place a more positive value upon self, that they give more healthy responses to projective tests. Perhaps it should be stressed that these generalizations regarding the direction of the process in which they are engaged exist in a context of enormously diverse specific behaviors, with different meanings for different individuals. Thus, progress toward maturity for one means developing sufficient autonomy to divorce himself from an unsuitable marriage partner; in another it means living more constructively with the partner he has. For one student it means working hard to obtain better grades; for another it means a lessened compulsiveness and a willingness to accept poorer grades. So we must recognize that the generalizations about this process of change are abstractions drawn from a very complex diversified picture.

But the nagging question over the years has been: What is it that initiates this process? Every therapist knows that it does not occur in each of his clients. What are the conditions, in the client, in the therapist, in the interaction, which are antecedent to this process of change? In trying to formulate hypotheses in regard to this, I believe that there is no substitute for close observation—with as much openness to unexpected facts and possibilities as the observer can bring to bear, with as much laying aside of defensiveness and rigidity as he can achieve. As I continued to observe therapy, the formulation at which I gradually arrived was very different from the views with which I started, though how much defensive inability to see the facts is still involved no man can say of himself. At any rate, the theoretical position to which I came hypothesized that the process of change was initiated primarily by the psychological climate created by the therapist, and not by his techniques, his therapeutic orientation, or his scholarly knowledge of personality dynamics. I have spelled out these hypotheses in different publications (Rogers, 1962a, 1959, 1957).

The point to which I would call attention is that when you become interested in the conditions which are antecedent to a given complex of behaviors, it becomes quite clear that questions regarding specific motives seem futile as leads for further work. Are differing therapist behaviors due to varying degrees of altruistic motive? or to differing amounts of the need for affiliation? or to the need for dominance? Are the client's behaviors due to his competence motive? or his need for dependence? or is there a self-exploration motive which is tapped? To me these do not seem to be heuristic questions.

On the other hand, when I begin, on the basis of observation, to hypothesize specific conditions or determinants of change, then, it seems to me, research progress is stimulated in two ways. In the first place, one attempts to describe the specific conditions which appear to operate, not to consult a list of motives. The specific conditions may conceivably be genetic or physiological or environmental. They may be strictly observable behaviors, or may be phenomenological states inferred from the behaviors. They may be interactional, although in my experience interactional variables are difficult to make operational. In the second place, it is, I believe, considerably easier to give operational definitions of observed conditions than to measure a general motivational state such as need for affiliation.

In any event, to continue with my account, the conditions which appeared on the basis of observation to be antecedent to and relevant to the process of developmental change in the client, were of quite different sorts. There were essentially five—four of them attitudinal sets in the therapist, one an element in the client.

An accurate and sensitive empathy communicated by the therapist appeared crucial. This is a variable which falls in the class of directly observable behaviors. It has been possible to assess it from the verbal behavior of the therapist and from his vocal inflections.

The warmth of positive regard for the client experienced by the therapist was postulated as a second variable of significance.

This is a complex factor existing in the phenomenal field of the therapist, which may be inferred from the quality and tone of his voice. It can also be inferred from his posture and gestures, if moving pictures or direct observation can be employed.

Third, the unconditionality of the therapist's regard is a related factor deemed to be important. Is the therapist's regard relatively conditional, that is, valuing certain aspects of the client and his behavior, and devaluing other aspects, or is it unconditional?

Assessment of such a variable must to some degree be an inference regarding the phenomenal field of the therapist, but to the extent that the regard is conditional, it constitutes observable behavior, evident in verbalizations, inflections, gestures.

A fourth element hypothesized to be important was the congruence of the therapist—the extent to which, in the relationship, he is integrated, whole, real, his conscious attitudes and behavior congruent with the experiencing going on in him. Assessment must be based entirely on behavioral observation—the voice qualities particularly—since a lack of congruence is usually unknown to the therapist himself at the time, being essentially a defense against feelings in himself which he senses as threatening. Thus, this seems like an extremely subtle assessment to make. We are assisted in this, however, by the fact that this type of assessment is made by everyone from childhood up, as he evaluates each relationship as to whether the person is being real, or is acting a role, putting up a façade, or being a 'phony.'

The fifth and final condition is purely phenomenological—the client's perception of at least a minimal degree of these qualities in the therapist. We have used a paper-and-pencil inventory to get at this client perception.

Now it should be clear that these are very crude formulations of variables hypothesized to be significant. In this respect they are, I believe, representative of the primitive state of psychological science as it relates to human beings. It is a tragedy that we have not achieved any rational scientific methodology which is adequate for the study of organisms with their wholistic nature and their basic process characteristics. So these formulations I have given represent only a first awkward attempt to define the elements which nourish and facilitate psychological change, growth, development toward maturity, in the human person. I see them as roughly analogous to the early attempts to isolate the nutritional elements which promote physical growth. Just as a maturing science can now define with very considerable precision the elements necessary for physical growth, so I believe a maturing psychological science will eventually define the psychological nutriments which promote personal growth.

When I ask myself if this attempt would have proceeded more rapidly or more accurately if we had hypotheses based upon some theory of specific motives, rather than upon naturalistic observation, my answer is strongly negative. In my judgment, assessment of therapist motives, such as need for affiliation, for altruism, for dominance or mastery or competence, would have approached only very indirectly, if at all, the problem of the conditions which facilitate change. And if I turn the question around and ask myself what motive lies behind the therapist's genuineness or his sensitive empathy in the relationship, I must answer that I do not know. Nor does the question have any real importance for me. So I reiterate the idea voiced previously, that a theory involving specific motivations, no matter how they are categorized or sliced, does not seem to me to be helpful in the empirical investigations which alone can determine the patterning which exists in human behavior.

Yet when the variables are selected through subjective observation, when the scientist is willing to use his own disciplined sensitivity to his experience in the selection of variables, when he is willing to trust his experience as a tentative and perhaps intuitive guide in the formulation of hypotheses, positive results can emerge. I think we often fail to recognize the truth of Polanyi's (1958) thesis that if it were not for the pattern which the disciplined scientist senses long before he can confirm or disconfirm it, there would be no such thing as an advancing science.

So to complete very briefly the story of these particular formulations about the conditions necessary for the therapeutic process, I will attempt to summarize the results of a number of completed studies in this field, several of which are moving toward publication (Barrett-Lennard, in press; Halkides, 1958; Spotts, 1962; Truax, 1962; Truax, Liccione and Rosenberg 1962). The studies deal with two rather different groups of clients: on the one hand, students and other adults who come voluntarily for help; and on the other hand, schizophrenic individuals who have been in a state hospital for periods ranging from a few months to many years. The first group is above the socioeducational average, well motivated, and ranging from mildly to seriously disturbed in their functioning. The second group is below the socioeducational average, not only unmotivated but resistant, unable to cope with life in the community, and often out of contact with reality.

In the different studies there have been three ways of measuring the relationship elements I have described. The first method is through the rating of brief segments of the recorded interviews, usually four minutes in length, taken in a randomized fashion from the interview. Raters, listening to these segments, judge the degree to which the therapist is, for example, being accurately empathic, and make a rating on a carefully defined scale. The raters have no knowledge as to whether the segment is from an early or late interview, or a more or less successful case. In the most recent of the studies a different group of raters has made the ratings for each of the qualities.

A second method of measurement has been through the use of the Relationship Inventory, an instrument designed to capture the client's perception of the qualities of the relationship. The third method is also based on this Inventory, filled out by the therapist to obtain his perception of the relationship qualities.

Various criteria of change have been used in these studies, to assess the degree of positive or negative change in personality. In all cases the criteria of change have been independent of the measures of the attitudinal elements. Some of the measures have been: assessment by clinicians, working 'blind,' of the changes between pre- and post-projective and other tests; changes in various MMPI scales; changes in Q-sort adjustment score and in a measure of anxiety. There have also been measures of process movement in some of the studies, based upon a process analysis of the interview segments made entirely independently of the attitudinal assessment.

The major finding from all of the studies is that clients in relationships marked by a high level of therapist congruence, empathy, and positive regard of an unconditional sort, tend to show a significant degree of constructive personality change and development. Clients in relationships characterized by a low level of these attitudinal conditions show significantly less positive change on the indices described above. In the schizophrenic group, the individuals in relationships low in these qualities show *negative* personality change. They are, at the end, worse off than their matched nontherapy controls. Clinically, this is a very sobering finding; scientifically, it is of great importance. There are various other findings which are of interest but not relevant to our present topic.

I have given this much of the findings simply to indicate that variables abstracted from observation, quite without regard to motivational constructs, have proven to be significantly related to personality change. They are of the order which I believe has usually been of the most importance in science, namely 'x is a function of y.' In this case, personality change is a function of certain measured relationship qualities.

But this is not all. One of our staff has also abstracted out the construct of client likability, and has shown that the likability of the client is also associated with the degree of change (Stoler, in press). Again, motivational constructs have, I am sure, played no part in this research. In some further work we seem to be teasing out a factor which perhaps we could call client readiness, as still another predictor of change. What I am saying is that in our efforts to understand objectively a complex process of change in the personality and behavior of the individual we are making progress, but that progress has in no way come from theories of specific motivations. In fact, to have operated from a base of such theories would, I believe, only have clouded the difficult task of discovering the elements which, empirically, are associated with change.

A RESTATEMENT

Let me summarize very briefly what I have been saying up to this point. The human organism is active, actualizing, and directional. This is the basis for all of my thinking. Once this fact is accepted, I see no virtue in imposing abstractions regarding specific motives upon man's complex and multiform behavior. It is certainly possible to categorize the behavioral phenomena into many different motives and, in fact, these phenomena may be sliced in a variety of ways, but that this is desirable or heuristic seems dubious to me. I have tried to indicate by illustration that in any actual attempt to understand the conditions antecedent to behavior it may be preferable to formulate our hypotheses on the basis of close observation of the phenomena, rather than upon a previously constructed series of motives.

THE PROBLEM OF INCONGRUENCE OR DISSOCIATION

I should like now to turn to a very different and very puzzling cluster of questions. These questions are certainly related to the issue of motivation, but to many other aspects of personality theory as well. Anyone who delves at all into the dynamics of human behavior must deal with them in some way. I have myself found them very perplexing, and have felt quite dissatisfied with the all too easy 'explanations' which have been given. They have to do with what I think of as incongruence or dissociation. In general, the questions are of this sort. How is it that man is so frequently at war within himself? How do we account for the all too common rift which we observe between the conscious aspects of man and his organismic aspects? How do we account for what appears to be two conflicting motivational systems in man?

To take a very simple example, how is it that a woman can consciously be a very submissive and compliant person, very sure that this is her goal, that such behavior represents her true values, and then at times blow up in abnormally hostile and resentful behavior which greatly surprises her, and which she does not own as a part of herself? Clearly her organism has been experiencing both submission and aggression, and moving toward the expression of both. Yet at the conscious level she has no awareness and no acceptance of one aspect of this process going on within her. This is a simple example of the rift with which every psychologist interested in human behavior must come to terms.

In the theory I advanced a decade ago I saw the rift as an incongruence between the self-perceptions held by the individual and his organismic experiencing. I said that this was brought about by distorted perceptions of self and experience, which in turn grew out of conditions of worth introjected from significant others. I expressed the view that the actualizing tendency promoted the fulfillment of the organism on the one hand, but that as the self developed it also tended to actualize the self, and that frequently the self and the experience of the organism were decidedly incongruent. Thus, we have the actualizing tendency splitting into two systems at least partially antagonistic in their directions (Rogers, 1959: 196–7). I am not at all sure that this captures the facts in the way most effective for promoting investigation. I do not see any clear solution to the problem, but I think perhaps I see the issues in a larger context. So I should like to share my puzzlement with you. To do so, I would like to back away and look at the broad picture.

In nature, the working out of the actualizing tendency shows a surprising efficiency. The organism makes errors, to be sure, but these are corrected on the basis of feedback. Even the human infant, faced with natural, unflavored foods, does a quite satisfactory job of balancing his diet over time, and thus both maintains and enhances his development. This type of relatively integrated, self-regulating behavior, directed toward maintenance and fulfillment, seems to be the rule in nature rather than the exception. One can, of course, point to serious mistakes over evolutionary time. Evidently the dinosaurs, by becoming very efficiently and rigidly actualized in terms of a given environment, could not adapt, and thus effectively destroyed themselves through the perfection with which they had fulfilled themselves in a given environment. But this is the exception. On the whole, organisms behave in ways which make an awesome degree of directional sense.

In man, however—perhaps particularly in our culture—the potentiality for awareness of his functioning can go so persistently awry as to make him truly estranged from his organismic experiencing. He can become self-defeating as in neurosis, incapable of coping with life as in psychosis, unhappy and divided as in the maladjustments which occur in all of us. Why this division? How is it that a man can be consciously struggling toward one goal, while his whole organic direction is at cross purposes with this?

In puzzling over this issue, I find myself trying to take a fresh look at the place and function of awareness in the life of man. The ability to focus conscious attention seems to be one of the latest evolutionary developments in our species. It is, we might say, a tiny peak of awareness, of symbolizing capacity, based on a vast pyramid of nonconscious organismic functioning. Perhaps a better analogy more indicative of the continual change going on, is to think of man's functioning as a large, pyramidal fountain in which the very tip of the fountain is intermittently illuminated with the flickering light of consciousness, but the constant flow goes on in darkness or in the light.

In the person who is functioning well, awareness tends to be reflexive, rather than the sharp spotlight of focused attention. Perhaps it is more accurate to say that in such a person awareness is simply a reflection of something of the flow of the organism at that moment. It is only when the functioning is disrupted that a sharply self-conscious awareness arises. Speaking of the different aspects of awareness in this well-functioning person, I have said, 'I do not mean that this individual would be self-consciously aware of all that was going on within himself, like the centipede who became aware of all his legs. On the contrary, he would be free to live a feeling subjectively, as well as be aware of it. He might experience love or pain or fear, living in this attitude subjectively. Or he might abstract himself from this subjectivity and realize in awareness, "I am in pain"; "I am afraid"; "I do love." The crucial point is that there would be no barriers, no inhibitions, which would prevent the full experiencing of whatever was organismically present' (Rogers, 1962b: 25).

In this way, as in various other ways, my thinking is similar to that of Lancelot Whyte, who comes at the same problem from a very different perspective, that of the philosopher of science and historian of ideas. He too feels that in the person who is functioning well 'the free play of spontaneous vitality—as in the transitory rhythms of eating, drinking, walking, loving, making things, working well, thinking, and dreaming—evokes no persistent differentiated awareness. We feel right while it is going on, and then forget it, as a rule' (Whyte, 1960: 35).

When functioning in this manner the person is whole, integrated, unitary. This appears to be the desirable and efficient human way. Sharpened self-consciousness in such functioning arises, according to Whyte, only as a result of contrast or clash between the organism and its environment, and the function of such self-awareness is to eliminate the clash by modifying the environment or altering the behavior of the individual. His viewpoint is startling but challenging when he says, 'The main purpose of conscious thought, its neobiological function, may be first to identify, and then to eliminate, the factors which evoke it' (Whyte, 1960: 37).

It will probably be evident that such views as the foregoing could be held only by individuals who see the nonconscious aspect of man's living in a positive light. I have myself stressed the idea that man is wiser than his intellect, and that well-functioning persons 'accept the realization that the meanings implicit in their experiencing of a situation constitute the wisest and most satisfying indication of appropriate behavior.' They have come to 'trust their experiencing' (Rogers, 1962b: 28). Whyte places this same idea in a larger context when he says, 'Crystals, plants, and animals grow without any conscious fuss, and the strangeness of our own history disappears once we assume that the same kind of natural ordering process that guides their growth also guided the development of man and of his mind, and does so still' (1960: 5). It is clear that these views are very remote from Freud's distrust of the unconscious, and his general view that it was antisocial in its direction. Instead, as developed in these paragraphs, when man is functioning in an integrated, unified, effective manner, he has confidence in the directions which he unconsciously chooses, and trusts his experiencing, of which, even if he is fortunate, he has only partial glimpses in his awareness.

If this is a reasonable description of the functioning of consciousness when all is going well, why does the rift develop in so many of us, to the point that organismically we are moving in one direction, and in our conscious life are struggling in another?

I am interested that Whyte and I give sharply different explanations of the way in which this dissociation comes about, but very similar descriptions of the condition itself. A brief summary can scarcely do justice to his thought, but he believes that the tendency of European or Western man to lose his proper organic integration has come about through the peculiarly Western development of static concepts—in the formation of our language, in our thought, in our philosophy. Though nature is clearly process, man has been caught in his own fixed forms of thought: 'Deliberate behavior was organized by the use of static concepts, while spontaneous behavior continued to express a formative process; that special part of nature which we call thought thus became alien in form to the rest of nature …' (Whyte, 1949: 39). It is in this fashion, he believes, that a dissociation develops in which 'mutually incompatible systems of behavior compete for control' (Whyte, 1949: 44). It is his judgment that this rift is more profound in men than in women because for various reasons, woman's special functions 'link her thought more closely to those organic processes which maintain the animal harmony' (Whyte, 1949: 40).

My own explanation has more to do with the personal dynamics of the individual. Love by the parent or significant other is made conditional. It is given only on the condition that the child introject certain constructs and values as his own, otherwise he will not be perceived as worthwhile, as worthy of love. These constructs are rigid and static since they are not a part of the child's normal process of evaluating his experience. He tends to disregard his own experiencing process wherever it conflicts with these constructs, and thus to this degree cuts himself off from his organic functioning, becoming to this degree dissociated. If the conditions of worth imposed on him are numerous and significant, then the dissociation can become very great, and the psychological consequences serious indeed (Rogers, 1959: 221–33).

I have gradually come to see this dissociation, rift, estrangement, as something learned, a perverse channeling of some of the actualizing tendency into behaviors which do not actualize. In this respect it would be similar to the situation in which sexual urges can, through learning, be channeled perversely into behaviors far removed from the physiological and evolutionary ends of these impulses. In this respect my thinking has changed during the past decade. Ten years ago I was endeavoring to explain the rift between self and experience, between conscious goals and organismic directions, as something natural and necessary, albeit unfortunate. Now I believe that individuals are culturally conditioned, rewarded, reinforced, for behaviors which are in fact perversions of the natural directions of the unitary actualizing tendency. As Whyte says, 'The conflict between spontaneous and deliberate behavior would never have represented more than a normal difficulty of choice had the influence of the social tradition been favorable to the maintenance of the overriding coordination' (1949: 44).

Both Whyte and I see the end result as similar, in that dissociated man is best described as man consciously behaving in terms of static constructs and abstractions and unconsciously behaving in terms of the actualizing tendency. This is in sharp contrast to the healthy, well-functioning person who lives in close and confident relationship to his own ongoing organismic process, nonconscious as well as conscious. I see constructive outcomes in therapy and Whyte sees constructive developments in society as possible only in terms of the human individual who trusts his own inner directions and whose awareness is a part of and integrated with the process nature of his organic functioning. Whyte states the goal as being 'the recovery of animal harmony in the differentiated form appropriate to man at this stage of history' (1949: 199). I have described the functioning of the psychologically mature individual as being similar in many ways to that of the infant, except that the fluid process of experiencing has more scope and sweep, and that the mature individual, like the child, 'trusts and uses the wisdom of his organism, with the difference that he is able to do so knowingly' (Rogers, 1962c: 14).

Let me endeavor to summarize my thoughts on this matter. I have said that the extremely common estrangement of conscious man from his directional organismic processes is not a necessary part of man's nature. It is instead something learned, and to an especially high degree in our Western culture. It is characterized by behaviors which are guided by rigid concepts and constructs, interrupted at times by behaviors guided by the organismic processes. The satisfaction or fulfillment of the actualizing tendency has become bifurcated into incompatible behavioral systems, of which one may be dominant at one moment, and the other dominant at another moment, but at a continual cost of strain and inefficiency. This dissociation which exists in most of us is the pattern and the basis of all psychological pathology in man, and the basis of all his social pathology as well. This, at least, is my view.

The natural and efficient mode of living as a human being, however, a mode partially achieved by individuals whom we term psychologically mature, does not involve this dissociation, this bifurcation. Instead, such a person exhibits a trust in the directions of his inner organismic processes which, with consciousness participating in a coordinated rather than a competitive fashion, carry him forward in a total, unified, integrated, adaptive, and changing encounter with life and its challenges.

I trust that the significance which I attach to the function of the actualizing tendency is indicated by the preceding paragraph. The tragic condition of man is that he has lost confidence in his own nonconscious inner directions. Again, I cannot refrain from quoting Whyte's words which express my own view: 'Western man stands out as a highly developed but bizarre distortion of the human animal' (1949: 46). To me the remedy for this situation is the incredibly difficult but not impossible task of permitting the human individual to grow and develop in a continuing confident relationship to the formative actualizing tendency and process in himself. If awareness and conscious thought are seen as a part of life—not its master nor its opponent, but an illumination of the developing processes within the individual—then man's total life can be the unified and unifying experience which seems characteristic in nature. If man's magnificent symbolizing capacity can develop as a part of and guided by the tendency toward fulfillment which exists in him as in every creature, then the 'animal harmony' is never lost, and becomes a human harmony and human wholeness simply because our species is capable of greater richness of experience than any other.

And if the skeptical and natural question is raised, 'Yes, but how? How could this possibly come about?' then it seems to me that the illustration I gave of research regarding the therapeutic relationship is a very small but hopefully a significant signpost in this respect. Our capacity for scientific investigation can help us. It seems very probable that the conditions which promote dissociation, which bifurcate the actualizing tendency, can be empirically identified. I have pointed out two types of hypotheses already formulated by Whyte and myself, which lie at hand for testing. The conditions which are associated with the restoration of unity and integration in the individual are, as I have indicated, already in process of being identified. The conditions which would promote a continuing internal harmony in children, without the all too common learning of dissociation, can also be identified and put to preventive use. We can, if we will, I believe, use our scientific skills to help us keep man whole and unified, a creature whose actualizing tendency will be continually forming him in the direction of a richer and more fulfilling relationship to life.

SUMMARY

I have endeavored to say three things. First, there is a tendency toward fulfillment which is the most basic aspect of the life of any organism. It is the substratum of anything we might term motivation.

Second, I have questioned whether the formulation of theories of specific motives moves us forward in research. Since the major usefulness of theories is to stimulate research, I question the value of specific motivational constructs. Through an illustration, I have endeavored to indicate that the determinants of any given set of complex behaviors may perhaps be more accurately hypothesized from careful naturalistic observation than from thinking in terms of 'motives.'

Third, and finally, I have pointed out that in nature the actualizing tendency usually brings about a unified and integrated behavioral process, often highly complex in character. Why in man does it so often produce bifurcated systems—conscious versus unconscious, self versus the experiencing process, conceived values versus experienced values? I have hypothesized that this is due to specific types of social learning, especially predominant in Western culture, and not a *necessary* part of human living. If this type of learning is not a necessary element of human life, there would seem to be some possibility that it might be changed.

REFERENCES

Barrett-Lennard GT (in press) Dimensions of therapist response as causal factors in therapeutic change. (Published 1962, *Psychological Monographs, 76* (43, Whole No. 562).)

Beach FA (1955) The descent of instinct. *Psychologocal. Review, 62*, 401–10.

Berlyne DE (1960) *Conflict, Arousal, and Curiosity.* New York: McGraw-Hill.

Bertalanffy L (1960) *Problems of Life.* New York: Harper Torchbooks. (First published 1952.)

Dember WN, Earl RW & Paradise N (1957) Response by rats to differential stimulus complexity. *J. Comp. Physiol. Psychol., 50*, 514–18.

Freud S (1953) Instincts and their vicissitudes. *Collected Papers Vol. IV.* London: Hogarth Press and Institute of Psychoanalysis pp. 60–83.

Goldstein K (1947) *Human Nature in the Light of Psychopathology.* Cambridge: Harvard University Press.

Halkides G (1958) An experimental study of four conditions necessary for therapeutic change. Unpublished doctoral dissertation, University of Chicago.

Harlow HF (1953) Motivation as a factor in the acquisition of new responses. *Current Theory and Research in Motivation: A symposium.* Lincoln, NE: University of Nebraska Press, pp. 24–49.

Polanyi M (1958) *Personal Knowledge.* Chicago: University of Chicago Press.

Rogers CR (1957) The necessary and sufficient conditions of therapeutic personality change. *Journal of Consulting Psychology, 21*, 95–103.

Rogers CR (1959) A theory of therapy, personality, and interpersonal relationships. In S Koch (Ed) *Psychology: A study of a science. Vol III: Formulations of the person and the social context.* New York: McGraw-Hill, pp. 184–256.

Rogers CR (1962a) The interpersonal relationship: The core of guidance. *Harvard Educucation Review, 32*, 416–29.

Rogers CR (1962b) Toward becoming a fully functioning person. In *Perceiving, Behaving, Becoming.* Washington, DC: Association for Supervision and Curriculum Development, 1962 yearbook, pp. 21–33.

Rogers CR (1962c) Toward a modern approach to values. Unpublished manuscript. (Subsequently published 1964, *Journal of Abnormal and Social Psychology, 68* (2), 160–7.)

Spotts JE (1962) The perception of positive regard by relatively successful and relatively unsuccessful clients. Wisconsin Psychiatric Institute: Research Reports. Unpublished manuscript.

Stoler N (in press) Client likability: A variable in the study of psychotherapy *Journal of Consulting Psychology.* (Subsequently published 1963, *Journal of Consulting Psychology, 27*, 175–8.)

Truax CB (1962) The relationship between the level of accurate empathy offered in psychotherapy and case outcome. Wisconsin Psychiatric Institute: Research Reports. Unpublished manuscript.

Truax CB, Liccione J & Rosenberg M (1962) Psychological test evaluations of personality change in high conditions therapy, low conditions therapy, and control patients. Wisconsin Psychiatric Institute: Research Reports. Unpublished manuscript.

White RW (1959) Motivation reconsidered: The concept of competence. *Psychological Review, 66*, 297–331.

Whyte LL (1949) *The Next Development in Man.* New York: Mentor Books.

Whyte LL (1960) *The Unconscious before Freud.* London: Tavistock Publications.

Author's note: The author is indebted to many persons in the writing of this paper, but would like to acknowledge special indebtedness to Lancelot L. Whyte, for valuable conversations at the Center for Advanced Study in the Behavioral Sciences, and to Wesley Westman for stimulating suggestions.

CHAPTER 2

ACTUALIZATION: A FUNCTIONAL CONCEPT IN CLIENT-CENTERED THERAPY

JEROLD D. BOZARTH AND
BARBARA TEMANER BRODLEY

Abstract

This paper reviews Carl R. Rogers' concept of the actualizing tendency as an operational premise in client-centered therapy. Rogers' view of actualization is clarified including the relationship of the concept to Rogers' speculations about the 'fully functioning person.' The function of the actualizing concept in therapy is demonstrated by reviewing segments of a therapy session. The client-centered therapist implements the actualizing tendency by creating a specific interpersonal climate during the therapy session. This climate is created by means of the therapist experiencing and communicating certain attitudes toward the client. These attitudes are identified as congruency, unconditional positive regard, and empathic understanding. Rather than intervening and thereby assuming therapeutic expertise about the client, the client-centered therapist trusts the client to move forward in a constructive direction. The constructive forward movement of the client is propelled by the sole and inherent motivation in human beings; that is, the actualizing tendency.

Actualization is a concept that has been discussed at length by many psychologists including Erich Fromm, Karen Horney, Robert White, Abraham Maslow, Andras Angyal, Kurt Goldstein, and Carl Rogers. *Only in client-centered therapy (also identified as person-centered therapy) is the concept of actualization a practical and functional premise for the work of the therapist.*

The intent of this paper is to clarify Carl Rogers' view of the actualizing tendency as the foundation block of client-centered therapy and to discuss the implications of actualization as a pragmatic and functional concept in this therapeutic approach. Specifically, the paper (1) examines Rogers' view on actualization and his rationale for therapy; (2) clarifies the relation between Rogers' concepts of the actualizing tendency and the fully functioning person; (3) discusses the function of Rogers' concept of actualization in the practice of psychotherapy; and (4) presents a therapy segment in order to illustrate the function of a therapist who operates with the cognitive underpinning of the actualizing tendency.

The client-centered approach has generated extensive research (Lambert, Shapiro and Bergin, 1986) and has been the most research-supported model of psychotherapy

---

First published (1991) in A Jones and R Crandall (Eds) Handbook of self-actualization. [Special Issue]. *Journal of Social Behavior and Personality*, 6 (5), 45–60.

(Goodyear, 1987; Patterson, 1984). However, there has been a sparsity of research on, and limited understanding of, the concept and functional implications of Rogers' actualizing tendency.

ROGERS' VIEWS ON ACTUALIZATION AND HIS RATIONALE FOR PSYCHOTHERAPY

One of Rogers' earliest writings on psychotherapy (Rogers, 1942) assumed the natural growth tendency as the healing factor. Later Rogers (1980) added the concept of the 'formative tendency' as the broader foundation block of the person-centered approach. He referred to the formative tendency as the directional tendency in the universe. The actualizing tendency is more specifically that tendency in organisms and is the foundation block for client-centered therapy. In 1942, Rogers wrote:

> Therapy is not a matter of doing something to the individual, or of inducing him to do something about himself. It is instead a matter of freeing him for normal growth and development. (p. 29)

Rogers acknowledged that his ideas about actualization were influenced by the work of Kurt Goldstein, Maslow, Angyal and others but noted that his formulation emerged primarily from his own naturalistic observations. Only after formulating his own theory did he become aware of some of the supporting work in biology (e.g., Bertalanffy, 1960).

Rogers observed that behaviors of organisms (including individuals in therapy) move in the direction of maintaining and enhancing themselves. Emphasizing this observation he asserted the idea of the actualizing tendency as involving all motivation, expansion and enhancement. The basis for all of his thinking about therapy, human development, personality and interpersonal relationships (1959) was the actualization tendency (1963). He stated:

> In client-centered therapy, the person is free to choose any directions, but actually selects positive and constructive pathways. I can only explain this in terms of a directional tendency inherent in the human organism—a tendency to grow, to develop, to realize its full potential. (Rogers, 1986a: 127)

The rationale for client-centered therapy and the person-centered approach in interpersonal interactions rests on the actualizing construct in the following ways: (1) The actualizing tendency is the basic and sole motivation of persons. (2) The actualizing tendency is constructively directional, aiming toward increasing differentiation and complexity and resulting in growth, development and fulfillment of potentialities. (3) The effects of this sole motivational tendency on the person's experience and behavior can be distorted or stunted by interaction with unfavorable, inadequate or destructive environmental circumstances. (4) These distorted or stunted realizations of the person create the need for psychotherapy. (5) Client-centered therapy is an attempt to create an optimal psychological climate for the person by means of the therapist providing a special kind of relationship that involves certain attitudinal qualities of the therapist. (6) This relationship fosters the person's natural actualizing tendency to function in ways that overcome the effects on his/her organism of unfavorable or destructive circumstances. (7) The result of therapy is that the person's experience and behavior become more purely constructive and more powerfully developmental and enhancing. Using the same logic, the promotion of a person's constructive growth tendency was extended beyond psychotherapy to include any interpersonal relationship where one individual can create a climate that promotes the other individual's actualizing tendency.

CHARACTERISTICS OF THE ACTUALIZING TENDENCY IN ROGERS' THEORY

Rogers' construct of the actualizing tendency is an organismic theory with the fundamental qualities in human nature being viewed as those of growth, process and change. In Rogers' theory, *'Man is an actualizing process'* (Van Belle, 1980: 70). Actualization is the motivational construct in organismic theory and, thus, is embedded in the organismic growth process and is *the* motivator for change. The organism/person is the basic unit of inquiry in Rogers' thought. The principle characteristics of all organisms, including the human, have this tendency in common although Rogers' term 'person' is the one used for the distinctly human realization of organismic nature.

In describing this motivational principle, the other main characteristics of organisms and those peculiar to persons are necessarily brought into view. The major properties of Rogers' 'actualizing tendency' construct in organisms/persons are as follows:

1. *The actualizing tendency is individual and universal* (Rogers, 1980). The expression of the tendency is always unique to the individual and also the presence of the tendency is a motivating tendency for all organisms.

2. *The actualizing tendency is holistic* (Rogers, 1959). The organism/person is a fluid, changing gestalt with different aspects assuming figure and ground relations depending upon the momentary specific aims of the person and upon the immediate demands of the environment. The actualizing tendency as the motivational force functions throughout all systems of the person. It is expressed in a variable, dynamic and fluctuating manner through the subsystems of the whole person while maintaining wholeness and organization.

3. *The actualizing tendency is ubiquitous and constant* (Rogers, 1963; Rogers and Sanford, 1984). It is the motivation for all activity of the person, under all circumstances, favorable and unfavorable to the specific person. It functions as long as the person is alive. The moment-by-moment living—the moving, responding, maintaining of wholeness, feeling, thinking, striving—are all manifestations of the actualizing tendency.

4. *The actualizing tendency is a directional process*. Although it involves assimilation and differentiation activities while maintaining wholeness, the wholeness is perpetually

changing. It is a tendency towards realization, fulfillment and perfection of inherent capabilities and potentialities of the individual (Rogers, 1963). It is a selective process in that it is directional and constructive. It tends to enhance and maintain the whole organism/person.

5. *The actualizing tendency is tension increasing* (Rogers, 1959). The organism/person is not a drive-reduction system but one which inherently and spontaneously increases tension levels to expand, grow and further realize inherent capabilities. The directionality of the actualizing tendency requires its tension-increasing characteristic.

6. *The actualizing tendency is a tendency toward autonomy and away from heteronomy* (Rogers, 1963). The person moves inherently toward self-regulation and away from being controlled.

7. *The actualizing tendency is vulnerable to environmental circumstances* (Rogers, 1980; Rogers and Sanford, 1984). Under unfavorable circumstances to the organism the expression of the actualizing tendency may be affected such that the organism becomes distorted although the tendency remains as constructive as possible under the circumstances. Rogers (1980) uses the metaphor of the potato sprout growing towards the tiny source of light in the dark cellar to clarify his point. He said:

> The conditions were unfavorable, but the potatoes would begin to sprout— pale white sprouts, so unlike the healthy green shoots they sent up when planted in the soil in the spring. But these sad, spindly sprouts would grow 2 or 3 feet in length as they reached toward the distant light of the window. The sprouts were, in their bizarre futile growth, a sort of desperate expression of the directional tendency I have been describing. They would never become plants, never mature, never fulfill their real potential. But under the most adverse circumstances, they were striving to become. Life would not give up, even if it could not flourish. (p. 118)

8. *The concept identified as 'self-actualization' is a construct referring to the actualization tendency manifest in the 'self'—a sub-system that becomes differentiated within the whole person* (Rogers, 1951, 1959). This construct is crucial to Rogers' theory of the development of normal personality and psychological disturbances. He theorizes that under unfavorable conditions the actualization of the self sub-system (dictated by self-concepts) may become discrepant from and in conflict with organismic experiencing. Such conflict results in loss of the person's wholeness and integration with consequent disturbance. Alternatively, under favorable developmental circumstances, persons are theorized as remaining open to experience and as developing self-concepts which are harmonious with organismic experiencing, with the consequence that wholeness and integration of the person is fostered.

9. *The concept of consciousness, in the sense of capacity for self-awareness, is viewed as a distinctive human channel of the actualizing tendency* (Rogers, 1980). Consciousness gives the person a greater range of choices for self-regulation and permits potentialities not present in other organisms.

10. *Human beings have a social nature; consequently a basic directionality of the actualizing tendency in humans is toward constructive social behavior* (Rogers, 1982). It is true of all directional characteristics of individuals and species, that the better the environmental/social conditions of the organism, the stronger the expression of the directional characteristic. Thus, in humans, the capacities of empathy, affiliation and language result in constructive social behavior under adequate (or better than adequate) conditions. It is important to recognize that in Rogers' thinking all potentialities of individuals and of species are not aspects of the directionality of the actualizing tendency (Rogers, 1989). For example, people have the potential to vomit or to commit murder. In Rogers' view, these potentials do not show expression under such favorable circumstances as the interpersonal climate of client-centered therapy.

The first seven of the above characteristics of the actualizing tendency, according to Rogers, are common to organisms. The last three characteristics, points eight, nine and ten, are considered distinctive to the human organism and are crucial in his theories of personality and psychological disturbance as well as relevant to therapeutic process.

Rogers (1980), while viewing the actualization tendency from the stance of his scientific orientation, always asserted that it is a hypothesis, 'open to disproof.' Nevertheless, the conception of actualization functions in Rogers' theory as an axiom; that is, it functions as a principle that directs therapist behaviors. Specifically, the organism/person is always actualizing because actualization is the motivational concept that accounts for all living activity. In effect, the person is always actualizing him/herself as best as he/she can under the circumstances. Whenever destructive or self-limiting behavior is observed, the actualizing tendency concept directs inquiry toward the circumstances that have distorted or limited constructiveness.

THE RELATION BETWEEN ROGERS' CONCEPTS OF THE ACTUALIZING TENDENCY AND THE FULLY FUNCTIONING PERSON

Rogers' concept of the 'fully functioning person' is often misunderstood as being a goal for clients in Rogers' therapy. In fact, Rogers is presenting his views on the meaning of 'the good life' and clarifying the manner in which the actualizing tendency functions in human beings. Rogers formulated his concept of the 'fully functioning person' as well as his whole theory from the context and vantage point of his experience as a client-centered therapist. The characteristics of the fully functioning person are an extrapolation from concrete observation of his individual clients and are based on the common features of his clients who progressed in therapy. The common features which Rogers expressed as the 'fully functioning person' are features of directional development in persons. Rogers (1961) said:

> If I attempt to capture in a few words what seems to me to be true of these people *(who showed positive movement in client-centered therapy)* [italics added], I believe it will come out something like this: The good life is a process, not a state of being. It is a direction, not a destination. It is not ... a state of virtue, or contentment, or nirvana or happiness. It is not a condition in which the individual is adjusted, or fulfilled or actualized. (pp. 186–7)

In other words, the 'fully functioning person' does not represent a state of being, a class of persons, as in Maslow's (1970) 'actualizing personalities,' nor a developmental level in Rogers' theory. Instead, Rogers is expressing dimensions of directionality that he believes are inherent and ubiquitous in human beings but which show obvious and accelerated development under favorable psychological conditions. Such conditions are described by Rogers as the necessary and sufficient conditions for constructive personality change and notably associated with client-centered therapy.

There are three major dimensions of the directionality in Rogers' description of the fully functioning person. These are: (1) 'an increasing openness to experience'; (2) 'increasingly existential living'; and (3) 'an increasing trust in his (or her) organism' (Rogers, 1961: 187–9). It is the extent of the development of the three directions in an individual that determines the extent of the psychological freedom of the individual. Psychological freedom is a process of growth, development and realization. Thus, it is through increasing openness to experience, increasingly existential living and increasing trust in one's organism that the inherent actualizing tendency operates more effectively and fully. Rogers has described the psychological dimensions of the expression of the actualizing tendency in human beings in his description of the fully functioning person (Rogers, 1961).

Rogers' and Maslow's theories of actualization are often mistakenly equated. In addition to the differences in their views concerning the fully functioning person, Rogers (1959) clarified a major difference between the theories early in his formulations when he defined the 'actualizing tendency' as the *sole* motivational construct. The motivations conceptualized as 'deficiency needs,' i.e., the physiological needs, needs for safety, belonging, love and esteem, hypothesized by Maslow (1970) as preceding the self-actualization of persons, are included in Rogers' sole motivational construct.

THE FUNCTIONAL ROLE OF THE ACTUALIZING TENDENCY IN CLIENT-CENTERED THERAPY

The fundamental notion of client-centered therapy is that the therapist can trust the tendency of the client, and the only role of the therapist is to create an interpersonal climate that promotes the individual's actualizing tendency. Rogers adopted the construct of the actualizing tendency principle as a cognitive underpinning that implied attitudes of trust in and respect for the client in a helping relationship. When a person has emotional disturbances and problems, according to Rogers' organismic theory, what is required to help the person is a situation or conditions that foster and facilitate the vitality of the person's innate recuperative and growth capabilities.

The therapeutic attitudes of trust and respect and the desirability of a fostering situation which can free the person's capacities for health and growth created some logical parameters for the therapist's approach. These parameters, in effect, eschew standard clinical thinking about psychotherapy, such as the need for diagnosis and treatment plans with treatment goals and strategies. Instead, it followed from the idea of the actualizing tendency and the therapeutic attitudes of trust and respect that the therapist need not conceptualize the client's illness, nor conceptualize any concrete goals that might affect the therapist's attitudes or behavior in relation to the client. It also followed that the therapist need not engage in interventions, strategies or manipulations based upon speculations concerning the client's disturbance or upon ideas about what would constitute healthy directions for the client. It was also logically consistent that the therapist need not determine the frequency of therapy interviews, the length of the therapy, nor when the client should stop therapy. Instead, Rogers thought the client should be approached naïvely, without preconceptions, as a unique individual and be allowed to develop his/her own therapy process. The assumption was that the client's innate actualizing tendency could be fostered most effectively by the creation of a distinctive interpersonal environment fundamentally based on the trust and respect that was implied by belief in the actualizing tendency. The client would be given, in effect, control over the therapeutic situation and therapeutic process up to the limits of the therapist's capacity (and the demands of the work situation). The therapist's basic task is to listen with respect and understanding and help the client to clarify his/her feelings and thoughts as they are expressed to the therapist.

Rogers and his colleagues functioned with this philosophy of trust in the client and, as well, systematically researched their work (Cartwright, 1957). Out of all these endeavors Rogers conceptualized his theory of client-centered therapy. The specific features of the theory evolved out of and continued to be based on the organismic theory of the actualizing tendency and the fundamental philosophy and attitudes of trust in and respect for persons.

THE THEORY

Client-centered theory posits the presence of a client who is incongruent, vulnerable and anxious, but who is also in psychological contact with an attentive therapist. The therapist experiences and manifests three basic attitudes in the relationship. These attitudes are labeled as (1) congruency (or genuineness); (2) unconditional positive regard; and (3) empathic understanding of the client's internal frame of reference (Rogers, 1957, 1959). The particular manifestations or implementation of these attitudes is variable, within limits, depending upon the personal characteristics of both therapist and client. The theory also asserts that the therapeutic attitudes must be perceived to some degree by the client. Rogers hypothesized that the more fully and consistently the therapeutic attitudes are provided by the therapist and perceived by the client, the greater the constructive movement that will occur in the client (Rogers, 1959). The actualizing concept functions in the practice of therapy by influencing the attitudes that are experienced and expressed by the therapist in relation to the client/other.

The client-centered therapist operates on a number of assumptions associated with the actualizing tendency. These assumptions include:

1. Motivation is considered intrinsic, directional, and constructive; the person's tendency is for self-regulation and self-knowledge. The therapist is, thus, oriented to the world of the whole person. *The therapist eschews knowledge 'about' the client, relates as an equal to the client, trusts and respects the client's perceptions as authority about him/herself and trusts the client.*

2. The conception of therapy is one which provides a favorable to optimal psychological and personal environment for the client. *The therapist is not precipitating change by manipulating or directing the client.*

3. Consciousness/perceptions affect the person's behavior. This assumption results in *the need for the therapist's empathic atunement to the phenomenal world of the client.*

4. *The therapist attitude of unconditional positive regard is based on the organismic assumption that the person is always doing the best that he/she can under the particular existing inner and outer circumstances.* The actualizing tendency is the motive for changing circumstances that result in 'doing better.'

5. The disease or disturbance of an individual which responds to psychotherapy is due to inadequate environments (inner/perceptual; outer/physical-social) that distort or stunt realization of inherent capabilities. *The therapist uses no other theoretical models to explain behaviors.*

The basic client/person-centered value is that the authority about the person rests in the person, not in an outside expert. This value emphasizes the internal (i.e., the client's) rather than the external (i.e., the therapist's) view. The client is viewed as going in his/her own way, allowed to go at his/her own pace, and to pursue his/her growth in his/her unique way. The external view is meaningless in a constructive therapy process since the only function of the therapist is to facilitate the client's actualizing process. Bozarth (1985) contends that client-centered therapy operates within a different paradigm than other therapies because of the extreme focus on the 'self-authority' of the client. This focus on self-authority is buttressed in the therapist's trust and belief in the actualizing tendency. Rogers (1986b) stated:

> Practice, theory and research make it clear that the person-centered approach is built on a basic trust in the person ... [It] depends on the actualizing tendency present in every living organism's tendency to grow, to develop, to realize its full potential. This way of being trusts the constructive directional flow of the human being toward a more complex and complete development. It is this directional flow that we aim to release. (p. 198)

THE FUNCTIONAL ROLE OF THE ACTUALIZING TENDENCY IN THERAPY PRACTICE

In the day-to-day work of the client-centered therapist, the idea of the actualizing tendency remains a conscious cognitive foundation. It continuously supports the therapist's trust in, and respect for, the client and supports the therapist's inner activity of generating and maintaining the therapeutic attitudes of congruency, unconditional positive regard and empathic understanding in relation to clients. The remainder of this paper presents a segment from a therapy session that demonstrates the application of the trust and respect of the therapist that is predicated upon the fundamental notion of the actualizing tendency.

THERAPY SESSION SEGMENT

This session is presented and then discussed in terms of the actualizing tendency. The session is that of a female client with a female therapist. The female client is identified as 'Angela.' The client is depicted as 'C' and the therapist as 'T.'

> C1: *Over the weekend … it's hard to explain. I noticed my pain, it was still there and I couldn't believe that I was functioning and feeling like a whole person. Even though I had the pain.*
>
> T1: *It was a new experience to have the pain coexist with a sense of wholeness.*
>
> C2: *Right. Yeah, and I'm still not comfortable with that. If I don't keep after my doctors and myself … you know, things still aren't perfect … I just say OK, it's livable, so I can live like this. And I might end up living with the pain when I could have gotten rid of it. I feel, if I don't keep after it, if I don't keep it in mind, and I don't keep bitching at my doctors, that somehow it's going to get lost … and I'll live that way.*
>
> T2: *But you won't have had to, (C: Yeah) you won't have had to have that pain continue but it will continue because you didn't keep at it.*
>
> C3: *Right.*
>
> T3: *If you don't keep* vigilant.
>
> C4: *Yeah, that's it. And this other thing … when I don't feel good about my physical self … like … I went to the doctor and I gained a few more pounds and I'm upset about that. I was doing so well and so I decided OK, that's it! You know, I know I can do it, so I'm depressed that I even let myself gain a few pounds. It goes the other way, too. When I look in the mirror and I'll go, 'God, you look so good today, why do you feel so shitty?' I have this mental image with my weight too, if it's not where I want it to be, it's kind of like I walk around in my head, when my head hurts. I feel fragmented. If this is the way my inside feels, then this is the way my outside self is going to look to others. But it doesn't, I know that, but it feels like it is not right …*
>
> T4: *How you look and feel should be consistent, but it isn't that way and somehow you can't …*
>
> C5: *Yeah, It's like … sometimes I used to just look in the mirror and say, 'God, how come*

my pain doesn't show?' (T: Uh huh) Where my pain is, I imagine like cracks in my face, something concrete that I can see.

T5: *You would be shocked, 'how could it be?'*

C6: *Yeah, I'd look in the mirror and I'd flip myself out, I'd just stand there ...*

T6: *'How could it be?'*

C7: *Yeah ... And when I'm feeling like that or when I'm feeling overweight or whatever, when I don't feel my body is physically in check, something feels, um, it feels like ... I don't know ... it feels like I'm not a whole person ... Which is, I guess, what's different about this past weekend, how I perceived myself, because ... It's like I don't feel like a whole person when I'm like that and even though others can't tell ... I feel like I'm being dishonest, because they can't see what's really inside of me. I have a big problem with that, talking to people when I feel like shit, I feel dishonest because I really don't feel like I'm me. I feel angry, I feel depressed, I feel fragmented ... I got the word, it's a good client-centered word, I just thought, 'congruent', I don't feel congruent. That's what it is.*

T7: *In your appearance and your behavior, your appearance is one kind of person ... but inside you're ...*

C8: *It's that they're not congruent, they're different. And to me that's why I can't feel like a whole person. But this weekend, I did feel like a whole person, even though I was still incongruent. And it felt good, but, yet, it was upsetting too. Because then, I guess, I feel if I'm not vigilant that I never am going to be congruent.*

T8: *The thing is you felt congruent, you felt (C: Right) a whole person in spite of the fact that you still have the pain. So, you had the same combination of contradictory realities and yet you had a feeling of wholeness. (C: Right) But there was the worry that you would, in feeling whole, let the pain stay by giving up on doing your utmost to get rid of it.*

C9: *That's it.*

A more detailed analysis of this therapy segment is presented in order to identify the relationship of the therapist's efforts to be consistent with the underpinning of the actualizing tendency. The segment is from the fortieth therapy session. Angela's first response (C1) illustrates her experience of surprise during the previous weekend. She says: 'It's hard to explain' and, indeed, it is, at this point, not clear exactly what Angela means by 'whole person' nor what her typical experience of herself may have been that made the weekend experiences so surprising. The therapist's first response (T1) simply checks or tests understanding with a brief restatement for Angela to verify or correct. The therapist makes no attempt to pursue clarification or elaboration through questions or guesses. *She simply expresses her understanding of the client as far as it goes. The therapist's trust is that the open acceptance of the client's statements will cumulate to foster the client's natural process of actualization.*

Angela (C2) reveals that there is more to this surprising feeling of wholeness co-existing with physical pain. She says it was accompanied by a feeling of fear. The therapist (T2) again tests her understanding by expressing Angela's point that she expects she would have to continue to live with pain if she were to accept the pain. Wholeness apparently involves accepting the pain. Accepting the pain means, to Angela, that she would give up pushing to find treatments.

Angela (C3) verifies the correctness of her therapist's response (in T2). The therapist then (T3) responds with an emphasis on Angela's felt need for vigilance. The word 'vigilance' was not used by Angela but is used by the therapist in her effort to understand the importance, to Angela, of keeping on the lookout for, and seeking treatment for, her pain. *To this point, the therapist has consistently tried to follow the client's meanings and feelings by checking or testing her understanding with Angela. The therapist continues to trust Angela's own capacity for forward movement.*

Next, in C4, Angela expresses two new points. The first point is that she doesn't feel good about herself. For example, because she gained weight, she says she must gain control. She expresses this as 'OK, that's it!' meaning that she must stop eating too much. She says that she can do what she needs to do when she reaches that point. The second point is expressed when she harks back to her first statement which had implied that previous to the weekend she had not ever been able to feel whole when in pain. Here (in C4) she is expressing a sense of confusion and disturbance when she feels 'shitty' and at the same time is looking good. Apparently, previously she had not been able to reconcile this discrepancy between her feelings and her appearance into an experience of wholeness. Instead she would feel 'fragmented.'

The therapist is not able to complete her response (T4) to Angela's C4. But she again is trying to test her understanding. She does this in the form of a restatement of Angela's expectation of being consistent in her feelings and her appearance that is not realized in her actual experience of herself. *The therapist does not attempt to explain or push Angela towards closure or resolution.*

Angela (C5) then vividly re-presents her previous point by quoting her thoughts when looking in her mirror and by stating the image she expects to see in her mirror. The therapist (T5) responds by re-presenting herself as Angela, stating, in her own words, what might be Angela's words of shock when she finds her face in the mirror is not cracked and distorted as her pain makes her feel it might be.

Angela (C6) further expresses her distress about the event of seeing she looks good while she's in pain. The therapist responds (T6) by repeating what she said in T5 as if they were Angela's thoughts or words, 'How could it be?'

Angela (C7) continues with a complex statement in which she first summarizes the basis for not feeling like a whole person. Then she restates the fact that the preceding weekend she felt whole while still experiencing pain. She then elaborates on the problem of feeling pain while looking good. She says it stimulates a feeling of being dishonest with people. Finally, still in C7, Angela expresses her awareness of the therapist's client-centered approach with a positive emotional tone. She uses the Rogerian term 'congruence' while explaining her new, recent, feeling of wholeness in the context of pain. In her response (T7), the therapist starts to check her understanding by restatement, but is interrupted. Angela (C9) verifies the therapist's grasp of what she has been expressing. *Through the entire interview segment the actualizing tendency construct has been functioning as an intellectual underpinning for the therapist's attitudes of trust in and respect for the client. These basic attitudes toward the client are channeled directly into the therapist's efforts to experience and express the specific therapeutic therapist attitudes identified by Rogers as congruency, unconditional positive regard and empathic understanding.*

In the sequence of interactions between Angela and her therapist, Angela leads as she fills out the meanings of her initial statement (C1) and adds other feelings that are related (e.g., C2, C4, C5). Angela's leading is a process of developing awareness, recollections and unfolding associations. How and what is revealed emanate from the process within Angela rather than from ideas put forth by the therapist. *The therapist is not intervening with any theoretical conceptions whatsoever in Angela's actualizing process (which includes self-awareness and self-disclosure for Angela). The actualizing tendency is immediately functional in the therapist's interaction with Angela. It is the basis underlying the attitudes that result in the therapist's non-interfering and non-directive empathic following of Angela's responses.* The therapist's only verbal behavior is her attempt to check or test her understanding of what Angela expresses. The question that is implicit in all of the therapist's restatements is, 'Do I understand you correctly?' or 'Is this what you are telling me?' Angela's responses indicate that she does feel understood. *The therapist, thus, does not intervene, bring in 'expert' suggestions or prescribe treatments. The therapist trusts the natural constructive direction of the client and strives only to implement the atmosphere that will foster the actualizing tendency.*

SUMMARY

This paper reviews Carl R. Rogers' concept of the actualizing tendency as an operational premise in client-centered therapy. Rogers' concept of the relation of the actualizing tendency and the fully functioning person is clarified. The role of the actualizing tendency as a functional cognitive underpinning in client-centered therapy is demonstrated by reviewing and commenting upon a client-centered therapy segment.

The client-centered therapist implements the actualizing tendency by creating a specific interpersonal climate during the therapy session. This climate is created by means of the therapist experiencing and communicating certain attitudes toward the client. These attitudes are identified as the qualities of congruency, unconditional positive regard, and accurate empathy. These were considered by Rogers to be the necessary and sufficient conditions for constructive personality change. Since the experience of these attitudes by the client fosters an individual's actualizing tendency, the client-centered therapist trusts the client to move forward in a constructive direction without intervening and assuming therapeutic expertise about the client. The constructive forward movement of the client is propelled by the sole and inherent motivation in human beings; that is, the actualizing tendency.

REFERENCES

Bertalanffy L (1960) *Problems in Life*. New York: Harper Torchbooks.

Bozarth JD (1985) Quantum theory and the person-centered approach. *Journal of Counseling and Development, 64* (3), 179–82.

Cartwright DS (1957) Annotated bibliography of research and theory construction in client-centered therapy. *Journal of Counseling Psychology, 4*, 82–100.

Ford JG (1991) Rogers's theory of personality: Review and perspectives. In A Jones & R Crandall (Eds) Handbook of self-actualization. [Special Issue]. *Journal of Social Behavior and Personality, 6* (5), 19–44.

Goodyear RK (1987) In memory of Carl Ransom Rogers (January 8, 1902–February 4, 1987). *Journal of Counseling and Development, 63*, 561–4.

Lambert MI, Shapiro DA & Bergin AE (1986) The effectiveness of psychotherapy. In SL Garfield & AE Bergin (Eds) *Handbook of Psychotherapy and Behavior Change*. New York: Wiley and Sons, pp. 157–211.

Maslow AH (1970) *Motivation and Personality* (2nd edn). New York: Harper and Row.

Patterson CH (1984) Empathy, warmth, and genuineness in psychotherapy: A review of reviews. *Psychotherapy, 21* (4), 431–8.

Rogers CR (1942) *Counseling and Psychotherapy*. Boston: Houghton Mifflin.

Rogers CR (1951) *Client-Centered Therapy*. Boston: Houghton Mifflin.

Rogers CR (1957) The necessary and sufficient conditions of therapeutic personality change. *Journal of Consulting Psychology, 21*, 95–103.

Rogers CR (1959) A theory of therapy, personality, and interpersonal relationships, as developed in the client-centered framework. In S Koch (Ed) *Psychology: A study of a science: Study 1. Conceptual and systematic: Vol. 3: Formulations of the person and the social context*. New York: McGraw-Hill, pp. 184–256.

Rogers CR (1961) A therapist's view of the good life: The fully functioning person. In CR Rogers (Ed) *Becoming a Person*. Boston: Houghton Mifflin, pp. 183–96.

Rogers CR (1963) The actualizing tendency in relation to 'motive' and to consciousness. In M Jones (Ed) *Nebraska Symposium on Motivation*. Lincoln, NE: University of Nebraska Press, pp. 1–24.

Rogers CR (1980) *A Way of Being*. Boston: Houghton Mifflin.

Rogers CR (1982) Reply to Rollo May's letter. *Journal of Humanistic Psychology, 22*, 85–9.

Rogers CR (1986a) Rogers, Kohut, and Erickson. *Person-Centered Review, 1* (2), 125–40.

Rogers CR (1986b) Client-centered approach to therapy. In IL Kutash & A Wolf (Eds) *Psychotherapist's Casebook: Theory and technique in practice*. San Francisco: Jossey Bass, pp. 197–208.

Rogers CR (1989) Rollo May. In H Kirschienbaum & VL Henderson (Eds) *Carl Rogers: Dialogues*. Boston: Houghton Mifflin, pp. 229–55.

Rogers CR & Sanford R (1984) Client-centered psychotherapy. In HI Kaplan & BJ Sadock (Eds) *Comprehensive Textbook of Psychiatry IV*. Baltimore, MD: Williams and Wilkins, pp. 1374–88.

Van Belle HA (1980) *Basic Intent and Therapeutic Approach of Carl R. Rogers*. Toronto: Wedge.

Chapter 3

THE ACTUALISATION CONUNDRUM

Tony Merry

Actualisation is a central concept within person-centred psychology. It is the only motivation for the growth and development of organisms, including humans, postulated by Rogers. Actualisation is a 'tendency' or a process that occurs universally in the biological world. It is a directional tendency towards greater differentiation and the fulfilment of constructive potential. That all organisms 'actualise' can be observed around us every day. The fact that an organism is alive and engaged in goal-directed behaviour (in the case of animals) is evidence of an actualising tendency. At the cellular level, recent research demonstrates, for example, that so-called 'stem cells' are capable of actualising in a variety of 'directions' according to the needs of the organism as a whole, though most cells fulfil a more limited set of potentials. This, too, is evidence for the existence of a tendency for organisms to actualise their potential in a way that is not dependent on consciously directing attention towards the process. Actualisation can be regarded as the non-conscious and inherent property of living organisms to become whatever they are capable of becoming. Individuals are actualising organisms; they are not entities which, at a certain point, engage in actualisation. Without actualisation there is no organism.

Actualisation implies differentiation. The tendency to fulfil potential includes the capacity to develop systems and subsystems (like a temperature regulatory system and a sensory system), all of which contribute to the development of the potentials inherent in the organism as a whole. At the psychological level, actualisation is evidenced by the development of a self and self-concept, a capacity to experience emotion and to think, create, and plan, among other things. Actualisation is manifested through the growth, development and enhancement of the organism and, ultimately, ensures its survival.

Prior to 1959, and including the 1951 book *Client-Centered Therapy: Its current practice, implications and theory*, Rogers, (as Guthrie Ford points out, 1989), referred to 'self-actualisation' as providing the motivation for personal growth and change. For example, 'the self-actualization of the organism appears in the direction of socialization, broadly defined' (Rogers, 1951: 488). However, by the time the 1959 statement of theory was published, Rogers' view had changed significantly. 'Self-actualization' had been replaced as the sole motivational construct with 'the actualizing tendency' (Rogers, 1959: 196). The significance of this shift is hard to underestimate. Firstly, self-actualisation

---

First published (2003) in *Person-Centred Practice, 11* (2), 83–91.

was no longer viewed as a process leading to optimal functioning, and, secondly, self-actualisation had become a 'sub-aspect of motivation' (Rogers, 1959: 197). The single motivational construct, according to person-centred theory, became 'this basic actualizing tendency' (p. 196), with the tendency toward self-actualisation appearing only after the development of the self-structure, and regarded as a 'sub-aspect of motivation' (p. 197). In other words the 'basic actualizing tendency' results in the development of a self-structure, and every individual self-actualises because it has a self-structure to maintain.

This shift was important since it provided an explanation for how a person can become psychologically malfunctioning, even though the underlying tendency of the person is to develop towards greater integration and psychological health. It is often assumed that it is the conflictual relationship between actualisation and self-actualisation that accounts for incongruence, but, in fact, the theory is more subtle than this.

Person-centred theory suggests that it is tension between self-actualisation and organismic experiencing that accounts for the development of incongruence. Organismic experiencing is the experience of the organism as a whole, but part of the organism (the self) interprets, symbolises and gives meaning to the experience. It is assumed that the self, as a result of past experiencing, is conditioned to process new experiences in the light of that conditioning. The actualising tendency prompts the organism to allow all experience into awareness and to symbolise it accurately, but the self-actualising process can sabotage this 'openness to experience' as the self selects certain experiences for 'special treatment', i.e., their denial or distortion. In other words, once a self or self-concept has begun to form, the organism is equipped to discriminate between experiences and respond to them differently according to the extent to which an experience either reinforces the existing self-concept or is in conflict with it. Those experiences that reinforce the self-concept are assimilated accurately into the self-structure; those that conflict with it are either denied completely or distorted in some way to make them 'fit'. Leaving aside those experiences that are never (or only rarely) available to awareness, such as the transmission of nerve impulses, or the routine beating of the heart, the potential for accurate symbolisation in awareness of all experiencing remains present, even as the self is assigning values to experience in accordance with the degree to which those experiences create or avoid dissonance.

Since we have used the terms 'self' and 'self-structure', it is helpful to be reminded of what Rogers meant by these terms:

> The self-structure is an organized configuration of perceptions of the self which are admissible to awareness. It is composed of such elements as the perceptions of one's characteristics and abilities; the precepts and concepts of the self in relation to others and to the environment; the value qualities which are perceived as associated with experiences and objects; and the goals and ideals which are perceived as having positive or negative valence. It is, then, the organized picture, existing in awareness either as figure or ground, of the self and the self-in-relationship, together with the positive or negative values which are associated with those qualities and relationships, as they are perceived as existing in the past, present or future. (Rogers, 1951: 501)

The 'self-structure' is an organisation of perceptions, precepts, concepts, values and qualities that are either currently in awareness or easily available to awareness. The particular characteristics of these factors, together with the way in which they are organised, determine the kinds of experiences that are made available to awareness, or are distorted or denied.

Mearns and Thorne (2000) have recently offered a revised theory of the self. While the Rogers definition (above) includes only those experiences etc. that are in awareness at any given time, Mearns and Thorne suggest an expanded definition to include 'edge of awareness' material (p. 175). The term 'edge of awareness' implies that some emotional material is not fully in the person's awareness, and so not a functional component of the self in Rogers' terms. However, Mearns and Thorne view edge of awareness material as having some influence and theoretically a component of the self even though it is not in direct awareness.

The problem with using the word 'edge' in this context is that it implies 'awareness' as being, metaphorically, a kind of geographical 'space' or 'area' with some experiences residing in the 'city centre' and others in the suburbs. To avoid this metaphor problem, it is perhaps better to consider 'edge of awareness' phenomena as those experiences against which the defences of distortion or denial are not totally successful. This is important because edge of awareness material must include at least some of those experiences that are perceived by the self as potentially threatening to its consistency. Such experiences may be 'dimly perceived' and are a source of some anxiety, but the individual will not be aware of the source of that anxiety.

To recap for a moment—the actualising tendency, as part of its manifestation, results in the differentiation of some experiences into a 'self' or 'self-concept'. A self-structure is created which, in the absence of threat or perceived threat during its formation, would be entirely open to admitting all experience accurately into awareness. However, some experiences are denied or distorted because they are perceived as threatening the current consistency of the self-concept. This sets up a cyclical series of events. The conditioned self discriminates between experiences and regards some as threatening, but others as entirely or partially acceptable. The self thus becomes further conditioned and more likely to defend against further experience perceived as threatening or potentially so.

THE ROLE OF ACTUALISATION IN THE CREATION OF CONDITIONS OF WORTH

It is usually assumed that conditions of worth result from the introjection or internalisation into the self-structure of evaluations (usually negative) of 'worth' originating with significant others in the person's immediate environment. The existence of conditions of worth is indication of the degree to which a person is incongruent, disturbed or malfunctioning in some way. But since 'actualisation' (not self-actualisation) is the sole motivational construct in person-centred psychology, the creation of conditions of worth must be a manifestation of actualisation. The logical problem here is that this does not seem to be consistent with a concept of actualisation that allows only for constructive change if conditions of worth are regarded as having only a negative or destructive effect on the person as a whole.

However, it is possible to conceive of conditions of worth as acting to the individual's benefit in that they serve to guide the person's behaviour away from the possibility of further 'hurt' or psychological damage. The existence of the condition of worth that says, 'It is not acceptable openly to express my anger, because to do so risks the withdrawal of love and protection', while closing down the individual's expressive potential in this realm, also serves to neutralise the risk (as perceived) of the withdrawal of protection should that potential become actualised.

In the above example, the general actualising tendency is protecting the person from further perceived threat by reinforcing the consistency of the self-structure ('I do not experience or express anger') at the expense of admitting some experiences into awareness. In other words, actualisation results (in conditions of perceived threat) in the ongoing development of a conditioned self that is defended against the possibility of allowing experiences into awareness that would subvert the consistency of the self-concept as it currently exists.

In this way, it is possible to view the actualising tendency as always manifesting to maintain self-consistency, especially in the face of external circumstances that are perceived as threatening. The consistently constructive direction of actualisation includes the tendency to protect and defend the person against threat originating in the environment, or the individual's perception of the environment. The continuing process of the actualisation of a conditioned self is a self-defence, but one that comes at a price. The underlying imperative of the person is his or her continuing survival, not 'openness to experience'.

It thus becomes appropriate to respect an individual's conditions of worth as evidence of the actualising tendency's capacity for self-defence and self-maintenance, as well as evidence of disturbance or incongruence. The positive benefits of conditions of worth, at least at one time, outweighed the benefits of 'openness to experience' in the individual's life experience. Such conditions of worth become embedded in the individual's self-structure because they serve a positive purpose. Self-actualisation, incorporating those conditions of worth, continues even though their self-defence properties become dysfunctional. Only when their self-defence properties are experienced as dysfunctional and redundant does it become possible for the actualising tendency to correct the self-structure in line with this new experience. It follows that only when an individual experiences a psychological environment significantly free of threat will dysfunctional defences tend to dissolve as the actualising tendency manifests in the fulfilment of constructive potentials.

ACTUALISATION AND THE EXPRESSION OF POTENTIAL

Rogers' descriptions of the person amount to a dynamic, experimental organism actively exploring new situations and new experiences. Humans seek out experiences that are likely to result in increased levels of positive self-regard, and avoid those experiences that do not. They are not passive 'consumers' of experience, but active creators of experience continually in negotiation with the environment, balancing the need for creativity and self-enhancement on the one hand, with the need to protect, maintain and survive on the other. At a more basic level, humans do not only seek experiences in terms of their positive self-regard 'payoff'. For example, they actively search for sustenance, physical safety and warmth which are not directly related to psychological needs, but are 'organismic' needs—they help maintain the organism as a whole. But humans do more than select experiences that maintain them; they also look for experiences that enhance them. In other words, humans are not tension-reducing organisms, but in seeking new experiences, levels of tension increase within the organism. An increase in tension enables the human organism to expand its capabilities and to actualise more potential than if the person were simply interested in neutralising tension.

The actualising tendency prompts the individual to experience novel and unpredictable situations, because these represent a 'growing edge', whereas familiar and 'safe' situations represent a status quo. However, we know from the phenomenological basis of person-centred theory that situations are responded to as perceived, rather than as they 'really are', or as they might be perceived by another individual. Whilst the actualising tendency may be urging the individual to experience novelty to enable growth to take place, the self-actualising tendency of that same individual may inhibit this motivation because the new situation is perceived as being too risky. For example, a client in therapy may face the novel situation of 'opening up' and becoming psychologically vulnerable in the company of another (in this case, a therapist). But the 'self' may contain a warning bell, based on previous experience that such an opening up is likely to result in further hurt. A tension now exists between the actualising tendency ('go for it, it will be good for you'), and the experience as perceived, i.e., as interpreted or assigned significance by the self as it is currently configured ('pull back, you know what will happen'). If this tension is experienced as unbearable in that it creates a high level of anxiety, the organismic experiencing process may be 'intercepted' by the conditioned self and given a value, in this case a negative one. The self remains free to continue actualising without undergoing change because the experience has been denied to awareness. Actualisation is manifested both through its tendency to protect and maintain the organism in situations of threat, and to enhance it in situations where threat is not perceived or is experienced as manageable.

Rogers makes it clear that the actualising tendency can drive the individual in one direction, but the need to maintain the consistency of even a maladaptive self-structure in the presence of threat (or the perception of threat) leads it in another, '… in some respects the individual's behavior will be regulated by the actualizing tendency, and in other respects by the self-actualizing tendency, thus promoting discordant or incomprehensible behaviors' (Rogers, 1959: 203).

SOME DIFFICULTIES WITH LOGIC

The Rogers position appears to some to be illogical or inconsistent. How can a 'tendency' be in conflict with a 'part' or 'subsystem' of itself? If the actualising tendency is the only source of motivation, how can it give rise to a part of itself that provides a second (and conflicting) motivation? Finally, if the actualising tendency is constructively directional, trustworthy and moving always in the direction of maturation, how does it create a secondary system that can sabotage it?

This apparent logical inconsistency is resolved if actualisation is conceptualised as manifesting (that is, actualising) the self-defence potentials of the individual. If the primary need is for survival, everything else is secondary. It is better to close down some potentials if the alternative threatens survival. The actualising tendency allows for the person to overcome perceived or actual threats to survival by creating a self-structure that is wise enough to avoid threatened extinction.

Mick Cooper has recently tried to find a way of dealing with apparent flaws in the theory of actualisation. Cooper (2000) has suggested 'a more logically consistent way of understanding Rogers' fundamental conflict' (p. 89), i.e., that between the general actualising tendency on the one hand, and the self-actualising imperative on the other. In contrast, he suggests 'a conflict between the self-actualising tendency and non-self-actualising subsystems of the actualising tendency … In other words, Rogers' developmental model can be understood as proposing that the organism inhabits a world in which to actualise one potential—its 'self'—it must inhibit the actualisation of other potentials' (pp. 89–90). But logical difficulties emerge here when the obvious questions are asked. How can a self-actualising tendency be composed, at least in part, of subsystems that are non-self-actualising? From where do these subsystems emerge and how do they develop? How can a directional actualising tendency which serves to maximise potential and is always constructive 'create' a subsystem of a subsystem that inhibits the actualisation of some potentials, some of which may be constructive and creative for the organism?

It is beyond doubt that an individual inhibits the actualisation of some of its potential in some circumstances. For example, a person has the potential to commit murder, but this potential (for most people) is inhibited because not to do so would place the individual in intolerable conflict with his or her (internalised) system of values, or might result in lengthy imprisonment or worse. Even then, this potential may become actualised in extreme circumstances (for example by redefining the act of murder into a justifiable act of self-defence, or to further a particular 'cause' which is regarded as being of greater value than the sanctity of individual human life). Any such inhibition, however, must (according to the theory of actualisation) be a product of the actualising tendency, because this provides the sole motivational direction. The actualisation of any potential will be inhibited if this inhibition serves the purpose of maintaining survival.

Cooper (2000) goes further by suggesting a 'plurality of self-concepts' (p. 92) with each self-concept existing in relation to certain experiences, but not others. In other words, one self-concept may emerge in relation to say, mother and father, but a different self-concept may emerge in relation to, say, schoolteachers or police officers.

Cooper is proposing that not only does the actualising tendency have a 'sub-aspect' (self-actualisation), but that this sub-aspect itself has any number of 'subsystems', some of which are in conflict with or antagonistic to the subsystem of which they are part. In order to resolve these conflicts, the human organism has developed a system where some experiences can be 'allocated' to one self-concept, whilst other experiences are 'allocated' to other self-concepts.

Once again, if actualisation includes the manifestation of self-defence potentials, as is being suggested here, then Cooper's complaint of a 'fundamental conflict' ceases to exist. There is no fundamental conflict, and there is no need to propose a set of subsystems to resolve the logical dilemma because no such dilemma exists.

Mearns and Thorne (2000) have suggested a revision of the self in person-centred psychology that has some similarities with Cooper's position, but also a major difference. Whereas Cooper suggests multiple 'selves' or self-concepts, Mearns and Thorne hold to the traditional position of a single self. Coining the term 'configurations of self', they propose the self as consisting of multiple configurations which themselves are composed of 'elements which form a coherent pattern generally reflective of a dimension of existence within the Self' (p. 102). The 'configurations' idea does not require the existence of multiple self-concepts, but does allow for the individual to be adaptive and flexible. It offers an explanation for how individuals can respond to different situations by allowing different sets of personal characteristics, values and attitudes to coalesce as a functioning unit in ways that are appropriate to the situation while maintaining self-consistency. For example, I do not consider myself to be a generally competitive person in most circumstances, but I know that I have the capability to become competitive when, for example, I am playing cricket. A set of configurations that enable me to express my competitive characteristics coalesces on the cricket field, but not in other contexts. I do not regard myself as in possession of two 'selves' because other underlying values and attitudes remain consistent.

The various 'configurations of self' available demonstrate the creativity and flexibility of actualisation. The 'self' is able to call upon different qualities in different situations. This idea also maintains the person-centred concept of the importance of a single 'self' in personality theory and is a more parsimonious theory than the Cooper alternative.

ACTUALISATION AND THE ENVIRONMENT

The environment contains both 'self-enhancing' and 'self-limiting' factors. Not all self-limiting factors are problematic if these limitations can be overcome successfully, or if the individual can act to accommodate them. Indeed, the existence of problems enables the individual to express creative abilities in overcoming them, to learn from the process and to 'grow' as a result. For example, we can safely assume that the need to reproduce is a fundamental one inherent in our biological make-up as 'organisms'. The need for sexual gratification may be present, even if the need for reproduction is not, and vice versa. The environment, however, contains many limitations to an uninhibited expression of either the reproductive potential or the potential for sexual gratification. In learning how to express sexual and/or reproductive needs appropriately, the person learns how to balance individual needs with those of others.

Rogers' use of the term 'self-actualisation' up to 1959 may account, at least in part, for the misperception that client-centred counselling was concerned only with the maximisation of 'self-potential', and that 'self-actualisation' represented the pinnacle of human achievement. Whilst 'the self' was (and remains) a pivotal concept in person-centred psychology, the problems of conceiving the 'self' in entirely individualistic terms quickly became apparent. Where 'self-actualisation' is (wrongly) assumed to be the goal of therapy (or even life itself), then the 'environment' becomes regarded as being made up of antagonistic features that, somehow, thwart individual expressions of 'self' and sabotage attempts at 'individuality' or 'autonomy'. It is a case of 'me' versus' my environment', containing (as it does) all kinds of hazards that conspire to prevent my 'actualisation' into becoming a 'fully functioning person'.

Mearns and Thorne (2000) have gone some way towards dealing with this misconception. They suggest that,

> There will be times when the pressure of the actualising tendency will inspire a resistance. Such resistance is intimately related both to the actualising tendency and to the person's current existence as a social being. The effect of the resistance serves to maintain a balance which allows for a degree of expression for the actualising tendency while taking care to preserve the viability of the social context within the person's 'life space'. (p. 182)

In Mearns and Thorne's' reframing of the theory, disorder is created when the individual is unable to achieve a balance (or homeostasis) between the conflicting demands of actualisation and the need to preserve 'the life space'. The emphasis is on the process by which this balance is achieved, and the ability of the individual to respond to changes in the social environment. Mearns and Thorne capture this concept in formal language as follows:

> 'Disorder' is caused when the person becomes chronically stuck within his own process such that the homeostatic balance cannot reconfigure to respond to changing circumstances. (2000: 184)

Note that it is the actualising tendency that inspires this resistance, not 'self-actualisation'. Whereas Rogers viewed antagonism between actualisation and self-actualisation as the source of disturbance, Mearns and Thorne provide a new dimension in suggesting that it is tension between the actualising tendency and the environment that upsets the balance between the actualisation of potential and a 'person's current existence as a social being'. Disorder is created when a person's self-structure is unable to cope with environmental factors, not when the actualising tendency finds itself in conflict with the need for self-actualisation or with the organismic experiencing process. Of course, there may be many occasions when these are merely different sides of the same coin or, to all intents and purposes, are the same thing, but there may also be other occasions when they are not. The difference between Rogers and Mearns and Thorne appears to be that whereas Rogers saw disturbance as being the outcome of an actualising tendency in conflict with itself (self-actualisation being a component or subsystem of actualisation), Mearns and Thorne see disturbance resulting from a conflict between an organismic process (actualisation) and external (or environmental) factors.

The strength of this position is that it places the individual squarely within his or her environmental context and views the person as being in negotiation with that environment, both shaping and being shaped by it. It regards the environment as both hostile and friendly in turn, and sees the person as resourceful and adaptable, or potentially so. It sees actualisation in process terms, and not something that either 'happens' or doesn't 'happen'. It also implies (though does not make specific) the idea (discussed above) of the actualising tendency serving, at times, to strengthen the individual's defences against threat and hurt, in this case by recognising the importance of the preservation of the life space as a critical component of the 'negotiation'.

The problem with the Mearns and Thorne concept is the notion of a 'degree of expression of the actualising tendency'. This implies that expression of the actualising tendency is somehow under the control of the environment, and can be switched on or off at times, or at least be slowed down or changed in some way. Consistent with other arguments presented here, I think this to be inaccurate or misleading to some extent. The actualising tendency, in my view, always 'works' at 'full volume'. It is the motivation for the individual to operate at the highest or most fully functioning level possible at all times in response to and taking into account prevailing environmental conditions. The fact that the actualisation of any particular potential becomes inhibited because of environmental circumstances is itself motivated by the actualising tendency. In other words, the inhibition itself is a manifestation of actualisation because actualisation fulfils self-defence potentials as well as self-enhancing ones.

CONCLUSION

Actualisation is a central component of person-centred theory and must remain so because it provides the basis of a process theory of human development. Since it is posited as the only source of motivation, then all aspects of human behaviour, change and development occur as manifestations of this one central tendency. To assume 'ulterior motives' or secondary motives of other systems or subsystems (like self-actualisation') is inconsistent with person-centred theory.

The most parsimonious view is of one motivation resulting in a single 'self'. Self-actualisation does not provide any motivation, but is an outcome of the general actualising tendency. Actualisation manifests in either self-defence and self-maintenance or in self-enhancement according to the experienced and perceived characteristics of environmental demands at any one time. The 'self' is best conceptualised as a single gestalt where different configurations become 'field' according to the needs of the individual at the time.

REFERENCES

Cooper M (2000) Person-centred developmental theory: Reflections and revisions. *Person-Centred Practice,* 8 (2), 87–94.

Guthrie Ford J (1989) On actualizing person-centered theory: A critique of textbook treatments of Rogers's motivational constructs. *Teaching of Psychology,* 16 (1), 30–1.

Mearns D & Thorne B (2000) *Person-Centred Therapy Today.* London: Sage.

Rogers CR (1951) *Client-Centered Therapy.* London: Constable.

Rogers CR (1959) A theory of therapy, personality and interpersonal relationships, as developed in the client-centered framework. In S Koch (Ed) *Psychology: a Study of Science, Vol. 3: Formulations of the person and the social context.* New York: McGraw-Hill, pp. 184–256.

Chapter 4

THE MYTH OF THE ACTUALIZING TENDENCY: THE ACTUALIZING TENDENCY CONCEPT AS A GUIDING STORY

Brian E. Levitt

> Indeed, the first and most essential service of mythology is this one, of opening the mind and heart to the utter wonder of all being.
>
> Joseph Campbell

INTRODUCTION

We are storytellers. We express ourselves through stories. We understand each other and the world around us through stories. Stories entertain us. Stories comfort us. Stories transport us. Stories wake us up to life and to ourselves. Some stories are woven into the fabric of our belief systems, and they serve to guide us (or blind us). They help us to navigate life, to understand the world, others, and ourselves. They can be especially useful in helping us come to terms with that which is frightening, strange, or clearly different. These stories can also take on a mythic dimension. They can wake us up to the fullness of life, or as Joseph Campbell would say, 'to the utter wonder of all being' (2002: xx).

Though myths may be seen as lies, or more benignly as entertainment, they have the power to point to truths. The danger, ever present, is seeing the myth itself as truth, or worse yet, as The Truth. Myths are not lies, nor are they truths, though they certainly have the potential to reinforce lies or guide us towards truths. A myth can be a compass when we find ourselves lost. Though myths are often seen as outdated, they are always waiting for us to find new life in them, to reinterpret them and create new maps with them. The potential held within a myth has everything to do with our ability to find its place in our modern context, and to be guided by it without being blinded by it. The value in a myth lies in what we do with it.

THE ACTUALIZING TENDENCY AS A GUIDING STORY

The actualizing tendency is a myth. I do not mean this as dismissive—I have no intention of painting this theoretical construct as rigid, outdated, or meaningless. In saying that the actualizing tendency is a myth, I am suggesting that it is a story that has the power to point to a truth. The actualizing tendency is a guiding story, if understood well, that is practical, useful, meaningful, and important as one means of following and remaining on a non-directive path. This chapter is an exploration of this idea, an attempt to empathically understand the actualizing tendency concept itself by seeing its power as a myth. But first I explore two other myths from two very different belief systems, in part to shed light on the way that myths can inhabit belief systems and can become reified as Truth. One of these myths I will explore is from the Bible, and one is from medicine.

THE MYTH OF JACOB IN THE DESERT

The story of Jacob and his dream in the desert, a part of his journey to Haram, is a guiding story. It is a myth. It is a very ancient and rich instructive tale found in the Torah (the first five books of Jewish scripture). Jacob is one of the most intriguing personalities of the ancient Torah. The major figures who come before him in the mythic stories of the Bible know and speak to God directly. Jacob does not have this facility of his ancestors. He is a man with many flaws who struggles through life. As a young man, he secures a blessing from his blind father under false pretenses—a blessing that should not really be his. His legendary journey through the desert tells of his securing a blessing of an entirely different kind. It is the story of a man who comes to a new awareness of what is around him, experiencing a consciousness-raising that changes his life.

In this story we are told that Jacob traveled through the desert from Be'er-Sheba to Haram. During his journey, the sun set, so he stopped for the night. He was in the middle of the desert, and lay down on the ground, as there were no rest stops. We are also told he set some stones at his head, which does not sound all that comfortable. Nonetheless, that is the story we are given, and he was apparently comfortable enough to fall asleep and have a dream. In his dream, Jacob saw 'messengers of God' going up and down a ladder connecting heaven and earth. He then saw God in his dream, and God spoke to him. After God speaks to him in his dream, Jacob awakes, stunned, and expresses his new awareness in one of the richest couplets found in the Bible:

YHWH [Yahweh] is in this place,
and I, I did not know it! (Fox, 1995: 131)

Jacob no longer sees the place he is in as simply a desert. He is, in fact, as the story tells us 'awestruck,' and recognizes that 'This is none other than a house of God, and that is the gate of heaven!' (ibid.: 131).

Whether this myth is still meaningful depends on our ability to see it with fresh eyes. It may be for many that the language, even in a modern and poetic translation is too out of step with our times. It may be that the religious context is simply too off-putting for some to see it in an alive way. However, this ancient Bible story is entirely relevant in our quest to understand the place of myth in belief systems, and to better see the actualizing tendency as a myth. As such, I ask for your patience and an open mind as you accompany me through these pages in this exploration.

There are many interpretations of Jacob's story, ranging from the literal (that it actually happened exactly as written), to various explorations that go beyond the literal facts and point to greater meanings. Jacob's story is a very human story of alienation and life-changing awareness. This is the story of a man who finds himself alone in a very dangerous and unforgiving place—the desert—and realizes that far more is there than he once thought. He awakens to the present moment and the fullness of the desert that confronts him, his dream signaling a new awareness. In the ancient world, and still today, a journey through the desert can be a very real flirtation with death. The desert is a place where life seems to have retreated, a place that looked to Jacob to be utterly abandoned. A place seemingly with no meaning. Or in Jacob's world, a place with no God. Yet, in this 'Godless' place, Jacob has a life-altering, consciousness-raising experience. He discovers that the desert is filled with meaning. In Jacob's new awareness, God is present *even* in the desert. In other words, he discovers meaningfulness (or in his way of understanding, God's presence) even in the most forbidding of places. He comes to life, suddenly and in full, with the awareness that even in the most barren wasteland God is present. His words are the words of a person experiencing a stunning epiphany—'YHWH is in this place and I, I did not know it!' He comes to a new awareness or understanding of life and the world around him; a new awareness of the meaning and potential that is everywhere and in all things, despite appearances to the contrary. And, as Jacob may have come to know, it is a heroic struggle to see and hold on to a new awareness such as this in a frightening place. As a myth, this story is a touchstone. It can still remind us today that things are not always as they appear, and that even in the worst, most seemingly empty places, something miraculous and extraordinary is present. We do not have to believe in God to get this meaning. Through this ancient narrative, we are reminded in very simple terms that something good and meaningful, that some potential, can actually be present where everything seems to be so clearly bad or devoid of meaning or hope.

The Jacob story is a central Biblical myth. It contains the core idea that God is One (or God is Oneness). It is a guiding story that reminds those following a spiritual belief system that God is everywhere and in all things and their ongoing unfolding. This realization can guide behaviors and provide the foundation for an ethical stance. Meditating on this myth and the idea that we are all interconnected in oneness has led many spiritual thinkers to recognize the importance of loving the stranger. It is the basis for the belief in embracing the enemy. The story itself does not have to be true to serve this purpose.

THE MYTH OF MENTAL ILLNESS

Moving ahead several thousand years, we find ourselves confronting a myth of a different kind. Szasz (1974) called it the myth of mental illness. Szasz systematically analyzed the application of the medical illness model in modern psychiatry to understand psychological distress. He asserted that mental illness is a myth, or guiding story, and not an actual fact. There is no such thing as mental illness. It is a metaphorical notion, a guiding construct. He argued that this myth became the foundation for a theory of professional conduct. It is used to give the air of scientific authority to psychiatrists (and psychologists) and their approaches to treating human beings who are emotionally distressed. Over the years, the 'mental illness' stories that psychiatrists and psychologists have told themselves about their 'patients' and their emotional distress began to find a home in a new Bible. This Bible is the *Diagnostic and Statistical Manual of Mental Disorders*, and the latest canon is in the form of a text revision of the fourth edition (*DSM-IV-TR*) (First, Frances and Pincus, 2004).

DSM AS BIBLE

The *DSM-IV-TR* is a wide-ranging collection of constructs under the umbrella of 'mental disorders.' The inclusion of 'Diagnostic' and 'Statistical' in the title tells us that this book serves at least two masters, clinicians and researchers. As such, the diagnostic constructs, or stories of 'mental illness,' that inhabit the *DSM* must be exclusive and objective (and thus objectifying) with regard to discrete symptom clusters. This specificity is necessary in order to use diagnostic labels meaningfully in designating 'subject' groups for research purposes, to generate statistics about them and the efficacy of various treatments, and to use them as meaningful anchors for directive psychological treatment plans. At the same time, there must be enough flexibility to account for what most clinicians hopefully know, which is that people who present with psychological distress vary to such a great extent that their experience cannot possibly fit neatly into and be described fully by the shorthand nomenclature provided by a finite number of diagnostic categories. This dilemma has led to a sharp increase in the number of diagnostic labels listed in the *DSM* over the years, as well as the inclusion of diagnoses to be used when 'patients' cannot be crammed into the more commonly used diagnostic categories. The 'Adjustment Disorder' diagnosis and the 'Not Otherwise Specified' qualifier provide some elbowroom for clinicians wishing to use a diagnostic label when a 'patient' does not meet all of the criteria for another diagnosis but still presents with significant psychological distress.

The diagnostic constructs in the *DSM* have become so entrenched in the health professions in the United States and Canada that it is now fairly commonplace for health professionals to speak of someone 'having' an adjustment disorder or a post-traumatic stress disorder, as if it is an actual disease entity, a 'mental illness.' Other diagnoses in the *DSM* do more clearly capture injury and disease processes, such as the cognitive disorders (e.g., vascular dementia) or some of the primary sleep disorders (e.g., breathing-related sleep disorder). Diagnoses of affective disorders and the schizophrenias may also describe potential biological disease processes. However, such diagnoses do not reflect the wide variety of human experiences held by the individual clients who carry them. These diagnoses cannot possibly tell the whole story, and may tell the wrong story or a misleading story. More often than not, psychological distress is reified as if it were an actual disease entity, and the individual is objectified and brought under the control of an expert other.

A *DSM* HORROR STORY—HOMOSEXUALITY AS A 'MENTAL ILLNESS'

For years, homosexuality was classified in the *DSM* as an illness, a mental disorder. Though momentum has been building towards a more affirming view of homosexuality, it was not until 1974 that the American Psychiatric Association removed it from its list of psychiatric disorders. The American Psychological Association followed suit in 1975. The former pathological status of homosexuality as a diagnosis sheds light on the power of 'mental illness' diagnostic categories as stories that can mislead and do harm. With a diagnosis to lend legitimacy, homosexuality can be seen as an illness in the individual to be cured. Indeed treatments have been developed to cure gay people and subdue their gayness. When a gay person was distressed over being gay, this was seen as an indicator that treatment should ensue to subdue or change the homosexuality in order to relieve that distress. The psychological distress thus becomes the justification for treating homosexuality as an illness, and the diagnostic label provides scientific backing, making this abuse appear acceptable. Most of us now can see how society is let off the hook for the distress that an individual experiences when coming to terms with a queer identity in a homophobic world. The individual is pathologized, rather than understanding homophobia as a significant source of distress—or, borrowing from the *DSM* medical-model metaphor, rather than understanding homophobia as a social 'illness' that causes a great deal of individual distress in someone who may be perfectly healthy.

MENTAL ILLNESS AS A GUIDING STORY

Knowing the potential for serious harm, why do clinicians conceptualize psychological distress as an illness? There are a number of reasons to conceptualize diagnostically, some of which are perhaps more supportable than others (for a more complete discussion, see Boyle, 2002; First, Frances and Pincus, 2004). Differential diagnosis can guide a clinician so that a life-threatening condition, such as a delirium is detected. There are also medications that many people find helpful in coping with their emotional distress, and differential diagnosis (e.g., depression vs. bipolar) can help people and their doctors steer clear of medications that are likely to be contraindicated and potentially hazardous. For some people, a diagnosis brings relief that what they are struggling with is understood and experienced by others, bringing a sense of normalization. Diagnosis serves as shorthand for professional communication, though this usage can and often does result in objectification and distancing during professional discourse and subsequent interactions with clients. Diagnosis—identifying a 'mental illness'—is also used by many professionals as a part of treatment planning. This usage generally keeps the therapist in an expert position, undermining the client's power to self-direct.

The mental illness myth, as it is interwoven with the medical model, is foundational in that it serves to remind practitioners that all 'clinically significant' psychological distress is classifiable and quantifiable as illness. It becomes a very basic guide for behavior in clinical practice—'illnesses' come under the control of the expert practitioner who hopes to effect a cure. Some good certainly comes from this. 'Patients' are often cured. However, the myth of mental illness, like any guiding story, has its limits and potential pitfalls. There are those who argue that this myth does not serve as a meaningful or useful guiding story (see Szasz, 1974; Boyle, 2002; Maddux, Snyder and Lopez, 2004; Joseph and Linley, 2004; Sanders, 2005). Shlien (1989/2002) went so far as to say it is evil. To be sure, diagnosis can get in the way of hearing our clients for who they really are and for how they are experiencing their distress. It can serve to keep health professionals at a distance from their patients, objectifying them and their distress and potentially isolating and alienating them. It is a myth with limitations. The editor, chairperson, and vice-chairperson of *DSM-IV-TR* show their awareness of the limits of diagnosis when they state, 'Most, if not all, mental disorders are better conceived of as no more than (but no less than) valuable heuristic constructs' (First, Frances and Pincus, 2004: 12).

'Mental illness' must be understood as a guiding story in order to understand its value as well as its significant potential for harm. Whatever can be said to support diagnosis, the fact remains that it is a story that reduces or simplifies the fullness of individual experience. Diagnosis reifies. It tells a story that keeps clients and therapists chained to the past, rather than a story that allows us to join our clients *unconditionally* in their continual unfolding from the present moment into the future.

THE MYTH OF THE ACTUALIZING TENDENCY

Rogers proposed a stunning change to the myth of mental illness. His 'newer therapy' essentially promoted giving power back to clients, as Rogers suggested that clients have both the right and the ability to self-direct in psychotherapy. The role of the doctor as the expert over the 'patient' was radically challenged. The client's right to self-define was emphasized over the doctor's act of imposing a definition or diagnosis on the client. Over the next two decades, Rogers refined his thinking and a fuller theory emerged. This theory placed central importance on the therapeutic relationship as curative (1959). Rogers theorized that psychopathology was the result of the impact of external relational conditions of worth (such as social pressures and conditional love from family) experienced by the individual. Therefore, a relationship with a therapist who does not impose conditions of worth on the client is not only healing, but has the potential to enhance growth beyond traditional, or medical model, notions of cure. The potential for cure, healing, and growth are all located in the individual client, not in the power of therapeutic techniques controlled by an expert professional. The therapeutic relationship can provide the conditions that allow clients to access their own power to change and grow.

The necessary conditions of therapeutic personality change were derived from observations, clinical experience, and extensive research (Rogers, 1957, 1959). With the advent of the actualizing tendency concept, Rogers further grounded an essentially ethical theory (one based on relationships and values/attitudes) in scientific thinking. The actualizing tendency appeared as an integral part of his 1959 theory statement, which he considered to be his 'magnum opus' theoretical formulation (Bozarth and Wang, 2008). Rogers (1959) described the actualizing tendency as 'the inherent tendency of the organism to develop all its capacities in ways which serve to maintain or enhance the organism' (p. 196). Rogers (1963) emphasized that the actualizing tendency is the *only* motive underlying all human behaviors. This is an important idea, and it is worth pausing for a moment to consider briefly the implications. As a fundamental organismic trait, it exists as long as the organism is alive. As the *only* motive, all behaviors (including the client's 'process') are expressions of the actualizing tendency. No matter how things may appear, there is always an organismic movement towards ensuring its own survival and fulfilling its own potential.

The actualizing tendency concept is basically a story of ever-present human potential that accompanies the non-directive story of the value of the individual and the right to self-direct. Whatever the merits of the actualizing tendency as a scientific concept, it is ultimately a myth, a guiding story. It can become the foundation of a theory of personal conduct. In person-centered practice, the actualizing tendency concept can serve the purpose of being a guiding story that supports a therapist in following the individual client's direction. Reflecting on this story can guide therapists' behaviors in relation to clients, enhancing their ability to embody the core conditions of unconditional positive regard, empathic understanding, and congruence. As attitudes, unconditional positive regard, empathic understanding, and congruence are elaborations and expressions of non-directivity (Levitt, 2005). One attitude feeds into the other, and it is in some ways a rather artificial distinction to see them as entirely separate. Nonetheless, the remainder of this paper is an exploration of these attitudes and how they can be shaped and guided by an awareness and understanding of the actualizing tendency myth.

UNCONDITIONAL POSITIVE REGARD

One way of interpreting the actualizing tendency story is that humans are always doing the best they can in any particular moment—whether they are complaining, angry, suicidal, engaged in addictive behaviors, or apparently stuck and doing nothing. Remembering that this potential is always present in the client's process, behaviors, and expressions can help the therapist to return to the fullness of the client's moment, embracing them with unconditional positive regard. Using the actualizing tendency as a compass, the therapist may be able to steer clear of judgments that place conditions of worth on clients.

In the present moment, clients may be observed and judged by someone who does not hold unconditional positive regard for them as 'complaining' or 'whining' or 'stuck.' From a non-directive perspective, clients are doing the best they can, even if it does not obviously look like it. Actualization may be thwarted, but its seeds are still present and expressed in a twisted form. Some may view clients as 'complaining' about the same things session after session. However, the non-directive stance is that these client expressions are never truly the same from one moment to the next. These expressions always carry the seeds of growth—they are always an expression of the client's actualizing tendency, no matter how it is obstructed or twisted. It is easy to believe there is nothing positive happening in these moments—no forward movement. Yet something is happening in these moments, and it can be easily overlooked. What might look like complaining with no movement and no end to someone else, to a non-directive therapist is an essential expression of the client's forward movement in the moment, and a very powerful one. As Rogers would say, the client is 'always motivated, always up to something, always seeking' (1963: 7).

The non-directive perspective places great importance on sitting with the unknown, sitting with discomfort, and not judging it as bad. We aim to retain unconditional positive regard in the face of anything, even apparent evil, without having to subdue and contain it with a diagnosis or other objectifying act. Unconditional means unconditional. An understanding of the actualizing tendency concept as a guiding story can be enough for some non-directive therapists to remain non-directive, and grounded in the core conditions—confident in their ability to face what is in front of them without needing to run in fear, boredom, or disgust. When we say we 'believe' in the actualizing tendency, what we really may be saying is that we believe in our clients at all times—we affirm their existence as inherently valuable without reservation or judgment. As such, we see them warmly and embrace whatever they bring from moment to moment. The actualizing tendency story can serve as a gentle reminder of our clients' unwavering worth and continual forward movement, bringing us back to a stance of complete acceptance of them when we stray. Put simply, being heard truly and being accepted fully by someone else is a precious and powerful thing—it is the heart of unconditional positive regard.

EMPATHIC UNDERSTANDING

Empathic understanding and unconditional positive regard go hand in hand. If the actualizing tendency story reminds us that the other person is always doing the best they can in any given moment, then we are reminded to put aside our judgments and provide unconditional positive regard. When we put aside our judgments, we are putting aside our tendency to objectify the other. Objectifying the other can be a very subtle thing, but it occurs when we place our understanding of the other within our own frame of reference or another frame of reference external to the client. Diagnosing mental illness places our understanding of the client in an external frame of reference. Other external frames can include such things as interpretations, psychodynamic formulations, or (perhaps more commonly) over-identification with our clients (i.e., assuming their experience to be like our own).

Awareness of the actualizing tendency myth can help the therapist move beyond judgments that are blocks to empathic understanding of who is really in front of us—to get beyond the surface appearance of a barren or hostile desert. Empathic understanding is a movement away from alienation. When we are more comfortable with what we encounter in others, our empathic understanding can be more accurate. The therapist does not attempt to contain or negate the client, but to embrace them as they experience themselves and the world. Being aware that a creative force or potential for forward movement is always there, even in an apparent wasteland, can allow us to see what is before us, rather than being blinded by fear, boredom, or judgment. Believing the person in front of us always has the capacity to change and grow, and trusting what is happening as an expression of the organism reaching towards its potential, helps the therapist to be more open to receiving whatever the client brings, without having to rip it from the client's frame of reference and contain it within the therapist's frame—without having to reify it and chain it to the past. This is the essence of maintaining the attitude of empathic understanding—'true empathy is always free of any evaluative or diagnostic quality' (Rogers, 1975: 6–7).

CONGRUENCE

It may be a little more obvious how the actualizing tendency myth can guide us in maintaining unconditional positive regard and remaining accurate or attuned in our empathic understanding. Perhaps a little more subtle is how this story impacts upon the therapist's ability to remain congruent—the ability to remain whole and accurately symbolize experience—in the presence of something fearful, negative, or 'bad.' Using the actualizing tendency story as a compass can aid our ability to overcome our inner struggles and blocks to discover more accurately what is right in front of us.

Some client processes may be harder to trust than others (e.g., 'psychotic' processes, so-called borderline processes, suicidal or homicidal impulses, or intense grief). This is often where the work is for the therapist. Without trust in the other, the therapist's ability to accurately symbolize their own experience will be compromised. Congruence is in many ways the bedrock of the core therapist attitudes, supporting unconditional positive regard and empathic understanding. Of course, congruence has to start with therapists believing in themselves. Letting one's guard down allows an accurate symbolization of experience—despite fear, disgust, etc. Believing in the other person, I can let my guard down and experience them.

Congruence is reflected in our knowledge of the things that fool us into thinking that the actualizing tendency is not present—our awareness of what makes us unable to be present for the fullness of someone else's reality—and having the discipline to be mindful of this. Even boredom may be signaling us to wake up to a very live moment in the middle of an apparent wasteland. It is a human shortcoming that it is easier to label things as bad (perhaps to reassure us that we are good), and sadly, it is easier to find ways to control the other and encounter them from a distance. It takes courage to enter a desert and allow ourselves to recognize what is really before us without needing to change it or run from it.

Understanding the actualizing tendency story can keep us from feeling or being alienated in a situation that is potentially alienating in many ways. The movement towards alienation can be very alluring in the face of fear. Withdrawing, whether through boredom, disgust, anger, or the need to define the other, is a form of protecting ourselves, a way of reasserting a sense of power and control out of fear. When afraid of the desert we have found ourselves in, we may find the need to assert our belief in our own goodness in order to feel powerful and in control. This will always lead to an empathic break and alienation. On a deeper level, whether we are aware of it or not, we are likely to be running from what we fear is potentially within us. This flight results in alienation, not only from the other, but also from ourselves. Alienation ultimately gets in the way of our recognizing positive strivings in another being, and gets in the way of being able to accurately symbolize our experience—it gets in the way of being congruent.

CONCLUSIONS

As people who work with other people who are in distress, we are often on a journey through the desert from Be'er Sheba to Haram when we encounter our clients. The deserts of our clients' worlds are often vast, dangerous, and frightening places. Places we might want to run from in disgust, anger, horror, or boredom. Places that seem devoid of meaning, where may we lose our bearings entirely, and wonder if we will in some sense survive the experience. The actualizing tendency concept is a reminder, an instructive tale, that informs us that something else is there in front of us, no matter how seemingly bad or meaningless. We are reminded that somehow there is something creative, a positive striving, a constant unfolding, right in front of us, no matter how well it is disguised and perverted. We might find ourselves saying something akin to Jacob when he declared, 'YHWH is in this place, and I, I did not know it!' In other words, the actualizing tendency is always present—our clients always have worth. Human potential is always there, even in the desert places we sometimes encounter in our clients—as Rogers noted, it is only absent when the organism is dead (Rogers, 1963). If we are guided by the idea of an actualizing tendency in all living things, in all people, we may find ourselves more capable of remaining centered, recognizing that clients not only have the right to self-direct, but indeed, they also have the capacity to do so.

The actualizing tendency myth informs us that all people have constructive potential, no matter how they may appear to us. Emotional distress contains within it the seeds of potential change and growth. People have the power to heal themselves and grow if they find themselves in the right 'soil.' Of further importance, the person-centered model not only sees the individual as capable of growth, but also respects the individual's right to self-determine, to find their own path. The client becomes her own ever-changing Bible, her own myth, her own guiding story. The flip side of the theory, often unexplored, is that there is great power in others and in society as a whole to bring about healing—as individuals we all live in a broader social context, in relation to each other. The actualizing tendency story not only suggests that individuals have the power and right to self-direct, but also that we all have responsibility in creating conditions that make this more likely. The individual is focused upon in theory and therapy—however, the theory also makes it clear that social or external factors inhibit individual potential. In other words, the 'problem' is not located solely in the individual, rather it is in the relationship between the individual and their environment—we all share responsibility. Therapy, on an individual scale, provides a potentially corrective relationship that may allow for the emergence of individual direction, healing, and growth. Though arguments can be made for the selfishness or limited impact of individual psychotherapy (see, for example, Wallach and Wallach, 1983; Proctor, 2006), I am reminded of the simple power of thinking globally and acting locally.

The actualizing tendency myth reminds us that as long as there is life there is the potential for growth and forward movement—only after death do we see the absence of the actualizing tendency. If the actualizing tendency is truly present across the entire lifespan, then it is present even in the desert places of our lives. The actualizing tendency construct is a story that transcends stories of mental illness as located in the individual (medical model) and even stories of growth beyond cure (positive psychology). In other words, client-centred theory goes beyond a duality of negative and positive psychologies, placing illness and health on equal footing. The theoretical concept of the actualizing tendency is really a restatement of the age-old belief that everyone is doing the best they are capable of in the moment. If we are able to go beyond just paying lip service to this notion and really take it to heart, we see that even in the most unlikely places there is always potential for growth. Symptoms of 'mental illness' become reframed as seeds of potential growth or forward movement. Because some expressions of distress are rather frightening, they may be more easily contained and distanced from ourselves when seen as symptoms of 'mental illness'—that they are actually the expressions of a potential for forward movement is not immediately obvious.

Whether the actualizing tendency exists is ultimately not important—just as it is not important whether 'Jacob' existed, or whether 'PTSD' exists. These are all just constructs, stories that we tell each other. What is important is how these constructs guide us in our relationships and actions; how they guide us in our efforts to relieve human suffering and promote growth and individual freedom. We all tell ourselves guiding stories. The actualizing tendency myth is just one of many possible guiding stories. While other guiding stories, such as the myth of mental illness, may objectify others, the myth of the actualizing tendency holds the promise of leading us to the client's reality as our ultimate guiding story. The actualizing tendency as a guiding story supports the therapist on a journey of forever following the potential in others, and believing in the ultimate value of doing so.

REFERENCES

Boyle M (2002) Diagnosis. In C Newnes, G Holmes & C Dunn (Eds) *This is Madness: A critical look at psychiatry and the future of mental health services.* Ross-on-Wye: PCCS Books, pp. 75–90.

Bozarth JD & Wang C-C (2008) The 'Unitary Actualizing Tendency' and congruence in client-centered theory. In BE Levitt (Ed) *Reflections on Human Potential: Bridging the person-centered approach and positive psychology.* Ross-on-Wye: PCCS Books, pp. 102–15.

Campbell J (2002) *The Inner Reaches of Outer Space: Metaphor as myth and as religion.* Novato, CA: New World Library.

First MB, Frances A & Pincus HA (2004) *DSM-IV-TR Guidebook.* Washington, DC: American Psychiatric Publishing.

Fox F (1995) (trans) *The five books of Moses: Genesis, Exodus, Leviticus, Numbers, Deureronomy. The Schocken Bible, Volume 1*, Standard Edition. New York: Schocken Books.

Joseph S & Linley PA (2004) Positive therapy: A positive psychological theory of therapeutic practice. In PA Linley & S Joseph (Eds) *Positive Psychology in Practice*. Hoboken, NJ: John Wiley & Sons, pp. 354–68.

Levitt BE (2005) Non-directivity: The foundational attitude. In BE Levitt (Ed) *Embracing Non-directivity: Reassessing person-centered theory and practice in the 21st century*. Ross-on-Wye: PCCS Books, pp. 5–16.

Maddux JE, Snyder CR & Lopez SJ (2004) Toward a positive clinical psychology: Deconstructing the illness ideology and constructing an ideology of human strengths and potential. In PA Linley & S Joseph (Eds) *Positive Psychology in Practice*. Hoboken, NJ: John Wiley & Sons, pp. 320–34.

Morrison J (1995) *DSM-IV Made Easy: The clinicians guide to diagnosis*. New York: The Guilford Press.

Proctor G (2006) Therapy: Opium for the masses or help for those who least need it? In G Proctor, M Cooper, P Sanders & B Malcolm (Eds) *Politicizing the Person-Centred Approach: An agenda for social change*. Ross-on-Wye: PCCS Books, pp. 66–79.

Rogers CR (1957) The necessary and sufficient conditions of personality change. *Journal of Consulting Psychology, 21* (2), 95–103.

Rogers CR (1959) A theory of therapy, personality and interpersonal relationships, as developed in the client-centered framework. In S Koch (Ed) *Psychology: A study of a science. Vol. 3: Formulations of the person and the social context*. New York: McGraw-Hill, pp. 184–256.

Rogers CR (1963) The actualizing tendency in relation to 'motives' and to consciousness. In M Jones (Ed) *Nebraska Symposium on Motivation*. Lincoln, NE: University of Nebraska Press, pp. 1–24.

Rogers CR (1975) Empathic: An unappreciated way of being. *The Counseling Psychologist, 5* (2), 2–10.

Sanders P (2005) Principled and strategic opposition to the medicalisation of distress and all its apparatus. In S Joseph & R Worsley (Eds) *Person-Centred Psychopathology: A positive psychology of mental health*. Ross-on-Wye: PCCS Books, pp. 21–42.

Shlien J (1989/2002) Response to Boy's symposium on psychodiagnosis. *Person-Centered Review, 4* (2), 157–62. Reproduced in DJ Cain (Ed) (2002) *Classics in the Person-Centered Approach*. Ross-on-Wye: PCCS Books, pp. 400–2.

Szasz T (1974) *The Myth of Mental Illness: Foundations of a theory of personal conduct*. New York: Harper and Row.

Wallach MA & Wallach L (1983) *Psychology's Sanction for Selfishness: The error of egoism in theory and therapy*. San Francisco: WH Freeman & Co.

Chapter 5

VERBAL BEING: FROM BEING HUMAN TO HUMAN BEING

Keith Tudor

Abstract

Each system of psychology and psychotherapy has a view about what it is to be human, and to be motivated. In the broader tradition of organismic psychology and, specifically, the work of Carl Rogers, person-centred psychology asserts that, as human organisms, we have one, unitary motivation: to maintain, enhance and reproduce the experiencing organism. This motivational force is usually referred to as 'the actualising tendency'. However, when practitioners and theorists talk about *the* actualising tendency in this way, as a noun, they reify it. Such objectification is contrary to person-centred views of the person in process (Rogers, 1954/1967e), and of life itself as an active process (Rogers, 1963).

This chapter explores the implications of reframing our thinking about the actualising tendency or 'the tendency to actualise' by changing the noun 'tendency' to a verb, thus: 'the organism *tends* to actualise'. This change to the verb form emphasises that human *being* is an ongoing *process* of motivation and movement. The chapter begins with some comments about the significance and importance of language and how it shapes our thinking about human being and relating. This is followed by a consideration of human motivation from a person-centred perspective, which, as with the book as a whole, is framed in the context of human potential and positive psychology. The chapter concludes with some thoughts about the implications of 'verbal being', especially for our understanding of what it means to be being, becoming and belonging.

LANGUAGE MATTERS

Language, as distinct from communication, is verbal, systematic and symbolic. It is verbal in that it is spoken and heard and, potentially, written. It is systematic in that it is structured in terms of the relationship between words, or the grammar of a language, which may be identified as different parts of speech such as nouns, adjectives, verbs, and so on. It is symbolic in that we use words as symbols to stand for things: cat, Sheffield, integrity, group (words/symbols which represent different kinds of nouns); this, each, some, which, our, robust (different kinds of adjectives); and so on. In this sense all symbols and words are abstract. The function of language is communication and, as human beings, we can communicate with each other precisely because we can understand and manipulate such symbols. For example, anyone who reads this chapter and who has a basic understanding of English or a dictionary will understand the symbols 'cat', 'this' and so on—and, I hope, a lot more! In other words, language is possible because human beings are capable of symbolic activity. Communication, of course, may be verbal or non-verbal through gestures, dress, style and so on.

Language thus shapes and constructs the way we understand the world. It is not so much a way of reporting experience as a way of framing and defining it—which is why the words we choose to describe things and experiences are so important. To give some examples:

- In 1492 Christopher Columbus discovered the New World. This sentence presents Columbus' 'discovery' of the 'New World' 'in 1492' as a fact. From a constructivist perspective it is a sentence which implies:

    a) A discounting of what was already there, especially with regard to the indigenous populations or First Nations peoples.

    b) A discounting of existing, 'old' cultures, including different perspectives on time. '1492' represents a particular construction of time and date—which the use of CE (Common Era), for instance, acknowledges.

This discounting has serious consequences in terms of how people think and act about history, land, ownership, other peoples, rights and so on. In this case, another construction would be to say that the so-called 'land of the free' was founded on the genocide of most of its indigenous population.

- Northern Ireland. This phrase, used to refer to a particular geographical area, represents a particular frame of reference, in this case, a political and a Protestant one which links it to the United Kingdom as it is presently constituted. When we refer to the same geographical area as 'The Six Counties' this frames them as a part of a traditional 32-county Irish Republic and the land mass of the island of Ireland. The same point may be made about many areas and, indeed, countries, such as Aotearoa (Maori) and New Zealand (English). Again these are not simply semantic differences or the niceties of political correctness. In these and many other cases, thousands of people have died over the centuries for what these different frames of reference represent.

- The Self. The self is the subject and stuff of much of modern day psychology. It is also a construct that influences how we view our*selves* and, despite numerous books on the subject, there is no agreed definition of the word. Moreover, the capitalisation of the—or even The—Self implies a core, higher or organising part of the whole, holistic human being. This tends to lead to further abstract speculation on its nature or construction and away from organismic experiencing. For a fuller critique of this concept, see Tudor and Worrall (2006). Moreover, as Mathews (1991: 143) puts it: 'The paradigm instance of the self realizing system—or "self"—is the organism' from primitive amoeba to highest mammal. Just as language socialises people into a way of thinking about ourselves and the environment, so too the language and constructs of psychology influence us psychologically. Keen (1983: 233) puts it more strongly: 'Language governs perception.' This is why language, grammar, constructs and metaphors matter.

Nouns name objects, persons and places, and ideas, including collective items (such as 'crowd'). Verbs describe an action or state of being. There are two principal advantages to the formulation 'the human organism tends to actualise' or 'actualis-ing' over 'tendency' or 'actualisation':

1. It describes actualising as an action, rather than an object or abstract noun. This is consistent with a process view of the person and of psychotherapy (see Rogers, 1958/1967c) and of life (Rogers, 1963), and clarifies the distinction between Rogers' concept of this tendency (Rogers' tended to use the noun) and Maslow's (1954) more outcome-focused and hierarchical concept of self-actualisation.

2. A noun, having no tense, has no temporality. As human beings we exist in time. A verb has tense (present, past, perfect, future) and thus represents temporality. The verb form—actualises, actualising, to actualise, and so on—gives a time frame and context to the human organism, which the abstract noun 'the actualising tendency' does not. The same may be said of 'to be' and 'being' (see p. 78).

The change from noun (the actualising tendency) to verb (the organism tends to actualise) is not simply a semantic one, but one which, literally, represents a change in the grammar of our understanding of the human organism or human being. A person does not *have* an actualising tendency in the same way that she has organs in her body; as an organism she is and she, including her organs, tends to actualise. Cooper (1997: 69) makes the same point in his book about Kabbalah when he describes and proposes that we conceive God as a verb:

> The closest we can come to thinking about God is as a process rather than a being. We can think of it as 'be-ing', as verb rather than a noun. Perhaps we would understand this concept better if we renamed God. We might call it God-ing, a process, rather than God, which suggests a noun.

Having argued that the concepts within person-centred psychology represented by the words 'actualisation', 'tendency' and 'actualising tendency' are more usefully translated into verb forms, I now consider the implications of this for the person-centred theory of motivation.

MOTIVATION—THE ORGANISM TENDS TO ACTUALISE

As an organismic theory, person-centred psychology has a unitary and holistic theory of motivation. It is important to place person-centred psychology in this broader theoretical context because it is historically accurate; because it begins to reclaim this lost tradition of twentieth-century psychology; and because it places the concept of motivation in the context of the positive psychology of human potential.

ORGANISMIC PSYCHOLOGY

The organism is holistic, and experiential. It construes reality, differentiates, is dialogic, is in a constant process of becoming, is regulatory, behaves according to need, is interdependent, and has an internal valuing process, direction and what Whitehead (1929/1978) refers to as 'appetition'. Interestingly, from a perspective which places organism rather than self at the heart of our understanding of what it is to be a person, current research in neuroscience and in developmental psychology supports and elaborates these qualities of the biological entity that is the organism (for details of which see Kriz, 2006; Tudor and Worrall, 2006). When Rogers writes about the organism he generally refers to it as maintaining, enhancing *and* reproducing itself (see, for example, Rogers, 1963). Interestingly, when others in person-centred psychology write about the organism or cite Rogers they generally tend to omit the reference to reproduction.

There is a rich tradition of organismic psychology, on some of which Rogers drew in developing his theory of therapy and personality (Rogers, 1951, 1959). This tradition is represented by Kantor (1924a, 1924b), Brunswik (see Tolman and Brunswik, 1935), Wheeler (1940), Angyal (1941, 1965/1973), Murphy (1947), Werner (1948) and, more recently, by Brown (1990) and Tudor and Worrall (2006). Apart from Kantor, all of these draw on the two principal organismic theorists: Whitehead (1929/1978), the philosopher of the organism and founder of process philosophy, and Goldstein (1934/1995) who wrote a seminal text on *The Organism*.

Organismic theory is holistic and views the organism as a whole, organised system. It is all-encompassing in that it takes a holistic approach to the study of the person and, therefore, offers a broad base for understanding the total organism, and for research. This links organismic theory with psychobiology, psychosomatics, neurology, neuropsychiatry, neuroscience and evolutionary psychology. Organismic theory is integrative and, as such, according to Hall and Lindzey (1978: 298), it 'emphasizes the unity, integration, consistency, and coherence of the normal personality. Organization is the natural state of the organism; disorganization is pathological and is usually brought about by the impact of an oppressive or threatening environment.' On this basis, a person-centred theory of psychopathology is—or should be—based on a theory of alienation (see Tudor and Worrall, 2006). Organismic theory is based on a unitary drive theory, and emphasises the inherent potentiality of the organism for growth (maintaining, enhancing and reproducing itself). This view of the human organism as having potential connects organismic psychology to ideas about human potential and to positive psychology.

HUMAN POTENTIAL

The idea that humans have potential goes back to Aristotle who uses the word *nous* to describe the human intellect, which gives a person the ability to realise her own potential as well as that of her environment. Interestingly, in Yorkshire dialect, the same word *nous* is used to denote a person's good common sense. In this way, Aristotle prefigures Whitehead as a philosopher of process in that he posited that all life is a process of moving toward one's potential or, in modern psychological parlance, a process of becoming. Furthermore, for Aristotle, the goodness or morality of someone or something is measured only in terms of its progress toward its particular potential, a view which forms the basis of his ethics, and one which implies a social as well as an individual responsibility to be the best we can be.

These ideas from Aristotle find their expression in humanism and, more recently, in humanistic psychology and the human potential movement. Although there is no agreed definition of humanistic psychology, Abraham Maslow (1962) suggests that it is concerned more with human motivation, self-development and aesthetics, and less with pathology and disturbance (as is psychoanalysis, at least according to Maslow), and with what can be explained in terms of mechanistic theory and metaphors (as is behaviourism). In a statement written in 1998, The British Association for Humanistic Psychology Practitioners (AHPP) suggests that humanistic practitioners share certain fundamental core beliefs about:

- The theory of human nature and of self—that it is unique, relational, OK, aspirational, holistic, self-regulating, autonomous and responsible.
- The aims of therapy and growth—self-awareness, wholeness, authenticity, creativity, etc.
- The nature of the therapeutic relationship—as the primary agent of change, and based on the therapist's genuineness, empathy, and non-judgemental acceptance of the client, etc.

It is clear from these beliefs and concepts that Rogers, and his theory and practice, deserves his place alongside Maslow and Rollo May, the existentialist philosopher, as one of the 'founding fathers' of humanistic psychology and, more broadly, the human potential movement. With regard to our specific present interest, Finke (2002) writes about aspects of the actualising tendency from a humanistic perspective. He argues that Rogers was influenced by humanistic and Romantic ideas about the actualising tendency, and wrote about it in rather metaphoric descriptions which had their roots more in biology than psychology.

POSITIVE PSYCHOLOGY

The roots of positive psychology can also be traced back to Ancient Greek philosophy and, specifically, the study of happiness and 'the good life', a phrase Rogers uses when writing (in 1957/1967b) about 'the fully functioning person'. Although psychology is generally more concerned with illness than with health, and mental illness as distinct from mental health, some psychologists, going back to William James (1842–1910), have been talking about positive health and well-being. Moreover, positive psychology is not confined to psychologists. Other professionals in health and social work, as well as lay people (see Pavis, Masters and Cunningham-Burley, 1996) have contributed to our understanding of this broad field, which encompasses positive mental health (e.g., Jahoda,

1958; Tudor, 1996) and complete mental health (see Keyes, 2003). This is a particularly important and topical point in the UK in the light of Layard's (2005) work on happiness, and his (2006) report on depression and anxiety which recommends a seven-year plan to fund the training of 10,000 extra 'therapists' across the country, and which the present UK government has taken up. These briefly trained 'therapists', mostly psychologists and other (medical) health care professionals, will deliver brief cognitive-behavioural therapy, with an explicit agenda to get people back to work and, thereby, to be happier.

Drawing on differences elucidated by different Greek words, positive psychology distinguishes between:

- The 'pleasant life' (*hedonia*), or emotional well-being, which, in its extreme form, consists in having as many pleasures as possible (and hence hedonism). Research into this examines how people experience, forecast and savour the positive feelings that are part of normal and healthy living such as happiness, life satisfaction, affect balance and so on.

- The 'good life' (*eudaimonia*), or psychological well-being. Rogers (1957/1967b) describes this as a *process*, not a state of being, a direction, not a destination, and an organismically selected direction at that. He summarises (p. 187) the good life as: 'the process of movement in a direction which the human organism selects when it is inwardly free to move in any direction', and comments that: 'the general qualities of this selected direction appear to have a certain universality'. In his view of fluidity, which he acknowledges as a social value judgement, Rogers (1958/1967a) is close to Aristotle's view of the good life as one of contemplation, and to Csikszentmihalyi's (1990) concept of flow. This, for Rogers, is the essence—or, more accurately, the *process*—of the fully functioning person: a being in process, experiencing life with immediacy, and is a very different vision from Maslow's teleological view of the self-actualised, 'sorted' individual. It follows that research into the good life investigates the beneficial effects of such contemplation or flow. Seligman (2002) suggests that, for an individual, the good life consists in knowing what her 'signature strengths' are and then using those strengths to have more flow.

- The 'meaningful life' (also *eudaimonia*), or social well-being. Despite his emphasis on the therapeutic relationship, Rogers consistently undervalues the social dimension and implications of his work. One example of this is his incomplete reference to the work of Angyal (1941) on which he drew. In his 1963 paper Rogers refers to his earlier (1959) paper in which he summarises the development of the actualising tendency as toward autonomy and away from heteronomy or control by external forces. What he omits is that, according to Angyal, the human organism also tends or has a trend towards homonomy, or connection, participation, and belonging. These organismic trends exist in the context of and response to heteronomy or difference and external laws. Rogers' partial reading of Angyal contributes towards a more individualistic view of the human organism and life than a social one. In their paper, Bozarth and Brodley (1991) make the same mistake. Keyes (2007) makes a similar criticism, that: 'Within the eudaimonic tradition, there was scant recognition of the social dimensions of an individual's functioning in life' —and, in his research, Keyes has made a major contribution in developing a social dimension to the understanding of and research into subjective well-being (Keyes, 1998, 2005, 2007; Keyes and Shapiro, 2004). With reference to the concept of signature strengths, Seligman's (2002) view of this dimension is when the individual uses her strengths in the service of something greater. Research into this 'life of affiliation' asks how individuals derive a positive sense of well-being, meaning and purpose from belonging, being part of, and contributing to something larger and more permanent than themselves.

THE ACTUALISING TENDENCY

In order to elaborate the argument that the actualising tendency is better understood as a verb, I refer to the three key, historical papers, reproduced in the first part of this volume, on the actualising tendency and actualisation (Rogers, 1963; Bozarth and Brodley, 1991; and Merry, 2003), and quote from the original versions.

Rogers (1963)
In his major paper on the theory of therapy, personality and interpersonal relationships, published in 1959 (though written as early as 1956), Rogers formulated the actualising tendency as *the* motivational construct in his theory. In his 1963 paper he revisits this and, citing supporting evidence from a number of different fields, and especially biology, states (p. 6) that: 'It is clear that the actualizing tendency is selective and directional, a constructive tendency if you will.' As with much of Rogers' writings, this idea is not new. It appears in Aristotle's writings and in a number of psychological and spiritual traditions. What was innovative about Rogers was the way in which he brought ideas together from a wide range of sources, synthesised them and used them as a basis for a new psychotherapy (see Tudor and Worrall, 2006). However, as far as the actualising tendency is concerned, he didn't take the implication of his process view of human life and of therapy to its logical conclusion by writing in the language of process and specifically the language of verbs.

In his 1963 paper Rogers makes a number of points about the organism and its actualising tendency, three of which, I think, help us to develop a verbal view of 'tend' and 'actualise':

1. That *the organism is naturally in tension* and, therefore, is not in itself a tension or drive reduction system. This means that being tense, nervous, anxious and upset are not negative *states* (tension, nervousness, anxiety, etc.) to be cured or ameliorated but, rather, are *processes* (and adjectives) which are descriptive of the organism's needs driven and goal-directed behaviour (see Rogers, 1951). Whitehead's (1929/1978) concept of appetition, with its principle of unrest, carries a similar sense of tension, with the added emphasis that the organism seeks, and has direction and

purpose (see Tudor and Worrall, 2006). This view that the organism is in tension also supports the therapist's trust in the wisdom of the organism and her embodiment of a non-directive attitude towards her clients and their behaviour. The person-centred therapist is non-directive towards the fact that her client tends to actualise.

2. That, in its tendency to fulfilment, *the organism is active* in its transactions with the environment, and expresses its need to explore and to produce change in the environment. Thus, as human organisms we are active, interactive and contributing. In effect, we aggress on and in our environment. As Perls, Hefferline and Goodman (1951/1973: 100–1) put it, aggression 'includes everything that an organism does to initiate contact with its environment'. Anything less is likely to be the result of the organism being thwarted in or conditioned about its natural activity. To take a political example: for many people being an active, engaged citizen involves exercising their right to vote. However, if people's votes do not count, or if politicians consistently ignore the expression of their constituents, those same citizens may become disempowered, disillusioned and apathetic, or, being in a state/process of unrest, may equally agitate, object and organise.

3. That *the actualising tendency is a sole motivational construct* and as such does not require more specific sets of motives (love, sex, death, and so on). I think it is possible to maintain this together with the view, from Angyal (1941), that the organism has two trends: towards autonomy *and* homonomy. Whilst this may initially appear as contradictory (one tendency, two trends), it isn't if we follow Rogers' (1963) argument that the actualising tendency is a *functional* construct which describes functional relationships. Also, viewing the actualising tendency as a functional construct provides the basis for empirical investigations (Rogers, 1963: 12) 'which alone can determine the patterning which exists in human behavior'. In this sense Angyal is simply reflecting the presence of two functional trends of one organism, motivated by virtue of being alive. As Patterson (1964/2000: 16) puts it: 'There's no such thing as a lack of or absence of motivation. To be alive is to be motivated, to be unmotivated is to be dead. Thus we cannot say that a client is unmotivated.' Angyal (1941: 218) himself sees no problem with this: 'Human behavior, as a rule, is multiply motivated: a given activity may express more than one tendency at the same time.'

Bozarth and Brodley (1991)

In their paper, originally published as a chapter in a *Handbook of Self-Actualization* (edited by Jones and Crandall, 1991), Bozarth and Brodley make two important points:

1. That (p. 47) 'the organism/person is the basic unity of inquiry in Rogers' thought'. This is an important statement and by no means a given in person-centred writing and theory (see Tudor and Worrall, 2006). However, Bozarth and Brodley somewhat undermine the clarity of this statement by their inconsistent use of language. They refer to 'characteristics' and 'properties' of the organism, words which are more

associated with mechanistic metaphors of the person (for the significance of which, see Leary, 1990). They also use these words as if they are synonymous, which they are not.

2. That the concept of *actualisation is a practical and functional premise* for the work of the therapist. In stating this they echo and develop Rogers' (1963) argument, asserting (p. 53) that 'the only function of the therapist is to facilitate the client's actualizing process'. Apart from the warranted confidence of this assertion, it is also an interesting statement in terms of our current concern about language. The therapist is verbal: she facilitates. Similarly, Taft (1933: 3) says that the therapist must, above all, '*be* a therapist'.

In both papers, Rogers and Bozarth and Brodley refer to the therapeutic conditions. However, in both papers the authors write in terms of 'supplying' (Rogers) and 'providing' (Bozarth and Brodley) these conditions. Rogers (1963: 4) says that: 'I cannot think of a better analogy for psychotherapy where, if I can *supply* [my emphasis] a psychological amniotic fluid, forward movement of a constructive sort will occur.' Bozarth and Brodley (1991) talk in terms of taking responsibility 'to create' 'an optimal psychological climate *for* the person' (p. 47, my emphasis) and, later (p. 51), 'an interpersonal climate'. Both papers were written under the influence of the 'if …, then …' formulation, an approximation of the material conditional of propositional logic. However, there are a number of problems with this formulation:

a) Firstly, the language does not appear or sound appropriate to describe how people relate.

b) Secondly, the formula encourages somewhat linear, unidirectional thinking, i.e., 'if (first) the *therapist* does (something), *then* the client does (something in response to the therapist)'.

c) Thirdly, it discourages thinking about the therapeutic relationship, or therapeutic relat*ing*, as co-created and mutual, albeit asymmetrical.

On the first point, Tudor and Worrall (2006) critique Rogers' use of philosophical terms. The second and third points appear to contradict Bozarth and Brodley's (1991: 53) own assertion of client/person-centred values: that 'the authority rests in the person [of the client], not in an outside expert'.

Merry (2003)

This paper is an important contribution to person-centred thinking about the view that human beings tend to actualise. Although, like Rogers and Bozarth and Brodley, Merry in the main views actualisation as a tendency (noun), at one point in his paper he also refers (p. 83) to the fact that 'all organisms "actualise"' (verb).

In his paper Merry makes a number of salient points:

1. That the actualising tendency has a capacity for defence, maintenance and, ultimately, survival; the latter of which is, for Merry, more of an imperative than 'openness to experience'. I suggest, however, that these are the same, i.e., that the organism is open to experiencing its need to survive.

2. That our search as human beings for new experiences, through which we enhance ourselves and develop our potential, is also based on organismic need and, indeed, often increases levels of tension.

3. That (p. 87) 'actualisation is conceptualised as manifesting (that is, actualising) the self-defence potentials of the individual'—which, Merry proposes, resolves the logical inconsistency in Rogers' thinking of a tendency in conflict with a part or subsystem within itself. I think this point is as easily resolved if we use the verb form: the human organism tends to actualise towards being autonomous and towards being homonomous; when it is not tending to actualise for some reason, in response to some interruption or disturbance in the environmental and organism/environmental relational field, then it tends to self-actualise.

The human organism tends to actualise. This sentence is both simple and rich with meaning. The *human organism* has a number of qualities (holistic, experiential, dialogic, interdependent, directional, needs-driven, goal-directed), which imply action (experiencing, construing reality, differentiating, being in dialogue, being in a constant process of becoming, regulating, behaving according to need, valuing, aggressing, and so on). That it *tends* to actualise is a statement which acknowledges the organism's inherent directionality—towards autonomy and homonomy. As a verb *'to actualise'* not only carries a sense of action but also is future-oriented. To actualise means to make actual, to realise in action—which implies a realisation of what is inherent, implicit, and immanent but not yet realised, and hence the sense of future. The present and future sense of what is and is to be actual is reflected in the two most common verbal constructs in person-centred practice, philosophy and theory: being and becoming. In the final part of this chapter I briefly discuss these concepts, together with the equally important although less common concept of belonging and, again, consider their value in the verbal form.

BEING, BECOMING AND BELONGING

These concepts describe, respectively, the ontology or essence of what it is to be human (a human being), as well as our potential (becoming), and social connectedness (belonging).

BEING

Philosophers down the ages have grappled with these concepts, and especially the nature of 'being'. This word carries different meanings in the work of Aristotle and within materialism, idealism, existentialism, and in Islam and Marxism, as well as different nuances in different languages. Of these Rogers drew explicitly on existential philosophy, although he himself was not an existentialist (see Kirschenbaum, 1979; Van Belle, 1980; Tudor and Worrall, 2006).

'Being' generally refers to the nature, state and process of active existence and, in person-centred psychology, to a focus on and acceptance of being in the present. Aristotle argues that there is an important distinction between the actual and the potential, and that being or actuality emerges from becoming or potentiality, a distinction which has influenced and has been developed in humanistic psychology by Maslow (1954), Allport (1955/1983), and Rogers (1958/1967a). Organismic philosophy and psychology, however, take a different view, arguing that becoming emerges from being. As Whitehead (1929/1978: 22) puts it: 'it belongs to the nature of a "being" that it has potential for every "becoming"'.

In his discussion of being, Gilson (1952: 2–3) argues that:

> In a first acceptation, the word being is a noun. As such, it signifies either a being (that is, the substance, nature, and essence of anything existent), or being itself, a property common to all that which can rightly be said to be. In a second acceptation, the same word is the present participle of the verb 'to be'. As a verb, it no longer signifies something that is, nor even existence in general, but rather the very act whereby any given reality actually is, or exists. Let us call this act a 'to be', in contradistinction to what is commonly called 'a being'. It appears at once that, at least to the mind, the relation of 'to be' to 'being' is not a reciprocal one. 'Being' is conceivable, 'to be' is not. We cannot possibly conceive an 'is' except as belonging to some thing that is, or exists.

Whilst Gilson is arguing for 'being' being conceivable and 'is' inconceivable, his argument also supports the value of the verbal form precisely because it is grounded in experiencing; in other words, it has to have a subject: 'I', 'You', 'She', 'Rogers' and so on.

BECOMING

If we accept the Aristotelian distinction between actuality and potentiality, then becoming describes the potential of the individual and, in psychological terms, the process of that potentiality as distinct from its outcome. In this sense, as Tudor and Worrall (2006: 145) observe: 'Becoming ... stands in the same relation to "be" as the actualising tendency does to self-actualisation.' Again, from an organismic perspective, whilst Maslow's view of self-actualisation is as an *outcome* of growth and change, Rogers, who emphasises the actualising tendency, generally talks more in terms of the *process* of becoming. He describes, for example, the fully functioning person as a person in process: being open to experience, trusting in her organism, having an internal locus of evaluation, and being willing to be a process and a complexity of process (Rogers, 1960/1967d). Both process (literally, a 'going forward') and becoming (or what process philosophers and psychologists refer to as 'concrescence') carry a sense of future (see Whitehead 1929/1978; Roy, 2000). In his paper on 'The Characteristics of a Helping Relationship' Rogers (1958/1967c) puts forward a number of questions and considerations which, he says, guides his behaviour in helping relationships. In the last of these questions, he asks (p. 55): 'Can I meet this other individual as a person who is in the process of *becoming*, or will I be bound by his past and by my past?' Here Rogers is concerned that conditional acceptance, such as that implied by a diagnosis, is based on a fixed, past-centred view of the person. Although he focuses on the present, Rogers implies an interest in the future. Bohart *et al.* (1993) are more explicit about this in their suggestion that human beings tend naturally to look to the future rather than the past.

In the same article Rogers follows this question with a quote from Martin Buber, the existentialist philosopher and theologian, with whom he had a dialogue in 1957. Rogers quotes, approvingly, Buber's use of the word 'confirmation', viewing it as similar to his own concept of acceptance. However, in a new transcript and commentary on this dialogue, Anderson and Cissna (1997: 92) clarify the differences between the two, commenting that:

> Rogers uses 'acceptance' to include both accepting the other's present self and his or her potential, while Buber reserves 'acceptance' to acknowledge who the other is now, but prefers 'confirmation' to refer to the overall process that includes the possibility of affecting the potential of the other.

BELONGING

Although, especially in his later years and writing, Rogers emphasises the social nature of human beings, and demonstrated his interest in groups, communities and conflict resolution, he doesn't talk explicitly about belonging or the process of belonging. Whilst other contemporary theorists and therapists did develop concepts such as *Gemeinschaftsgefuehl* or 'community feeling' (Adler); 'affiliation needs' (Murray); homonomy (Angyal); and belonging, which Maslow includes in his hierarchy of needs, after basic needs and security, Rogers didn't develop this logic of his 'relationship therapy'.

In effect, belonging describes social being and social becoming. As a word/symbol it catches something of our need for affiliation, connection and community, as it were, a longing for belonging. Interestingly, Whitehead (1929/1978) describes the philosophy of the organism as concerned exclusively with 'the becoming, the being, and the relatedness of actual entities.' Moreover, according to Lukács (1920/1967: §5), a Marxist philosopher:

> It is only when the core of being has shown itself as social becoming, that the being itself can appear as a product, so far unconscious, of human activity, and this activity, in turn, as the decisive element of the transformation of being.

This argues that 'the being' in Marxism is the historical product of human activity or labour, and that neither being nor becoming can be understood outside of belonging or social becoming.

When we focus on belonging we emphasise the interrelatedness of human beings and, in the context of therapy, our need for encounter, intersubjectivity, and therapeutic relat*ing*. The concept of encounter is a familiar one to person-centred therapists, and has been developed in the last ten years particularly through the work of Schmid (1998; Schmid and Mearns, 2006). Intersubjectivity, or the meeting of the two subjective worlds of client and therapist, has its origins in self-psychology (Stolorow, Brandchaft and Atwood, 1987), and may be found in some recent person-centred literature (see Peters, 2006; Tudor and Worrall, 2006). The concept of therapeutic relating brings these two points together. There is now an extensive literature on the therapeutic relationship, its nature and influence on psychotherapy outcome. This literature is, to a great extent, influenced by Rogers' work, although this influence is generally understated and undervalued. However, the therapeutic 'relationship' (noun) is, as such, a fixed thing and, in my view, is more accurately and usefully described as therapeutic relating (see Summers and Tudor, 2000; Tudor and Worrall, 2006). This is based on what Siegel (2003: 6) refers to as 'contingent communication', i.e., 'the ability of one person to perceive, make sense of, and respond to the signals of the other person … [which] creates a sense of communion, of joining, in the attuned, resonating pair of minds'. It is in this moment-to-moment therapeutic relating that a sense of belonging is co-created, maintained, enhanced and sometimes ruptured. This *is* therapy.

BEING VERBAL

Although the words 'being', 'belonging' and 'becoming' derive like verbs, they may also be used as nouns. When we use the present (indicative) tense of the verb 'to be' to describe ourselves, as in the example 'I am tired', we describe a fixed state. If we want to describe this as an ongoing present process we must use the present continuous, i.e., 'I am being tired' or, more usually we change the verb and say, 'I am feeling tired'. This process-oriented language has been developed in the therapeutic field especially by gestalt psychologists (see Stevens, 1971/1989), the purpose of which is to change one's awareness of reality from a collection of *things* to a process of *experiencing*. Instead of saying 'I've got a headache' or even 'I've got a tension in my head', we may say 'I am tensing my head'. As Roy (2000: 12) puts it in his book *Toward a Process Psychology*: '[This] perspective drives towards the conclusion that people ultimately are responsible for their experience, that they are not filled with things but are ultimately their own, self-determined experience.' Whilst too much can be made of personal responsibility and self-determination and even a particular form of words, the exercise can be a useful one and the point well made, and both can have a positive therapeutic impact in terms of the client's greater appreciation of his potential for change.

In the same way, if we say: 'I am being', 'I am becoming' or 'I am belonging', we are emphasising our present continuous process. This is different from the use of these words as nouns, as in 'Rogers emphasises the process of becoming' where 'becoming' is the gerund form of the verb used as a noun. In some languages other than English this distinction is clearer. For instance, in Spanish, in order to use an infinitive as a noun it must be preceded by an article, in this instance, *el* (the), in which case the infinitive *ser* (to be) becomes *el ser* (the being), used as a noun. Thus, when referring to these concepts as nouns, we may usefully name them: 'the being', 'the belonging' and 'the becoming'. Taking this further, in an article on the opening Surah of the Qur'an, Mir (2003) comments that the first three verses make up a nominal sentence, whereas the last two verses are a verbal sentence. He argues that: 'Grammatically, the nominal sentence signifies *Dawam* ("permanence"—or, in philosophical language: "being"), whereas the verbal sentence signifies *Huduth* ("happening"—philosophically: "becoming").' In other words, a verbal sentence about being, such as 'I am being', signifies or implies becoming.

This has two principle advantages:

1. It echoes the definition of 'to actualise' (and, indeed, 'actualisation') as carrying the sense of both present and future.
2. It clarifies the interrelation between being and becoming.

Person-centred psychology proposes that, as persons, we are in process—of being, becoming, and belonging. In order that the process of therapeutic relating matches the theory of process, and that the medium of our language matches our message, we need to adopt more verbal language: that we are being, becoming, and belonging human beings.

REFERENCES

Allport GW (1983) *Becoming: Basic considerations for a psychology of personality*. New Haven, NJ: Yale University Press. (Original work published 1955.)

Anderson R & Cissna K (1997) *The Martin Buber–Carl Rogers Dialogue: A new transcript with commentary*. Albany, NY: Suny Press.

Angyal A (1941) *Foundations for a Science of Personality*. New York: Commonwealth Fund.

Angyal A (1973) *Neurosis and Treatment: A holistic theory*. New York: John Wiley & Sons. (Original work published 1965.)

Association for Humanistic Psychology Practitioners (1998) The AHPP statement of core beliefs. *Self & Society, 26* (3), 3–6.

Bohart AC, Humphrey A, Magallanes M, Guzman R, Smiljanich K & Aguallo S (1993) Emphasizing the future in empathy responses. *Journal of Humanistic Psychology, 33* (2), 12–29.

Bozarth JD & Brodley BT (1991) Actualization: A functional concept in client-centered therapy. In A Jones and R Crandall (Eds) Handbook of Self-Actualization [Special issue] *Journal of Social Behavior and Personality, 6* (5), 45–59.

Brown M (1990) *The Healing Touch: An introduction to organismic psychotherapy*. Mendocino, CA: Liferhythm.

Cooper DA (1997) *God is a Verb: Kabbalah and the practice of mystical Judaism*. New York: Riverhead Books.

Csikszentmihalyi M (1990) *Flow: The psychology of optimal experience*. New York: HarperCollins.

Finke J (2002) Aspects of the actualizing tendency from a humanistic psychology perspective. *Person-Centered and Experiential Psychotherapies, 1* (1&2), 28–40.

Gilson E (1952) *Being and Some Philosophers* (2nd edn). Toronto: Pontifical Institute of Mediaeval Studies.
Goldstein K (1995) *The Organism.* New York: Zone Books. (Original work published 1934.)
Hall C & Lindzey G (1978) *Theories of Personality* (3rd edn). New York: Wiley.
Jahoda M (1958) *Current Concepts of Positive Mental Health.* New York: Basic Books.
Jones A & Crandall R (Eds) (1991) Handbook of Self-Actualization [Special issue] *Journal of Social Behavior and Personality, 6* (5).
Kantor JR (1924a) *Principles of Psychology. Vol. 1.* New York: Knopf.
Kantor JR (1924b) *Principles of Psychology. Vol. 2.* New York: Knopf.
Keen S (1983) *The Passionate Life: Stages of loving.* London: Gateway Books.
Keyes CLM (1998) Social well-being. *Social Psychology Quarterly, 61,* 121–40.
Keyes CLM (2003) Complete mental health: An agenda for the 21st century. In CLM Keyes & J Haidt (Eds) *Flourishing: Positive psychology and the life well-lived.* Washington, DC: American Psychological Association Press, pp. 293–312.
Keyes CLM (2005) Mental health and/or mental illness? Investigating axioms of the complete state model of health. *Journal of Consulting and Clinical Psychology, 73,* 539–48.
Keyes CLM (2007) Promoting and protecting mental health as flourishing: A complementary strategy for improving national mental health. *American Psychologist, 62* (2), 95–108.
Keyes CLM & Shapiro A (2004) Social well-being in the United States: A descriptive epidemiology. In OG Brim, C Ryff & R Kessler (Eds) *How Healthy Are We? A national study of well-being at midlife.* Chicago: University of Chicago Press, pp. 350–72.
Kirschenbaum H (1979) *On Becoming Carl Rogers.* New York: Delacorte Press. Republished (2007) as *The Life and Work of Carl Rogers.* Ross-on-Wye: PCCS Books.
Kriz J (2006) *Self-Actualization.* Norderstedt: Herstellung und Verlag.
Layard R (2005) *Happiness: Lessons from a new science.* New York: Penguin.
Layard R (2006) *The Depression Report: A new deal for depression and anxiety disorders.* Centre for Economic Performance, London School of Economics, London.
Leary DE (Ed) (1990) *Metaphors in the History of Psychology.* Cambridge: Cambridge University Press.
Lukács, G (1967) What is orthodoxical Marxism? In *History and Class Consciousness.* London: Merlin Press. (Original work published 1920.)
Maslow AH (1954) *Motivation and Personality.* New York: Harper & Row.
Maslow AH (1962) *Towards a Psychology of Being.* New York: Van Nostrand.
Mathews F (1991) *The Ecological Self.* London: Routledge.
Merry T (2003). The actualisation conundrum. *Person-Centred Practice, 11* (2), 83–91.
Mir M (2003) *Contrapuntal Harmony in the Thought, Mood and Structure of Surah Fatihah.* Online article available at: <www.quranicstudies.com/article65.html> (published 10 December 2003).
Murphy G (1947) *Personality: A biosocial approach to origins and structure.* New York: Harper.
Patterson CH (2000) A unitary theory of motivation and its counseling implications. In CH Patterson *Understanding Psychotherapy: Fifty years of client-centred theory and practice.* Ross-on-Wye: PCCS Books, pp. 10–21. (Original work published 1964.)
Pavis S, Masters H & Cunningham-Burley S (1996) *Lay Concepts of Mental Health and How It Can Be Maintained.* Department of Public Health Sciences, University of Edinburgh, Edinburgh.
Perls F, Hefferline RF & Goodman P (1973) *Gestalt Therapy: Excitement and growth in the human personality.* (Original work published 1951.)

Peters H (2006) The development of intersubjectivity in relation to psychotherapy and its importance for Pre-Therapy. *Person-Centered and Experiential Psychotherapies, 5* (3), 191–207.

Rogers CR (1951) *Client-Centered Therapy*. London: Constable.

Rogers CR (1959) A theory of therapy, personality and interpersonal relationships, as developed in the client-centred framework. In S Koch (Ed) *Psychology: A study of a science. Vol. 3: Formulations of the person and the social context*. New York: McGraw-Hill, pp. 184–256.

Rogers CR (1963) The actualizing tendency in relation to 'motive' and to consciousness. In M Jones (Ed) *Nebraska Symposium on Motivation*. Lincoln, NE: University of Nebraska Press, pp. 1–24.

Rogers CR (1967a) A process conception of psychotherapy. In *On Becoming a Person*. London: Constable, pp. 125–59. (Original work published in 1958.)

Rogers CR (1967b) A therapist's view of the good life: The fully functioning person. In *On Becoming a Person*. London: Constable, pp. 183–96. (Original work published in 1957.)

Rogers CR (1967c) The characteristics of a helping relationship. In *On Becoming a Person*. London: Constable, pp. 39–57. (Original work published in 1958.)

Rogers CR (1967d) 'To be that self which one truly is': A therapist's view of personal goals. In *On Becoming a Person*. London: Constable, pp. 163–82. (Original work published in 1960.)

Rogers CR (1967e) What it means to become a person. In *On Becoming a Person*. London: Constable, pp. 107–24. (Original work published 1954.)

Roy DE (2000) *Toward a Process Psychology: A model of integration*. Fresno, CA: Adobe Creations Press.

Schmid PF (1998) 'Face to face': The art of encounter. In B Thorne & E Lambers (Eds) *Person-Centred Therapy: A European perspective*. London: Sage, pp. 94–90.

Schmid PF & Mearns D (2006) Being-with and being-counter: Person-centred psychotherapy as an in-depth co-creative process of personalization. *Person-Centered and Experiential Psychotherapies, 5* (3), 174–90.

Seligman MP (2002) *Authentic Happiness*. New York: Free Press.

Siegel DJ (2003) An interpersonal neurobiology of psychotherapy: The developing mind and the resolution of trauma. In MF Solomon & DJ Siegel (Eds) *Healing Trauma: Attachment, mind, body, and brain*. New York: WW Norton, pp.1–56.

Stevens JO (1989) *Awareness*. London: Eden Grove Editions. (Original work published 1971.)

Stolorow RD, Brandchaft B & Atwood G (1987) *Psychoanalytic Treatment: An intersubjective approach*. Hillsdale, NJ: Analytic Press.

Summers G & Tudor K (2000) Cocreative transactional analysis. *Transactional Analysis Journal, 30* (1), 23–40.

Taft J (1933) *The Dynamics of Therapy in a Controlled Relationship*. New York: Macmillan.

Tolman EC & Brunswik E (1935) The organism and the causal texture of the environment. *Psychological Review, 42*, 43–77.

Tudor K (1996) *Mental Health Promotion: Paradigms and practice*. London: Routledge.

Tudor K & Worrall M (2006) *Person-Centred Therapy: A clinical philosophy*. London: Routledge.

Van Belle HA (1980) *Basic Intent and Therapeutic Approach of Carl R Rogers*. Toronto: Wedge Publishing Foundation.

Werner H (1948) *Comparative Psychology of Mental Development* (rev edn). Chicago, IL: Follett.

Wheeler RH (1940) *The Science of Psychology* (2nd edn). New York: Crowell.

Whitehead AN (1978) *Process and Reality* (DR Griffin & DW Sherburne, Eds) (corrected edn). New York: The Free Press. (Original work published 1929.)

CHAPTER 6

A PERSONALIZING TENDENCY: DIALOGICAL AND THERAPEUTIC CONSEQUENCES OF THE ACTUALIZING TENDENCY AXIOM

PETER F. SCHMID

Abstract

How do we become the personality that we are? How does personal development come about? How do we realise our being-a-person? These questions are fundamental to the person-centered image of the human being and its consequences for the theory and practice of psychotherapy and counseling. The focus of the following chapter is on a better understanding of the specifically human process of actualization, and therefore on the substantial aspect of personhood and its relation to the dialectical nature of being a person.

THE RELATIONSHIP PERSON TO PERSON: PERSONALIZATION AS AN ONGOING PROCESS OF ENCOUNTER

Recent developments in person-centered theory and practice have brought about an increased interest in and understanding of the relationship between client(s) and therapist(s). They have led to a deeper comprehension of the foundational dialogical nature of the therapeutic relationship and the encounter quality of this liaison. The following précis of this major step in the development of person-centered therapy and counseling also shows how profoundly person-centered anthropology is rooted in occidental philosophy. Thus it will not come as a surprise that we will also find the roots of the dialectical nature of the actualizing tendency in this tradition.

I have been applying anthropological and phenomenological perspectives in trying to understand what a person-centered approach really means. In my explorations, I have become aware that in this unique approach to therapy and related fields, initiated by Carl Rogers and further elaborated around the world, we find an image of the human being that is deeply embedded in traditions developed over millennia in the Middle East and Europe (Schmid, 1991, 1994, 1996, 1998a, 2001a, 2007a). I have, as have others, extensively described the development of a relational understanding of the person and the consequences thereof for person-centered theory and practice (see the bibliography in Schmid and Mearns 2006: 177–8). This relational understanding has gained popular acceptance (see the Special Issue of *Person-Centered and Experiential Psychotherapies*, 5 (4), 2006; Cooper et al., 2007).

It is regarded by many as the state of the art of genuine person-centered anthropology, theory and practice.

THE DIALECTICAL MEANING OF BEING A PERSON

The person-centered approach is founded philosophically upon the conviction that the image of the human being most adequate to our experience is based on regarding him or her as a *person*. This means that the human being is intrinsically and dialectically both substantial and relational: being *from* oneself and thus autonomous, *and* being *from* relationship and thus interdependent with others. Human beings have an innate capacity, need and tendency to develop on their own *and* in relationships. Both autonomy and interrelatedness constitute a single human nature as a substantial-relational being. In a summary of Carl Rogers' words: the human is motivated by the actualizing tendency—the inner force and resource to lead one's own life out of one's own capabilities. This can be tapped only if the individual is facilitated by a special kind of relationship.

This image of the human being is so challenging that all too often it was and continues to be reduced to only one of its dimensions. Accordingly, different orientations in psychotherapy tend to rely one-sidedly either on the inner powerful resources of the individual or on the effective quality of the relationship between therapist and client. It is important to be aware that the person-centered view is grounded in the conviction that the human being is both independent, living out of its own resources, and interdependent, inevitably connected with others. This notion of the human being as a person not only gave birth to the name of the approach; the image of men and women as persons is also the foundation of humanistic personality and developmental theory, including the theory of so-called disorders and the theory of therapy (Schmid, 2004). Nowhere else in the therapeutic and related fields is the respective understanding of the human being so consequently realized than in what genuinely is called a *person*-centered approach.

THE DIALOGICAL NATURE OF THE THERAPEUTIC RELATIONSHIP

The therapeutic relationship is an encounter relationship. The term *encounter* denotes a relationship where the other person is not regarded as an alter ego, but met as truly being an *Other*. This means that I cannot simply draw conclusions from myself and my experience about the self and experience of the other person. Rather the therapeutic attitude is to open up, accept genuinely and try to comprehend empathically what the partner in the relationship is disclosing. Thus the respective epistemology can be named correctly a Thou–I relationship (Schmid, 1994, 1998b, 2001b, c, d, 2002a, 2003, 2006), because it has its origin in the opening up of the 'Thou.'

Carl Rogers (1962) was convinced that 'the interpersonal relationship' is 'the core of guidance.' As early as 1939 he wrote in the context of child guidance that 'the relationship between the worker and the parent is the essential feature' (Rogers, 1939: 197). This 'encounter person to person'—as he later described the psychotherapeutic enterprise (Rogers, 1962)—is the core of an *intersubjective, co-creative process of personalization* (see below) through meeting 'at relational depth,' to use Mearns and Cooper's (2005) terminology. Therefore, therapy springs from a *fundamental We* (Schmid, 2003); its nature is to respond to the given situation of the client. This denotes that therapist and client are co-responding to the relationship they find themselves in within the very moment of their being-together. So they are co-creating the relationship out of mutual encounter. The contribution on the therapist's part is to be present. The client's contribution to this joint process is to make use actively of their inherent capacity to make the therapist's acknowledgement and empathy work. This is carefully and convincingly described by Bohart and others (Bohart, 2004; Bohart and Tallman, 1999). The client is the one who 'in–forms' the therapist (from the Latin *informare*, to give shape to, to fashion, to describe), which means that they bring the therapist into a form in which understanding can take place (Schmid, 2005b)—a stance that indeed allows the formulation that the client is the therapist.

Presence—literally the underlying Latin word '*prae-esse*' means 'to be fully there'—is the existential foundation and deeper meaning of the well known, yet all too often superficially misunderstood 'core conditions' of authenticity, acknowledgment and comprehension (to use Martin Buber's terms for the attitudes described by Rogers as congruence, unconditional positive regard and empathy; see Schmid, 2001b, c, d, 2002a). The therapist's task is to realize these continuously and in any given situation—thus responding to the challenge of the relationship in its concrete context. This provides a climate of safety, trust and respect for the client enabling them to increasingly face and develop themselves, their self in all its plurality (Mearns, 1999; Mearns and Thorne, 2000). With this stance, a genuine, person-centered *bi- (or multi-) polar model of psychotherapy has been developed*—both (or all) persons involved as a part of the focus of reflection, forming a fundamentally *dialogical* process of co-creating the therapy (Schmid, 2006).

In many psychotherapeutic orientations the relationship is only 'used,' i.e., seen as a means or a precondition to do the actual and true therapeutic work on or with the client. The unique stance of person-centered psychotherapy, based on experience and supported by research, is that therapy does not *use* relationship as a basis or an introduction; on the contrary, relationship itself *is* therapy (Rogers, 1962; see Barrett-Lennard, 2007). Therapy is a co-creative process of becoming a person (Schmid and Mearns, 2006; Mearns and Schmid, 2006), it is the art of encounter, it is dialogue from the very outset (Schmid, 2006).

In short, as persons we are not only *in* relationships, but we *are* relationships (Schmid, 2002b). This means that the person is developing when the relationship is developing. Therefore the quality of relationship is crucial for personality development.

THE ACTUALIZING TENDENCY: PERSONALIZATION AS AN ONGOING PROCESS OF THE REALIZATION OF INHERENT POTENTIAL

The elements mentioned above illustrate the relational dimension of being, which we understand much better now. In order to keep the balance of both dimensions of personhood (substantial and relational) following these theoretical and practical developments, the question arises anew as to how the substantial aspect must be comprehended and how it is connected with the relational aspect.

CARL ROGERS' CONCEPT OF THE ACTUALIZING TENDENCY

Rogers thought of the human organism as active, actualizing and directional. The central idea and term characteristic of the *substantial* dimension of being a person is the *actualizing tendency*. This aspect was central to Rogers' focus in the early stage of his ongoing exploration of the nature of psychotherapy, where he mainly concentrated on the view of the person as an individual. His 1959 chapter with the theoretical definitions, his 1963 paper on motivation and its political aspects, and his extension of the actualizing tendency axiom to a formative tendency in his 1979 paper on the foundations of the person-centered approach are essential writings.

With the actualizing tendency, Rogers postulates an inherent tendency in all organisms, including human beings, to develop 'all its capacities in ways which serve to maintain or enhance the organism' (Rogers, 1959: 196; see 1980: cols. 2181–2). It is a tendency to 'more complex organization, the fulfilment of potential and, in human beings, the actualization of the self' (Tudor and Merry, 2002: 2). This is an active tendency, not a passive one or one that becomes active only if there are deficits to correct (as traditional drive theories usually posit). It is seen as the central source of energy (Rogers, 1963: 3; see Schmid, 1991: 129), the sole motivational force, the substratum of all motivation (Rogers, 1963). Thus, it is the answer to the question of what makes the human organism tick, what causes us to live in the way we do. Human nature is basically trustworthy in its tendency to develop individually and socially (Rogers, 1963, 1977: ch. 11) in the direction of a 'fully functioning person' (see below). It is a tendency, not a guarantee of full realization (Brodley, 1999: 113). It is individual and universal, holistic and ubiquitous (Brodley, 1999). It is a constant tendency: the organism is always motivated, 'up to something,' always seeking (Rogers, 1963).

As a paradigm Rogers liked to refer to the infant who wants to learn how to walk, and therefore overcomes all obstacles in spite of the fact that crawling would be so much easier. The same thing happens psychologically as well as biologically if an appropriate growth climate is given. The tendency includes the differentiation of organs and functions, as well as the enhancement of efficiency, and a movement towards autonomy, away from external control and towards wholeness and integration (Wilkins, 2003). It is a proactive tendency in order both to keep the organism functioning optimally under given conditions and to develop it (Bohart, 2007). This is a biological and psychological concept that must not be (mis)understood in a moral sense! (Brodley, 1999: 116; Mearns and Thorne, 2000: 181–2). Rogers (1961: 26) is convinced that the direction is basically constructive: 'It is my opinion that persons have a basically positive direction.' This does not mean that human beings are simply 'good.' They also have the potential to develop asocially and destructively, if the necessary facilitative relationship climate is missing. This means that a constructive, prosocial tendency needs not necessarily produce constructiveness and a prosocial behaviour. Inhibiting influences from outside the individual, or the lack of external facilitative influences may hinder such a development or steer development in a different direction.

The claim that there is an actualizing tendency at work in all organisms is, of course, a matter of belief. In spite of all parallels, analogies, plausibility and seeming support from different realms of science (see, for example, Rogers, 1963; Kriz, 2007) the actualizing tendency is an axiom, as Rogers (1959) stated, and not verifiable. It is the fundamental idea of the person-centered image of the human being, underlying all person-centered theory and practice. It cannot scientifically be proved as Kriz (2007) seems to suggest, not even from a systemic-dynamic (as opposed to a mechanistic) point of view, because it is not simply a description of processes but an interpretation. Furthermore, it does not make sense to try to explain the actualizing tendency from the point of view of natural science, because it is human science that we are talking about.

SOME FURTHER DEVELOPMENTS OF THE CONCEPT

Many scholars clarified, refined and elaborated the concept further (e.g., Bozarth and Brodley, 1991; Gendlin, 1996; Brodley, 1999; Cornelius-White, 2007). Mearns and Thorne developed 'a dialogical model where both the forces towards growth, and the restraint of social mediation, are valued as contributing to the fundamental dialectic of the social being' (Mearns and Thorne, 2000: 180) and thus shifted the focus to the actualizing *process*. This represents an important counter-position or corrective to a simplistic moral misunderstanding of the actualizing tendency as 'the good' within us as opposed to an evil, oppressing social environment.

I agree with Tudor and Worrall (2006: 87) that it is more accurate to say that an organism *is* a tendency to actualize, than to say it *has* this tendency. This perspective prevents us from thinking the actualizing tendency could be a thing or an entity. Rather it is a force that is inevitably at work in all organisms.

Finke (2002) puts the emphasis on the humanistic quality of the concept, emphasizing intentionality, self-determination and, relying on Sartre (1965), the freedom of choice of the self-concept. He emphasizes the personal quality of the decision-making process of the human being for his own life and questions descriptions of the actualizing tendency that refer to natural scientific explanations, among them the a-personal concepts of self-organizing and self-regulating processes as can be found in biology and systems theory. Instead he refers to the cultural history of the human being and their creativity as a basis for the understanding of individual and collective development. (This is discussed controversially in Kriz et al., 2003.)

LIFE MEANS TO BECOME WHAT YOU ARE, TOGETHER WITH OTHERS: THE UNDERLYING PHILOSOPHICAL IDEA OF CENTRAL PERSON-CENTERED CONCEPTIONS

Consequently, the person-centered approach is based on the idea that life is an active process, that there is a reliable, fundamental organismic tendency toward fulfilment, a potential inherent in the human being, to constructively and pro-socially realize their possibilities towards growth, maturity, and life enrichment (Rogers, 1980: col. 2160). Therefore, the central statement of person-centered therapy is that the individual has immeasurably rich abilities (substantial dimension) which can be tapped in a clearly defined psychological climate (relational dimension).

Exploring historical trains of thought that underlie the actualizing tendency axiom sheds light on this principle concept of the person-centered approach and helps us to understand it further. We can trace these strands back to the great philosopher Aristotle (384–322 BC) in ancient Greece. According to Aristotle, all being is interconnected. He postulated that a living being is not a mere accumulation of parts or a machine—it is an organism, which means that it is a whole that gives meaning to its parts. Specific to an organism is the idea that it is held together and directed by an aim or an end, which is not introduced from the outside but is intrinsic to the organism. This end, for an organism, is to strive for the actualization of its potentialities. Aristotle is convinced that all living has an inner purposefulness (called *entelechy*, see p. 93), which means that he postulates a concept of universal teleology, i.e., of self-actualization and self-perfecting. The same basic striving is true for the human being: they aim at becoming fully what they are. In *Ethics*, Aristole (1955) assumes that the human being is basically good. To realize this means to strive towards 'the good'—and 'the good' is to actualize oneself as much as possible to become what one is, namely truly a human being. According to Aristotle, that is what life is about, what the purpose of life is. (See Weischedel, 1997: 55–6) This is why Aristotle is called the father of humanism.

THE ACTUAL AND THE POTENTIAL: THE PERSON IS MORE THAN THEY ACTUALLY REALIZE

So the original idea that underlies the actualizing tendency concept is nearly two and a half thousand years old. The view of an actualizing tendency held by many humanistic thinkers is rooted in Aristotle's doctrine of ενεργεια *[energeia]* and δυναμις *[dynamis]* and the similar doctrine of *actus* [act] and *potentia* [potency] put forth by the medieval scholastic theologian and philosopher Thomas Aquinas (1225–1274) (Aristotle, 1966; Thomas Aquinas, 1976; see Anzenbacher, 1992; Hirschberger, 1965; Ricken, 1996; Weischedel, 1997).

Aristotle and Thomas Aquinas started from a question that appears to be as relevant to twenty-first century psychotherapy as it was to their own philosophical problems: How is it possible that something can become something else, something different? Or generally: How does change come about? In classical Greek thinking the idea of *energeia* and *dynamis* served to explain movement (and thus motivation) and change (and thus development).

According to the Aristotelian and Thomasian worldview, the two foundational modalities of being are 'act' and 'potency.' The Latin *agere* means 'to do' and *posse* means 'being able to.' 'Act' denotes the reality, the present development of all possibilities, capabilities, talents, the actual (real) being 'as is,' the realized present. 'Potency' stands for the possibility, the not-unfolded, the mere being possible. Act is what is already there; act is what something or somebody has already become. Potency is what it or they still can become. Synonyms for act are reality, actuality, action, deed, performance, activity, operation; synonyms for potency are possibility, potential, ability, aptitude, talent, capacity, power, force, effectiveness.

Dynamis is, according to Aristotle, the principle of movement, the potentiality of something to become something else. It is the principle of change or development to become something different. Accordingly *energeia*—coined by Aristotle from the words εν εργω ειναι [*en ergô einai:* to be at work]—is the act of 'being at work' of something, the real (actual) 'working' of the potential. Therefore each change is the realization or actualization of a potential. But this assumes, requires, presupposes another real being triggering this actualization, i.e., an other thing. Change happens through something different, through 'a third,' through another (see below).

Potentiality is what a thing is capable of doing, or being acted upon. As an example Aristotle takes the seed of a plant in the soil. It is potentially a plant. Actuality is the fulfilment of the end of the potentiality. Because the end (*telos*, see p. 93) is the principle of every change, and potentiality exists for the sake of the end, therefore actuality is the end. Referring then to the example of the seed, we could say that actuality is when the seed of the plant becomes a plant (Aristotle, 1966, IX).

To give some more examples: A young woman is a possible mother; if she becomes pregnant and gives birth to a child, she is an actual mother. An idea is a possible revolution; if it is adopted and taken over by enough people, it may become a real revolution. A dependent client, relying on the therapist's advice is possibly somebody who can decide and take responsibility for themselves; if the therapist not only pays attention to what is missing but also acknowledges the person of the client with this potential, the client is likely to acknowledge themselves in that way and thus actually become the responsible person.

But what exactly is the potency, the potential, the potentiality? The act is 'what is.' Is the potential only 'what can be' and nothing else? It was Aristotle's conception—contrary to Protagoras and others who only considered the actual as being, as existing—to regard the potency also as something being (*ens*), as existing. Aristotle recorded the view that potency, although not being (*esse*) in the full sense (*actus*), is more than a mere possibility in the mind. The potential is not only in someone's head, it is really there.

It is clear that the same idea is the underlying intention of those philosophers, psychologists and psychotherapists who consider the human being's potential as at least of equal importance, because of its mere existence, as their actual doing and their actual consciousness of themselves.

The therapist, for instance, does not only look at the actual but also at the possible, not only at the 'reality' but also at the 'potentiality' which they also consider to be real. Thus they trigger a movement that means change, because the client does not only show them the obvious but also the possible, not only the actual thinking and doing but also potential directions of thinking and doing. This, by the way, is another proof that the client is the one who starts the change by disclosing potential, by referring to potential (even if still quite unaware of it); it is another proof of the fact that it is always the client 'who makes therapy work' (Bohart and Tallman, 1999, see below).

All that is real has within itself the difference between actual and potential being. It comes from this difference. It is what it is through the *Aufhebung* of this difference. The Hegelian German term *aufheben* means (1) to preserve, (2) to abolish and dissolve, and (3) to supersede, transcend and give new meaning on a higher level. *Aufhebung* is the combination of these meanings: the former is preserved as well as dissolved by being superseded and transcended. To become is to be transcended to being fully (Schmid, 2001b, c, d, 2002a). Here we can see easily that concepts like Rogers' process scale of psychotherapy and his idea of the fully functioning person (see p. 93) are rooted in this understanding of becoming real and becoming fully.

Many centuries later Thomas Aquinas, referring to Aristotle, understood the essence (*essentia*) of a finite being (*ens*) as potency, which means the possibility and the determination to become the appropriate being (*esse*). This being (*esse*) of a being (*ens*) is interpreted by Thomas as an act, i.e., as the realization of its essence. In other words: To be is the actualization of inherent possibilities. And, again, Thomas also stresses the necessity of the other. In order to come into being, another is needed.

THE EFFICIENT CAUSE: ACTUALIZATION DEPENDS ON THE RELATIONSHIP WITH 'THE OTHER'

What makes the possible become real? What makes a being in the state of 'can be' develop to the state of 'really being there'? The answer is that change, development, actualization needs something from the outside, something different, 'a third,' 'an other.'

To understand the character of potency it is important to note that it 'waits,' so to speak, for the actualizing stimulus or 'kick,' for the action that makes it possible to become real. Potency cannot actualize itself by itself; it cannot become an act without an extrinsic cause that makes this happen. It needs something (or somebody) that causes the difference, that brings about this effect.

This is called the efficient cause (*causa efficiens*). According to Aristotle's theory of causality the efficient cause is that from which the change or the ending of the change first starts. An example of an efficient cause is the artist who creates a statue, or the carpenter who is the cause of wood becoming a table. This principle of causality became the universal explanatory model of modern natural sciences.

For the image of the human being and the understanding of personality development this means that life is the actualization (realization) of the given possibilities (potential, potency), which needs an 'influence' from outside, i.e., by somebody else, by another human being. *This is the foundation of the essential importance of relationship*—also from a substantial viewpoint. Although the actualizing tendency is an inherent (substantial, or in the substance of the being) tendency, to become effective it needs something else; in other words: it needs interconnection, relatedness, relationship.

It is important to note that with the very idea of actualization, the 'outside effect' is inevitably connected. Realization or actualization is not possible without influence from outside. This implies that the idea of self-actualization in the meaning of 'actualization only by or through oneself' (i.e., without something or somebody else) is impossible. All individualistic ways of understanding the humanistic tradition in general and the person-centered approach in particular must be wrong, because they make no sense in the light of the idea of actualization as what is possible becoming real. As it is not possible for a plant to become the flower or tree it can become without outside influence (i.e., water, light, etc.), without the necessary circumstances, it is also not possible for a human being to grow and develop without the necessary conditions or climate. In this case the necessary 'third' is another human being or other human beings, and the appropriate facilitative relationship that was described precisely by Carl Rogers.

Thus the often uttered reproaches against *self*-actualization, *self*-development, *self*-determination (and many of the other self terms of a one-sided understanding of the humanistic ideals) are correct and well-founded, if 'self' is meant in the sense of 'totally by itself.' Amongst others this criticism was prominently voiced by the Lithuanian philosopher Emmanuel Levinas, when he confronted 'totality' with 'infinity' in his most well-known book *Totalité et Infini* (Levinas, 1961). All encounter philosophers (or philosophers of dialogue or personalistic philosophers) never tire of repeatedly stressing that there is no human being without other humans. Fichte (1965, Vol. III: 39) had already written that 'the human only becomes human among humans.' And, as a matter of fact, long before the emerging of an explicitly systemic perspective in psychotherapy the relational dimension of being a person—the fact that a person cannot exist without other persons, that one cannot even think of a person without thinking of their relationships—anticipated a systems theory view (Schmid, 1996: 77–112).

These considerations show that the relational and the substantial are not independent dimensions but two sides of the same coin, two aspects from which we can look at one and the same phenomenon. There is no 'becoming the self that one truly is' (Kierkegaard, 1924: 17) without relationships that foster this development in an adequate way. There is no human relationship that is worthy of the name 'presence', i.e., an authentic-empathic-acknowledging human relationship, without development of both (or all) persons involved. In other words, the substantial and the relational dimension are one and the same: the person.

For the comprehension and conception of the actualizing tendency this means that it must be seen as a dialectical axiom of independence and interdependence, autonomy and interconnectedness (Schmid, 1999). It is wrong to think of it only as an inner force of the individual. *It must also be regarded as a relationship-oriented and therefore a social construct.* Another way of stating this is that we are not only *in* relationships but that we *are* relationships.

This also means that the motivational theory built on the actualizing tendency is not as simplistic as it might look at first glance and was quite often understood: *the process of actualization is a substantial-relational process.* The idea of the person rests not just on the actualizing tendency but on the relationship that frees it—or the other way around: the idea of the actualizing tendency would have no meaning without the interconnectedness of the person (see also Cornelius-White, 2007, who sees the actualizing tendency as 'inherently and non-directively relational').

So, interestingly, by taking a closer look at the main assumption of the substantial dimension of becoming a person, the actualizing tendency, we again end up with the dialectical nature of being a person. There is no actualization without relationship. The substantial and the relational dimension of being and becoming a person are two sides of the same coin.

ENTELECHY: THE TELEOLOGICAL IMPLICATIONS OF THE FORMATIVE TENDENCY AND THE FULLY FUNCTIONING PERSON ASSUME AN ACTIVE, DIRECTIONAL STRIVING TOWARDS A FORM

There is yet another interesting aspect of the Greek understanding of *energeia* and *dynamis*. As mentioned above, potentiality aims at realization, at actualization. According to these concepts, each change, each development, each actualization strives for a goal and its realization. Ultimately this implies a teleological idea: nature as a whole is aimed at an end (a stance opposed to a mechanistic worldview). This is closely related to the concept of entelechy, which deserves a closer examination.

In its original meaning entelechy refers to a philosophical concept of Aristotle who was influenced by Plato on this matter. The term can be traced to the ancient Greek word εντελεχεια [*entelecheia*], also coined by Aristotle himself. In English the term is roughly translated as 'having the end within itself.'

The concept of entelechy is closely related to the idea of *energeia*: entelechy is the possibility given in a certain reality. But it emphasizes an active moment. To Aristotle, *entelecheia* referred to a certain state or sort of being, in which a thing was actively working to be itself (1966, Metaphysics IX: 8). To use the Latin translation, the word denotes actuality or realization as opposed to potentiality. However, the terms actuality and realization should not be taken to imply that an *entelecheia* is inert or completed, but that the *entelecheia* is in some way actively being itself.

Actually, the words included in the term *entelecheia* can be combined in two ways: the first combination of the Greek words is *en* (in), *telos* (end, purpose, completion) and *echein* (to have); the other possibility is to join *enteles* (complete), *telos* and *echein*. According to these two possibilities of combinations you get two different meanings of *entelecheia* (which are also considered by Heron, 1998: 52, when he discusses the actualizing tendency). The term can be understood as the 'mature gestalt, as an individual in the state of completion' (according to the first combination) or as 'possession of the potential to reach one's completion' (the second combination).

In the first meaning entelechy denotes an individual that has come to its perfect end, the form that realizes itself in the matter. In this sense, the butterfly is the entelechy of the caterpillar. Here entelechy is the condition in which a potentiality has become an actuality.

In the second meaning entelechy denotes possessing the complete possibilities that can be actualized on principle at any given moment. In this case, entelechy signifies a possibility of an individual, not the individual itself. Entelechy here means the immanent formative potential of what is actual, the force in the organism that causes its development and completion. In this sense, the possibility of flying would be called the entelechy of the butterfly. It is the entelechy of a flower to blossom and of a bird to fly. And it is definitely this meaning that underlies Rogers' idea of an actualizing and a formative tendency. The teleological nature of these ideas (see also Brodley, 1999: 109; Tudor and Worrall, 2006: 24–6) also finds expression in Carl Rogers' well-known concepts of the formative tendency and the fully functioning person.

This is not the place to discuss whether these teleological conceptions satisfy diverse contemporary views of anthropological theories, and in particular questions regarding the philosophy of science implicitly and explicitly connected with them (for a discussion see Finke, 2002 and Kriz et al., 2003)—for instance, the leap from an actualizing tendency in the individual via a similar tendency in groups and society to a formative tendency in the universe. I am convinced that the actualizing tendency and the formative tendency can best be understood if treated as analogies, not as scientific proofs.

Rogers definitely was influenced by the idea of entelechy when he came to understand the actualizing tendency in human beings, and organisms generally, in the frame of an overall *formative tendency*, as part of a more universal force at work in the universe (Rogers, 1979). According to Rogers, a universal developmental movement, an evolutionary tendency toward greater order, more differentiation and integration, as well as greater complexity and greater interrelatedness (Rogers, 1980: 133), including the production of something new and creative, can be observed in the whole universe from the smallest to the largest levels, 'a formative directional tendency in the universe, which can be traced and observed in stellar space, in crystals, in microorganisms, in organic life, in human beings' (Rogers, 1978: 26). According to Rogers, this formative tendency realizes itself in organisms as actualizing tendency. Here we find the old philosophical idea that 'becoming is striving towards a form' (Hirschberger, 1965, Vol. I: 205)—hence the term 'formative tendency.' Entelechy clearly is the underlying idea of the formative tendency as a directional tendency. In *Ethics*, Aristotle (1955) says that the products of nature have an innate tendency in the direction of the best condition of which they are capable (see Tudor and Worrall, 2006: 86).[1]

---

1. It is important to mention that the idea of entelechy has been understood and used in different ways, which must not be confused with each other. In some philosophical systems, the concept of entelechy denotes a force propelling one to self-fulfilment. This concept occupies a central position in the metaphysics of Leibniz. It is closely related to his monadology, according to which each sentient entity contains, in a sense, its own entire universe within it. Each sentient entity is a monad, an absolutely independent thing that has no contact with any other sentient entity except through the mediating agency of God. It is obvious that this is different from the concept being described in the main text. Goethe also referred to the idea of entelechy …

What is the 'end' of the actualizing process in human beings? According to Rogers, the 'aim' of the actualizing tendency—as a subset of the formative tendency—is what he called the *fully functioning person* (Rogers, 1961), which also can be termed (and may be less liable to be misunderstood in a 'functional' way) as *the fully realized or actualized person*. Different from Maslow's understanding of actualization, this is a hypothetical process term that illustrates which direction optimal development takes (see Bohart, 2003)—there actually are no fully functioning or fully actualized persons in real life. Accordingly, Rogers (1961: 27) emphasizes: 'Life, at its best, is a flowing, changing process, in which nothing is fixed.' Thus the person is always a process (which parallels the second meaning of entelechy), never something static, fixed or finished (the first meaning of entelechy).

Although human beings change continuously, from moment to moment, there is continuity. As Bohart (2007) says, human beings are 'structures-in-process.' We use our experiences to enable ourselves to cope with new situations, although past experiences are never entirely sufficient. We can never deal with a new situation exactly in the same way as with a past one. Therefore we continuously need to learn. Continuous learning out of experience and openness for the ongoing process of immediate present experiencing are foundational characteristics of the construct of the 'fully functioning person.' In other words, the 'twin principles' (Moreno, 1991: 546) creativity and spontaneity are also essential characteristics of the fully functioning person.

PERSONALIZATION: THE ACTUALIZING TENDENCY AS CREATIVITY

It is important to distinguish clearly between the different levels (person, group, society, organic nature, inorganic nature, universe) where actualizing/formative tendencies are assumed. In the rest of this chapter, for the sake of a *person*-centered understanding, I shall follow the question of the specific human quality of the actualizing tendency in the human being.

If humans are seen as characterized by freedom, learning and openness, and particularly as interrelated beings, it is clear that a concept postulating a rigid direction and an end, set in advance within the individual, which only needs to be unfolded, cannot satisfy the person-centered anthropological understanding. The metaphor of a bulb or seed or potato which only has to come up and sprout or blossom is of very limited use, if we talk about

---

(Continued ...) [Neo-]vitalism is the biological doctrine which holds that the processes of life are not explicable by the laws of physics and chemistry alone—that life is in some part self-determining, based on an *élan vital* (Bergson, 1962), a life force. In other words, according to Hans Driesch (1905), living things are animated by an entelechy. Entelechy here is seen as a holistic, process-steering natural factor in organic life. Rogers (1963) refers to Driesch when he uses the growth potential of divided sea urchin eggs as an analogy for his experience with the directional tendency toward wholeness and toward actualization of the client's potentialities in psychotherapy. Here it is very important to distinguish between using such examples as an analogy and a biologically based interpretation as a proof.

human beings. A metaphor that really fits the conditions of human life has to be taken from somewhere else. Here we may take our lead from Aristotle. It is assumed and indeed seems quite likely that Aristotle became clear about the difference between actuality and potentiality from his observations of the creative act of an artist.

THE HUMAN WAY OF ACTUALIZATION: A PERSONALIZING TENDENCY

In a chapter entitled 'Personalization—the actualizing tendency as creativity' (Schmid 1994: 413–23; see Teilhard de Chardin, 1956) I suggested calling the actualizing tendency of a human being 'personalization.' The human being's freedom is the quality that makes its actualizing tendency different from that in other organisms. This specific quality lies within the human being's capability of 'freedom to,' as opposed to a 'freedom from,' which enables the human being to choose their actualization among different possibilities. That possibility to choose makes a creative process possible, which is to be regarded as a lifelong, ongoing actualizing process to become the person that one can become, within certain limits. It goes without saying that this does not mean that the human being can do anything they wish—to quote Martin Buber (1984: 259–60): 'The human being is the potentiality in its actual restriction.'

Thus personalization is the human way of actualization. One might very well speak of a *personalizing tendency,* characterized by freedom, creativity and personal interrelatedness (Schmid, 1994, 2007b). Personalization, i.e., to become a person, is a creative process. Creativity is the production of something new. The products of creativity qualitatively transcend the status quo (Schmid, 1994: 413–23)—new qualities are created and there is a breakthrough of something that did not exist before, of a new reality. It is the opposite of a mere reaction to situations and relationships. It qualifies the human being as a person in free action and interaction, as opposed to and beyond simple reaction. Carl Rogers (1959) understood creativity as an aspect of the actualizing tendency, and was convinced that it is absolutely necessary for human development and the continued existence of our culture (Rogers, 1954). Interestingly in his paper, which is based on a talk given in 1952, quite early in the development of person-centered theory, he defines creativity as relational, when he defines the creative process as 'the emergence in action of a novel relational product, growing out of the uniqueness of the individual on the one hand, and the materials, events, people, or circumstances of life on the other' (Rogers, 1961: 350; see also Rogers, 1986). Rogers also links creativity to the formative tendency, which he calls 'creative' (1979). Ned Gaylin (1974) argues that 'creativeness' is the same process that Rogers calls actualizing tendency. Doug Land (1984), describing the creative act of an artist, stresses the non-directedness and spontaneity of it, and understands psychotherapy as the re-establishing of personal creativity. Bohart and Associates (1986) explored the relationship between experiencing, change, and creativity. The artistic quality of therapeutic work has also been described by many other authors (see Schmid, 1994).

For Rogers (1961: 350–1) a deep link between the actualizing tendency and creativity was a given fact.

> The mainspring of creativity appears to be the same tendency which we discover so deeply as the curative force in psychotherapy—*man's tendency to actualize himself, to become his potentialities* [original italics]. By this I mean the directional trend which is evident in all organic and human life ... the tendency to express and activate all the [human] capacities ... it ... awaits only the proper conditions to be released .... It is this tendency which is the primary motivation for creativity as the organism forms new relationships to the environment in its endeavor most fully to be itself.

Again, we see the dialectical notion of the actualizing tendency as embracing both—uniqueness of the individual and interrelatedness with the environment—a personal encounter with other persons.

THERAPY AS PERSONALIZATION

What is true for life is true for psychotherapy and counseling. The most important consequence of the actualizing idea is that under appropriate circumstances human beings move towards solutions of what they regard as problems; they move towards becoming a 'more fully functioning person,' which includes openness as well as the reduction of fears and defences. The actualizing tendency is the 'motor' that keeps this process going. Therefore, the psychotherapist does not need to teach someone to move in a specific direction or direct them. Therapy is thus, by definition, 'non-directive' (for an explanation of 'non-directivity' see Schmid, 2005a). Its task is to foster and facilitate the innate pro-active and constructive tendency. As Rogers (1974: 8) points out: Therapy 'relies much more heavily on the individual drive toward growth, health, and adjustment.' The task is to free the client 'for normal growth and development' (see Bohart, 2007).

Supported by research, Bohart and Tallman (1999) accordingly stressed that 'it is the client who makes therapy work.' In other words, the client makes it function by using the therapist and their remarks and expressions to actively and productively support their inner growth. In this view, therapy—being indeed 'client-centered'—is really self-healing in terms of actualization of the given potential in a relationship and in terms of new developments and enhanced capacities (as opposed to reparation or restoration). The focus is on the possibilities of facilitating the process of life. In other words, the focus is on the self-healing capacities (Schmid, 2004: 40).

This is exactly what is meant by the substantial dimension of the notion of 'person', which stresses the autonomy of the human being. The actualizing tendency is a concept that rests on the idea of an autonomous and interdependent human being, themselves capable of living their life. Or the other way round: With the concept of the actualizing tendency, the phenomenological fact is taken into account that human beings are capable of living their lives and finding ways of dealing with their problems—not independently, but interdependently.

CONCLUSION: THE ACTUALIZING PROCESS IS A DIALOGICAL PROCESS

Without a doubt, Carl Rogers, person-centered and other humanistic scholars find themselves within the philosophical tradition that appreciates the possible as highly as the actual. They stress both the directionality of human motivation and the essential dialectic interconnection of the substantial and the relational dimension of being a person. Actualization is not possible without an impetus from outside. In contrast to any individualistic, egoistic, or even narcissistic misunderstandings of self-realization, it is necessary to state clearly that the idea underlying actualization is not that of an individual realizing themselves from and by themselves. Rather the point is that realization (actualization) of intrinsic potentialities can only take place if and when the appropriate extrinsic conditions are given. These appropriate extrinsic conditions are found in a facilitative relationship. Therefore personality development and psychotherapeutic change require encounter with the Other.

Actualization is a social process as much as it is an individual (that is, substantial) process—it is a dialogical process. The basic motivational construct of the person-centered approach is not only about autonomy and self-determination; it is also about interconnectedness, encounter, interaction and co-operation. Person-centered therapy is the only approach that holds the conviction that actualization is a dialectical process of the realization of the person's potential and the encounter relationship with the therapist—and nothing else. Actualization in and through therapy needs *nothing but* the presence of the therapist in order for it to unfold. The presence of the therapist provides the necessary conditions in the encounter with the client, such that, if the client is capable and willing to enter this relationship, the process of actualization ensues. Actualization is an encounter process. In other words: psychotherapy is dialogue from the very beginning (Schmid, 2006).

REFERENCES

Anzenbacher A (1992) *Einführung in die Philosophie* (2nd edn). Wien: Herder.
Aquinas, St Thomas (1976) Leonine Edition of Aquinas' works (Vol. 43) *Sancti Thomae De Aquino Opera Omnia*. Rome: Leonine Comm., pp. 368–81.
Aristotle (1955) *Ethics*. Harmondsworth: Penguin.
Aristotle (1966) *Metaphysics*. Bloomington, IN: Indiana University Press.
Barrett-Lennard GT (2007) Human relationship: Linkage or life form? *Person-Centered and Experiential Psychotherapies, 6* (3), 183–95.
Bergson H (1962) *L'Energie Spirituelle*. Paris: Presses Universitaires de France.
Bohart AC (2003) Person-centered psychotherapy and related experiential approaches. In AS Gurman & SB Messer (Eds) *Essential Psychotherapies* (2nd edn). New York: Guilford, pp. 107–48.
Bohart AC (2004) How do clients make empathy work? *Person-Centered and Experiential Psychotherapies, 3* (2), 102–16.
Bohart AC (2007) The actualizing person. In M Cooper, M O'Hara, PF Schmid & G Wyatt

(Eds) *The Handbook of Person-Centred Psychotherapy and Counselling*. Houndsmill: Palgrave, pp. 47–63.

Bohart AC & Associates (1986) Experiencing, knowing, and change. In R Hutterer, G Pawlowsky, PF Schmid & R Stipsits (Eds) *Client-Centered and Experiential Psychotherapy: A paradigm in motion*. Vienna: Peter Lang, pp. 199–212.

Bohart AC & Tallman K (1999) *How Clients Make Therapy Work*. Washington: APA.

Bozarth JD & Brodley BT (1991) Actualization: A functional concept in client-centered therapy. In A Jones & R Crandall (Eds) *Handbook of Self-Actualization*. [Special Issue]. *Journal of Social Behavior and Personality*, 6, 45–60.

Brodley BT (1999) The actualizing tendency concept in client-centered therapy. *Person-Centered Journal*, 6 (2), 108–20.

Buber M (1984) *Das dialogische Prinzip* (5th edn). Heidelberg: Lambert Schneider.

Cooper M, O'Hara M, Schmid PF & Wyatt G (Eds) (2007) *The Handbook of Person-Centred Psychotherapy and Counselling*. Houndsmill: Palgrave.

Cornelius-White JHD (2007) The actualizing and formative tendencies: Prioritizing the motivational constructs of the person-centered approach. *Person-Centered and Experiential Psychotherapies*, 6 (2), 129–40.

Driesch HAE (1905) *Der Vitalismus als Geschichte und als Lehre*. Leipzig: Barth.

Fichte JH (1965) *Werke*. Berlin: de Gruyter.

Finke J (2002) Das Menschenbild des Personzentrierten Ansatzes zwischen Humanismus und Naturalismus. *PERSON*, 6 (2), 26–34.

Gaylin NL (1974) On creativeness and a psychology of well-being In DA Wexler & LN Rice (Eds) *Innovations in Client-Centered Therapy*. New York: John Wiley, pp. 339–66.

Gendlin, ET (1996) *Focusing-Oriented Psychotherapy: A manual of the experiential method*. New York: Guilford.

Heron J (1998) *Sacred Science. Person-centred inquiry into the spiritual and the subtle*. Ross-on-Wye: PCCS Books.

Hirschberger J (1965) *Geschichte der Philosophie*. 2 vols. Freiburg i. Br.: Herder.

Kierkegaard S (1924) *Die Krankheit zum Tode* (2nd edn). Jena: Eugen Diederichs.

Kriz J, Eckert J, Zurhorst G, Fehringer C & Finke J (2003) Humanismus und/oder Naturalismus: Eine Auseinandersetzung zum Menschenbild und zum Verständnis der Aktualisierungstendenz im PCA. *PERSON*, 7 (1), 81–92.

Kriz J (2007) Actualizing tendency: The link between person-centered and experiential psychotherapy and interdisciplinary systems theory. *Person-Centered and Experiential Psychotherapies*, 6 (1), 30–44.

Land D (1984) Psychotherapie als Kunstform. In APG (Ed) *Persönlichkeitsentwicklung durch Begegnung: das personenzentrierte Konzept in Psychotherapie, Erziehung und Wissenschaft*. Vienna: Deuticke, pp. 176–83.

Levinas E (1961) *Totalité et Infini: Essais sur l'exteriorité*. Den Haag: Nijhoff.

Mearns D (1999) Person-centred therapy with configuration of self. *Counselling*, 10, 125–30.

Mearns D & Cooper M (2005) (Eds) *Working at Relational Depth in Counselling and Psychotherapy*. London: Sage.

Mearns D & Schmid PF (2006) Being-with and being-counter: Relational depth: The challenge of fully meeting the client. *Person-Centered and Experiential Psychotherapies*, 5 (4), 255–65.

Mearns D & Thorne B (2000) *Person-Centred Therapy Today: New frontiers in theory and practice*. London: Sage.

Moreno ZT (1991) Psychodrama: Rollentheorie und das Konzept des sozialen Atoms. In JK Zeig (Ed) *Psychotherapie: Entwicklungslinien und Geschichte.* Tübingen: dgvt, pp. 545–70.
Ricken F (1996) (Ed) *Philosophen der Antike I.* Stuttgart: Kohlhammer.
Rogers CR (1939) *The Clinical Treatment of the Problem Child.* Boston: Houghton Mifflin.
Rogers CR (1954) Towards a theory of creativity. *ETC: A Review of General Semantics, 11,* 249–60. Also chapter 19 of *On Becoming a Person* (Rogers, 1961).
Rogers CR (1959) A theory of therapy, personality and interpersonal relationships as developed in the client-centered framework. In S Koch (Ed) *Psychology: A study of science. Vol. 3: Formulations of the person and the social context.* New York: McGraw-Hill, pp. 184–256.
Rogers CR (1961) *On Becoming a Person: A therapist's view of psychotherapy.* Boston: Houghton Mifflin.
Rogers CR (1962) The interpersonal relationship: The core of guidance. In CR Rogers & B Stevens *Person to Person: The problem of being human.* Moab: Real People, pp. 89–104.
Rogers CR (1963) The actualizing tendency in relation to 'motives' and to consciousness. In MR Jones (Ed) *Nebraska Symposium on Motivation.* Lincoln, NE: University of Nebraska Press, pp. 1–24.
Rogers CR (1974) Remarks on the future of client-centered therapy. In DA Wexler & LN Rice (Eds) *Innovations in Client-Centered Therapy.* New York: John Wiley, pp. 7–13.
Rogers CR (1977) *On Personal Power: Inner strength and its revolutionary impact.* New York: Delacorte.
Rogers CR (1978) The formative tendency. *Journal of Humanistic Psychology, 18,* 23–6.
Rogers CR (1979) The foundations of the person-centered approach. *Education, 100* (2), 98–107.
Rogers CR (1980) *A Way of Being.* New York: Houghton Mifflin.
Rogers CR (1986) Fostering creativity. Unpublished manuscript.
Schmid PF (1991) Souveränität und Engagement: Zu einem personzentrierten Verständnis von 'Person'. In CR Rogers & PF Schmid, *Person-zentriert: Grundlagen von Theorie und Praxis* (6th edn, 2006). Mainz: Grünewald, pp. 15–164.
Schmid PF (1994) *Personzentrierte Gruppenpsychotherapie. Vol. I: Solidarität und Autonomie.* Cologne: EHP.
Schmid PF (1996) *Personzentrierte Gruppenpsychotherapie in der Praxis. Vol. II: Die Kunst der Begegnung.* Paderborn: Junfermann.
Schmid PF (1998a) 'On becoming a *Person*-Centred Approach': A person-centred understanding of the person. In B Thorne & E Lambers (Eds) *Person-Centred Therapy: A European perspective.* London: Sage, pp 38–52.
Schmid PF (1998b) 'Face to face': The art of encounter. In B Thorne & E Lambers (Eds) *Person-Centred Therapy: A European perspective.* London: Sage, pp. 74–90.
Schmid PF (1999) Personzentrierte Psychotherapie. In T Slunecko & G Sonneck (Eds) *Einführung in die Psychotherapie.* Vienna: UTB/WUV, pp. 169–211.
Schmid PF (2001a) Personzentrierte Persönlichkeits- und Beziehungstheorie. In P Frenzel, W Keil, PF Schmid & N Stölzl (Eds) *Klienten-/Personzentrierte Psychotherapie: Kontexte, Konzepte, Konkretisierungen.* Vienna: Facultas, pp. 57–95.
Schmid PF (2001b) Authenticity: The person as his or her own author. Dialogical and ethical perspectives on therapy as an encounter relationship. And beyond. In G Wyatt (Ed) *Rogers' Therapeutic Conditions: Evolution, theory and practice. Vol. 1: Congruence.* Ross-on-Wye: PCCS Books, pp. 213–28.
Schmid PF (2001c) Comprehension: The art of not knowing. Dialogical and ethical perspectives

on empathy as dialogue in personal and person centered relationships. In S Haugh & T Merry (Eds) *Rogers' Therapeutic Conditions: Evolution, theory and practice. Vol. 2: Empathy.* Ross-on-Wye: PCCS Books, pp. 53–71.

Schmid PF (2001d) Acknowledgement: The art of responding. Dialogical and ethical perspectives on the challenge of unconditional relationships in therapy and beyond. In JD Bozarth & P Wilkins (Eds) *Rogers' Therapeutic Conditions: Evolution, theory and practice. Vol. 3: Unconditional Positive Regard.* Ross-on-Wye: PCCS Books, pp. 49–64.

Schmid PF (2002a) Presence: Im-media-te co-experiencing c-responding. Phenomenological, dialogical and ethical perspectives on contact and perception in person-centred therapy and beyond. In G Wyatt & P Sanders (Eds) *Rogers' Therapeutic Conditions: Evolution, theory and practice. Vol. 4: Contact and Perception.* Ross-on-Wye: PCCS Books, pp. 182–203.

Schmid PF (2002b) Knowledge or acknowledgement? Psychotherapy as 'the art of not-knowing'— Prospects on further developments of a radical paradigm. *Person-Centered and Experiential Psychotherapies, 1* (1&2), 56–70.

Schmid PF (2003) The characteristics of a person-centered approach to therapy and counseling: Criteria for identity and coherence. *Person-Centered and Experiential Psychotherapies, 2* (2), 104–20.

Schmid PF (2004) Back to the client. A phenomenological approach to the process of understanding and diagnosis. *Person-Centered and Experiential Psychotherapies, 3* (1), 36–51.

Schmid PF (2005a) Facilitative responsiveness. Non-directiveness from an anthropological, epistemological and ethical perspective. In B Levitt (Ed) *Embracing Non-directivity. Reassessing person-centered theory and practice in the 21st century.* Ross-on-Wye: PCCS Books, pp. 74–94.

Schmid PF (2005b) Authenticity and alienation. Towards an understanding of the person beyond the categories of order and disorder. In S Joseph & R Worsley (Eds) *Psychopathology and the Person-Centred Approach.* Ross-on-Wye: PCCS Books, pp. 75–90.

Schmid PF (2006) The challenge of the Other: Towards dialogical person-centered psychotherapy and counseling. *Person-Centered and Experiential Psychotherapies, 5* (4), 241–54.

Schmid PF (2007a) The anthropological and ethical foundations of person-centered therapy. In M Cooper, M O'Hara, PF Schmid & G Wyatt, (Eds) *The Handbook of Person-Centred Psychotherapy and Counselling.* Houndsmill: Palgrave, pp. 30–46.

Schmid PF (2007b) Psychotherapy is political or it is not psychotherapy. The actualizing tendency as personalizing tendency. Keynote lecture given at the 3rd BAPCA conference 'PCA— Past, Present and Future'. Unpublished manuscript. Cirencester, September 2007.

Schmid PF & Mearns D (2006) Being-with and being-counter: Person-centered psychotherapy as an in-depth co-creative process of personalization. *Person-Centered and Experiential Psychotherapies, 5* (3), 174–90.

Teilhard de Chardin, P (1956) *Le Phénomène Humain.* Paris: Les Éditions du Seuil.

Tudor K & Merry T (2002). *Dictionary of Person-Centred Psychology.* London: Routledge. Republished (2006) Ross-on-Wye: PCCS Books.

Tudor K & Worrall M (2006) *Person-Centred Therapy: A clinical philosophy.* London: Routledge.

Weischedel W (1997) *Die philosophische Hintertreppe. Die großen Phoilosophen in Alltag und Denken,* (27th edn). München: Deutscher Taschenbuch Verlag.

Wilkins P (2003) *Person-Centred Therapy in Focus.* London: Sage.

CHAPTER 7

THE 'UNITARY ACTUALIZING TENDENCY' AND CONGRUENCE IN CLIENT-CENTERED THEORY

JEROLD D. BOZARTH AND
CHUN-CHUAN WANG

Abstract

This chapter discusses the 'unitary actualizing tendency' postulated by Carl Rogers (1959) in his theory of therapy and clarified shortly thereafter (Rogers, 1963). Rogers (1951, 1959, 1963, 1980) more commonly used the term 'actualizing tendency' to describe this sole motivational force of individuals. We examine the integral connection of the actualizing tendency to other constructs in Rogers' theory of therapy; e.g., self-actualization as part of the unitary actualizing tendency, and unconditional positive regard and empathic understanding as the conditions that facilitate the unitary actualizing tendency. Therapist congruence is considered as the macro-facilitator of the actualizing tendency, and is also postulated as the manifestation of the actualizing process.

HISTORY

OBSERVATIONS IN THERAPY

Rogers identified one incident that symbolized the beginning of client-centered therapy. Concomitantly, this incident reflects the assumption of one directional, motivational tendency (Kirschenbaum, 1979: 89) of individuals in therapy. Rogers was working with the mother of a boy who was considered 'something of a hellion' (ibid.: 89). Rogers tried to help her realize her rejection of the boy and other influences that were thought to affect him. They 'got nowhere' with their discussions and mutually decided to give up. As the woman left, she asked whether or not he ever saw adult clients. When Rogers said, 'Yes,' she indicated that she would like some help. It was then that she returned and 'began to pour out her despair about her marriage, her troubled relationship with her husband, her sense of failure and confusion, all very different from the sterile "case history" she had given before' (ibid.: 89). This incident characterized Rogers' observations of hundreds of clients. Initiated by his observations of clients in therapy, and buttressed by further observations and research, Rogers' thinking moved towards a view of the internal constructive force of actualization as the sole motivating source that could be trusted in psychotherapy. Rogers' shift toward trust of the client and away from the therapist's expertise as the guide for the process of therapy is captured in the following statement:

> Individuals have within themselves vast resources for self-understanding and for altering their self-concepts, basic attitudes, and self-directed behavior; these resources can be tapped if a definable climate of facilitative psychological attitudes can be provided. (Rogers, 1980: 115)

OBSERVATIONS IN NATURE

Rogers' observations of 'organisms' in nature added to his thoughts about actualization as a foundation for therapy. The most notable example is his summary about potatoes kept in a cellar:

> The conditions were unfavorable, but the potatoes would begin to sprout—pale white sprouts, so unlike the healthy green shoots they sent up when planted in the soil in the spring. But these sad, spindly sprouts would grow 2 or 3 feet in length as they reached toward the distant light of the window. The sprouts were, in their bizarre, futile growth, a sort of desperate expression of the directional tendency I have been describing. They would never become plants, never mature, never fulfill their real potential. But under the most adverse circumstances, they were striving to become. Life would not give up, even if it could not flourish. (Rogers, 1980: 118)

He observed that this process was similar to the process of people in state mental hospitals, who would strive for growth regardless of the dire external and internal circumstances impinging on them. He saw humans as reflecting the behavioral direction of all organisms, in that the development of organisms could 'be counted on to be in the direction of maintaining, enhancing, and reproducing itself' (Rogers, 1963: 5).

COMPATIBLE THEORETICAL CONCEPTS

Rogers' consideration of the direction of clients in therapy and of organisms in nature led him to examine compatible theories of organismic growth. Theoretical concepts that supported the notion of trusting the client's self-direction were already established by others. He found the theories of Maslow, Goldstein, and Angyal comparable to his own observations. His understanding of their theories contributed to his own theoretical formulation. Rogers (1959) identified the actualizing tendency as the 'development toward autonomy and away from heteronomy, or control by external forces' (p. 196). He cited Angyal's explanation as a particularly comparable and relevant statement:

> Life processes do not merely tend to preserve life but transcend the momentary status quo of the organism, expanding itself continually and imposing its autonomous determination upon an ever increasing realm of events. (Rogers, 1959: 196)

INTEGRATION INTO THEORETICAL FRAMEWORK

Rogers' concept of the actualizing tendency was integrated into his developing theoretical framework. His ongoing examinations of psychotherapy began to reach fruition in theoretical form when Rogers (1951) changed the name (but not the intent) of Non-directive Therapy to Client-Centered Therapy. The term 'actualizing tendency' was not yet referenced in his first theoretical book on client-centered therapy (Rogers, 1951). Rather, self-actualization was equated with 'self-enhancement'. Though not explicitly named, the actualizing process was captured in the content of the propositions in his 1951 theory of therapy. These propositions were later integrated into Rogers' theory of personality (1959), a concomitant theory to the theory of therapy. Perhaps the first actual reference to the actualizing process was in Rogers' theory of personality, when he identified 'the organic experience' as 'something which occurs and is an organic fact' (Rogers, 1951: 505). Most of the nineteen propositions of the personality theory refer either directly or indirectly to organismic experiences in relation to self experiences. The most specific reference to what was to become *the* motivational source of growth was referred to in Proposition IV: '*The organism has one basic tendency and striving—to actualize, maintain, and enhance the experiencing organism*' (Rogers, 1951: 487). Rogers referred to 'self-actualization' in the discussion of this proposition by indicating that: 'self-actualization of the organism appears to be in the direction of socialization, broadly defined' (p. 488). The self-actualizing individual, similar to Maslow's (1970) concept, referred to the individual's movement toward the development of potentialities. The meaning of self-actualization changed in 1959 and is discussed later.

THE ACTUALIZING TENDENCY

MEANING OF THE ACTUALIZING TENDENCY

According to Rogers, the actualizing tendency exists in all organisms. It is a directional tendency for an organism to maintain, enhance, and reproduce itself. It operates at all times, and its presence or absence demonstrates the life and death of an organism. Discussion of the actualizing tendency in client-centered therapy by Barbara Brodley (1999) is, arguably, the most comprehensive clarification of the concept available outside of Rogers' (1959, 1963) writings.

The functional meaning of the actualizing tendency was present in Rogers' assessment that the best therapy occurs when clients are allowed to go in their own direction, identify which problems are crucial for them, and to identify their own deeply buried experiences. Rogers believed that he 'would do better to rely on the client for the direction of movement in the process' (Kirschenbaum, 1979: 89). Elaboration of the functional meaning of the actualizing tendency is reproduced (Bozarth and Brodley, 1991) elsewhere in this book (Chapter 2). However, we would briefly note here that client-centered theory holds that the actualizing tendency is a first principle in the practice of client centered therapy (Bozarth & Brodley, 1991; Brodley, 1999). The actualizing tendency leads client-centered therapists 'to hold two fundamental beliefs'. These beliefs are: '(1) the therapist can trust the client's tendency to grow, develop, and heal', and '(2) all of the therapist's actions must express respect for the client—viewing the client as a person who is capable of self-determination with capacities for self-understanding and constructive change' (Brodley, 1999: 119).

The actualizing tendency is the only motive that is postulated in the theoretical system of client-centered therapy (Rogers, 1959: 196). Later, Rogers (1978, 1980) emphasized the actualizing tendency as 'a characteristic of organic life' and added the concept of the 'formative tendency' as a 'tendency in the universe as a whole' (1980: 114). He referred to these concepts 'taken together' as the foundation blocks of the person-centered approach. This chapter focuses on the actualizing tendency, since we are concentrating on this tendency as a characteristic of organic life, and to its interrelationship with the therapeutic constructs (i.e., the core conditions) of the theory of therapy.

SHIFT FROM SELF-ACTUALIZATION TO THE ACTUALIZING TENDENCY

Self-actualization was the motivating construct in Rogers' theoretical formulations in 1951. As noted earlier, the concept of the actualizing tendency would not be formalized in Rogers' work until 1959. The self-actualized individual was optimally healthy and growth-oriented. The term was used in a way similar to Maslow and Goldstein. Maslow's definition was not included in Rogers' (1951) book, but Maslow's enumeration of attributes that characterize 'self-actualizing' individuals was one source that buttressed Rogers' deliberations, and was especially similar to Rogers' hypothesis of the ideal 'Fully Functioning Person' (Rogers, 1959: 234). Goldstein described self-actualization as 'this one basic striving' (Goldstein,1995: 489). Clients were described as going in the 'ultimately rewarding path of self-actualization or growth' (*ibid.*: 490). Goldstein's studies of severely brain-injured individuals led him to conclude that: 'we have *to assume only one drive, the drive of self-actualization*' (Goldstein, *ibid.*: 197). Goldstein's conclusion was later reflected by Rogers with the term 'actualizing tendency,' rather than 'self-actualization'.

A succinct definition of the actualizing tendency emerges in Rogers' (1959) self-proclaimed magnum opus as: 'the inherent tendency of the organism to develop all its capacities in ways which serve to maintain or enhance the organism' (Rogers, 1959: 196). In more pragmatic terminology, the process of client change can be described 'as moving in the direction of actualization of their potentialities, moving away from rigidity and toward flexibility, moving toward more process living, moving toward autonomy, and the like' (Rogers, 1963: 8). It is, however, only when the self-concept is congruent with organismic experiences that constructive direction is facilitated; that is, organismic actualization and self-actualization are synchronized to become the 'unitary actualizing tendency' (Rogers, 1963: 20). Indeed, the self can actualize in a direction contrary to the actualization of the organism. The discrepancy between the organismic actualization and self-actualization is, in fact, the cause of problems, anxiety, denial, and distortions (Rogers, 1959: 197).

ACTUALIZATION AND THE THERAPEUTIC PRINCIPLES

Rogers' (1959) theory of therapy is straightforward: A congruent therapist experiencing unconditional positive regard toward the client and empathic understanding of the client's frame of reference, when perceived by the client, will result in increased client congruence. Increased congruence, whether in the client or therapist, is associated with: (1) openness to experience; (2) psychological adjustment; that is, congruence viewed from a social point of view; (3) extensional behaviors, e. g., the capacity to evaluate in multiple ways; and (4) maturity, which describes personality characteristics and behaviors of congruent individuals. In addition, congruence includes those characteristics that promote increased congruence; namely, empathic understanding and unconditional positive regard (Rogers, 1959: 215).

Several features of Rogers' theory are often not included in theoretical or practical discourses. The interrelationship of the conditions with each other and with the actualizing tendency (AT) is not explicitly considered. Elsewhere, Levitt (2005) offers the view that unconditional positive regard, empathic understanding, and congruence are unified as expressions or elaborations of a fundamental non-directive stance towards the other, though he does not take this further and integrate them with the actualizing tendency concept. In a rare attempt at such examination, Bozarth (1996, 1998/2002) reconceptualizes the interrelationship by casting congruence as the therapist's state of readiness, empathic understanding as the active mode of reception, and unconditional positive regard as the primary change agent (1998/2002: 47). Such an attempt only touches on the whole integration of the theory. The conditions and the actualizing tendency usually are discussed as 'states', rather than as processes. This diminishes the dynamic considerations of the relationship of all variables to the actualizing tendency.

Rogers (1975, 1980) took a step towards shifting from 'states' to processes when he reconsidered the concept of empathy and recognized it as a 'process' rather than as a 'state'. Nevertheless, congruence and unconditional positive regard were seldom, if ever, discussed as process variables. Perhaps, Rogers considered this to be obvious because of his frequent references to the 'organism' being 'always motivated, always up to something, always seeking' (Rogers, 1963: 4). The therapeutic conditions in relationship to the actualizing tendency are briefly examined below. It might at the outset be noted that these characteristics are also associated with 'self-actualized' individuals in Maslow's delineation of such individuals, even though the definition of self-actualization by Rogers is different from Maslow's definition. As well, Rogers' ideal of the fully functioning person presents a picture that is part and parcel of congruence and of higher levels of the actualizing tendency.

POSITIVE REGARD

The assumption that individuals have a need for positive regard is a crucial psychological variable that is seldom focused on in client-centered therapy. It is a critical formulation in the definition of self-actualization as it evolved from 1951 to 1959. In 1951, self-actualization was posited as *the* motivational tendency in humans. The self-actualizing individual was increasingly healthy and growth-oriented. The self-actualizing individual was moving toward her potentialities. In 1959, self-actualization became a 'subsystem' of the actualizing tendency. When the need for positive regard is influenced by conditions of worth, the actualization of the self is incongruent with the actualizing tendency and the person behaves with denial and distortion of the organismic experiences that are not in accordance with her self-concept. The actualizing tendency is thwarted when the self and the organism are not integrated.

Generally, positive regard includes 'such attitudes as warmth, liking, respect, sympathy, acceptance' (Rogers, 1959: 208). However, careful consideration of the operational definition of positive regard is revealing. Rogers (1959) states:

> If the perception by me [as a therapist] of some self-experience in another makes a positive difference in my experiential field, then I am experiencing positive regard for that individual … To perceive oneself [as a client] as receiving positive regard is to experience oneself as making a positive difference in the experiential field of another. (pp. 207–8)

Does this pragmatically mean that the therapist's positive regard is predicated upon the client making a positive difference in the therapist? Likewise, does it mean that the client experiences positive regard when she has made a positive difference in the therapist? The following statements re-frame these questions in more personal terms: 'When I experience a positive difference from the client, I am experiencing positive regard for her.' 'When I experience myself making a positive difference for the therapist, I am receiving positive regard.' This realization may have particular implications in relation to unitary actualization, which will be explored later in this paper.

UNCONDITIONAL POSITIVE REGARD

Conditional positive self-regard results in a disconnection between the self-experiences and the inherent organismic actualizing process of the person. Specifically, it is 'because of the distorted perceptions arising from the conditions of worth that the individual departs from the integration which characterizes his infant state' (Rogers, 1959: 226). According to client-centered theory, this is the 'basic estrangement' (ibid.: 226) in humans.

The curative feature, in Rogers' theory of therapy, is the integration of organismic and self-experiences through the experiencing of unconditional positive regard (Bozarth, 2001a). That is, as conditions for experiencing positive regard are reduced, the individual becomes increasingly connected with her organismic experiences and this experience is synchronized with the self-concept. (The individual says to herself: 'I am worthwhile even though I have these "irresponsible" feelings.') Conditions of positive regard are reduced and the individual increasingly develops unconditional positive self-regard. The self-concept is increasingly congruent with organismic experiences and in harmony with the actualizing tendency. Unconditional positive regard can be defined as the client making a consistent positive difference in the therapist. As Rogers (1959: 208) stated, 'To perceive oneself as receiving positive regard is to perceive that of one's self-experiences none can be discriminated by the other individual as more or less worthy of positive regard.' Van Belle (1980) offers a cogent summary:

> We are only actualized by others and ourselves at the regard level. If/when the regard that others show us and which consequently we show ourselves, is unconditionally positive, that is, if/when it is such that personality development can be interpersonally assimilated. (p. 90)

Here, the connection to the actualizing tendency is readily apparent. The freedom from conditional constraints on one's experiencing allows the individual to assimilate her organismic experiences. This freedom enables the individual to operate in an integrated and whole manner.

EMPATHIC UNDERSTANDING

Empathic understanding or *empathy* is used interchangeably by Rogers. He defines 'empathy' but refers to the term 'empathic understanding' in his formulation of the necessary and sufficient conditions. *Empathy, the state of empathy, or being empathic*, may be defined as perceiving 'the internal frame of reference of another with accuracy, and with the emotional components and meanings which pertain thereto, as if one were the other person, but without ever losing the "as if" condition' (Rogers, 1959: 210). The total dedication to the individual's frame of reference reflects a trust in the client's direction, which is a result of increased actualization. It is only through the client's perception of being trusted to direct her own life (i.e., perceiving unconditional positive regard and empathic understanding from the therapist) that her individual experiences can be integrated with her organismic experiences.

CONGRUENCE

Congruence is one of the therapist conditions identified in the 'conditions of the therapeutic process' (Rogers, 1959: 213). Congruence of the individual's self-experiences and organismic experiences results in the individual being attuned to the actualizing tendency. Generally, the term is synonymous with the individual being integrated, whole, and genuine. A succinct definition of congruence is as follows: 'When self experiences are accurately symbolized, and are included in the self-concept in this accurately symbolized form, then the state is one of congruence of self and experience' (Rogers, 1959: 206). Rogers (1957) also offers a slightly broader definition in his 'integration' statement that applies to all therapies and helping relationships: 'It means that within the relationship he [the therapist] is freely and deeply himself, with his actual experience accurately represented by his awareness of himself' (p. 99).

For Rogers, *experience* includes 'all that is going on within the envelope of the organism at any given moment which is potentially available to awareness' (Rogers, 1959: 197). Experience is, in the person-centered framework, the dynamic that is changing from moment to moment. It encompasses what an organism can or cannot perceive consciously but is always ready for the organism to symbolize.

Self-experience is coined by Standal (1954) and first appears publicly in Rogers' 1959 work. According to Rogers (1959), self-experience refers to 'any event or entity in the phenomenal field discriminated by the individual which is also discriminated as "self," "me," "I," or related thereto' (p. 200). He discussed 'self' as 'the concept of self' or 'the structure of self.' The self is: 'the fluid but consistent organization that does not permit the intrusion of a perception at variance with it, except under certain conditions' (Rogers, 1951: 505). For example, a social scenario in which a woman is characterized as a friendly individual might clarify the difference. This woman might greet people warmly and receptively in a public meeting while experiencing such feelings toward them. This could indicate the consistency of experiences and self-concept of an individual (i.e., congruence) in a social situation. In another situation, she meets her ex-boyfriend at a party and greets him with friendliness and warmth because she views herself as being a friendly and receptive person, but also feels angry with him without consciously realizing her anger. Her organismic experience is distorted by her behavior that is 'guided' by her self-concept. At this moment she is 'incongruent.' To offer a simplistic extension, her actualizing tendency might operate by her 'accidentally' spilling a drink on her ex-boyfriend. It is when the self experiences and the organismic experiences of an individual are consistent that the actualizing tendency activates and enhances to the utmost. That is, congruence of the moment is the manifestation of the actualizing tendency. In an examination of the construct of congruence in relation to Rogers' client-centered theory and practice, Bozarth (2001b) offers the following definition:

> Congruence is the manifestation of unconditional positive self-regard (UPSR) and can be identified as the therapist's presence in client-centered therapy. Unconditional positive regard toward and empathic understanding of the client's frame of reference characterize this presence. (p. 185)

It is this same presence that characterizes the fully functioning person.

THE FULLY FUNCTIONING PERSON

The fully functioning person is included as a 'peripheral theory in relation to the theory of client-centered therapy' (Rogers, 1959: 234). The fully functioning person refers to a hypothetical person when therapy reaches its maximal success (Rogers, 1961). To this point, when all self-experiences 'are accurately symbolized, and are included in the self-concept in this accurately symbolized form,' an individual is then a fully functioning person (Rogers, 1959: 206). A fully functioning person is living freely and is open to all his experiences without any defensiveness. There is congruence between his organismic experiences and self-experiences, and both of which are fluid and constantly changing. A fully functioning person also activates his organismic valuing process to live all experiences in awareness.

Fully functioning individuals become increasingly congruent and encompass the characteristics of 'actualized individuals.' That is, individuals move toward greater harmony of their self-concept with their organismic tendencies. They move toward the ideal of the fully functioning person. In short, they develop increased unconditional positive self-regard and unconditional positive regard for others. They are more empathic toward themselves and others. They have greater internal locus of evaluation and work more harmoniously with others. They are more efficient; less anxious and vulnerable, and more creative. They are hypothetically 'actualized' individuals; that is, operating at an advanced process of actualization.

CONGRUENCE AS A MANIFESTATION OF THE ACTUALIZING TENDENCY

The theory of the fully functioning person in client-centered theory offers an example of the 'ultimate' actualization of the human being. This person 'would be synonymous with "the goal of social evolution," "the end point of optimal psychotherapy," etc.' (Rogers, 1959: 234). Likewise, congruence represents the simultaneous constructive directionality of self and organismic experiences. When the therapist's self-concept and organismic experiences are congruent in the therapeutic relationship, the therapist is also embodying the necessary and sufficient conditions for personality change to take place. Part of the therapist's congruence includes the experiencing of unconditional positive regard toward the client and the experiencing of empathic understanding towards the internal frame of reference of the client (Rogers, 1959: 215). All of these principles combine to engage the unitary actualizing tendency. *Congruence* is a representation of the *unitary actualizing tendency*.

A BRIEF VIGNETTE

A vignette from a clinical setting that sheds further light on congruence as a manifestation of the actualizing tendency is offered by Rogers (1977). A young adolescent boy, brought up in a strictly religious home, where it was clear that he was acceptable to his parents only if he believed that sexual thoughts, impulses, and behaviors were evil and awful. When he was caught one night in the home of the next-door neighbor, trying to tear the nightdress off of their sleeping daughter, he could say, with a firm belief that he was telling the truth, that he had not done it—it was not his behavior. Here, his organism—with its natural curiosity, fantasies, and impulses in the area of sex—had been so thoroughly denied that he was quite unaware of these aspects of his physical being (p. 247).

In short, the positive regard is conditional or dependent on his 'appropriate behavior'. The boy develops conditional self-regard. He is only worthwhile if he meets certain conditions. The incongruence between his felt organismic experiences and his conditional positive self-regard is the culprit that creates problems and dysfunction. The individual is incongruent; that is, his organismic and self-experiences are incompatible. The curative feature is for the boy to become more congruent; specifically, to increase his unconditional positive self-regard. It is when the boy can accept all aspects of his experience as existing that he no longer says: 'I am worthwhile as long as I am responsible and sober.' Rather, he says: 'I am worthwhile regardless of my feelings of irresponsibility and giddiness.' He can accept his experiences as existing in him and still experience himself as being a worthy human being. Congruence can be seen here as a manifestation of the actualizing tendency.

AN EXTENDED VIGNETTE

Here we offer a more detailed vignette to add to our exploration of congruence as a manifestation of the actualizing tendency. Joan, a college student, was referred to a university counseling center by her academic advisor for an intelligence test. A professor identified her as having 'low motivation for life, and probably mentally retarded.' Joan expressed her view of this professor as 'kind-hearted.' However, the way she described her professor's kindness appeared distant and emotionless. In her first session with the counselor, the only time Joan got excited was when she talked about becoming a cartoonist. Her counselor was not aware of the professor's comments about Joan until after this session, just minutes before their second session.

Joan spent most of her early sessions talking about her favorite topics: online video games, cartoons and comic books. Gradually Joan discussed her friends, acquaintances, and even her parents as not being supportive of her interests. Joan also told her counselor that she loved sketching and would sketch whenever possible, especially when she felt particularly sad, happy, or angry.

In her third session, Joan shared some of her artwork with her counselor. Her counselor viewed the art as quite good aesthetically. In her fifth session, Joan discussed her middle-school years, when she played with her younger brother. They sometimes acted spontaneously and created new stories by mixing numerous characters from cartoons and comic books. Joan described this as if performing a play. Her spontaneity and creativity with unlimited characters greatly impressed her counselor. The counselor looked for words to reflect her own experience of Joan, and offered, 'Your creativity … no, your … imagination is totally unbelievable!' Even though the counselor was aware of the professor's comment that Joan could be mentally retarded, the counselor spontaneously expressed exactly how she experienced Joan.

Joan commented about her 'imagination' in her eleventh session. Her counselor said to her, 'You do know a lot!' after she told the counselor several long stories from comic books. Joan responded by recalling one of her professor's statements, 'the foundation of imagination is knowledge.' Joan reflected that she knew herself to be a person of imagination, although she was not clear what knowledge she possessed. This was the first time Joan ever positively described herself.

Joan continued sharing her knowledge of cartoons and comic books, prompting her counselor to say spontaneously, 'Maybe you should be in the Department of Art?'

Joan responded that she had thought seriously about this possibility, and had also given consideration to biology. This was a somewhat unusual interaction for the counselor, as she expressed more of her spontaneous experiences than she usually would. The counselor made such comments as: 'Your … imagination is totally unbelievable!' and 'You do know a lot!' The counselor's comment that perhaps Joan could enter the Art Department might appear to be a directive suggestion. However, this comment was more of an expression of her reaction to her client's frame of reference. This was one way the counselor allowed herself to be congruent with her own experiences arising from her experience of unconditional positive regard for and empathic understanding of Joan. Such expressions of her experience accelerated the counselor's capacity to understand Joan's experienced disconnection between a 'conditioned' self-concept as incompetent and wasting her time with her experience of success and competence in her artistic efforts. She became more aware of the satisfaction 'in her gut' while involved in artistic pursuits, as well as the pure satisfaction from learning certain things in art and biology. This 'retarded girl's' self-actualization was facilitated as her relationship with a congruent therapist (providing unconditional positive regard) helped her to regain congruence with her self-concept and her organismic experiences. Joan found success in art and biology. This success, an expression of her actualizing tendency, can be explained as a manifestation of her emerging congruence.

SYNTHESIS AND DISCUSSION

The intent of this chapter was to examine client-centered therapy in relation to the actualizing tendency. In this endeavor, we emphasize the 'unitary actualizing tendency' (Rogers, 1963: 20) as a more precise representation of the actualizing tendency in client-centered theory (Rogers, 1959). Attention to this nomenclature leads us to consider unitary aspects of the theory beyond the integration of organismic and self-experiences. That is, the integral connection of the attitudes of unconditional positive regard and empathic understanding to the actualizing tendency is suggested. Moreover, we hold that the construct of congruence is the macro-facilitator of the actualizing tendency (i.e., therapist congruence facilitates client congruence). We also postulate that congruence is the manifestation of the actualizing process.

The 'necessary and sufficient conditions' of unconditional positive regard and empathic understanding are process constructs integrally related to the actualizing tendency. *Unconditional positive regard* is the curative factor of the approach. *Empathic understanding* is a critical part of unconditional positive regard, 'always necessary if unconditional positive regard is to be fully communicated' (Rogers, 1959: 231). As the two attitudes to be experienced by the therapist, they are part of and also emergent from the congruent therapist. As such, these are the therapist attitudes that facilitate congruence. Unconditional positive regard from the therapist frees the client to assimilate organismic experiences with self-experiences. In other words, the person increasingly lives the actualizing process as a *congruent* (ideally fully functioning) individual.

Rogers (1959: 213, 1963: 12) spoke of the therapist condition of congruence as an antecedent relevant to the process of developmental change for the client. Client incongruence is presented as a condition of anxiety and vulnerability (Rogers, 1959: 213). Somehow, Rogers seems to neglect discussing the construct of congruence as an integral part of other constructs in his theory. However, he does acknowledge that when self-experiences are accurately symbolized and incorporated in the self-concept there is congruence of self and experience. He notes that if this congruence were true of all self-experiences that the person would be 'fully functioning' (ibid.: 206).

'Fully functioning' is considered synonymous with optimal psychological adjustment and maturity, complete openness to experience, and *complete congruence* (ibid.: 235). The fully functioning person is also the fully 'actualized person.' This, then, brings us to a confounding complexity of simplicity. *Therapist congruence begets client congruence.* That is, the more congruent the therapist or the more fully functioning or the more embedded the characteristics of unconditional positive regard and empathic understanding (as prominent characteristics of congruence), the more apt the client will integrate her organismic and self-experiences. That is, the more integrated and whole (actualized) the therapist, the more likely the client will become more integrated and whole (actualized).

IMPLICATIONS

Consideration of the unitary actualizing tendency in Rogers' theory of therapy confirms it as an organismic theory with basic qualities viewed as those of growth, process and change. Our conclusions agree with Van Belle's (1980) contention that, in Rogers' theory, '*Man (the human being) is an actualizing process*' (p. 70). More specifically, we can say that: *Congruence represents the self-actualizing tendency* in humans. That is, the human being at the more advanced process of actualization, self-actualization, *is* the congruent individual. Congruence can also be referred to as the manifestation of the actualizing tendency.

Two particular implications emerge from viewing the motivational foundation of the theory as the 'unitary actualizing tendency.' One is that the conditions of unconditional positive regard and empathic understanding are implicit characteristics of congruence. The other is that therapist congruence facilitates client congruence (primarily because the congruent/actualized person is at a high level of experiencing unconditional positive regard and empathic understanding).

The view we offer of Rogers' theory of therapy focuses on the integration and wholeness of the therapist in relation to the client. It is an interactive, albeit non-directive, view since it is the constructive growth of the client that is emphasized. With emphasis on the influence of a congruent therapist, there is less apt to be confusion about different modes of interaction (i.e., directive techniques) being substituted for the therapeutic capacity of congruence. The importance of the therapist's attitudes which are associated with increased congruence, namely, unconditional positive regard and empathic understanding, are less apt to be confused with response repertoire, therapist-determined directions of inquiry or process, or certain 'rules of engagement.' Congruence as a manifestation of the actualizing tendency offers a conceptual schema for theoretical expansion and empirical examination, as well as a unifying perspective for understanding non-directive practice.

REFERENCES

Bozarth JD (1996) A theoretical reconsideration of the necessary and sufficient conditions for therapeutic personality change. *The Person-Centered Journal, 3* (1), 44–51.

Bozarth JD (1998/2002) *Person-Centered Therapy: A revolutionary paradigm* (2nd edn). Ross-on-Wye: PCCS Books.

Bozarth JD (2001a) Client-centered unconditional positive regard: A historical perspective. In J Bozarth & P Wilkins (Eds) *Rogers' Therapeutic Conditions: Evolution, Theory and Practice. Vol. 3: Unconditional Positive Regard.* Ross-On-Wye: PCCS Books, pp. 5–18.

Bozarth JD (2001b) Congruence: A special way of being. In G Wyatt (Ed) *Rogers' Therapeutic Conditions: Evolution, Theory and Practice. Vol. 1: Congruence.* Ross-On Wye: PCCS Books, pp. 184–9.

Bozarth JD & Brodley BT (1986) Client-centered psychotherapy: A statement. *Person-Centered Review, 1* (3), 262–71.

Bozarth JD & Brodley BT (1991) Actualization: A functional concept in client-centered therapy. In A Jones & R Crandall (Eds) Handbook of self-actualization. [Special Issue]. *Journal of Social Behavior and Personality, 6* (5), 45–60.

Brodley BT (1999) The actualizing tendency concept in client-centered theory. *The Person-Centered Journal, 6* (2), 108–19.

Goldstein K (1995) *The Organism: A holistic approach to biology derived from pathological data in man.* New York: Zone Books.

Kirschenbaum H (1979) *On Becoming Carl Rogers.* New York: Dell.

Levitt BE (2005) Non-directivity: The foundational attitude. In BE Levitt (Ed) *Embracing Non-directivity: Reassessing person-centered theory and practice in the 21st century.* Ross-on-Wye: PCCS Books, pp. 5–16.

Maslow AH (1970) *Motivation and Personality* (2nd edn). New York: Harper and Row.

Rogers CR (1951) *Client-Centered Therapy: Its current practice, implications, and theory.* Boston: Houghton Mifflin.

Rogers CR (1957) The necessary and sufficient conditions of therapeutic personality change. *Journal of Consulting Psychology, 21* (2), 95–103.

Rogers CR (1959) A theory of therapy, personality, and interpersonal relationships as developed in the client-centered framework. In S Koch (Ed) *Psychology: A study of science. Vol. 3: Formulations of the person and the social context.* New York: McGraw-Hill, pp. 184–256.

Rogers CR (1961) *On Becoming a Person: A therapist's view of psychotherapy.* Boston: Houghton Mifflin.

Rogers CR (1963) The actualizing tendency in relation to 'motives' and to consciousness. In M Jones (Ed) *Nebraska Symposium on Motivation.* Lincoln, NE: University of Nebraska Press, pp. 1–24.

Rogers CR (1975) Empathic: An unappreciated way of being. *The Counseling Psychologist, 5* (2), 2–10.

Rogers CR (1977) *Carl Rogers on Personal Power: Inner strength and its revolutionary impact.* New York: Delacorte.

Rogers CR (1978) The formative tendency. *Journal of Humanistic Psychology, 18* (1), 23–6.

Rogers CR (1980) The foundations of a person-centered approach. In *A Way of Being.* Boston: Houghton Mifflin, pp. 113–36.

Standal SW (1954) The need for positive regard: A contribution to client-centered theory. Unpublished doctoral dissertation, University of Chicago.

Van Belle HA (1980) *Basic Intent and Therapeutic Approach of Carl R. Rogers: A study of his view of man in relation to his view of therapy, personality and interpersonal relations.* Toronto, Canada: Wedge Publishing.

CHAPTER 8

THE FORMATIVE TENDENCY: PERSON-CENTERED SYSTEMS THEORY, INTERDEPENDENCE AND HUMAN POTENTIAL

JEFFREY H.D. CORNELIUS-WHITE
AND
JÜRGEN KRIZ

Abstract

Even though Rogers wrote that the formative tendency 'definitely forms a base for the person-centered approach' (1980: 133), it has remained a seldom-explored construct. For example, a PsycINFO search on November12, 2006 using the term 'formative tendency' accounted for only 8 of the 5,190 references yielded by the term 'client-centered'. While the formative tendency rarely has been explored directly, recent writings concerning the person-centered approach from the perspective of systems theory (e.g., Cornelius-White, 2007a; Kriz, 2006, 2007; O'Hara, 2006/2007; Seeman, 2001, Wyatt, 2001) are rich ground for understanding how the formative tendency has been a silent but salient participant in 'the quiet revolution' that is the person-centered approach.

With the postulation of the formative tendency, Rogers expanded his lifelong attempt to understand phenomena where order emerges, changes and develops in a system without the imposition of that order from the outside, or without someone explicitly making that order. Today, in the interdisciplinary discourse of systems theory, we speak of these phenomena as 'self-organization'. This discourse includes sub-concepts such as 'emergence' (the self-organized formation of order, patterns or structure) and 'phase transition' (the self-organized change of order, patterns or structure), which are based on 'interconnectedness' (interactive, reciprocal feedback loops). The 'formative tendency' concept forces a recognition that actualization processes are relevant as a challenging perspective on epistemology (the study of knowing), as well as to the development of a psychology (the study of individual people). Further, it offers a means to knowledge not just of individual persons but also of groups, social forces, biodiversity, chemistry and many other areas. The following section will trace the development of Rogers' thinking regarding actualization processes from the person to increasingly larger systems.

THE DEVELOPMENT OF THE FORMATIVE TENDENCY

Rogers was aware that the phenomena of emerging and (self-organized) changing of order must be explained by totally different principles than those of classical behaviorism and Western, mechanistic science. Yet, these behavioral concepts still govern the overarching Western understanding of the world, including its living beings, in everyday psychology and worldview. While the concept of control, or external imposition of order to a system, may function well if one has to repair a defective engine or beat out the dents in a tin can, intevening with a living being, such as with a client in psychotherapy, is better explained with different principles. These principles describe the phenomena of self-organized order and take reciprocal change processes into account (Kriz, 2006).

Over 50 years ago, in *Client-Centered Therapy*, Rogers (1951) refers to the 'self' as a 'Gestalt.' Gestalt Psychology (especially the Berlin School) had already developed its core concept of 'Gestalt,' which stresses that a structural whole integrates several elements in a dynamic manner (the 'bottom up' perspective) while special features of the elements get their meaning primarily through being parts of the whole (the 'top down' perspective). For example, a melody integrates individual tones, and can remain 'the same melody' when transposed into another key because of the structural invariance of the relationships among the tones. A melody also gives special meaning to many of its tones—for example, the 'key tone,' the 'leading tone,' etc. Because Rogers was especially interested in the *developmental* perspective—how persons can change themselves and under what facilitating conditions—he focused not only on the dynamic stability of the Gestalt but more so on the concept of 'self-actualization,' coined by Kurt Goldstein (1939). As a physiologist, Goldstein was referring to the self-organizing processes of a biological organism, particularly the human organism.[1] Following Goldstein, Rogers (1951) uses the term 'self-actualization' to stress that the development of a human being, and his or her functioning, is based mostly on *inherent* structural possibilities. Human development—including development that is facilitated by the support of a therapist—is towards 'increasing self-government, self-regulation, and autonomy, and away from heteronymous control, or control by external forces' (Rogers, 1951: 488).

As his theory of personality developed, the 'self' as a psychological construct became so important that Rogers made an analytical distinction between the actualization of the 'self', termed 'self-actualization', and the actualization of the organism, now referred to simply as 'actualization.' Although 'self-actualization' is a part or aspect of the actualization of the whole human being, the meaning of the term 'self-actualization' changed. In Rogers' theory 'self-actualization' is not actualization by one*self* in contrast to external imposed order. Rather, it involves the actualization of a 'self-concept' in contrast to the whole phenomenal field of the person's experience. Hence, 'self-actualization' refers to the psychological level, while 'actualization' refers to the holistic level, including the body-based or biological.

Because this idea either was not understood or was rejected by those psychologists who still believed only in the classical control principles of Western science—and even devalued by some as not being in tune with 'science'—Rogers looks for support of his theoretical descriptions and explanations in the hard sciences of physics, chemistry, and biology. He, in fact, found this support for his principles among certain theories in science that already had been formulated:

---

1. Indeed, after his forced emigration from Germany to the USA due to the Nazi regime, Goldstein became famous as one of the founders of the American 'organismic approach.'

> I am not alone in seeing such an actualizing tendency as the fundamental answer to the question of what makes an organism 'tick.' Goldstein (1947), Maslow (1954), Angyal (1941, 1965), Szent Gyoergyi (1974), and others have held similar views and have influenced my own thinking. (Rogers, 1980: 119)

He got further support from the rise of Interdisciplinary Systems Theory in the 1970s, which was validated by the award of Nobel prizes to its leading proponents. Rogers, unlike most psychologists, was aware of this highly significant paradigm change in science. He broadened his concept of actualization to include phenomena exceeding the psychological and somatic level to phenomena of self-organization on the interpersonal levels and beyond. He called this broader notion the 'formative tendency.' As a consequence, in person-centered theory, the 'self-actualization tendency' (on the psychological level) is a special aspect of the 'actualization tendency' (on the organismic level), which in turn is a special aspect of the 'formative tendency' (on the universal level).

THE INCONSISTENCY OF THE FORMATIVE TENDENCY WITH WESTERN SOCIETY

Client-centered therapy is best seen as a transformational paradigm (Rogers, 1977, 1980). However, it has been described typically within the context of Western culture. Western society is largely concerned with 'power over' a person's environment, including other people, animals, minerals, and plants. Science and Enlightenment values are externally imposed values that put control at the center of the discovery of 'knowledge.' In particular, the behavioral paradigm of control through reinforcement still dominates psychology.

This paradigm, which involves the isolation of behavior by or toward the individual person, like the isolation of the individual variable in traditional science, is not an appropriate way of describing our world if one takes the interrelationship of material entities into account. The understanding of 'the world,' even in physics or chemistry, had to change to account for these phenomena, where feedback and interrelationship are important. In the arena of living beings, especially for human beings, interrelationship is ubiquitous. Mechanistic science, therefore, explains only 'a special artificial area of our world'. It is a nineteenth-century belief that this approach would give a sufficient description not only of mechanistic arrangements of matter, but of the whole world, including biological phenomena and even human beings. Modern science, by contrast, has proven that 'these principles work only under very restricted conditions and constraints, which are adequate for machines but, as it turned out, inadequate for entities where complex recursive processes are essential' (Kriz, 2006: 126).

THE CONSISTENCY OF THE FORMATIVE TENDENCY WITH INTERDISCIPLINARY SYSTEMS THEORY

Interdisciplinary systems theory shows that in the developmental dynamics of a system—i.e., for an entity where the interrelationship of parts is crucial—order can emerge ('emergence') and change ('phase transition') due to the changing conditions of the surroundings. However, these 'conditions' neither impose order nor transport order from outside into the system, as would be understood by the classical approach and interventions. In contrast to a classical understanding, these 'conditions' can only support or facilitate the process of emergence or phase transition of order, which are due to inherent possibilities. Therefore, in dealing with such systems, even physicists and chemists have to respect their inherent structural possibilities and cannot 'shape' their structure and order through will or force alone.

Other principles are important in dynamic systems. For example, the emergence and phase transition of order shows that the classical understanding of bigger inputs resulting in bigger outputs (or bigger stimuli resulting in bigger responses) does not hold. For any particular system, with its own unique history and special status, strong influences might result in almost no effects due to a smoothing away of the 'perturbations' (attractor effects). In other states, and/or due to other historical pathways, even very small influences can result in very big (or 'qualitative') changes ('butterfly effects'). These phenomena are typical in the area of the development of living beings, and in particular human beings. In these living human systems, 'jumps' to new levels after a period of nearly no (observable) progress is typical, such as a sudden change in the understanding of a complex problem after collecting many pieces of disperate information (the 'Aha' experience described by Gestalt Psychology). In literature and tales of wisdom, these sudden jumps in the dynamics of structure have been referred to by the principle of 'die and become!', stressing that a new (partial) order, pattern or structure is only possible by overcoming the old one and passing the gate (or state) of chaotic instability. The idea of 'growth' in Humanistic Psychology refers to this same principle of 'die and become.' This is opposed to the notion of growth as accumulating more and more, which Westerrn cultures might advocate.

In systems science one has to respect (or at least take into account) the history of the system, as the same conditions of the surroundings can often be associated with very different states in the system. An example of this is the principle of 'hysteresis' (also called 'homeostasis'). Hysteresis refers to an over-stability of a system's state against the change of the surroundings. The inner status and potentials of the system are at least as important as the influence of the surroundings. A system does not just 'react' to external stimuli, as the classical approach assumes.

The phenomena of emergence and phase transition are related to a connection between bottom-up and top-down dynamics (see also Kriz, 2006). We explored this through the example of a melody and its individual notes. The parts contribute, bottom up, to the emergence of order. Order structures or 'field forces,' top down, further the dynamics of the parts. This holds true for and can be seen in human beings. For example, cultural rules are continued over time and generations by human action (bottom up), while cultural rules (patterns, order) in turn structure the behavioral learning of people, particularly in each new generation (top down). The relationship between top-down and bottom-up dynamics can also be seen in prejudice. Individuals focusing on 'strange' and 'untrustworthy' behaviors of other people may, bottom up, create an 'attitude' and 'worldview' of mistrust or prejudice. At the same time, these worldviews can act as 'field forces' that, top down, influence the cognitive processes of individuals to focus on 'strange' and 'untrustworthy' actions of others.

Cornelius-White (2006a) describes how the purpose of the book *Carl Rogers On Personal Power* was to explore 'the ways in which control is exercised, consciously or unconsciously' (Rogers, 1977: 56). Rogers used the concept of subtle veils of cultural conditioning to explain how a social consciousness, outside our individual awareness, can shape our individual views. Social forces like gender, race, and nationality structure top down our individual attitudes towards the bottom-up behaviors of individuals with particular genders, races, or nationalities. Whiteness, patriarchy and language are strong systemic attractors and explanatory concepts for much injustice and suffering. Rogers (1977) aimed for the PCA to 'do away with discrimination,' offering examples of a subtle veil of sexism, including 'less obvious situations like our language—*man*kind, chair*man*, homage to *Him*' (p. 45).

The principles of interdisciplinary systems science obviously are much more adequate than the principles of classical Western science in refering to, describing, and understanding many phenomena regarded central to the life processes of human beings. However, we want to stress that such an assertion is not an ontological statement. We totally dislike statements that are reductionistic conceptualizations without qualification, such as: 'The human being is non-linear and, therefore, a self-organizing system.' The human being is a human being. Period. When a human being jumps out of the window of a skyscraper, the principles of classical physics would suffice when answering questions concerning the nature of the fall (such as trajectory and speed). For some inquiries, for example the analysis of a small piece of flesh under a microscope, classical biology would also suffice. For some other questions the behavioral approach also may be adequate. However, if one does not take a living being as an isolated system, but takes into account its interrelationships, the principles of systems theory are more complete and satisfying descriptors than the principles of classical Western science. The 'formative tendency' in the person-centered approach is a central construct that reflects the principles of systems theory.

We should be aware that even the principles of systems theory do not adequately answer all questions regarding human beings. However, we can use these principles to explore the dynamics of many cognitive and interpersonal processes. We can even use mathematics to express these principles with a high degree of precision (e.g., Kriz, 2006). However, to understand the essence of a human being in contrast to other living beings or entities in the world, we must turn to philosophy, such as the descriptions and principles of Existentialism. According to Heidegger, we have to accept that a human being cannot be understood as a category or class like all other 'things' in the world, which are defined by their 'whatness,' because 'man is never a what—his essence (self) lies in his existence' (King, 1964: 66). The human being, as a reflexive being, can—and must—meaningfully define his own existence and his own presence in this world. His different mode of being frees him from categorization. And from this point of view, a person can be understood best 'from the inside'—through one's personal understanding and narratives of one's biographical past, one's meaning and value structures, as well as one's ideas of one's future. Psychology is the science that must face both of these perspectives—a science in which the inner and outer views of life's processes meet.

Interdisciplinary systems theory and its principles do not attempt to answer all questions that might be important in the realm of a human being. Neither the movement of a human falling from a skyscraper, nor the essence of existence and freedom can or should be described by these principles. However, there are many important phenomena, especially related to developmental or psychotherapeutic aspects of human beings (including their relationships in couples, families or organizations), which we claim can be described and understood best by these principles of self-organization (and more poorly, for example, by principles of stimulus-response analysis, or other mechanistic principles).

FACILITATION AND IMAGINATION

Actualization 'is neither a belief nor an assumption in Rogers' theory, but a simple description of the consequences of seriously taking interconnectedness and relationships into account'(Kriz, 2007: 40). This understanding of the actualizing tendency must be considered when we refer to real-world, non-artificial or isolated processes. However, we must also take into account other aspects, which are in tune with interdisciplinary systems theory. Facilitation and imagination are two such aspects, which ask us in particular to 'trust' rather than to 'do or control.' With the formative tendency, we are focusing more on fluid boundaries and categories. We are open to possibilities, contrasting 'planning' with 'imagining the future' (Kriz, 2006). Planning means that development starts from a clearly analyzed status and proceeds in well-defined steps in order to reach an explicitly given aim. Deviation or departure from these steps is interpreted as failure or error and, therefore, it is corrected or eliminated. If goals or conditions change, planning must begin again. Imagination, on the other hand, means that development proceeds towards a roughly specified goal. Moving in a general direction, decisions have to be made and the goal becomes more and more clear along the way. Decisions are generated and goals become more clear in a reciprocal manner. The whole path is adaptive to changing needs or conditions, and the goal may change a great deal in the process.

Non-directivity is a crucial aspect of trust. The non-directive therapist is not an expert in content, but an expert in facilitating developmental processes of emergence and transition of inherent potentials. This stance is obviously at odds with the perspective of medical-model, disorder-specific treatments, of training the right behavior, or of teaching self-control. Instead of reducing the client to a carrier or manifestation of a disorder category, the non-directive perspective respects the uniqueness of individual human beings, including their specific potentials and biographies. Angyal (1951) wrote, 'it is incongruous with the nature of love to try to reduce the loved person to an item in one's personal world, or to try to make him comply with one's demands, or to try to exert power over him in whatever way' (p. 131).

The person-centered approach is not the only way to bring about change. However, we also assert that the healing power of the person-centered approach is due to respect for the formative tendency. This stance is in contrast to a stance of imposing order, and is an ethical resolution. Imposing order from outside and controlling the results can work rather well. For example, after a concert, a rhythmic clapping, a synchronizing of all of the individual clapping rhythms in the audience, very often will spontaneously emerge from the initial chaos of applause. This synchronized clapping rhythm can also be imposed by means of 'classical' intervention. Imagine a concert for an army. At the end, an officer jumps on stage. He has learned in the army, and heard from politicians, teachers, or even a therapist with a 'classical' worldview, that order has to be imposed. Shouting 'wasn't it a nice concert?' he might make big clapping movements, adding 'let's clap—now, now, now!' If the soldiers follow, order is imposed from the outside.

EMERGENCE AND EMERGENCY

The top-down power of ordering fields can reduce or restrict potential in individuals to find new solutions to meet new requirements. In natural science systems theory this is known by the principle of 'enslaving.' Kriz (2006) addresses this dynamic in his discussion of 'meaning fields,' which can impose order, top down, and restrict individual creativity. The structural forces of narratives, terms, categories, or assumptions may then configure the processes of perception, rational-emotive mediation, and behavior of single human beings as well as of couples, families, organizations and other systems. New situations can be responded to reactively (emergency) or with appreciation of the possibilities they engender (emergence). Many structural forces are presesnt in narratives due to the individual's personal biography, the history of a couple, and the more far-reaching histories of families over generations and even in our culture as a whole.

Rogers (1951) highlighted the importance of the structural forces of a distorted symbolization in the self with regard to the experience of a single person:

> The accurate symbolization would be: 'I perceive my parents as experiencing this behavior as unsatisfying to them.' The distorted symbolization, distorted to preserve the threatened concept of self, is: 'I perceive this behavior as unsatisfying.' It is in this way, it would seem, that parental attitudes are not only introjected, but what is much more important, are experienced not as the attitude of another, but in distorted fashion, *as if* based on the evidence of one's own sensory and visceral equipment. (p. 500)

The forces of distorted symbolization can be seen also in a couple's communications. A couple's history gives rise to patterns of meaning that influence how communications are received and interpreted. These 'emerged patterns' reduce the ability of individuals in a couple to listen carefully to what is said here and now. The potential for change (e.g., improved communication) is thereby reduced, or enslaved. A typical situation in couples therapy is that a therapist asks one partner: 'Did you hear what your partner just said?' The client answers, 'No, I didn't—but by the way my partner looked at me, I already knew what he would say!'

Similarly, the common diagnosis, or narrative, that little Peter 'has a behavior disorder' reduces the highly complex space of situations and interpretations to one single static and inflexible focus: 'behavior disorder.' But there may be situations in which his behavior appears to be a natural reaction to provocation from his sister. In other situations, it could be a signal asking for more attention. Sometimes, it might serve to distract attention away from conflict between his parents. Of course, there will certainly also be situations in which he is simply outrageously impossible, but even this can be described more accurately and poetically than simply resorting to a diagnostic label of 'behavior disorder.' It is of crucial importance to move beyond the constraints of the 'behavior disorder' label and restore awareness of the complexity and breadth of situations and their significance.

Kriz (2006) described the complex attracting forces in our '*Lebenswelt,*' defined as 'our personal experience and understanding of the world, including the individual, social, political, and environmental perspectives.' These structures function in our everyday experience without being explicitly conscious or even an object of reflection' (p. 62). In this sense, even the principles of Western science and behaviorism serve as structural forces ordering the thought of many people in our culture. We see this when clients come to therapy with the 'idea' that they should be 'fixed' like a machine, or at least that the therapist should give some advice or 'answer' from 'expertise' or 'knowledge' and thereby bring some order to their life.

TOWARD GREATER ORDER AND GREATER COMPLEXITY: ON CHAOS AND ORGANIZATION—THE PARADOX OF THE EVOLUTIONARY TENDENCY

The attracting forces of 'subtle veils,' concepts, narratives, and rules of our culture are indeed powerful. They reduce the complexity of possible interpretations and meaning of 'what is going on' to categories of content and explanatory rules. 'Ordering,' even by the formative tendency or self-organization, is always a reduction of complexity. In this sense, Rogers' definition of the formative tendency as an 'evolutionary tendency' not only toward 'greater order,' but also toward 'greater complexity,' would appear to be a contradiction. But it is not. We would find a dominance of attracting (and thereby complexity-reducing) forces only in meta-stable system-environment relationships; i.e., when the conditions of the environment are rather stable. However, in contrast to stable mechanistic 'things'—such as a tin can—systems adequately described by non-linear dynamics, like self-organization and emergence of order, are typically highly adaptive to changes in environmental conditions. To be clear, this does not at all mean that *order* is imported from the outside. In contrast, phase transition, the self-organized change of order, patterns, and structure, always means that complexity increases, that the dynamic stability of the attractor becomes unstable. From this unstable point, a multitude of possibilities opens up. In further development, the system again reduces complexity; i.e., it develops another attractor, finding new order, patterns, and structure (for details see Kriz, 1992; Matthes et al., 2001).

This description of change by phase transition corresponds exactly with the principle of 'die and become!' This principle is a valid description of 'growth' in humanistic psychologies, such as the person-centered approach. Normally, this adaptive change of order/patterns takes place without the help of psychotherapists. For example, imagine a family of a father, a mother and a 3-year-old daughter. The patterns of interaction that have emerged in this small family may be very good at present, and adequate for each family member. However, if we continue to see these same patterns twenty years later, some people, including the family members, might refer to the situation with terms like 'crazy' or 'pathological.' Twenty years later, treating a (now) 23-year-old woman as if she were still three years old is, of course, mad. Normally this does not happen: due to changing environmental conditions in which the interaction patterns are embedded—maturation, changing demands and requests of the daughter from other people, expectations that the daughter should make her own decisions, etc.—the patterns of interaction will make one (or more) phase transitions in adapting to changed or changing demands. In other words, some of the patterns really 'die' while others 'become.'

Patterns do not only change on the level of interaction. They also change on the level of cognitive and emotive processes change. This change typically occurs through increasing complexity (e.g., 'passing the gate of chaos'), leaving previous attractors of order behind. New attractors are established as the system finds new order, patterns, and meaning. The formative tendency, with its movement toward 'greater order', as well as toward 'greater complexity', works in a 'breathing' rhythm: the 'die and become!' of growth means that order (in other words, reduced complexity) actually becomes more complex due to the changing environment. It becomes unstable (and increasingly presents more possibilities). It leaves the 'old' order (it 'dies') and reduces complexity again by finding a new order, which is more adaptive to the changed demands of the environment (for more details, see Kriz, 1997, 1999, 2006).[2]

---

2. These descriptions are still somewhat simplistic. The processes relevant for a human being, whom we describe by way of systems theory, have many aspects, and must be described in a multidimensional space. In some dimensions in this multidimensional space we may find that a process has attracting, order increasing, and complexity reducing aspects. At the same time, in other dimensions in this same space, the opposite may be true. Readers who are familiar with modern systems theory in detail may be aware of the notion of a 'phase space.' Such readers should think of the famous 'Lorenz Attractor' which, although only in a phase space of three dimensions, shows that attractive and 'chaotic' dimensions exist together in one process.

There are situations where no change takes place, even though the 'conditions of the environment' obviously have changed. In other words, the system is 'maladaptive', (e.g., the family with a 23-year-old daughter interacting as if she were a three-year-old child). This situation does not contradict the notion of the 'formative tendency,' nor the notion of the actualizing tendency. It is not an adequate description if we say that the process got 'stuck,' is 'blocked' or is 'maladaptive.' If we speak in this way, we are not aware of all the conditions and different perspectives as they mix together. Even if a system appears maladaptive, it is always adapting and unfolding its formative potential to the whole array of environmental conditions. For the individual human being, and specifically in client-centered therapy, Rogers (1951) stressed:

I) Every individual exists in a continually changing world of experience of which he is the center.

II) The organism reacts to the field as it is experienced and perceived. This perceptual field is, for the individual, 'reality.'

III) The organism reacts as an organized whole to this phenomenal field.

(pp. 483–6)

Due to 'introjections,' 'traumatized perceptions,' and other idiosyncrasies, the observer's reality of the 'obvious conditions' may not be the same as the client's or family's reality of the conditions. In the extreme case of the extreme example with the 23-year-old daughter who is treated as if she is three years old, the 'objective' conditions may have changed drastically over the twenty years since she was actually three years old, due to such factors as maturation and new demands. However, perhaps the daughter has had, since the age of three, severe and life-threatening asthma. The changing conditions of maturation and new demands may be rather unimportant compared the family's 'views' and beliefs that every 'change' is dangerous. In such a case, the pattern we see is actually adapted to *that reality*, which is the family's 'real reality.' The pattern or order is established not *in spite* of the actualizing tendency, but *because* of it. Nothing got 'stuck.' The system is not 'maladaptive.' It is, in actuality, working very well with respect to a *particular* reality, that of the family. As person-centered therapists, we trust that the pattern will change in the context of a relationship with a therapist who brings new conditions to this reality, due to the formative tendency. A 'reality' structured by abstract categories is much more stable and reduced than a 'reality' full of here-and-now experiences. Person-centered therapy facilitates movement toward *experiencing* the world in more vivid, complex, and creative encounter that is in tune with the here and now. It facilitates the conditions whereby reduced, abstract descriptions are broken down and 'die,' allowing for a more full here-and-now experience to 'become.'

UPHEAVAL, LEARNING TO LEARN, AND ADAPTING TO CHANGINGNESS

The example of the 23-year-old daughter is, of course, rather extreme and artificial. But it should make the point clear that 'upheaval' can give rise to a new stage of development. In other words, instability creates a challenge to be creative and grow. This, of course, necessitates a condition of trust. Upheaval can also lead to reductive abstraction—the fear of uncertainty can establish narrative structures that limit scrutiny because of this reductive abstraction. In *Lebenswelt in Upheaval* (Kriz, 2004, partly in English in Kriz, 2006) it is shown how 'symptoms' are interwoven in such processes on different levels. Different levels of meaning for individuals, families and the whole culture influence each other.

Our shared '*Lebenswelt* in upheaval' includes endless wars, environmental degradation, genocides,[3] species extinctions,[4] gender violence, avoidable famine, oppression and terrorism. It presents both an extreme vulnerability and a 'path to social and psychological evolution' (O'Hara, 2006/2007: 47). O'Hara (2006/2007) argues, 'No one is "native" in this new culture; "culture shock" and cognitive dissonance are pandemic, bewilderment is normal and—with the rapid pace of change—is likely ever to be' (p. 50). The principles of Western science, particulary control instead of trust, imposing order instead of facilitating and imagining inherent possibilities, has run to its edge. Respecting the formative tendency offers an alternative by which to adapt.

Rogers' (1951, 1969, 1983) educational writings highlight the broader formative tendency, whereas his psychotherapy writings highlight the narrower actualizing tendency. Rogers discusses the necessity of learning to learn, or adapting to 'changingness,' for humanity to survive (Cornelius-White, 2006c, 2007b; Cornelius-White and Harbaugh, in press). If changingness is seen as the reality for our future, as Rogers, O'Hara and others have suggested, then the concepts of emergence, phase transitions, and interrelatedness become core constructs for a humanistic 'response-ability.' Even in 1951, Rogers wrote of the intention to 'release the group' to actualize (p. 59) and of situations where 'the group took responsibility upon itself' (p. 56).

HUMAN POTENTIAL: ECOLOGICAL BALANCE AND DE-CENTERING THERAPY

ECOLOGICAL BALANCE: ORGANISMIC INTEGRATION AND ENVIRONMENTAL RESPONSIBILITY

Seeman (2001) has for over 50 years described how the person can be understood best from a combination of biochemical, physiological, perceptual, precognitive, cognitive, interpersonal, and ecological perspectives. In this way the congruent (or to use Seeman's preferred term, organismically integrated) person is conceptualized as connected and communicated across all of these levels, simultaneously and non-reductionistically. A person is not thought of as just an individual but also a relationship between the body's parts and all that is around that body. In this way, one's 'phenomenal field,' to borrow Rogers' term, is visceral, subjective and co-created by larger systems. Similarly,

---

3. See <www.genocidewatch.org>.
4. See <www.overpopulation.org>.

Bronfenbrenner (1979) describes human ecology in terms of nested systems where a person is a person, but also part of their microsystem (such as the family or classroom), the mesosytem (which is two microsystems in interaction), the exosystem (which is a system influencing development, i.e., parental workplace), and the macrosystem (the larger cultural context). Each system contains roles, norms and rules that can powerfully shape development.

Rogers (1951), in lengthy citations, seems to acknowledge the salience of the ecology of organisms. He wrote, 'Angyal's statement [1941] could be used as a synonym for actualization: "Life is an autonomous event which takes place *between the organism and the environment* [italics added]. Life processes do not merely tend to preserve life but transcend the momentary status quo of the organism"' (Rogers, 1959: 196). He also cited Pearse and Williamson (1938: 38–40), 'the biologist conceives an order emanating from the organism *living in poise in its environment* [italics added]. Our necessity, therefore, is to secure the free flow of forces in the environment so that the order inherent in their material we are studying may emerge and change adaptivly. Our interest is in that *balance of forces* [italics added] which sustains naturally and spontaneously the forms of life we are studying' (1951: 62). Likewise, many ancestral worldviews, particularly those of people of color, view persons as embedded in connections with others, interdependent, part of their tribe or family before being seen as an individual (Cornelius-White, 2006b, 2006d).

Though a person is best understood from the 'inside' or personally, we also acknowledge that the personal is not an isolated phenomenon. For many people the personal is about their environment, especially their loved ones. In the context of his 'Person-Centered Systems Approach,' Kriz (1991) has shown how the internal cognitive-emotive processes which are essential for the 'self' and the 'person' are embedded in interactive and communicative processes of the family and the whole culture. The emergence and co-construction of 'meaning attractors' (Kriz, 2006) refer to meaning structures both of the person and of the social systems in a bottom-up as well as in a top-down relationship. The oft repeated phrase, 'the personal is political' captures some of this paradox, while Schmid's (2001) eloquent words describe it this way: there are 'two unrenounceable dimensions of human existence: the substantial or individual aspect of being a person and the relational or dialogical aspect of becoming a person' (p. 214). People are both individuals and their relationships.

Cornelius-White (2007c) writes:
> If the formative tendency is central to understanding the person-centered approach in concert with its sub-concept, the actualizing tendency, then the responsibility of person-centered practitioners shifts to releasing the natural tendency of not just individuals, but groups, other organisms, and perhaps most importantly the ecology ... The formative tendency and a corresponding nondirectivity values life not just individuals. As such, it becomes 'obvious that the approach needs further development towards a truly social approach' and to 'authentically implement the essence of it into all fields of life' (Schmid, 2001: 226) ... The formative person-centered approach is the practice of respecting the truth and diversity of life, including each person, each group,

each species, and the overall web itself. It is a profound relinquishment of control, not only over individual persons, but over all life. While implicit in the actualizing tendency, the formative tendency helps us realize that 'everythingisconnectedtoeverythingelse' in such a way that our ethical obligation must be greater than to the individual. (pp. 135, 137)

The formative tendency contributes to an appreciation of the interdependence that is instrumental to the self-organization and transformative aspects of the person-centered approach.

CONCLUSION

DE-CENTERING THERAPY: A COROLLARY OF THE FORMATIVE PERSON-CENTERED APPROACH

O'Hara (2006/2007) states, 'Rogers had lost interest in counseling and therapy almost entirely … He felt increasingly that the problems facing humanity were on a scale far beyond what could be helped through individual counseling [which had become] de-contextualized and alienated from the looming cultural issues' (p. 54). Nevertheless, Rogers was also clear that he did not see the old client-centered therapy and the new person-centered approach as inherently different (Rogers, Cornelius-White, and Cornelius-White, 2005). Rogers described 'persons of tomorrow' who will survive in the future. Cornelius-White (2007a) summarizes the values of persons of tomorrow as being 'open to experience, authentic, intimate, capable of living with change and ambiguity, altruistic, revering of nature, building of egalitarian institutions, internally moral, less materialistic, and yearning for harmonious spiritual and/or ecological connections' (p. 65). Beyond this, Cornelius-White (2007a) summarizes five themes that appear to be representative of the emerging person-centered paradigm, all of which are consistent with the formative tendency: '(1) being part of an ecological context; (2) balancing dialectics of rationality and emergence; (3) trusting and appreciating creativity; (4) facilitating in and adapting to the actual world beyond therapy; and (5) fundamentally transforming who we are' (p. 67). The person-centered approach must be lived in the wider world if it is not to be enslaved in the cultural conditioning in which it originated and limited to the problems of individuals in isolation (Cornelius-White, 2006b; Cornelius-White and Anderson, 2007). The person-centered approach is an approach to life, not just to therapy.

REFERENCES

Angyal A (1951) A theoretical model for personality studies. *Journal of Personality, 20*, 131–42.

Barrett-Lennard GT (2005) *Relationship at the Centre: Healing in a troubled world.* London: Whurr.

Bozarth JD (1985). Quantum theory and the person-centered approach. *Journal of Counseling and Development, 64*, 179–81.

Bronfenbrenner U (1979) *The Ecology of Human Development: Experiments by nature and design.* Cambridge, MA: Harvard University Press.

Cornelius-White JHD (2006a, May). Cultural congruence: Subtle veils of whiteness and patriarchy. *Person-Centred Quarterly*, 4–6.

Cornelius-White JHD (2006a) De-centering the theory of therapy in the person-centered approach: An implication of formative, multicultural nondirectivity Manuscript in preparation. Missouri State University.

Cornelius-White JHD (2006b) Environmental responsibility: A social justice mandate for counselors. Manuscript submitted for publication. Missouri State University.

Cornelius-White JHD (2006c) A Review and Evolution of Rogers' Theory of Education. Manuscript submitted for publication. Missouri State University.

Cornelius-White JHD (2006d, August). Environmental responsibility, the formative tendency and well-being. *Person-Centred Quarterly*, 11–12.

Cornelius-White JHD (2007a) Leading a good life: The evolving paradigm from the PCE 2006 Keynote Addresses. *Person-Centered and Experiential Psychotherapies, 6* (1), 61–71.

Cornelius-White JHD (2007b) Learner-centered teacher–student relationships are effective: A meta-analysis. *Review of Educational Research, 77*, 113–43.

Cornelius-White JHD (2007c) The actualizing and formative tendencies: Prioritizing the motivational constructs of the person-centered approach. *Person-Centered and Experiential Psychotherapies, 6* (2), 129–40.

Cornelius-White JHD (2007d). Congruence as extensionality. *Person-Centered and Experiential Psychotherapies, 6* (3), 196–204.

Cornelius-White JHD (2007e) Congruence. In M Cooper, PF Schmid, M O'Hara & G Wyatt (Eds) *The Handbook of Person-Centred Therapy.* New York: Palgrave Macmillan, pp. 168–81.

Cornelius-White JHD & Anderson AL (2007, February). Digging in the white soil of person-centered therapy. *Person-Centred Quarterly*, 5–8.

Cornelius-White JHD & Harbaugh AP (in press) *Learner-Centered Instruction: Building relationships for student success.* Thousand Oaks, CA: Sage.

Goldstein K (1939) *The Organism.* New York: American Book.

Johnson DW & Johnson R (1994) *Learning Together and Alone: Cooperative, competitive, and individualistic learning* (4th edn). Boston: Allyn & Bacon.

King M (1964) *Heidegger's Philosophy.* New York: Macmillan.

Kriz J (1991) Mental health: Its conception in Systems Theory. An outline of the Person-Centered Systems Approach. In MJ Pelaez (Ed) *Comparative Sociology of Family, Health and Education*, Vol. XX. Malaga, España: University of Malaga Press, pp. 6061–83.

Kriz J (1992) *Chaos und Struktur. Systemtheorie*, Vol. 1. München, Berlin: Quintessenz.

Kriz J (1997) On chaos and order. *Gestalt Theory, 19*, 197–212.

Kriz J (1999) *Systemtheorie für Psychotherapeuten, Psychologen und Mediziner.* (3rd edn). Wien: UTB/Facultas.

Kriz J (2004) *Lebenswelten im Umbruch*. Wien: Picus.

Kriz J (2006) *Self-actualization*. Norderstedt: BoD.

Kriz J (2007) Actualizing Tendency—The link between person-centered and experiential psychotherapy and interdisciplinary systems theory. *Person-Centered and Experiential Psychotherapies, 6* (1), 30–44.

Matthies M, Malchow H & Kriz J (Eds) (2001) *Integrative Systems Approaches to Natural and Social Dynamics*. Heidelberg: Springer.

O'Hara M (2006/2007) Psychological literacy for an uncertain world—Another look at Rogers' Persons of Tomorrow. *Person-Centered and Experiential Psychotherapies, 6* (1), 45–60.

O'Hara, M & Wood JK (1983) Patterns of awareness: Consciousness and the group mind. *The Gestalt Journal, 6,* 103–16.

Rogers CR (1951) *Client-Centered Therapy: Its current practice, implications, and theory*. Boston: Houghton Mifflin.

Rogers CR (1959) A theory of therapy, personality, and interpersonal relationship as developed in the client-centered framework. In S Koch (Ed) *Psychology: A study of science. Vol. 3: Formulations of the person and the social context*. New York: McGraw-Hill, pp. 184–256.

Rogers CR (1969). *Freedom to Learn*. New York: Merrill.

Rogers CR (1977) *Carl Rogers On Personal Power*. New York: Dell Publishing.

Rogers CR (1978) The formative tendency. *Journal of Humanistic Psychology, 18,* 23–6.

Rogers CR (1980) *A Way of Being*. Boston: Houghton Mifflin.

Rogers CR (1983). *Freedom to Learn for the 80s*. Columbus, OH: Charles E Merrill.

Rogers CR & Russell DE (2002) *Carl Rogers the Quiet Revolutionary: An oral history*. Roseville, CA: Panmarin Books.

Rogers CR, Cornelius-White JHD & Cornelius-White CF (2005) Reminiscing and Predicting: Rogers's Beyond Words speech and commentary. *Journal of Humanistic Psychology, 45,* 383–96.

Schmid PF (2001) Authenticity: The person as his or her own author: Dialogical and ethical perspectives on therapy as an encounter relationship. And beyond. In G Wyatt (Ed) *Rogers' Therapeutic Conditions: Evolution, theory, and practice. Vol. 1: Congruence*. Ross-on-Wye: PCCS Books, pp. 213–28.

Schmid PF (2005) Facilitative responsiveness: Non-directiveness from anthropological, epistemological and ethical perspectives. In BE Levitt (Ed) *Embracing Non-directivity: Reassessing person-centered theory and practice in the 21st century*. Ross-on-Wye: PCCS-Books, pp. 75–95.

Seeman J (2001) On congruence: A human system paradigm. In G Wyatt (Ed) *Rogers' Therapeutic Conditions: Evolution, theory, and practice. Vol. 1: Congruence*. Ross-on-Wye: PCCS Books, pp. 200–12.

Wyatt G (2001) Congruence: A synthesis and implications. In G Wyatt (Ed) *Rogers' Therapeutic Conditions: Evolution, theory, and practice. Vol. 1. Congruence*. Ross-on-Wye: PCCS Books, pp. 229–40.

Chapter 9

FROM ILLNESS TO HEALTH, WELL-BEING AND EMPOWERMENT: THE PERSON-CENTERED PARADIGM SHIFT FROM PATIENT TO CLIENT

Alberto Zucconi

The person-centered approach was founded by Carl Ransom Rogers, a clinical psychologist. It is a systemic, holistic approach that focuses on health rather than illness; empowering rather than curing. It promotes the development of potentialities of individuals, groups and organizations through the process of freeing people to be responsible for what they do, rather than encouraging passivity and dependency. The central hypothesis of the person-centered approach is that individuals have within themselves innate capacities for self-understanding and self-regulation. These resources can be tapped best in a psychological climate that has facilitating qualities. The helping relationship found in such a climate is characterized by acceptance, empathy and authenticity/congruence. This type of relationship promotes self-understanding and allows for the relationship with oneself, others and the world to change in a positive direction.

The person-centered approach sees and leaves the locus of responsibility for change with the client. It is important for both the client and the professional helper to recognize that the client, the person with the problem, must be the one entrusted to create change. Leaving the locus of responsibility, evaluation and control with the client reduces the likelihood of passive, rebellious or victim-like behavior, and sets up a process wherein the client develops an increasing sense of 'response-ability' for the problem, willingness to explore possible solutions to the problem, and willingness to initiate actions to solve the problem for him/herself. The person-centered approach recognizes the person as being in charge of her own life and problems, and as being the one with the most data about her personal situation. It recognizes that the role of the professional is that of a facilitator of change, providing an environment that fosters growth and empowerment, thus enabling the client to explore and find solutions to his/her problems.

Research shows that the therapeutic alliance is the strongest predictive variable for success in psychotherapy. The therapeutic alliance is comprised of Rogers' formulation of the necessary and sufficient conditions (1959), with the additional elements of client and therapist agreement regarding therapy goals and their capacity to repair ruptures in the therapeutic alliance (Norcross, 2002). The impact of the therapeutic alliance appears to be evident in pharmacotherapy outcomes, including placebo responses (Krupnick, et al., 1996).

Carl Rogers has been described eloquently by his colleague and friend, Richard Farson (1974), as a quiet revolutionary. This is a very fitting description of Carl's life and work. He brought a dramatic change to the fields of psychotherapy and human relations. His ideas still are considered fundamental. Practitioners and researchers agree on his impact in this regard. A survey conducted by *American Psychologist* (1982) found Carl Rogers to be the most influential psychologist. In 2006, 26 years later, a survey conducted by Joan Cook at Columbia University, through a grant from the National Institute of Mental Health (NIMH), reached the same conclusion regarding Rogers' influence (*Psychotherapy Networker*, 2007).

Rogers adopted a strikingly different viewpoint from his colleagues—instead of a mechanistic, reductionistic perspective he assumed a holistic-systemic frame of reference. His vision was ahead of his time. In the 1980s, the World Health Organization manifesto on health promotion, the Ottawa Charter (WHO, 1986: 1), seems to echo some of Rogers' tenets:

> Health promotion is the process of enabling people to increase control over, and to improve, their health. To reach a state of complete physical, mental and social well-being, an individual or group must be able to identify and to realize aspirations, to satisfy needs, and to change or cope with the environment. Health is, therefore, seen as a resource for everyday life, not the objective of living. Health is a positive concept emphasizing social and personal resources, as well as physical capacities. Therefore, health promotion is not just the responsibility of the health sector, but goes beyond healthy life-styles to well-being.

In order to fully appreciate the impact of Rogers' revolutionary work, this paper considers broader contexts, including aspects of the history and sociology of science, shifts in scientific paradigms, the sociology of knowledge, and the effects many years later of Rogers' original formulations in the field of health.

A SCIENTIFIC PARADIGM SHIFT

For Thomas Kuhn, a scientific paradigm is considered valid as long as it is able to function adequately in exploring that aspect of nature its use is intended to investigate. When evidence emerges of phenomena that cannot be understood or problems that cannot be explained by the current paradigm, this leads to intense research and scientific speculation. This leads eventually to the formulation of a new paradigm that is able to explain the new data better. It also leads to the creation of an array of more powerful tools and modes of intervention.

According to Kuhn, for paradigms to become accepted they must be innovative and open in ways that attract a sufficient part of the scientific community. The science produced by the new paradigm is not for the sake of change per se. Rather, its aim is the resolution of problems, extending the knowledge of key elements of the paradigm and providing experimental confirmation.

For this reason, it is evident that any focus on scientific problems without recognition of how the related research is dependent upon and oriented by the paradigm upon which it is based can be, paradoxically, a barrier to scientific development.

Kuhn sees scientific progress as proceeding not according to the successive accumulation of knowledge, but through scientific revolution. Such a revolution is heralded by a growing awareness that an existing paradigm has ceased to function adequately in the exploration of an aspect of nature for which the paradigm had previously been adequate. This awareness is felt first by only a small sector of the scientific community. 'Revolution' constitutes an exceptional moment with respect to what Kuhn (1962) calls *normal science*, the relatively routine work of scientists working within a paradigm, slowly accumulating detail in accord with established broad theory, not actually challenging or attempting to test the underlying assumptions of that theory. Kuhn also tells us:

> The success of a paradigm is at the start largely a promise of success discoverable in selected and still incomplete examples. Normal science consists in the actualization of that promise, an actualization achieved by extending the knowledge of those facts that the paradigm displays as particularly revealing, by increasing the extent of the match between those facts and the paradigm's predictions, and by further articulation of the paradigm itself. (1962: 23–4)

In the eighteenth century, light was considered to be composed of material particles. This was the understanding held within the field of optics, an important and integral part of Newtonian physics. Scientists of the time were convinced they understood the fundamental principles of nature: atoms were the bricks from which the natural world was built; motion was explained by Newton's laws; and the majority of physics problems seemed resolved. The Newtonian explanation of light held until the beginning of the twentieth century, when Einstein's and Planck's experiments contradicted certainties upon which Newtonian physics was based. A new theory emerged that light has a dual nature—both wave and particle. This theory was formalized under the new paradigm of Quantum Mechanics.

A BRIEF SUMMARY OF QUANTUM MECHANICS AND GENERAL SYSTEM THEORY

Albert Einstein's Theory of Relativity, along with Quantum Mechanics, constitutes one of the fundamental paradigms of contemporary physics. Einstein introduced the concept of time as a fourth dimension, along with the three spatial dimensions, specifying that the description of physical phenomena needs to be represented in four-dimensional space. The theory presented by Einstein in 1905 was not accepted immediately because of its revolutionary impact on the accepted scientific formulations of Newton and Galileo. Yet, the stunning advances in the scientific understanding of reality springing from his Theory of Relativity were supported by new instruments of observation such as electron microscopes and better telescopes that enabled physicists and astronomers to explore smaller realms and farther reaches of the universe. What they found were phenomena such as subatomic particles and black holes whose actions and characteristics bore little resemblance to those described by Newtonian mechanics or the Cartesian notion of reducing matter to understandable building blocks. Scientists such as Niels Bohr and Werner Heisenberg struggled with interpreting the seemingly chaotic and decidedly counter-intuitive phenomena found in the subatomic realm, and called their area of investigation quantum theory—'quanta' meaning the smallest possible quantity.

Gradually, scientists began to perceive order in the seemingly random and unpredictable behaviors of subatomic particles. Discoveries unfolded to generate a new, integrated view of the universe based on relationships. For example, physicist David Bohm discovered that every particle is part of a pair, mutually and instantly influencing each other even when separated by vast distances. The world appeared as an interacting, mutually influencing system made up of subsystems ranging from galaxies, to human beings, to the atom. More importantly scientists achieved a new breakthrough in awareness regarding the creation of scientific knowledge. This is illustrated by the Heisenberg' principle: the observer and the instruments he/she uses for observation interact with the phenomenon observed and co-construct it. This concept derived from the 'hard' science of physics helps us understand how Rogers' criticism of Freud's and Skinner's visions of human nature, as well as the dangers of psychopathological labeling, actually is grounded in a paradigm that had been known to top physicists and biologists since the 1930s.

Another significant paradigm shift tackled the concept of wholeness. This is the Systems paradigm. Biologist Ludwig von Bertalanffy, author of the fundamental text, *General System Theory*, intended to furnish an integrated structure for all scientific activities. Such theory allows for an integrative framework for scientific activity; e.g., viewing the biosphere as a whole. Rogers' work, within an integrative, organismic and relational framework carries similarly profound implications.

Systems theory, as developed by Bertalanffy and later by others, is *'based on awareness of the essential interrelatedness of all phenomena—physical, biological, psychological, social and cultural'* (Capra, 1996: 265). It can be seen as a *total ecology model* wherein the human organism is best understood as a system that is part of a bigger system (e.g., one's family of origin, community, socio-economic status, profession, culture, the environment, etc.). The human organism is also made up of smaller systems (e.g., one's genetic blueprint, cardiovascular system, lymphatic system, skeletal system, immune system, personality, emotional and cognitive systems). This ecological, systemic view has relevant implications for the understanding of the health of individuals and society.

Since systems theory sees all living structures as comprised of extensive subsystems that are in constant interaction with each other, any impact on society affects the family, the individual, and vice versa. The figure below illustrates this concept.

Figure 1

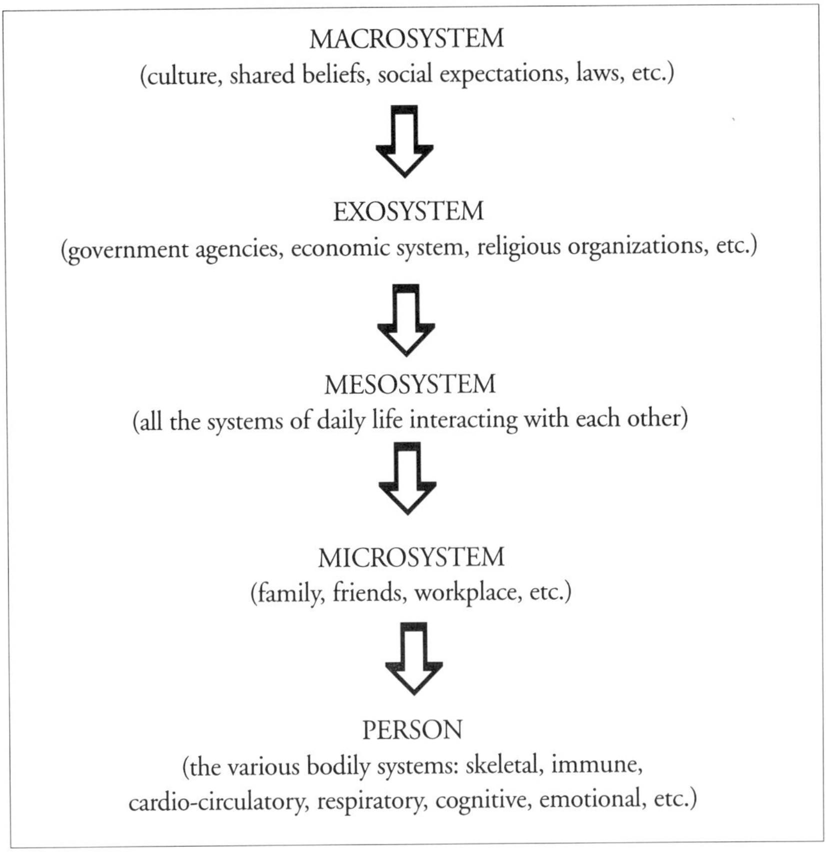

```
                            MACROSYSTEM
            (culture, shared beliefs, social expectations, laws, etc.)
                                 ⇩
                             EXOSYSTEM
        (government agencies, economic system, religious organizations, etc.)
                                 ⇩
                             MESOSYSTEM
              (all the systems of daily life interacting with each other)
                                 ⇩
                            MICROSYSTEM
                      (family, friends, workplace, etc.)
                                 ⇩
                               PERSON
                  (the various bodily systems: skeletal, immune,
            cardio-circulatory, respiratory, cognitive, emotional, etc.)
```

Adapted from Egan and Cowan, 1979

The following example illustrates the interconnectedness within a whole system:

If there is a shared cultural belief that women are inferior to men, legislation likely will reflect this and will not grant the same rights to all citizens based on gender. Women may lack even the right to elect their representatives in public elections, may not receive equal pay for equal work, and will be unlikely to receive equal treatment within society and within their own families. In such a scenario, women may even accept the cultural belief that they are inferior to men. This, in turn, will impact on their emotional and cognitive experiences, and it is likely that their potentialities will not be actualized fully. This will have far reaching consequences for women and the entire society within which they live. This leads us to consider another idea: the social construction of reality.

THE SOCIAL CONSTRUCTION OF REALITY

What is perceived as real varies from society to society and is produced, transmitted and conserved through social processes. In other words, our perception of reality is largely modeled from beliefs and a conceptual assumption that is typical of the society and culture to which we belong. What we know, what we consider true and right, the behaviors we adopt, all are influenced profoundly by the social/cultural environment in which we live. This process happens through the internalization of a 'reality' that occurs during the socialization process (by parents or other significant persons). This occurs largely without an awareness that 'The world of everyday life is not only taken for granted as reality by ordinary members of society in the subjectively meaningful conduct of their lives. It is a world originated in their thought and actions, and is maintained as real by these' (Berger and Luckmann, 1966: 19).

Our reality is largely determined by the roles that are played by the people who interact with us, by the roles that they give us, and from the ways in which we relate with ourselves, others, and society at large. The social environment influences individual behavior through the imposition or communication of societal norms and through individual adherence to and respect for the social model of control. The concept of health, for example, is a *social* construct in the sense that it is closely correlated with the dominant culture.

In every society the majority of people live their lives with experiences that have meanings that are socially shared, and where daily behavior is familiar and predictable. The social construction of reality is not perceived as socially constructed by the majority. Therefore, it is not easily criticized or modified when aspects of it are dysfunctional and not allowing for awareness of basic needs or their fulfillment. A consequence is the persistence of dysfunctional attitudes and behaviors—both in individuals and society. The influence of such unexamined beliefs and behaviors on an individual can be significant, as suggested in the following scenario:

> *When I was a child my mother (influenced by background and culture) served (as most mothers did) tasty, fat-filled food. She was worried if I looked 'skinny' and urged me to be a 'good boy' and eat more even if I was not hungry. My peers urged me to smoke and drink 'as real men do' as we saw Humphrey Bogart and all of the glamorous stars doing in the movies. I learned the social expectation of being a passive patient at the doctor's office and I was led to believe that health simply meant not being sick. All of these influences helped build my perception of 'reality'. These social experiences had real health consequences for my life, just as the accepted standard practice for better insulation that resulted in asbestos being put in my school building had real health consequences for many.*

Another example:

> *If a shared cultural belief is that gays, lesbians, and bisexuals are deviant and sick people, and their loving relationships are seen as sinful, we might see this pathologizing*

view mirrored in the diagnostic frameworks used by health professionals in that culture.[1] *Such a social construction of reality, reinforced by health processionals, easily would be considered the truth by the majority of people in that culture. Even large proportions of gay, lesbian, and bisexual citizens would adopt this belief. This would create untold suffering and lead to wasted human potentials for individuals and society. This scenario is in fact played out in many cultures in countless ways. This same process could be visualized for the impact of social constructs in discrimination towards racial or ethnic groups, women, older people or the 'mentally ill', among other groups of people.*

Carl Rogers challenged his colleagues to ask themselves if they were aware of the social construction they were creating actively with each consumer of their professional services. His work contained the implicit challenging question: As helping professionals, are we part of the solution or are we part of the problem? It was a stunning contribution during his time. His work affirmed that labeling people who were asking for help as 'patients', and framing them with psychopathological labels, would contribute to their problems, not to solutions. He recognized that such socially constructed labels automatically would put people in a passive, dependent role, and would risk the creation of self-fulfilling prophecies.

PARADIGM CHANGE IN THE HEALTH SCIENCES

As has happened in other fields, public health and medicine have been experiencing a paradigm shift over the last thirty years. The mechanistic, reductionistic medical paradigm has survived for many years. However, it is seen now as less likely to offer effective answers to emerging health problems. A new paradigm, grounded in the systemic approach, has emerged. This new framework takes every aspect of life into consideration, from individual awareness and lifestyles to the society and natural environment in which people live. This new vision of health, understood as a system composed of subsystems, hierarchically inclusive and functionally interdependent, allows us to better understand and impact health at every level: personal, familial, work, community and beyond. This new frame of reference is defined as a biopsychosocial model. It enables the integration of all the interdependent relationships that determine health: biological, psychological and social. Its dynamic field of action is called Health Promotion, and it is understood as a process of empowering individuals, groups, communities and institutions for the purpose of fostering maximal health.

The essential premise of this new paradigm is the concept that health and illness are determined by numerous interrelated biological, psychological and social factors. It is therefore necessary to design and take actions that help people to assume a proactive role in the protection and promotion of their health and well-being. Mental health is an

---

1. The *Diagnostic and Statistical Manual of Mental Disorders*, created and used widely by psychiatrists and psychologists in the Western world, listed homosexuality as a diagnosable pathology, a mental 'illness,' as late as 1973 (Cooper, 2004).

important variable in this new paradigm. As such, professionals who work in the health sector need to acquire a new view of their professions—one that encompasses seeing themselves as *agents for social change*. It necessitates a view of themselves as people who assist individuals, communities and institutions in weaning themselves from passivity and dependency; in other words, as people who become protagonists in the promotion of health and well-being.

The biopsychosocial model recognizes that health is socially constructed within the context of human behavior and relationships.

> Health is created and lived by people within the settings of their everyday life: where they learn, work, play and love. Health is created by caring for oneself, and others, by being able to take decisions and have control over one's life circumstances and by ensuring that the society one lives in creates conditions that allow the attainment of health by all its members.
>
> Caring, holism and ecology are essential issues in developing strategies for health promotion. Therefore, those involved should take as a guiding principle that, in each phase of planning, implementation and evaluation of health promotion activities, women and men should become equal partners. (WHO, 1986: 3–4)

This view of health and its determinants is a radical departure from the mechanistic biomedical approach. While this new approach certainly will continue to include medical doctors treating people with illnesses, it also will require that health professionals go beyond the focus on illness or the biomedical model. Health professionals must foster a significant change in the way people understand how health is created and promoted. They also must help people and their institutions become aware of some key concepts:

- Health is created by behaviors and actions that to a large extent are determined by human choices.
- These choices are important to individuals' lives, the lives of their loved ones, and to their communities.
- Decisions and actions that affect the environment have important consequences for health.
- The world of work must recognize that virtually every action taken will promote or damage health.
- Government leaders must support programs and regulations that benefit human health.
- Health and well-being must be a priority for society.

To help others become aware of these concepts, health professionals must adjust their perspectives and relinquish much of their expert status over those whom they serve. Health professionals must become practitioners of learning and empowerment. For the health promoter in this new paradigm, the focus on health includes individuals, the health system, the workplace, governmental agencies, communities and society in general.

THE BIOMEDICAL PARADIGM AND THE COSTS OF A MECHANISTIC, REDUCTIONISTIC APPROACH

The biomedical paradigm imposes limitations that are too costly to ignore. It is a mechanistic, reductionistic model that overlooks too many opportunities and entails too many dangers to remain acceptable. A systemic approach to health recognizes that human life is embedded in a constellation of biopsychosocial systems that work as a whole to impact the health of individuals, and helps us move beyond the costly limitations of the biomedical model.

After World War II, the development of pesticides and chemical fertilizers was seen as a scientific breakthrough for feeding humanity and building a better and more prosperous world. The unlimited use of these chemicals fit the prevailing expectation of scientific progress for the betterment of society. Unfortunately, this mechanistic, reductionistic view did not take into account the complex interrelationships of the world in which we live. The massive use of pesticides and chemical fertilizers initially expanded the production of food. However, success encouraged one-crop cultivation that soon impoverished the soil, necessitating an ever greater use of chemicals. This created a downward spiral of increasing chemical usage and decreasing soil vitality. Moreover, after boosting crop production and killing unwanted pests and weeds, it became apparent that the pesticides had a long period of continued action on the environment. They continued to affect the cohesiveness of the soil's organic matter, creating topsoil run-off and pollution of drinking water. This negatively impacted the whole food chain. For example, traces of DDT have been found in human breast milk and in the livers of penguins in the Antarctic, sites far removed from their original targets. The end result is the immeasurable, unanticipated degradation of the environment, as well as ongoing threats to human health and the whole food chain. It is now evident that our simplistic approach to the use of chemicals for the improvement of food production was tragically flawed. Our eyes are opening now to the costs of ignoring the complex web of relationships involved in growing our food.

Heart bypass surgery is another example of well-intentioned myopia generated by the biomedical model. 'Patients' often see this surgery as a miracle cure, a new lease on life. However, this procedure does nothing to improve the factors that create the problem—patients' arteries will eventually re-occlude if bypass surgery remains the only intervention. An ecological or systemic approach would promote awareness of interconnectedness and encourage changes in attitudes and lifestyle; e.g., a diet low in saturated fat and cholesterol, abstinence from tobacco use, undertaking appropriate exercise, and improving stress management. Such an approach has been shown to reverse the build-up of arterial plaque without surgical intervention (Pelletier, 1994). It allows the patient/client to understand and cope more effectively with his health problems and produce better long-term results (Ornish, 1990).

A PARADIGM SHIFT IN PSYCHOTHERAPY

> Can we build a *psychological* science or a *behavioral* science which grows out of the problems encountered in the study of the whole man in his subjective and objective being? or must we feel that our science can only be a copy of Newtonian science—a model already outdated in its own field? (Rogers, 1968: 69)

When Rogers started to propose a new holistic/systemic approach to psychotherapy, the health fields were dominated already by the 'biomedical model,' the traditional approach of Western medicine for 150 years. The biomedical model is a disease-based paradigm, founded upon a mechanistic, reductionistic view of biological systems. Illness is seen as arising from biological changes beyond individual control, either from outside the body, or as internal, involuntary physical changes caused by factors such as chemical imbalances, bacteria, viruses, or genetic predisposition. Treatments in this model involve medication, surgery, chemotherapy, vaccination and other interventions aimed at changing the physical state of the body. The mind and body are viewed as functioning independently from each other, with the mind incapable of influencing physical matters. Responsibility for treatment is seen as lying with the medical profession. The field of mental health was characterized by a mechanistic psychiatric model based on diagnosis and cure, solidly within the biomedical paradigm.

Even though there is still some resistance, our present day paradigm is the 'biopsychosocial model'. This model is a systemic paradigm recognizing that health is determined by a multiplicity of biological, psychological and social factors, all of which mutually interact. Health is promoted by empowering individuals as responsible for and capable of taking steps that support their own health. The mind and body are viewed as one, each strongly influencing the other. Illness is seen as the result of a combination of biological, psychological, social, lifestyle and environmental factors, over many of which each person has significant control. Individuals are seen as largely responsible (being *able to respond*) for their own health, with health professionals serving them as a valuable resource in their ability to respond (in their 'response-ability'). Treatment is given to the whole person, not just the physical symptoms associated with an illness. Treatment is provided with strategies of empowerment, and may include facilitation of awareness, attitudes, behavior and lifestyle changes, coping strategies, social and emotional support, and better compliance with medical recommendations.

Carl Rogers' work was revolutionary, moving the focus from illness to health and well-being. Rogers' formulation of an approach to psychotherapy and human relations is within a holistic-systemic paradigm. His view of the human being is as a unified organism, with somatic and psychic aspects. The mind-body separation typical of reductionistic paradigms, as well the notion of intrapsychic problems found in Freud, were gone. For Rogers, human nature is trustworthy, and the origin of individual problems is environmental (extrapsychic).

Rogers' actualizing tendency axiom was a natural articulation of his holistic viewpoint. Self-understanding, self-regulation, agency and free will flow from this model. Rogers' notion that the quality of the relationship was the principal variable promoting change is also within this holistic framework. Healthy change is a process in which a person becomes free by removing the obstacles to the development of her/his potentialities so that normal growth and development can proceed and independence and self-direction is achieved.

THE POLITICS OF PSYCHOTHERAPY

Rogers was aware that every organism is a complex system continuously interacting with other systems and affecting and being affected by them. He recognized that human beings may formulate self-fulfilling prophecies, and are highly susceptible to the influence of others in this regard. This made him wary of the way he was taught in the biomedical model to manage his relationships with patients. Clinical experience taught him that there was a need for a more democratic, more optimistic, respectful, authentic and effective approach.

The epistemology of Carl Rogers is grounded in trust of human nature. He viewed congruence as an essential source of knowledge, and emphasized the ultimate reliability of a congruent human organism's self-experience:

> not as a scientist to an object of study, but as a person to a person. He feels this client to be a person of self-worth; of value no matter what his condition, his behavior or his feelings. He respects him for what he is, and accepts him as he is, with his potentialities. (Rogers, 1965: 22)

Rogers tells us that organisms know what is good for them. Since self-regulation is adaptive for every living organism, why would it not be so for human beings?

Every approach to health is based on a view of human nature. If we compare an anatomic table based on allopathic medicine with one based on traditional Chinese medicine, the different underlying views of human nature are clear. Likewise, every approach in the helping professions is based on a specific vision of human nature, which in turn is based on values. Those values determine the politics of the helping relationship and influence outcomes. To be trained generally in the biomedical reductionistic model, or to be trained specifically as a psychiatrist, Freudian analyst, behaviorist or person-centered psychotherapist, is to enter into and belong to a construed world of values, to take on different roles, and to create clinical settings that actively promote different narratives. The definitions of disease, illness and cure, and the roles of therapist and consumer of the service provided are all influenced by differences in therapeutic approach. Different approaches are grounded in different worldviews, and most importantly, in different values and different politics. Any view of human nature assumes a set of values. That views of psychopathology and theories of therapy descend automatically from views of human nature is still not necessarily accepted by everybody, even among the different 'tribes' of person-centered practitioners and researchers. Perhaps this is one of the reasons it is difficult to find agreement among ourselves when assessing innovations in the client-centered and person-centered approaches.

One of the invited addresses at the 2006 World Conference for Person-Centered and Experiential Psychotherapies and Counseling focused on the promotion of health. The term patient was used consistently—the term client was not used once. For some colleagues this biomedical model terminology apparently is not at odds with the paradigm Rogers created. However, for me, this is entirely incongruous with the basic premises of client-centered psychotherapy and the person-centered approach.

Research shows us that psychotherapists from any orientation able to create a good working alliance with their clients have a good chance of being effective facilitators of change. This is not surprising, since different cultures are all effective in creating consensus realities. Realities are socially construed, whether in a culture or in a therapy relationship. However, different cultures differentially impact and 'mold' people's roles, differentially define what is good or bad, and differentially favor the introjection of different values and constructs. Different cultures show different kinds of respect or dignity, offering or negating equal opportunities for some of their members. For example, socially, women are defined very differently in different cultures, with different consequences for the women born and raised within these different constructions of cultural reality. In psychotherapy, whether theoreticians or practitioners are aware of it, the same process of social construction of reality is at work. It is an entirely different thing to assign the role of 'patient' and to label a service offered as a psychotherapeutic treatment from facilitating clients in their process of change. With all that we know presently, can we really believe that these two approaches or constructions of therapeutic reality will have identical impacts? Perhaps we should be asking such questions as whether psychotherapy is nowadays the best socially constructed concept for reaching our aims, or whether a more appropriate one can be found.

Profound differences and results are created by different narratives of symptom reduction, health promotion and self-realization. As such, the significant variables to be measured should not be limited only to symptom reduction and the usage of health care services. Worldviews rooted in different values, role models and ways of relating create vast differences in terms of impact on individuals. In all democratic societies there is continued negotiation around such issues. The person-centered community, along with other psychotherapeutic orientations, cannot afford to be unaware in this respect. Lack of attention to the issues of values and relational politics in psychotherapy settings before Rogers' revolution was a reflection of the level of awareness of the time. When the results of therapist behaviors become apparent, ethical codes and psychotherapy practice must take notice. Nowadays any exploration of psychotherapists' ethical responsibilities cannot ignore the politics of psychotherapy. Rogers' refusal to construct the role of 'patient' for his clients offered all professionals a profound learning: how we see and how we relate to clients influences them and also influences us. This is the premise of psychotherapy: some relationships can be debilitating, and other relationships can be healing and health-promoting. In this regard, Rogers offered this profound political statement:

> I object to the process of depersonalization and dehumanization of the individual which I see in our culture. I regret that the behavioral sciences seem to me promoting and reinforcing this trend. (1968: 59)

BEING A PATIENT MAY BE DANGEROUS TO YOUR HEALTH

In addition to the grim evidence that the health care system in developed nations is both more expensive and less effective than desirable, there is a further, more subtle cost in our way of relating to health care in the industrialized world: the hidden dangers of being a patient. Modern medical practice is structured with the doctor at the top of the ladder, other health care professionals below this, and the patient on the bottom rung. A consequence of this way of shaping reality is the disempowerment of the consumer of health services. This consumer is designated as the patient. There may be no simpler way to shed light on this disempowerment than to review synonyms of the word *patient*: submissive, calm, susceptible, long-suffering, invalid. Indeed, there is an essential invalidation of the person that occurs as a byproduct of our health care practices, including our ways of relating to 'patients' that discount their concerns, observations, needs, human dignity, and potential for regaining health.

The invalidation of patients is not just a matter of semantic cleverness. The helpless, passive role expected of patients is, in fact, bad for their health. Social critic Ivan Illich, writing as far back as 1976, saw modern technological medicine as overextending itself and becoming 'medical imperialism,' insisting that anything remotely connected with health belonged under the supervision or control of the medical profession. According to Illich (1976: 3), the disabling impact of professional control has already 'reached the proportions of an epidemic.' However, Illich went even further, seeing the way the medical establishment relates to people as a major threat to health itself.

People have learned to be patient, passive recipients of whatever health-affecting circumstances are meted out to them by the medical system and life in general—whether they be life-enhancing or life-damaging. The by-product of modern medical practice is that the locus of control for health has been handed over to the medical establishment. Most people do not view themselves as the person primarily responsible for their own health. Consciously or unconsciously, they have externalized that responsibility and assigned it to medical professionals, on whom they rely to cure them when they are ill. Typically, people go about their lives until illness arrives, following this each time by another trip to the medical center looking externally for another cure. Whether healthy or ill, most people in industrialized countries do not experience being in charge of their own health. They have fallen into a pattern of 'learned helplessness' in regard to their health and well-being.

> People have given their power over to the health care establishment—oftentimes without realizing it. To further compound the damage, people commonly commit an act of self-denial by thinking they do not have the power to create change. (Zucconi and Howell, 2003: 32–3)

A COMPASS FOR THE PERSON-CENTERED PSYCHOTHERAPIST

> ... at the basis of anything that a scientist undertakes is, first of all, an ethical and moral value judgment that he makes. (Rogers, in Rogers and Coulson, 1968: 200)

Relating to persons as patients or as clients brings about very different outcomes. According to the Heisenberg principle in physics, the observer and the instruments he uses for observation interact with the phenomenon observed and co-construct it. Understanding this concept allows us to appreciate the context and significance of Rogers' refusal to label people as 'patients,' and to avoid subjecting clients to a series of psychological 'tests', as this would have clear consequences. Many authors have emphasized that observing a person through psycho-pathological labels can produce harmful iatrogenic outcomes (Rogers, 1961; Rogers, et al., 1967; Kirk and Kutchins, 1992; McNamee and Gergen, 1992; Kutchins and Kirk, 1997; Neimeyer and Raskin, 2000; Wakefield, 1992a, 1992b).

Understanding how reality is constructed socially (Berger and Luckmann, 1966) enables us to pay attention to the messages and meta-messages we communicate to our clients. Grasping the relevance of the *social construction of reality* offers the practitioner a compass—it offers the practitioner a deep understanding of the difference between assuming the role of expert and assuming the role of a promoter of empowerment. Many professional failures begin with a lack of awareness of the politics of psychotherapy and a lack of awareness of the incongruent application of one's own paradigm. The politics of psychotherapy and the paradigm shift brought about by Carl Rogers necessitate an awareness of whether we are respecting our clients and their rights and empowering them, or unintentionally impeding personal and social change.

REFERENCES

Berger PL & Luckmann T (1966) *The Social Construction of Reality: A treatise in the sociology of knowledge.* New York: Anchor Books, Doubleday & Company, Inc.

Bertalanffy L von (1968) *General System Theory: Foundations, development, applications.* New York: George Braziller.

Bertalanffy L von (1975) *Perspectives on General System Theory: Scientific-Philosophical Studies.* New York: George Braziller.

Brendel DH (2003) Reductionism, eclecticism, and pragmatism in psychiatry: The dialectic of clinical explanation. *J Med Philos, 28*, 563–80.

Capra F (1996) *The Web of Life.* New York: Anchor Books/Doubleday.

Cooper R (2004) What is wrong with the DSM? *Hist Psychiatry, 15*, 5–25.

Egan G & Cowan M (1979) *People in Systems.* Monterey, CA: Brookes-Cole.

Elliott R & Zucconi A (2006) Doing research on the effectiveness of psychotherapy and psychotherapy training: A person-centered/experiential perspective. *Person-Centered and*

Experiential Psychotherapies, 5 (2), 82–100.
Farson R (1974) Carl Rogers, Quiet Revolutionary. *Education, 95* (2), 197–203.
Illich I (1976) *Medical Nemesis: The expropriation of health.* New York: Pantheon Books.
Kirk SA & Kutchins H (1992) *The Selling of DSM: The rhetoric of science in psychiatry.* New York: de Gruyter.
Krupnick JL et al. (1996) The role of therapeutic alliance in psychotherapy and pharmacotherapy outcome: Findings in the National Institute of Mental Health Treatment of Depression Collaborative Research Program. *J Consult Clin Psychol 64,* 532–9.
Kuhn TS (1962) *The Structure of Scientific Revolutions.* Chicago: University of Chicago Press.
Kutchins H & Kirk SA (1997) *Making us crazy. DSM: The psychiatric bible and the creation of mental disorder.* New York: Free Press.
McNamee S & Gergen KJ (1992) *Therapy as Social Construction.* London: Sage Publications.
Neimeyer RA & Raskin JD (2000) *Constructions of Disorder: Meaning-making frameworks for psychotherapy.* Washington, DC: American Psychological Association.
Norcross J (Ed) (2002) *Psychotherapy Relationships that Work.* New York: Oxford University Press.
Ornish D (1990) *Dr Dean Ornish's Program for Reversing Heart Disease.* New York: Random House.
Pelletier KR (1994) *Sound Mind, Sound Body: A new model for lifelong health.* New York: Simon & Schuster.
Psychotherapy Networker (2007) The Top 10: The most influential therapists of the past quarter-century. Washington, DC, March/April.
Rogers CR (1959) A theory of therapy, personality and interpersonal relationships, as developed in the client-centered framework. In S Koch (Ed) *Psychology: A study of science. Vol. 3: Formulations of the person and the social context.* New York: McGraw-Hill, pp. 184–256.
Rogers CR (1961) *On Becoming a Person.* Boston: Houghton Mifflin.
Rogers CR (1965) A humanistic conception of man. In RE Farson (Ed) *Science and Human Affairs.* Palo Alto, CA: Science and Behavior Books Inc, pp. 18–31.
Rogers, CR (1968) Some thoughts regarding the current presuppositions of the behavioral sciences. In CR Rogers & WR Coulson (Eds) *Man and the Science of Man.* Columbus OH: Charles E Merrill, pp. 55–72.
Rogers CR (1977) *Carl Rogers on Personal Power.* New York: Delacorte Press.
Rogers CR & Coulson WR (Eds) (1968) *Man and the Science of Man.* Columbus, OH: Charles E Merrill.
Rogers CR, Gendlin ET, Kiesler DJ & Truax CB (Eds) (1967) *The Therapeutic Relationship and Its Impact. A study of psychotherapy with schizophrenics.* Madison, WI: University of Wisconsin Press.
Rogers CR & Raskin N (1989) Person-centered therapy. In R Corsini & D Wedding (Eds) *Current Psychotherapies.* Itasca, IL: Peacock, pp. 155–94.
Rogers DE (1974) The Doctor himself must become the treatment. *Alpha Omega Honor Medical Society, 3* (4), 124–9.
Shorter E & Tyrer P (2003) Separation of anxiety and depressive disorders: blind alley in psychopharmacology and classification of disease. *BMJ, 327,* 158–60.
Wakefield JC (1992a) The concept of mental disorder: On the boundary between biological facts and social values. *American Psychologist, 47* (3), 373–88.
Wakefield JC (1992b) Diagnosing *DSM-IV-Part I: DSM-IV* and the concept of disorder. *Behaviour, Research and Therapy, 35* (7), 633–49.
WHO (1986) *Ottawa Charter for Health Promotion*: An International Conference on Health

Promotion, Ottawa, Canada. Geneva, CH: World Health Organization.

Zucconi A & Howel P (2003) *La Promozione della Salute: Un approccio globale per il benessere della persona e della società.* Bari, Italy: La Meridiana Editore.

CHAPTER 10

NON-DUALISM AND NON-DIRECTIVITY: A PERSON-CENTERED CONCEPT OF HEALTH AND THE FULLY FUNCTIONING PERSON

CAROL WOLTER-GUSTAFSON

LIZARD BRAINS, LANGUAGE, AND DESCARTES

The binary brain of the lizard suits its context. Lizard survival depends upon accurate answers to simple questions: Is this food, or not food? Is there danger, or no danger? As humans, we share this ancient, primitive, binary brain structure with lizards—yet the limited capacity of the binary brain does not, by itself, suit any human in the context of twenty-first century life. Questions of survival remain simple, but life-promoting strategies, in the sense of skillful or efficacious actions, require processing an exponential explosion of interdependent variables, themselves contingent upon shifting interpretations of ever-changing events.

The limitations of simple binary reasoning could never provide an adequately elaborated level of reasoning in the context of complex social, political, economic, and physical realities. Our need for higher-order reasoning increases proportionally to the degree of complexity we face. Antonio Damasio, author and world-renowned neurologist, describes the brain as a 'supersystem of systems' (Damasio, 1994: 87). Candace Pert, former Chief of Brain Biochemistry at the National Institute of Mental Health, helped create the field of psychoneuroimmunology to establish an understanding of the previously unimaginable interconnectivity of the brain, body, emotion, and mind (Pert, 1997).

Our understanding of the brain and the mind–body connection has revolutionized the sciences. Though the field of psychology is often change resistant, the philosophically dualistic model of reality must be recognized as obsolete. A radical theoretical upgrade is necessary and will represent more accurately the reality of our brain functioning and, with the help of person-centered theory, lead to the creation of an organismic conception of health.

This reconfiguration has been underway for more than a half-century throughout a wide spectrum of academic disciplines. Evelyn Fox Keller, mathematical biophysicist and author of *Reflections on Gender and Science* (1985) suggests that the end of dualistic attributions of female nature and male mind comes through renaming both nature *and* mind. Scientists like Pert, Austin, Damasio and countless others are furthering that renaming. Elizabeth Deeds Ermarth (1989) summarizes the redefinition of the epistemological critique underway. She writes:

[It is] a critique of Western discourse itself: its obsession with power, its ethic of winning, its quantifiable and objective knowledge and its association of knowledge with power, its preference of the symbolic and thetic function of language over the semiotic and ludic, its reliance on rationalist and categorical means of identification and inclusion, its belief in a linear and progressive history, its individual subject, and most powerfully its common media of exchange (time, space, money) which make possible certain ideas of political and social order (pp. 39-40)

The disciplines of psychoanalysis and clinical psychology, the latter in its most recent expression as cognitive behavioral theory, have been largely absent in this academic revolution. Theoreticians in these areas have shown little willingness to question their respective epistemological bases. It is anachronistic and troublesome that they have tied their authority to a scientific model that mainstream scientists, from research centers around the world, no longer hold.

DESCARTES AND THE WESTERN INTELLECTUAL TRADITION

How do we account for the persistence and the prevalence of binary-based intellectual theories in the Western intellectual tradition? Most scholars attribute dualism's ascendance and prominence in Western philosophy to René Descartes, the mathematician known as the founder of modern philosophy. Descartes reasoned that human knowledge of all the sciences and all eternal truths could be attained by following a reasoned method. That method was set down in his *Rules for the Direction of the Mind* in which complex operations were broken down into smaller, more simple bits to form an orderly pattern.

Genevieve Lloyd (1993) writes,
To see what is really distinctive and important about Descartes' method we must see it in the context of the metaphysical doctrine for which he is most notorious—the radical separateness of mind and body ... (p. 41)

His method would guide all humans who followed it faithfully, to pursue pure scientific investigation. 'He saw the encroachments of non-intellectual passion, sense or imagination ... as intrusions from the body' (Lloyd, 1993: 46). In this quest for pure reason we must transcend our corporality. As René Descartes put it in *his Discourse on Method* (1970/c. 1637),

Je pense, donc je suis. [*Later translated in Latin as: Cogito ergo sum; and in English as: I think, therefore I am.*]

Still, you and I are exploring forces that energize our bodily, passionate, intellectual, emotional selves, and support our fully functioning selves. We do so amidst the multiple forces attempting to shape our lives, starting with the The Western Intellectual Tradition and then a Client-Centered Model of Health.

The mainstream Western Intellectual Tradition (TWIT)[1] is founded upon dualistic descriptions of reality that set up, and insist upon, divisions between: mind–body, spirit–body, male–female, cause–effect, universal–particular, good–evil, black–white, gay–straight, health–disease, phenomena–noumena and so forth. What is essential to note here is that one side of the dualistic description is deemed more valuable than the other. Equally essential to understand is that this inequality of status is, for the most part, denied, and the ontological equality of both sides declared. Despite Descartes' egalitarian intentions, he could not overcome the prevailing assumptions that the mind was superior to the body. Genevieve Lloyd, Philosophy Professor at the University of New South Wales in Sydney, explains:

> In place of the older divisions within the soul he introduced a division between the soul—now identified again with the mind—and body; the non-rational was no longer part of the soul, but pertained entirely to the body. (1993: 45)

As a result, these divisions characterized by inequality have become codified throughout the history of philosophy, theology, and law developed in the West, and permeate both our language and social conventions. Our thought and language developed to espouse human equality while *simultaneously* maintaining the conventions that the prevailing culture deemed to be 'inherent' inequalities.

One example from political theory concerns the United States Declaration of Independence. Thomas Jefferson wrote, 'All men are created equal' and have 'inalienable rights.' Yet, 'all men' was never meant to include 'Negroes' who were considered property. Neither was it meant to include women, who, through marriage law, became property of their husbands. In both cases, acts of civil disobedience were required to throw off the inferior status conferred upon them by the dominant group.

Following the tradition of theological exegesis, Western philosophers interpreted authoritative texts and Scripture to accept both male–female equality 'in the sight of God' and in the cultural norms that gave to men rights and privileges over women. These arrangements were said to be natural, and ordained by God in Jewish and Christian patriarchal systems. For example, in the New Testament we find the following: 'Wives, submit to your husbands' (St. Paul, in Ephesians 5: 23); and 'A woman should learn in quietness and full submission. I do not permit a woman to teach or to have authority over a man; she must be silent' (from Timothy 2: 11–14). Also, in daily blessings of Orthodox and Conservative Jews, the men recite the prayer '*Baruch Atah Adonai, Eloheinu Melech ha-olam, shelo asani ishah*' (Blessed are You, O Lord our God, Ruler of the Universe, Who did not make me a woman).

The role of language in the reification of dualistic intellectual habits we have inherited is beyond the scope of this chapter's purposes. Yet, as Eugene Gendlin (1997: 5) points out, 'The traditional concepts inhere in all the words, and cannot be removed. Even when we have criticized and rejected them, they are still implicit in our words.' For

---

1. Robert Ornstein's abbreviation of The Western Intellectual Tradition as TWIT is meant to convey its limited representation of the world's knowledge base. In the English language a 'twit' means a silly or foolish person (Ornstein, 1986).

example, most of us concerned with congruent behavior recognize that it is one thing to use inclusive language, and quite another to shift all of our habitual associations with experiencing 'the other' so that we *are in our very being* inclusive. Gendlin's original contribution to this issue requires serious consideration and study.

Dualistic tendencies are literally 'in-corporated,' from the Latin, (pl. corpora, circa 1390, lit. 'body') in our lizard brains and then further embedded in scholasticisms' legacy in Western narratives. I contend that the judgments embedded in our inherited dualistic language that grants one side of the dualism superiority and the other inferiority persist, despite claims that those same conditions of worth do not exist, or conversely, are natural. This disparity in the valuing process creates strong conditions of worth.

Mainstream American psychology remains founded upon the dualistic biases that regularly exclude data from non-dominant sources and replicate the traditional TWIT. The positivist epistemological base on which it rests remains unchanged by, and dismissive of the seminal critiques of the twentieth century that are altering and expanding academic discourse. Regardless of a psychology's stated positive and progressive goals or its theories of health, happiness, or wholeness, if the processes proceed from a positivist epistemology, it represents no change at all. The person-centered model of health represents a change that is aligned with both current neurobiological science and the change progressing in other academic disciplines.

CONSTRUCTING THE CONCEPT OF HEALTH IN DUALISTIC AND NON-DUALISTIC PARADIGMS

The construct of health in the dualistic paradigm is familiar. We tend not to blink when the response to, 'How are you?' is, 'I am fine, but I have a killer headache.' We seldom consider the level of dissociation we tolerate. Of course, we *know* what this type of response means. But what we also seem to know *tacitly* is that a killer headache is an 'it'—some 'thing' that we 'have'—as opposed to some way that we *are* achingness in our unitary '*body-beingness*.'[2]

In our culturally normative way of speaking, we divide health from disease, in effect creating separate entities. This linguistic separation tends to obscure our view of the person as a complex and unitary organism interacting with a complex multi-causal, multi-layered environment, a view eloquently articulated in client-centered theory.

Person-centered theorists in concert with other humanistic psychologists have long noted that labeling a person carries no restoration of wellness. A person living with the 'negative' label can feel further isolated, more disintegrated, less likely to move toward any healing source. We are less likely to be empathic to the information arising from such an alien intrusion to our life, called a disease, which we see as separate from our

---

2. I have settled on the term 'body-beingness' to convey the dynamic organismic integrity that *is* a human being prior to all divisive biologically, theologically, philosophically, and culturally inscribed categories; and who is, nonetheless, inextricably interconnected with all manner of influence and conditions of worth. This is consistent with Eugene Gendlin's call for a new way of languaging our experience.

'self.' We are less likely to offer unconditional attention to the 'deficient' body or part of the body that is 'causing us trouble' or 'acting up.' And we are less likely to make contact and communicate with whatever 'the body' is 'doing to us.'

The complex, interactive elements that constitute *body-being* are more likely to be ignored. Negative judgments toward those who are labeled diseased may have served an evolutionary purpose in the survival of the fittest. But what actualizing purpose is served by carrying those conditions into our post-industrial, information age? What purpose is served by negatively judging persons with cancer who have been sold houses built on top of toxic waste sites? In client-centered terms, we tend to take on, and frequently are *helped* to take on, conditions of worth, for our failure to be 'good' and 'healthy.'

Neurologist and author Antonio Damasio writes, 'The brain and the body are indissociably integrated by mutually targeted biochemical neural activities' (1994: 87). The notion of health as opposite to and separate from disease repeats the illusion of separation between mind and body that has been fostered by the Western Intellectual Tradition. Although common sense dictates that we would rather be well than ill, if we do *fall* ill, it is as if we 'fall from grace.'

A number of contemporary social forces stoke the fires of judgment, and help create negative self-regard among those who have 'fallen.' First, the pioneering work of the Framingham Heart Study introduced the popular understanding of 'risk factors' influencing the onset of particularly deadly diseases, such as heart attacks, strokes, and some cancers. One positive outcome has been to raise public awareness of the role each of us plays in maintaining our own health. An unintended outcome has been the tendency of some to exaggerate of the amount of control we have over their own health. The impact of social constructionists, with emphasis placed on active creation rather than passive givenness as explanatory schemas, is another potent social force. It too has been used to popularize the idea that we create reality. Finally, there has been a steady mainstreaming of Eastern and Western spirituality, in the past half-century, that emphasizes making a right relationship with the Divine in order to create health. If you are unhealthy, you have done something wrong. All three of these social forces have, at times, conspired to blame the victim (Ryan, 1976; LeShan, 1994; Levine, 1987). In essence, all three assert that we create our own reality. This is an ontological premise highly worthy of the centuries of theological and philosophical discourse that consider variations on this theme. However, it is my contention that pronouncements about Ultimate Reality, or the lack thereof, at minimum, warrant a certain humility.

Unfortunately, humility is frequently missing when the frame of reference of the psychologist, doctor or healer takes on the expert role. Their interventions 'for the good of the patient' are externally proscribed. One person's story is illustrative of this approach to healing. Dr. Larry Lachman (Lachman and Masten, 2003) psychologist, had just learned he had prostate cancer. As part of his approach to the diagnosis, he sought out a Therapeutic Touch and Polarity practitioner. He describes his initial phone encounter, and what transpired made him furious. He writes: 'This young woman had the audacity to say to me, "So, Larry, why did you need to create this illness?" "What purpose is your tumor serving you?" and, "What feelings or unfinished business do you have that caused your cancer?'" He describes feeling kicked in the gut, as well as hurt, devastated and 'really angry.' He then asked, 'Are you telling me that it's my fault for getting cancer?' She, in not so many words, said, "Yes." ... At that moment, I "lost it!" ... and yelled, "How the hell do you expect any cancer patient, who is already feeling depressed and anxious, to 'heal,' and get their immune system boosted up if you blame them for their cancer?'" His experience would have been radically different had he consulted a client-centered practitioner who offers unconditional positive regard, empathy and authenticity and trusts the client to discover her or his own direction. Lawrence LeShan, psychologist, author and pioneer in the interconnectedness of mind and body, rejects the simplistic and destructive practice of assigning blaming to the person who is sick.[3]

> Anyone who even hints that the person with cancer is responsible for getting it and/or for not getting better is not only the rankest amateur and should be completely ignored, but is setting in motion confusion, anxiety, and anger at the self. (LeShan, 2007)

Growth is often cast in a positive light, as a 'good.' But growth for its own sake is the ideology of a cancer cell. As Maslow noted, growth is *one* element in human process, while safety, not risking more than can be tolerated, is also required so that an organism is not overwhelmed. It is the wisdom of the organism that Carl Rogers honors when he writes that the organism (that is, each of us) allows only what it/we perceive can be symbolized to awareness.

Each person is a unique being, whose biology, history, and relational situatedness will never be repeated. Our particular vantage point puts each of us in the best position to understand our own life. What Rogers postulated, researched, and published is that in the presence of a rich facilitative milieu, a person is free to make use of all the data available. It is in this definable climate that a person is empowered to make positive, self-directed constructive change. The organismic integrity of the person embedded in client-centered theory is fundamentally non-dualistic and shares some elements with Eastern traditions. One such element is a deep trust in the powerful capacity within the person for self-healing the person.

Inherent in Eastern thought is a commitment to restoring balance to the entire organism, rather than directing attention to one part of the organism, as if it were separate. According to Sukie Colgrave in *The Spirit of the Valley* (1979), there are paradigms from the East that predate hierarchical influences and have retained their inclusive, non-judgmental attitude. Buddhist author Steven Levine describes healing as actively cultivating wholeness, regardless of whether or not a person is cured from disease. While this perspective may not be considered mainstream, it is viable among increasing numbers of people who have turned from dualistic mind patterns and towards an uncharted 'third' way. Social researchers Ray and Anderson (2000) call this growing population of seekers, 'cultural creatives.'

---

3. See LeShan (1994), whose life-work on the creation of health has been consistently both non-dualistic and innovative.

In the United States, a record number of healthcare consumers are stepping outside the dualistic medical model and turning to more personal and empathic relationships with alternative practitioners. For example, with increasing frequency, a person seeking relief from a killer headache may choose to consult with an acupuncturist. Nearly one half of the Americans surveyed by *Consumer Reports* has 'some form of alternative treatment' to the Western model of healthcare provision (Consumer Reports, August 2005; 70: 39).

It is to our detriment in the West that we speak and think in terms of having a disease, an *it*, rather than being in a complex interactive disease process that is fluid and requires systemic attention, connection and communication. When a person is bound by limiting conditions of worth, he or she is more likely to feel isolated. With more isolation and depression, we are less likely to engage in movement. With less movement, messages of decay are sent to cells. Dr. Henry Lodge studies cellular and evolutionary biology, and is clinical faculty at Columbia University's Medical School. He writes,

> The hard reality of our biology is that we are built to move. Exercise is the master signaling system that tells our cells to grow instead of fade ... One of the most fascinating revelations of the last decade is that emotions change our cells through the same molecular pathways as exercise. Anger, stress and loneliness are signals for 'starvation' and chronic danger. (Lodge, 2007)

Thus, judgments and the societal pressures creating conditions of worth bring organismic, system-wide neurological messages to 'shut down': Seeman contends that the entire *DSM-IV* (*Diagnostic and Statistical Manual of Mental Disorders*) could be reduced to two primary sources, either failures of connection or failures of communication, both of which are common occurrences in a person experiencing conditions of worth.

> There are myriad ways of describing dysfunction, as volumes of abnormal psychology indicate. Yet the singular theme that characterizes the many modes of dysfunction refers to impeded access to one's own experiential data; that is, dysfunction in connectedness and communication is a major hallmark of dysfunction and psychopathology. (Seeman, 2001: 628)[4]

Organismic health results from an accurate flow of communication, taking information from the whole system into account. In contrast, hostile and inhospitable conditions inhibit full functioning. Seeman speaks from the integrated, organismic conception of health that he helped create with Rogers and colleagues almost 50 years ago. Inadequate or corrupted information, what Seeman calls 'blocked, impeded, and disturbed communication,' results in and increases the likelihood of dysfunction in the person.

---

4. In an earlier draft of Seeman's paper, sent to me in 1999, 'volumes of abnormal psychology' was followed by 'and listings in *DSM-IV*.' In personal communication Seeman was more blunt, saying (paraphrased), 'Carol, when you think about it, all of the dysfunction in the *DSM-IV* can be attributed to a breakdown in one of two processes, either a breakdown in connection or in communication, either at the molecular, intrapsychic or interpersonal levels that I write about in my Human-System's Model paper.'

WHY WE NEED A PERSON-CENTERED MODEL OF HEALTH

One of the chief reasons that we need a person-centered model of health is that our persistent dualistic habits of thought which are codified in language, misrepresent current knowledge of the role between psychology and health. We need to correct the TWIT's legacy of division, hierarchy, and patriarchy that fail to provide the following: (1) a more complex and accurate description of reality, (2) a more adequate and encompassing epistemology, and (3) a blueprint that supports and enhances our health and optimizes our innate actualizing tendency. Client-centered authors have more work to do explicating what Jerold Bozarth (1998) rightly names Rogers' 'revolutionary paradigm.'

The need for a non-dualistic model of health has spurred an academic revolution over the past several decades, as described by Evelyn Fox Keller earlier in this chapter. These academic critiques and reconceptualizations have developed largely outside the field of psychology. Within the person-centered approach, there have been some notable exceptions (Fairhurst, 1999; Natiello, 2001; Wilkins, 2003; Proctor and Napier, 2004; Schmid, 2004; Haugh, 2001; Cooper, 2001; O'Hara, 1997). However, there is still more work to do in order to make the features of person-centered theory of organismic actualization and health explicit to the larger academic world.

ORGANISMIC HEALTH AND INTEGRITY: THE PERSON-CENTERED MODEL

Central to Rogers' person-centered theory is that whether the organism is a person, a large group, or part of the universe's formative tendency, it operates as a whole. Rogers was vigorous in communicating his willingness for *all* aspects of experience to be acknowledged. My own experience with him in large groups is quite the opposite of other humanistic groups, where the cultivation of a 'positive' feeling was actively sought and celebrated as the right way to be. One memory of Rogers stands out for me as prototypical of the integrity of his life and work. Over one hundred of us had gathered together for more than a week in a large workshop. We were experiencing a good deal of conflict. Then, a significant shift occurred in the group climate, creating a discernable break away from self-promotion and defense and toward empathic understanding. Intimate expressions increased throughout the community. Each person speaking seemed to speak from heightened levels of caring attention and respect. One person said, 'I have never felt so alive.' Another said, 'This is the first time I have felt so safe and free to be myself.' … 'I have never felt closer to others.' … 'I feel as if we are all one.' A cascade of similar sentiments was expressed, one after another, in almost reverential tones. After several more heartfelt comments in the same vein, Carl spoke up. In a clear and plain voice, he said, 'I feel as if we have heard several strong statements that are all very positive. But I am quite certain that there are others here who are quite likely feeling just the opposite—feeling, "Well—*I* am *not* feeling closer to others"—but might be reluctant to express those feelings. I would be interested to hear from those who might *not* be feeling particularly safe and warm right now.'

Rogers consistently acknowledged and honored the presence of multiple realities in the creation of an inclusive construction of wholeness. For me, the group experience I am describing here stands as a clear demonstration of the congruence between his theory and practice of positive change through accurate understanding and unconditional regard for *what is*. What followed in that group was that people risked offering their feelings of hurt, anger, and other less 'positive' selves—a more genuinely inclusive and complex integrity of the group emerged. My experience is that this deep degree of integrity never emerges in groups that favor one type of feeling, spiritual or political path, or manner of expression over another. Excluding relevant data from the accurate representation of a phenomenon cannot result in wholeness. In other words, wholeness cannot result from the exclusion of relevant data that more fully and accurately represent the phenomena present. In Rogers' theory all phenomena must be received and regarded unconditionally. This phenomenological feature is of great importance, and is central to a person-centered theory of health and wholeness. It is essential

> ... that we consider all the data, real or unreal or doubtful, as having equal rights, and investigate them without fear or favor. This ... will help us to do justice to all of them, especially to those which are under the handicap of initial suspicion as to their existential claim. (Wolter-Gustafson, 1984: 49)

ORGANISMIC INTEGRITY AND THE FULLY FUNCTIONING PERSON

In *Client-Centered Therapy* (1951), Rogers systematically sets out his 'Theory of Personality and Behavior' in a series of 19 propositions, for which he won the first American Psychological Association Distinguished Scientific Contribution Award. In 1959 Rogers expanded his theories in his contribution to Sigmund Koch's *Psychology: A Study of a Science, Volume 3: Formulations of the Person and the Social Context*. This document, *A theory of therapy, personality and interpersonal relationships as developed in the client-centered framework*, should be read in its entirety in order to appreciate the intricacy and precision of Rogers' work. While each of the propositions builds on the others, for the purposes of this chapter I will outline only the first four.

The first proposition states, 'Every individual exists in a continually changing world of experience of which he is the center.' The second proposition states, 'The organism reacts to the field as it is experienced and perceived.' For that individual, that field is 'reality.' The third and fourth propositions build on these first two, and they are the ones that most concern our discussion here. The third proposition states, 'The organism acts as an organized whole to this phenomenal field.' The fourth proposition states, 'The organism has one basic tendency and striving—to actualize, maintain, and enhance the experiencing organism.' These two propositions capture the essence of Rogers' theory of the actualizing tendency and the fully functioning person. In 1961, with regard to organismic experiencing, Rogers wrote, 'I have learned that my total organismic sensing of a situation is more trustworthy than my intellect' (in Kirschenbaum and Henderson, 1989: 23).

As late as 1986 he continued to show this unflagging trust in the organism in noting that,

> In client-centered therapy, the person is free to choose any direction, but actually selects positive and constructive pathways. I can only explain this in terms of a directional tendency inherent in the human organism—a tendency to grow, to develop, to realize its full potential. (Rogers, 1986a: 127)

Carl Rogers' steadfast trust in the person remains consistent throughout his work. In one of the last articles he wrote, he asserts that,

> Practice, theory and research make it clear that the person-centered approach is built on a basic trust in the person. ... [It] depends on the actualizing tendency present in every living organism's tendency to grow, to develop, to realize its full potential. This way of being trusts the constructive directional flow of the human being toward a more complex and complete development. It is this directional flow that we aim to release. (1986b: 198)

ORGANISMIC INTEGRITY THEORY

The word 'health' comes from the Old English, 'whole.' Health is wholeness, an all-inclusive presence of every seemingly disparate part. Disease is separation from the whole. This root meaning of health is a vivid expression of the organismic theory of Rogers and colleagues and offers a significant shift for psychology.

Jules Seeman, theoretician and Carl Rogers' original chief officer for research conducted on the conditions that are necessary and sufficient for change, has created language critical to our current understanding of organismic integration. Seeman (1989) writes:

> Here the term *organismic* is intended to suggest a pervasive phenomenon that includes all of a person's behavioral subsystems: biochemical, physiological, perceptual, cognitive, and interpersonal. The term *integration* indicates a transactional process that blends these subsystem behaviors in ways that are congruent, harmonious, and adaptive. (p. 146)

Here is an example of the intricate and confounding effects of language and thought originating from a mechanistic model of reality from the mid-twentieth century. In attempting to offer an inclusive theory of the organism's complex interactivity, Seeman borrows the concept of 'subsystems' from systems theory. However, this language could be construed to suggest *solid entities,* which are then *blended* harmoniously, rather than infinitely complex organismic interactions. I believe this confusion reflects our legacy of linguistic limitations, rather than any intention to replicate a mechanistic or Newtonian worldview. This of course, was not Seeman's intent. Seeman's model is meant to express a level of organismic integration beyond the capacity of language to adequately express the integrity of the organism (Seeman, 2007).

In photographic terms, while mainstream psychology generally uses a micro lens to understand the client's world, Rogers and colleagues may be characterized as using both a micro *and* macro lens. Focusing attention on human beings through a wide-angle, organismic lens, Rogers could remain open to all data connected to the 'vast resources' and the indefatigable life force he had first observed in his childhood (Rogers, 1979: 3). Rogers explains that the central place that actualization is given in the theory came as a result of therapists' experience with clients in therapy, in concert with extensive research.

> The therapist becomes very much aware that the forward moving tendency of the human organism is the basis upon which he relies most deeply and fundamentally. It is evident not only in the general tendency of clients to move in the direction of growth when the factors in the situation are clear, but is most dramatically shown in very serious cases where the individual is on the brink of psychosis or suicide. (1951: 489)

BEYOND PSYCHOLOGICAL HEALTH

The client-centered approach has generated extensive research (Lambert, Shapiro and Bergin, 1986). It has been the most research-supported model of psychotherapy (Goodyear, 1987; Patterson, 1984). However, there has been a scarcity of research on, and limited understanding of, the concept and functional implications of Rogers' actualizing tendency. Jules Seeman headed the research team charged with designing the strongest possible quantitative studies to test the newly articulated (at the time) non-directive hypotheses. In his co-edited book *Humanistic Psychotherapies* (2001), he reflects on that time:

> Carl Rogers ... had a long-standing interest in what he so elegantly called the fully functioning person and described the fully functioning person in what are essentially human-system terms: [Rogers (1965) writes] 'He is making use of his organic equipment to sense, as accurately as possible, the existential situation within and without. He is using all of the data his nervous system can thus supply ... He is a fully functioning organism, and because of the awareness of himself which flows freely in and through his experiences, he is a fully functioning person'. (p. 628)

This position is supported by diverse research studies. The empirical studies originally carried out by Seeman (1983) and later with his students at Vanderbilt University led to the following summary:

> Persons who understand and trust their basic organismic self can listen to their own signals. They do not have the need to screen, shut out, or deflect

and distort signals in a way that characterizes more vulnerable persons. For the integrated person this ability to receive and process the data of their immediate experience results in the optimal receipt of information. ... This ability to receive and process the reality data of their world has portentious [sic] effects for the integrated person. Reality data serve as nutrition, fully as important to the psychological organism as food is to the biological organism. (2001: 628)

What is most consistent in all of these descriptions is the commanding role of communication in maintaining a healthy organism, and the key role of an 'open, fluid, and unimpeded communication system in maximizing effective human functioning.' (p. 628)

Organismic integrity forms the basis for how the actualizing tendency functions in human beings, and thus is central to client-centered therapy. Despite the prevailing persistent distrust of non-directivity, researchers and practitioners, persuaded by its power, have continued to develop theory and practice. They work to influence their respective fields toward respect for the trustworthy 'organismic integrity of the person.' Person-centered theory and practice represent a significant, one might say seismic, shift within the world of psychology and beyond, articulating a broader vision of optimal organismic health. Ultimately, the organismic theory of Carl Rogers and colleagues not only reveals the intricate processes by which positive change occurs, but also provides an epistemological framework that rejects the dualistic and linear limitations embedded in other psychological theories that limit our understanding of health and wholeness.

REFERENCES

Bozarth J (1998) *Person-Centered Therapy: A revolutionary paradigm.* Ross-on-Wye: PCCS Books.
Colgrave S (1979). *The Spirit of the Valley, Androgeny and Chinese Thought.* London: Virago.
Consumer Reports (2005) Which alternative treatments work? *Consumer Reports, 70,* 39–43.
Cooper M (2001) Embodied empathy. In S Haugh & T Merry (Eds) *Rogers' Therapeutic Conditions: Evolution, theory and practice. Vol. 2: Empathy.* Ross-on-Wye: PCCS Books, pp. 218–29.
Damasio A (1994) *Descartes' Error: Emotion, reason, and the human brain.* New York: Penguin Books.
Descartes R (1970/1637) In ES Haldane & GRT Ross (Translators) *The Philosophical Works of Descartes. Vol. 1.* New York: Cambridge University Press. (Original work published circa 1637.)
Ermarth ED (1989) The solitude of women and social time. In FJ Forman (Ed) *Taking Our Time: Feminist perspectives on temporality.* New York: Pergamon Press.
Fairhurst I (Ed) (1999) *Women Writing in the Person-Centred Approach.* Ross-on-Wye: PCCS Books.
Gendlin E (1997) How philosophy cannot appeal to experience, and how it can. In DM Levin (Ed) *Language beyond Postmodernism: Saying and thinking in Gendlin's philosophy.* Evanston, IL: Northwestern University Press, pp. 3–41.

Goodyear RK (1987) In memory of Carl Ransome Rogers (January 8, 1902–February 4, 1987). *Journal of Counseling and Development 63*, 561–4.

Haugh S (2001) The difficulties in the conceptualization of congruence: A way forward with complexity theory? In G Wyatt (Ed) *Rogers' Therapeutic Conditions: Evolution, theory and practice. Vol. 1: Congruence*. Ross-on-Wye: PCCS Books, pp. 116–30.

Keller EF (1985) *Reflection on Gender and Science*. New Haven: Yale University Press.

Kirschenbaum H & Henderson V (Eds) (1989) *The Carl Rogers Reader*. Boston: Houghton Mifflin.

Lachman L & Masten R (2003) *Parallel Journeys—A spirited approach to coping and living with cancer*. Carmel, CA: SunInk Presentations.

Lambert MJ, Shapiro DA & Bergin, AE (1986). The effectiveness of psychotherapy. In SL Garfield & AE Bergen (Eds) *Handbook of Psychotherapy and Behavior Change* (3rd ed). New York: Wiley, pp. 157–212).

LeShan L (1994) *Cancer as a Turning Point: A handbook for people with cancer, their families, and health professionals*. New York: Plume Books.

LeShan L (2007) retrieved August 6, 2007 from <http://www.paralleljourneys-cancer.com/poc/blame.html>.

Levant R & Shlien J (Eds) (1984) *Client-Centered Therapy and the Person-Centered Approach: New directions in theory, research, and practice*. New York: Praeger.

Levine S (1987) *Healing into Life and Death*. New York: Anchor Books.

Lloyd G (1993) *The Man of Reason: Male and female in Western philosophy*. Minneapolis, MN: University of Minnesota Press.

Lodge HS (2007) You can stop 'normal' aging. Excerpted in *Parade Newsmagazine* March 18, 2007 from C Crowley & HS Lodge *Younger Next Year for Women: Live strong, fit, and sexy: Until you're 80*. New York: Workman Publishing.

Maslow A (1968) *Towards a Psychology of Being*. New York: Van Nostrand Reinhold.

Natiello P (2001) *The Person-Centered Approach: A passionate presence*. Ross-on-Wye: PCCS Books.

O'Hara M (1997) Relational empathy: Beyond modernistic egocentrism to postmodern holistic contextualism. In A Bohart & L Greenberg (Eds) *Empathy Reconsidered: New directions in psychotherapy*. Washington, DC: APA, pp. 295–319.

Ornstein R (1986) *Multimind: A new way of looking at human behavior*. Boston: Houghton Mifflin.

Patterson CH (1984) Empathy, warmth, and genuineness in psychotherapy: A review of reviews. *Psychotherapy, 21* (4), 431–8.

Pert CB (1997) *Molecules of Emotion: Why you feel the way you feel*. New York: Scribner.

Proctor G & Napier MB (Eds) (2004) *Encountering Feminism*. Ross-on-Wye: PCCS Books.

Ray PH & Anderson SR (2000) *The Cultural Creatives*. New York: Three Rivers Press.

Rogers CR (1951) *Client-Centered Therapy*. Boston: Houghton Mifflin.

Rogers CR (1959) A theory of therapy, personality, and interpersonal relationships, as developed in the client-centered framework. In S Koch (Ed) *Psychology: A study of a science. Vol. 3: Formulations of the person and the social context*. New York: McGraw-Hill, pp. 184–256.

Rogers CR (1979) The foundations of the person-centered approach. Original unpublished manuscript, Center for Studies of the Person, La Jolla, CA, 22 pages. Published (1979) in *Education, 100* (2), 98–107.

Rogers CR (1986a) Rogers, Kohut, and Erickson. *Person-Centered Review, 1* (2), 125–40.

Rogers CR (1986b) Client-centered approach to therapy. In IL Kutash & A Wolf (Eds)

Psychotherapist's Casebook: Theory and technique in practice. San Francisco: Jossey Bass, pp. 197–208.

Rogers CR & Russell D (2002) *Carl Rogers: The quiet revolutionary: An oral history.* Roseville, CA: Penmarin Books.

Ryan W (1976) *Blaming the Victim.* New York: Vintage Books.

Schmid P (2004) New men?—A new image of man? Person-centered challenges to gender dialogue. In G Proctor & MB Napier (Eds) *Encountering Feminism: Intersections between feminism and the person-centred approach.* Ross-on-Wye: PCCS Books, pp. 179–90.

Seeman J (1959) Toward a model of positive health. *American Psychologist, 44,* 1099–109.

Seeman J (1983) *Personality Integration: Studies and reflections.* New York: Human Sciences Press.

Seeman J (2001) Looking back, looking ahead: A synthesis. In D Cain & J Seeman (Eds) *Humanistic Psychotherapies: Handbook of research and practice.* Washington, DC: APA, pp. 617–36.

Seeman J (2007) personal communication.

Wilkins P (2003) *Person-Centred Therapy in Focus.* London: Sage Publication.

Wolter-Gustafson C (1984) *Women's Lived Experience of Wholeness.* (Doctoral Dissertation, Boston University, 1984). Ann Arbor, MI: UMI Dissertation Services.

Wolter-Gustafson C (2004) Toward convergence: Client-centered and feminist assumptions about epistemology and power. In G Proctor & MB Napier (Eds) *Encountering Feminism: Intersections between feminism and the person-centred approach.* Ross-on-Wye: PCCS Books. pp. 97–115.

CHAPTER 11

PSYCHOLOGICAL HEALTH: AUTONOMY AND HOMONOMY

KEITH TUDOR

Health is more difficult to deal with than illness.
D.W. Winnicott

What is it, then, about sanity that makes it so difficult to talk about?
Adam Phillips

Abstract
These two epigrams point to the difficulty of talking about health or mental health separately from illness. It is perhaps significant that the writers are both psychoanalysts. In the field of psychotherapy, humanistic psychology is viewed as one which emphasises the creative, aesthetic, positive and healthy aspects of human beings and human existence, at least in theory. However, these aspects are generally underdeveloped in humanistic psychotherapy. This chapter argues that person-centred theory has a rare contribution to make to our understanding of health, functioning and well-being. It discusses the concept of psychological or mental health, and how this informs the process and outcomes of person-centred psychotherapy. Health is discussed with reference to philosophical ideas about health and the good life, concepts of mental health and positive psychology, and person-centred psychology. Drawing on the work of the Hungarian psychologist, Andras Angyal, whose ideas influenced Carl Rogers, the trend towards homonomy or belonging is viewed as just as much a part of human existence as the trend towards autonomy—and as an integral, if overlooked part of the concept of the fully functioning, authentic human being. The chapter considers the importance of viewing the client as both healthy and ill (if at all), or of having or holding healthy processes alongside psychopathological ones, and that the process of psychotherapy is—or should be—as much concerned with acknowledging healthy processes as defensive ones. The personal and social reality of a homonomic trend is central to an understanding of the fully functioning person and engaged citizen of today. This is especially true in an increasingly conflictual world in which dominant 'Western' societies and psychologies overemphasise autonomy.

This chapter is based on a paper delivered as a lecture at the 7th World Conference for Person-Centered and Experiential Psychotherapy and Counselling at Potsdam, Germany on 13th July 2006, an edited version of which was first published in the Dutch journal *Tijdschrift Cliëntgerichte Psychotherapie* (Tudor, 2007).

PHILOSOPHICAL IDEAS ABOUT HEALTH

> One cannot engage in psychotherapy without giving operational evidence of an underlying value orientation and view of human nature. It is definitely preferable, in my estimation, that such underlying views be open and explicit, rather than covert and implicit. (Rogers, 1957/1990a: 402)

Rogers argues for the importance of investigating and elaborating underlying values and philosophy when undertaking psychotherapy. Here, we examine three concepts which provide an underlying value orientation to human health that can be applied to this context.

HEALTH AND HOLISM

The roots of the English word for health, from Old English and Old High German, link it to wholeness and healing. As Graham (1992: 53) observes: 'etymologically speaking ... to be healthy is to be whole or holy, which clearly embraces both spiritual and physical features rather than merely the latter.' The grammar of health, then, is one that implies a holistic or integrative structure to our health and to our understanding of health. Thus, health may be taken as referring to mind (including thoughts, beliefs and feelings), body (including behaviour) and spirit. Bohm (1980/1983: 3) makes a similar point, viewing health, holy and whole as equivalent to the Hebrew word *shalem*. He concludes: 'all of this indicates that man has sensed always that wholeness or integrity is an absolute necessity to make life worth living. Yet, over the ages, he has generally lived in fragmentation.'

This view about the holistic nature of human being and health has prevailed for most of human history and in most cultures. It is only in Western thought from the seventeenth century that Cartesian dualism, represented by Descartes' famous dictum 'I think therefore I am', has had the effect (if not the intention) of conceptualising a split between the mind and the body. Ultimately, this split has given rise to the medical model and practice of referring to whole, if ill, people in hospital as 'the appendix in bed four'. It is a short step from bed four in a general hospital ward to the psychiatric back ward and to being referred to as '*the* schizophrenic' or, topically in the United Kingdom, as being a dangerous person with a severe personality disorder (DSPD). This particular diagnosis began life as a figment of the then Home Secretary's imagination, and unfortunately has gained some credence through the popular press. This reductionism of person to symptom and/or behaviour is not only limited and limiting, it is inaccurate, unhelpful and, ultimately, anti-human.

HEALTH AND HAPPINESS

Health is often linked with happiness, a link which has its roots in Aristotle's concept of *eudaemonia* or the good life. For Aristotle, perfect happiness is only to be found in intellectual contemplation. In this sense philosophy, or the love of wisdom (*philo*, love and *sophia*, wisdom), is the supreme intellectual virtue. When we have a good conversation in good company, or what the Irish refer to as 'the *craic*', when we contemplate well, we feel completely at one, or at home. In this state or process, we often have the sense that time stops and we are unselfconscious. Interestingly this is one of the qualities of the human organism, as distinct from 'self', which by definition is self-conscious.

Van Belle (2005) views the origins of the person-centred approach as a therapy movement as rooted in continental (European) rationalism (encompassing thinkers such as Descartes, Leibnitz and Kant). One of the central beliefs of rationalism is that human beings could perfect themselves through self-reflection. Reflecting on one of his own papers, Rogers (1960/1967d: 163) finds that he has crystallised two themes, the second of which he refers to as '*the existential quality of satisfying living*'. Rogers (1957/1967a) echoes this view of the good life in the title of a chapter in which he elaborates his concept of the fully functioning person. The pursuit of happiness or 'satisfying living' is also embedded in US American culture. It was written famously into the *American Declaration of Independence* by Thomas Jefferson, who was influenced by the English philosopher, John Locke. Jefferson viewed this pursuit, along with life and liberty, as an inalienable right of man and a self-evident truth. Interestingly it is framed in a constitution which extols individualism and autonomy, in contrast, for instance, to the Canadian constitution which refers to 'the common good', a sentiment which reflects a trend to homonomy or a sense of belonging. It is perhaps no coincidence that extreme, isolationist, US American culture, including the current President, is defensively aggressive about 'Old Europe' and its cultures, which have matured together through proximity, conflict, reconciliation, trade and union.

BEING HEALTHY, HEALTHY BEING

Even though Rogers says (1961/1967c: 199) that he 'was not a student of existential philosophy', he aligns himself and his ideas with both existentialism and phenomenology. He contributed, for instance, to a volume on existential psychology (May, 1961) and to another on behaviorism and phenomenology (Wann, 1964/1965). He held public dialogues with existential theologians Martin Buber (in 1957) and Paul Tillich (in 1965). Rogers says that he was encouraged to read the existential writers Kierkegaard and Buber in the early 1950s by some of his theological students in Chicago (Kirschenbaum, 1979). He describes them both as 'friends of mine that I never knew I had', and took especially to Kierkegaard (Evans, 1975). This influence is most apparent in Rogers' (1960/1967c) paper '"To be that self which one truly is": A therapist's views of personal goals', in which Rogers describes directions taken by clients in the context of a facilitative therapeutic relationship. He summarises these trends and tendencies as follows (pp. 175–6):

> It seems to mean that the individual moves towards *being*, knowingly and acceptingly, the process which he inwardly and actually *is*. He is moving away from being what he is not, from being a façade. He is not trying to be

more than he is, with the attendant feelings of insecurity or bombastic defensiveness. He is not trying to be less than he is, with attendant feelings of guilt or self-depreciation. He is increasingly listening to the deepest recesses of his physiological and emotional being and finds himself increasingly willing to be, with greater accuracy and depth, that self which he most truly is.

Thus, being and being in process may be viewed as synonymous to being healthy. In addition to its explicit existential reference, this passage refers to a necessary balance between less and more, a balance which echoes Aristotle's view, as expressed in his *Nichomachean Ethics*, that the virtuous habit of action is always an intermediate state between the opposed vices of excess and deficiency. Too much and too little are always wrong; the right kind of action always lies in the mean. Thus, with respect to relations with strangers, being friendly is a mean between the excess of being ingratiating and the deficiency of being surly. With respect to self-esteem, magnanimity is a mean between the excess of vanity and the deficiency of pusillanimity or small-mindedness. According to Aristotle, each of the virtues is a state of being that naturally seeks its mean, although the application of this theory of virtue requires flexibility—for example, friendliness is closer to its excess than to its deficiency—and, ultimately, is highly personal. This view of the mean is similar to Pestana's (1998) view of 'normal health' which is a neutral state between negative health and positive or optimal health.

CONCEPTS OF MENTAL HEALTH AND POSITIVE PSYCHOLOGY

As a term and a concept 'mental health' is often confused and conflated with 'mental illness'. This means that 'health' is often subsumed to illness, with the result, as Winnicott observes, that 'health is more difficult to deal with than illness'. Despite recent work that reclaims this distinction (e.g., Minister for National Health and Welfare, 1988; Tudor, 1996; McCulloch and Boxer, 1997; Joubert and Raeburn, 1998; Tengland, 1998), government initiatives in the UK and in other countries continue to confuse and conflate these two fields (see Tudor, 2004).

One of the early pioneers in the field of positive mental health was Marie Jahoda who, in a report to a United States Joint Commission on Mental Illness and Mental Health—note the distinction explicit in its title—identified six major categories of concepts of mental health (Jahoda, 1958):

- Mental health as indicated by the *attitudes of an individual towards themselves* (i.e., self-concept, self-esteem).

- Mental health as expressed in the individual's style and degree of *growth, development or self-actualisation.*

- Mental health as *integration* of the first two criteria, that is, the individual's ability to

integrate developing and different aspects of themselves over time (i.e., personality integration).
- Mental health based on the individual's relation to reality in terms of:
  - *Autonomy* (the development of internal standards and values, an internal valuing process);
  - *Perception of social and physical reality* (i.e., a maximum awareness free from distortion); and
  - *Environmental mastery* (framed in terms of performance, success and adaptation).

Jahoda's work and that of others who followed her has led to the identification of further concepts, such as the importance of social support, and their development within the field of mental health promotion (see Tudor, 1996). Interestingly, in his elaboration of Rogers' concept of the fully functioning person, Seeman (1984) also cites Jahoda's work and concepts.

In a separate strand of development, some psychologists and researchers have been moving forward the mental health agenda through studies of subjective well-being. Notable amongst these is Keyes in the United States who has developed a perspective on mental health, which he refers to as flourishing, and on mental ill-health and illness, which he refers to as languishing (Keyes, 2003). He identifies thirteen dimensions of subjective well-being which he divides between those which are *hedonic* (as in hedonistic) which are concerned with pleasure and positive emotions, and those which are *eudaimonic* which are to do with self-fulfilment and positive functioning, including positive *social* well-being (see Table 1 overleaf) (Keyes, 2007).

Keyes' work is particularly important—and compatible with a person-centred approach to the study and understanding of mental health—as it is based on subjective views of mental health, and it emphasises social functioning, both of which are central to person-centred psychology.

PERSON-CENTRED PSYCHOLOGY

In the history of psychology and psychotherapy, many theorists from the clinical tradition derived their data and their theories from observation and study of troubled, conflicted and disturbed individuals. Inevitably this informed the development of theories of conflict, disturbance and psychopathology. Historically, not as much research has focused on the psychology of health, well-being, 'positive' emotions, optimal functioning, and so on. Harry Stack Sullivan is reported to have lamented that he could not say much about human maturity as his patients finished with him just as they were approaching that stage! (see Seeman, 1984). Whilst person-centred psychology is not unique in having a theory of health and in promoting positive views of the person (see Tudor, 1997), Rogers was, as Seeman (1984) acknowledges, one of the first psychologists and counsellors to assume health and functioning alongside pathology and dysfunctional behaviour. From his initial research on personal adjustment in children (published in 1931) Rogers was

Table 1 Factors and thirteen dimensions reflecting mental health as flourishing (Keyes, 2007)

Positive Emotions (i.e. Emotional Well-Being)

1. *Positive Affect* – Regularly cheerful, interested in life, in good spirits, happy, calm and peaceful, full of life.
2. *Avowed Quality of Life* – Mostly or highly satisfied with life overall or in domains of life.

Positive Psychological Functioning (i.e. Psychological Well-Being)

3. *Self-Acceptance* – Holds positive attitudes toward self, acknowledges, likes most parts of self, personality.
4. *Personal Growth* – Seeks challenge, has insight into own potential, feels a sense of continued development.
5. *Purpose in Life* – Finds own life has a direction and meaning.
6. *Environmental Mastery* – Exercises ability to select, manage, and mould personal environs to suit needs.
7. *Autonomy* – Is guided by own, socially accepted, internal standards and values.
8. *Positive Relations with Others* – Has, or can form, warm, trusting personal relationships.

Positive Social Functioning (i.e. Social Well-Being)

9. *Social Acceptance* – Holds positive attitudes toward, acknowledges, and is accepting of human differences.
10. *Social Actualisation* – Believes people, groups, and society have potential and can evolve or grow positively.
11. *Social Contribution* – Sees own daily activities as useful to and valued by society and others.
12. *Social Coherence* – Interest in society and social life, and finds them meaningful and somewhat intelligible.
13. *Social Integration* – A sense of belonging to, and comfort and support from, a community.

---

interested in health, adjustment and maturity. He refers to mental hygiene services in *Counseling and Psychotherapy* (Rogers, 1942), and a report of research into mental health appears in Rogers and Dymond's (1954) book on *Psychotherapy and Personality Change* (Grummon and John, 1954).

PERSON-CENTRED PSYCHOLOGY AND HEALTH

If there is one concept which may be said to characterise the state or process of health from a person-centred perspective, it is authenticity. In *A Way of Being*, Rogers (1980) describes the person of tomorrow as having a desire for authenticity. However, earlier in his writings, and specifically in his major formulation of a theory of therapy, personality and interpersonal relationships (Rogers, 1959: 207), he describes fully functioning more in terms of a cluster of concepts related to congruence. Here I elaborate these with regard to health:

- Congruence

  For Rogers, congruence is synonymous with authenticity and in this context I think authenticity is a more precise word. Rogers (1975) sees a deep concern for authenticity as a quality of the multifaceted, emerging person. He goes on to describe this person in polemical and political terms, citing examples of people who are prepared to reject a culture they see as hypocritical, to confront those in authority, to refuse orders, to work for civil rights, and to take full personal responsibility in situations (p. 158): 'Such painful honesty, such willingness to confront, and the willingness to pay the price of such utterances are indications of the value this emerging person places on being authentic.' More recently, Schmid (2004: 38) puts it simply: 'To be a person can truly be called living the process of authenticity.'

- Openness to experience

  When we are not threatened, we are open to meeting and processing new experiences. This represents and requires a non-defensive attitude. With regard to health this involves being open to how we experience ourselves as a whole person. Rogers (1959: 206) suggests that this applies equally to some areas of experience and to the total experience of the organism: 'It signifies that every stimulus, whether originating within the organism or in the environment, is freely relayed through the nervous system without being distorted or channeled off by any defensive mechanism.' In terms of health this challenges us to be our health, to live in touch with our bodies, to account for rather than discount, deny or distort stimuli such as aches and pains. There is some evidence that this may be more challenging for men than for women, and that men tend to ignore symptoms of ill health until they get worse. One piece of research examined the use of a hospital Accident and Emergency (A&E) Department in an area in the UK comprising a population of 574,000, of which 49% are male and 51% are female. The research showed that the Department was used by more than 66,000 patients a year, of which 56 per cent were men and 44 per cent were women (see <www.nnuh.nhs.uk/news.asp?ID=93>).

- Psychological adjustment

  Rogers describes this as congruence viewed from a social point of view. I think this is confusing in that it implies that congruence may be assessed by an external person, an implication and confusion which has found its way on to a number of person-centred training courses and into the minds and practice of some trainers, students and therapists. In another passage Rogers (1959: 206) is clearer: 'Optimal psychological adjustment exists when the concept of the self is such that all experiences are or may be assimilated on a symbolic level into the gestalt of the self-structure.'

In terms of health, it is important to reclaim this subjective perspective, as otherwise psychological adjustment becomes the domain of so-called objective psychological measurements, and of a politicised psychiatry whereby dissent is pathologised. As Grummon (1954: 239) puts it, in an early critique of the notion of cure, 'no one can say with certainty what constitutes good psychological adjustment, and therefore there can be no fully accepted definitions of what constitutes improvement or a "cure".'

- Extensionality

    For Rogers this term describes the specific types of *behaviour* of a congruent individual, and has a particular meaning which, as he acknowledges, is derived from the field of semantics. It describes:

    - A person who sees experience in differentiated terms—which is a quality of the organism and of organismic development.

    - A person who is aware of the space-time anchorage of facts—a point which underlies Van Werde's (1998) use of the term 'anchorage' as a core concept in working with people diagnosed as psychotic.

    - A person who is able to evaluate in multiple ways—a quality which is seen by some educationalists (e.g., Bloom et al., 1956) as the highest objective in educational functioning.

    - A person who is aware of different levels of abstraction, and is able to test her or his inferences and abstractions against a perceived and consensual reality—a process which also is reflective of Rogers' approach to theory and practice.

- Maturity

    This final concept in the cluster of terms which grow out of the concept of congruence is, for Rogers, a broad term which describes the personality characteristics and behaviour of a person who is, in general, congruent. He (Rogers, 1959) goes on to describe this in terms of an individual perceiving things realistically, and in an extensional manner, being non-defensive, evaluating experience openly, accepting and prizing her or himself and others. Elsewhere in his writing (Rogers, 1964/1990b) he talks about maturity as the basis of a valuing process—and of values.

These concepts offer us a person-centred theory and description of health—and, by implication, its opposite, illness. However, as it stands, it describes health as an individualistic concept and the good life as one lived somewhat in isolation. In terms of Keyes' dimensions of flourishing, Rogers is describing the dimensions of positive *psychological* functioning or well-being but not the dimensions of positive *social* functioning. The interdependency of the organism and its environment is not explicit. In this sense Rogers stands accused, amongst others by Buber (Buber and Rogers, 1957/1990), Holland (1977) and Vitz (1977), of an undue emphasis on the self and of an overly individualistic approach to psychology. Rogers was alive to the interdependence of organism and environment, especially in his thinking about the therapeutic relationship—and, indeed, as early as 1942 had, following Jessie Taft, referred to his therapy as 'relationship therapy'. Nevertheless he does not emphasise interdependence in his work. To rediscover this emphasis we turn to the work of the Hungarian psychologist, Andras Angyal, whose ideas influenced Rogers and whom he cites.

HOMONOMY

Angyal (1941, 1965/1973) viewed the organism as having two related trends: one towards increased *autonomy* (a concept with which most of us are familiar), and one towards *homonomy* or a sense of belonging. Angyal (1941: 23) defines the organism as autonomous in the sense that it is 'to a large extent, a *self-governing* entity', and homonomous (p. 172) in the sense that it longs 'to be in harmony with superindividual units, the social group, nature, God, ethical world order, or whatever the person's formulation of it may be.' Angyal also acknowledges (p. 33) the notion of *heteronomy*: 'The organism lives in a world in which things happen according to laws which are heteronomous from the point of view of the organism.' Human beings live autonomously and homonomously in a world that is heteronomous or other. Angyal uses the term biosphere (from the German *Lebenskreis*), meaning the realm or sphere of life, to convey the concept of a holistic entity which includes both individual and environment. Indeed we could describe life as a continuous process of negotiating our need to be separate or different, and to belong, in the face of otherness, difference and diversity. Rogers (1959: 207) comes close to this when he describes an individual who is mature, in part, as an individual who 'accepts others as unique individuals different from himself'.

In general, psychology and psychotherapy in the West have focused predominantly on understanding the individual, individuality, *self*-actualisation, autonomy, the concept of the *self*, and the importance of *self*-development. Recently, criticisms has been levelled against the emphasis on the individual and our narcissistic culture (notably, by Lasch, 1979), and more specifically, regarding the emphasis on the individual (Hillman and Ventura, 1992). Criticism has also been directed against the focus on self-actualisation (Rigney, 1981; Lukas, 1989); autonomy (Whitney, 1982; LeVine, 1990); and self-development and individual *self*-concept (Nobles, 1973). Angyal's view of a homonomic trend addresses such criticisms. In his psychology, homonomy, or belonging, is viewed as just as much a part of human existence as the trend towards autonomy, and as an integral, if overlooked part of the concept of the fully functioning, authentic, healthy human being, living in the context of groups, relationships and community (see Tudor, 2006). As the English poet, T.S. Eliot (1934/1963: 168) puts it (in his play *The Rock*): 'What life have you if you have not life together? There is no life that is not in community.' In relation to mental health this balance between autonomy and homonomy is reflected in the notion that it requires both 'individual resilience' and 'supportive environments' (Joubert and Raeburn, 1998). Therefore, health policies and practices need to strike a necessary balance in focusing on the individual, say, in terms of personal physical and psychological healthcare, and on the environment, through the workplace, organisations, institutions, community, and at a cultural level (see, for example, Money, 1993). With respect to the environmental or social, Keyes' dimensions of positive social functioning—social acceptance, social actualisation, social contribution, social coherence, and social integration—offer us not only a description of our trend to homonomy, but also a link to research on these constructs.

IMPLICATIONS FOR PRACTICE

If homonomy is brought into focus alongside autonomy, and health alongside illness, as this paper argues is necessary, what are the implications for practice? Here, we identify six implications for health, the good life and a therapeutic approach which reclaims the importance of health and homonomy.

1. *People can be—and, indeed, are—well and ill at the same time.*
   If we acknowledge the importance of healthy processes alongside neurotic or even psychotic ones, then the process of psychotherapy is or should be as much concerned with dealing with the failure of a person's communication with her or himself about health as it is about neurosis or maladjustment (see Rogers, 1961/1967b). Phillips (1994: 49) puts this well when he says that 'In psychotherapy one always has to remember that anyone who is failing at one thing is always succeeding at another.'

2. *Being well and being ill are both trustworthy.*
   This is not only a person-centred perspective, it is, for instance, a homeopathic one. As if commenting on our propensity to flee into health, Rogers (1951: 48) challenges us as therapists, asking:
   > [I]s he willing for the client to choose regression rather than growth or maturity? to choose neuroticism rather than mental health? to choose to reject help rather than accept it? to choose death rather than life? To me, it appears that only as the therapist is completely willing that any outcome, any direction, may be chosen—only then does he realize the vital strength of the capacity and potentiality of the individual for constructive action.

3. *The person is best understood in the context of a holistic approach.*
   This, as Clarkson (1989: 8) describes it, 'embraces and affirms complexity, inclusion and diversity and resists reductionism'. The miracle of life is not how different we are in our selves, it is that we hang together at all! As Whitehead (1929/1978: 108), the philosopher of the organism, puts it:
   > All the life in the body is the life of the individual cells. There are thus millions upon millions of centers of life in each animal body. So what needs to be explained is not dissociation of personality but unifying control, by reason of which we not only have unified behaviour, which can be observed by others, but also consciousness of a unified experience.

It *appears* that we think in parts, as in: 'You know, there's a part of me that feels really loving, and yet there's another part of me that feels just angry.' However, if we conceptualise our experience in this way, we are already construing parts or even configurations of self. As we know, in person-centred psychology, self is a differentiated part of the organism, so what this compartmentalisation ignores or discounts is the holistic nature of the human organism including its inherent tension. Talking with one client, who was using the language of parts, I discovered that, far from being 'natural', they had introjected it from a previous therapist! In order to catch something of this holistic and unified approach, I am experimenting with using constructions such as: 'I am all loving, and all angry' and 'The whole of me wants (a), and the whole of me wants (b).' It may sound and initially feel a little awkward, but both I and some clients have found it interesting and useful, and it is certainly more reflective and compatible with Rogers' (1951) theory of personality and behaviour than theories which emphasise parts.

4. *The human organism/person can only be understood within their environment.*
   Half a century ago, Lewin (1952) argued that it was impossible to view a person except in the context of their environment or 'environmental field' (hence field theory), a perspective which, of course, includes the viewer/researcher/doctor/nurse/ etc. as part of this interactional field. As Perls and his colleagues (1951/1973: 19) put it: 'only the interplay of organism and environment … constitutes the psychological situation, not the organism and environment taken separately'. This view acknowledges the significance of a client's environment and relational field. Of course, as therapists we are a part of that relational field which I believe is best understood in terms of organism and environment, in which client and therapist co-create the therapeutic conditions of what is, in effect, an environmental therapy.

5. *Health can only be experienced and defined and, indeed, is dependent on relationship.*
   Keen (1983: 214) puts this succinctly: 'No matter how much we must struggle with the limits imposed upon us by families, there is no health possible apart from belonging within a circle of arms where we are known and accepted.' This is also true of therapeutic relationships, including those within groups and, in this context, Giesekus and Mente (1986) report significant research in which they identify the importance of the group members' empathy for each other. Healthy and health-promoting relationships are active and engaged ones. Interestingly in terms of his own autobiography—and the autobiographical nature of theory— Rogers (1951: 488) sees an autonomous organism moving 'away from heteronymous [sic] control'. Here, summarizing Angyal (incorrectly), Rogers' language is one of distance and separation. However, Angyal does not separate organism from environment. He sees (1941: 38) that 'The organism asserts itself against the heteronomous surroundings.' His language is, significantly, more a language of relational, assertive and contactful engagement with the heteronomous environment, including others.

6. *Just as our health and authenticity is relational, so too is our alienation or estrangement, inauthenticity and illness.*

As Karl Marx (1858/1964), the philosopher of alienation, puts it: 'Every self-estrangement of man from himself and nature is manifested in the relationship he sets up between other men and himself and nature.' Thus, whether we are estranged from our product, our productive capacity, other people, our species, or the Earth, we express that 'alienness' in our relationships, including therapeutic relationships. From this perspective, our task as therapists is one of dis-alienation, which as Bulhan (1980) states is impossible without a total restructuring of society.

Whether we get as far as such restructuring, we suggest that the acknowledgement of a homonomic trend is central for a more complete and holistic understanding of the healthy, fully functioning person, and the relational and engaged citizen of today—and tomorrow. This appears increasingly important in an increasingly conflictual world in which dominant 'Western' societies and psychology overemphasise self-actualisation and autonomy. Faced with sick societies and a mad world, our search for homonomy, health and sanity has never been so urgent or necessary.

REFERENCES

Angyal A (1941) *Foundations for a Science of Personality*. New York: Commonwealth Fund.

Angyal A (1973) *Neurosis and Treatment: A holistic theory*. New York: John Wiley & Sons. (Original work published 1965.)

Bloom BS, Engelhart MD, Furst EJ, Hill WD & Krathwohl DR (1956) *Taxonomy of Educational Objectives. Handbook I: Cognitive domain*. London: Longman.

Bohm D (1983) *Wholeness and the Implicate Order*. London: Ark. (Original work published 1980.)

Buber M & Rogers CR (1990) Martin Buber. In H Kirschenbaum & VL Henderson (Eds) *Carl Rogers: Dialogues*. London: Constable. (Original work 1957.)

Bulhan HA (1980) Fritz Fanon: the revolutionary psychiatrist. *Race and Class, 21*, 251–70.

Clarkson P (1989) *Gestalt Counselling in Action*. London: Sage.

Eliot TS (1963) Choruses from 'The Rock'. In *Collected Poems 1909–1963*. London: Faber & Faber, pp. 161–85. (Original work published 1934.)

Evans RI (1975) *Carl Rogers: The man and his ideas*. New York: EP Dutton & Co.

Giesekus U & Mente A (1986) Client empathic understanding in client-centered therapy. *Person-Centered Review, 1*, 163–71.

Graham H (1992) Imaginative assessment of personal health needs. In DR Trent (Ed) *Promotion of Mental Health. Vol. 1*. Aldershot: Avebury, pp. 53–62.

Grummon DL (1954) Personality changes as a function of time in persons motivated for therapy. In CR Rogers & RF Dymond (Eds) *Psychotherapy and Personality Change*. Chicago: The University of Chicago Press, pp. 238–55.

Grummon DL & John ES (1954) Changes over client-centered therapy evaluated on psychoanalytically based thematic apperception test scales. In CR Rogers & RF Dymond (Eds) *Psychotherapy and Personality Change*. Chicago: The University of Chicago Press, pp. 121–44.

Hillman J & Ventura M (1992) *We've Had a Hundred Years of Psychotherapy and the World's Getting Worse*. San Francisco, CA: Harper.
Holland R (1977) *Self in Social Context*. London: Macmillan.
Jahoda M (1958) *Current Concepts of Positive Mental Health*. New York: Basic Books.
Joubert N & Raeburn J (1998) Mental health promotion: People, power and passion. *International Journal of Mental Health Promotion, 1*, 15–22.
Keen S (1983) *The Passionate Life: Stages of loving*. London: Gateway Books.
Keyes CLM (2003) Complete mental health: An agenda for the 21st century. In CLM Keyes & J Haidt (Eds) *Flourishing: Positive psychology and the life well-lived*. Washington, DC: American Psychological Association Press, pp. 293–312.
Keyes CLM (2007) Promoting and protecting mental health as flourishing: A complementary strategy for improving national mental health. *American Psychologist, 62* (2), 95–108.
Kirschenbaum H (1979) *On Becoming Carl Rogers*. New York: Delacorte Press.
Lasch C (1979) *The Culture of Narcissism*. New York: Warner Books.
LeVine RA (1990) Infant environments in psychoanalysis: A cross-cultural view. In JW Stigler, RA Shweder & G Herdt (Eds) *Cultural Psychology*. Cambridge: Cambridge University Press, pp. 454–76.
Lewin K (1952) *Field Theory in Social Science*. New York: Harper & Row.
Lukas E (1989) From self-actualization to global responsibility. Paper presented at the Seventh World Congress of Logotherapy, Kansas City, KS, June.
Marx K (1964) *Pre-Capitalist Economic Formations*. London: Lawrence & Wishart. (Original work published 1858.)
May R (Ed) (1961) *Existential Psychology*. New York: Random House.
McCulloch GF & Boxer J (1997) *Mental Health Promotion: Policy, practice and partnerships*. London: Baillière Tindall.
Minister of National Health and Welfare (1988) *Mental Health for Canadians*. Ottawa: MNHW.
Money M (1993) *Health and Community*. Dartington: Green Books.
Nobles WW (1973) Psychological research and the black self-concept: A critical review. *Journal of Social Issues, 29*, 11–31.
Perls FS, Hefferline RF & Goodman P (1973) *Gestalt Therapy*. Harmondsworth: Penguin. (Original work published 1951.)
Pestana M (1998) *Moral Virtue or Mental Health*. New York: Peter Lang Press.
Phillips A (1994) *On Flirtation*. London: Faber & Faber.
Phillips A (2006) *Going Sane*. London: Penguin.
Rigney M (1981) *A Critique of Maslow's Self-Actualization Theory: The 'highest good' for the aboriginal is relationship*. Videotape. Aboriginal Open College, Adelaide, Australia.
Rogers CR (1931) *Measuring Personality Adjustment in Children Nine to Thirteen*. New York: Teachers College, Columbia University, Bureau of Publications.
Rogers CR (1942) *Counseling and Psychotherapy: Newer concepts in practice*. Boston: Houghton Mifflin.
Rogers CR (1951) *Client-Centered Therapy*. London: Constable.
Rogers CR (1959) A theory of therapy, personality and interpersonal relationships, as developed in the client-centred framework. In S Koch (Ed) *Psychology: A study of a science. Vol. 3: Formulations of the person and the social context*. New York: McGraw-Hill, pp. 184–256.
Rogers CR (1967a) A therapist's view of the good life: The fully functioning person. In *On Becoming a Person*. London: Constable, pp. 183–96. (Original work published in 1957)
Rogers CR (1967b) Dealing with breakdowns in communication—Interpersonal and intergroup. In

On Becoming a Person. London: Constable, pp. 329–37. (Original work published in 1961.)
Rogers CR (1967c) Persons or science? A philosophical question. In *On Becoming a Person*. London: Constable, pp. 199–224. (Original work published in 1961.)
Rogers CR (1967d) 'To be that self which one truly is': A therapist's view of personal goals. In *On Becoming a Person*. London: Constable, pp. 163–82. (Original work published in 1960.)
Rogers CR (1975) The emerging person: A new revolution. In RI Evans *Carl Rogers: The man and his ideas*. New York: EP Dutton & Co, pp. 147–75.
Rogers CR (1980) *A Way of Being*. Boston: Houghton Mifflin.
Rogers CR (1990a) A note on 'The nature of man'. In H Kirschenbaum & VL Henderson (Eds) *The Carl Rogers Reader*. London: Constable, pp. 401–8. (Original work published 1957.)
Rogers CR (1990b) Toward a modern approach to values: The valuing process in the mature person. In H Kirschenbaum & VL Henderson (Eds) *The Carl Rogers Reader*. London: Constable, pp. 168–85. (Original work published 1964.)
Rogers CR & Dymond RF (Eds) (1954) *Psychotherapy and Personality Change*. Chicago: The University of Chicago Press.
Schmid P (2004) Back to the client: A phenomenological approach to the process of understanding and diagnosis. *Person-Centered and Experiential Psychotherapies, 3* (1), 36–51.
Seeman J (1984) The fully functioning person: Theory and research. In RF Levant & J Shlien (Eds) *Client-Centered Therapy and the Person-Centered Approach: New directions in theory, research and practice*. New York: Praeger, pp. 131–52.
Tengland P-A (1998) *Mental Health: A philosophical analysis*. Linköping, Sweden: Linköping University.
Tudor K (1996) *Mental Health Promotion: Paradigms and practice*. London: Routledge.
Tudor K (1997) Mental health promotion: The contribution of psychotherapy. In M Money & L Buckley (Eds) *Positive Mental Health and its Promotion*. Liverpool: Institute for Health, John Moores University, pp. 21–4.
Tudor K (2004) Mental health promotion. In IJ Norman & I Ryrie (Eds) *The Art and Science of Mental Health Nursing: A textbook of principles and practice*. Buckingham: McGraw-Hill/Open University Press, pp. 35–65.
Tudor K (2006) We and Them: Working with difference in groups. Keynote speech. WPATA Australasian Transactional Analysis Conference, Sydney, Australia, 19th November.
Tudor K (2007) Geestelijk gezond; autonoom én homonoom [Psychological health: Autonomy and homonomy]. *Tijdshrift Cliëntgerichte Psychotherapie, 45* (1), 5–18.
Tudor K & Worrall M (2006) *Person-Centred Therapy: A clinical philosophy*. London: Routledge.
Van Belle HA (2005) Philosophical roots of person-centered therapy in the history of Western thought. *The Person-Centered Journal, 12* (1–2), 50–60.
Van Werde D (1998) 'Anchorage' as a core concept in working with psychotic people. In B Thorne & E Lambers (Eds) *Person-Centred Therapy*. London: Sage, pp. 195–205.
Vitz P (1977) *Psychology as Religion: The cult of self-worship*. Grand Rapids, MI: William B Eerdmans.
Wann TW (Ed) (1964/1965) *Behaviorism and Phenomenology: Contrasting bases for modern psychology*. Chicago & London: Phoenix Books. (Original work published 1964.)
Whitehead AN (1978) *Process and Reality* (DR Griffin & DW Sherburne, Eds) (corrected edn). New York: The Free Press. (Original work published 1929.)
Whitney NJ (1982) A critique of individual autonomy as the key to personhood. *Transactional Analysis Journal, 12*, 210–12.

Chapter 12

HOW CLIENTS SELF-HEAL IN PSYCHOTHERAPY

Arthur C. Bohart

In the dominant narratives of therapy, for instance, in cognitive-behavioral and psychodynamic theory, it is therapists who 'fix' clients by restructuring cognitions, extinguishing fears, teaching relaxation, shedding insight into childhoods, strengthening egos, or restructuring images of self–other relationships. In these models therapists 'operate on' clients to make change occur. In contrast, Karen Tallman and I have argued, in accord with Rogerian theory, that it is clients who 'operate on' what therapy provides to produce change (Bohart and Tallman, 1999). Clients are *active self-healers*. Clients make therapy work by investing their intelligence, efforts, and creativity. Therapist interventions do not have potency without clients' active efforts to engage, and invest energy and life, into them. Clients create change by selectively picking out from the therapy interaction aspects that are of use to them (which may not be the aspects therapists think are important), selectively construing the meaning and usefulness of therapist responses in ways that promote self-healing, actively and creatively operating on therapist input, working to shape the therapy interaction so that it is of benefit, and actively working to integrate what they learn in therapy with their everyday lives.

Clients' capacities to use therapy to self-heal is part of their more general capacity to actualize (Bohart, 2007a, 2007b). Actualization is the organismic thrust that leads individuals to grow, differentiate, integrate, learn, and creatively develop more organized, effective, and sensitive ways of dealing with self, world, and others. Self-healing is the process that occurs when individuals are blocked, develop personal problems, or are otherwise stuck. It consists of coping with these blocks, problems, or stuck points in such a way that the person finds ways of untangling them, resolving them, or growing from them. Ultimately it involves a matter of being open to new information, being willing to face up to failure or challenge, and looking for new, integrative solutions to life's problems (Bohart, 2007a, 2007b).

Many times individuals are able to self-right or self-heal in everyday life without the aid of professional therapists (Bohart and Tallman, 1999). At times they need assistance and so they seek out or are sent to psychotherapists. People come to therapy whenever they are stuck, when their own intrinsic self-healing processes are not able to lead to self-righting on their own. Therapists then provide assistance to help clients get unstuck so their own self-healing processes can operate. Therapists help by offering support, space within which clients can work, and useful tools and structure that clients can use to explore and resolve problems.

HOW DOES CHANGE OCCUR?

My premise is that we don't really know how therapy helps clients create change. Typical descriptions of how therapy works are 'top down.' They focus on the *conscious* activity of the client. In cognitive therapy clients consciously learn how to challenge dysfunctional cognitions and then use that ability in their everyday lives. In psychodynamic therapy clients consciously gain insight which they use to alter their ways of reacting to situations. In existential therapy clients become aware of how they are choosing safety over the courage to confront the uncertainty of life. This allows them to be able to *consciously* make better choices. In person-centered therapy clients consciously *explore* their experience, become *aware* of feelings, and become more (consciously) *accepting* of experience.

Our client as active self-healer theory also describes what clients do as if it is a conscious process. Clients actively *interpret* interventions, they deliberately shape the therapy environment to get what they need, they creatively modify interventions, and they actively blend what they have learned with their everyday lives. Although I believe there is some truth in these descriptions, in this paper I am going to argue that change is largely an unconscious process—that we know something about the conditions that facilitate it, but that we do not really know how it happens. I will offer a hypothesis about how I believe a core part of the process works.

THREE EXAMPLES

I start by presenting three examples of where change appears to include unconscious aspects. The first is drawn from Carl Rogers' and Maureen O'Hara's observations. Later in his life, Rogers believed that therapy was a meeting of persons and that therapeutic change was a by-product of this meeting (Cissna and Anderson, 1994; Maureen O'Hara, personal communication, 16th November 2007). According to O'Hara, 'We discussed this several times. He (and I) believed that therapeutic change is a (non-determinate) emergent outflow from a true meeting of persons' (Maureen O'Hara, personal communication, 16th November 2007).

Consider this equation: It says change does not result from anything intentionally designed to facilitate change. It does not even occur from facilitating client self-exploration through empathic listening and responding. Rather, it occurs from a meeting of persons. Something about this meeting of persons promotes change without either therapist or client necessarily consciously focusing on things like discussing problems, self-exploring, or whatever. Rather, it seems that Rogers and O'Hara are saying that change will occur from a certain kind of relationship where client learning, absorbing, and changing happens unconsciously.

The next example comes from my work with a client who was struggling with relationship issues. My experience was that all the client did was complain, session after session. I saw no process happening in terms of what I had learned should be happening, from any theoretical point of view, for therapy to work. I did not see the client deeply experiencing. I did not see him actively accessing emotion. I did not see him challenging his dysfunctional cognitions. I did not see him forging new understandings of the relationship of his present to his past. I did not see him becoming more open to experience. I did not seem him moving toward holding his constructs more tentatively. While he complained a lot, I did not see him *exploring* his experience, like I was used to seeing in Rogerian therapy. In fact, the complaints seemed the same from session to session and I felt thoroughly ineffective with this client. Yet, after a while, the client moved to make some definite and more functional choices about the relationship he had been struggling with. He terminated therapy, told me how helpful I had been and moved on with his life. Over time I have periodically heard from him. He is doing well, and he tells me how helpful I was!

The third example is taken from my own personal therapy. In my twenties I was plagued with severe anxiety. I saw a therapist who, although he labeled himself psychodynamic, operated a lot like a person-centered therapist. Mostly he listened empathically. Occasionally he would self-disclose. Each week I would go in to see him feeling very anxious. I would leave feeling calm. But over the week the anxiety would grow and grow so that by the time I saw him the next week I was very anxious again. This process went on for weeks. Then, one day, I went and saw him and left feeling calm, as always. But the anxiety never came back. Neither then nor since have I ever had any idea why it just vanished after that one session. Was there something he said? Even in the weeks that followed I could not think of anything special that had happened in that session. Yet it has been gone (mostly) for good—I am now 64.

Not only am I unaware of anything special or different that he did, I am unaware of anything special or different that I did. Nor am I aware of anything special that happened at that exact point in my life. In retrospect I can say that I had learned to become more self-accepting and less self-critical (it was self-criticism that was the source of my anxiety). But how did I do that and why was there a shift that particular day (if it was that particular day)? And: *was* there a shift that particular day? Or had it been a slow process of some kind of unconscious accumulation that finally just reached a critical mass, and then change occurred? I do not know.

If these were the only times these types of these things had happened to me, I would treat them as anomalies. But they are not. With clients I have had other experiences where the things that were supposed to work did not work. The client seems to have a major breakthrough—a great insight, a deep emotional experience—I am sure change will occur—and the next session she is the same as before. I have also had other experiences where seemingly trivial inconsequential things happened and clients change. (I am not alone in this, Rosenbaum and Talmon (2006) have reported something similar.) About four years ago I had a client who had several moments of deep emotional insight, yet her particular anxiety problem did not budge. After about a year of therapy I had to terminate the relationship because I was moving 400 miles away. Three years later I have heard that she considers me a 'lifesaver.' Yet the 'great moments' of her therapy *seemed* unfruitful at the time.

This is not to say there haven't been times when things work the way they are supposed to—where clients engage in a rich and deep self-exploration process that seems to relate to their making new experiential discoveries, becoming more process-oriented in how they live life, and finding new ways of being and behaving that work better for them. Of course I have not kept systematic records. If I had, I suspect I would find that on average clients change in accordance with theory and research findings. But what interests me are the exceptions. I think of a cartoon I saw many years ago. It is a famous cartoon and can be found on the internet. It shows a mathematician developing a proof on a blackboard. After several steps the mathematician has written 'and then a miracle occurs,' and then continues on with more of the proof. I think this is how therapy operates. We know many things that on average seem to help clients. But they don't always. And I suspect that even when they do we don't really know why. Instead, a miracle has occurred.

MY GUESS AT PART OF HOW THE CORE PROCESS OF THERAPY WORKS

Here is my model of how change works:

- The client comes into therapy feeling stuck. They have tried to solve their problems on their own unsuccessfully. They come in an organismic state that is not optimal to creative problem solving—they may feel helpless, discouraged, or defensive. Their proactive creative potential for self-healing, problem-solving, and growth is blocked.

- Therapy provides a context that should promote client self-healing. Clients encounter a situation that they experience as safe. They experience it as accepting. They experience it as one in which they can encounter new options. They experience it as one which allows them to open up, where they feel less defensive. Through their interactions with the therapist they begin to recover an experience of their own efficacy. The situation provides a context where they begin to perceive new options. It is also a context which promotes hope.

- Therapists provide this environment by acting in ways that are validating, encouraging, accepting, and understanding. If they use interventions they are ones that give the client the opportunity to experience a sense of mastery, gain a better understanding, and begin to feel more grounded in how they confront life's problems.

- Clients become more open and less defensive. In the therapy situation they are more open and attentive and begin to notice new options in both their own experience and in their interactions with the therapist.

- When they leave the therapy situation clients are more freely attentive and notice new options in their environment. In the context of their life problems they now become more creatively open and new solutions emerge. This becomes a self-fulfilling prophecy. As they have these experiences they feel more efficacious and open and continue the process of finding new solutions.

- Many of the new ideas and solutions 'bubble up' and are examples of creative emergence. This is what Rogers and O'Hara would describe as the 'emergent outflow from a true meeting of persons' (Maureen O'Hara, personal communication, 16th November 2007).

I will look at this model in more detail. First, I hypothesize that therapeutic events provide an experiential context in which the person responds by moving into a state of greater internal harmony and openness. This 'moving into' is not a conscious moving into. The person moves from a state in which he or she is stuck, feeling defensive, feeling hypervigilant, perhaps feeling helpless, all of which block openness to new information, into a state where he or she is more receptive and open.

The state shares similarities with states of relaxation, hypnotic states, states of flow (Csikszentmihalyi, 1990) or other states of absorption and involvement. However, the state is not necessarily a hypnotic state, and change does not necessarily happen from suggestion. The person enters into this state, *and* in this state, the whole organism—body and mind working together interactively—becomes more open to organismically generated growth and transformation, generated through interaction with the world. For instance, a person who has chronically experienced criticism from other people, and whose body has come to 'expect' criticism, may relax in an accepting environment and become more open to new experience. He or she may learn by noticing the accepting nature of the relationship and may automatically adjust to no longer expect criticism at a bodily level, without ever thinking about the fact that 'I am being accepted.'

An example of this type of movement can be seen in the film of Gloria working with Carl Rogers (Shostrom, 1965). Until near the end of the film, Gloria focuses on various issues in her life: her relationship with her daughter, her relationship to her own sexuality, her relationship to men, her divorce, her difficulties in knowing when she feels most in touch with herself. Suddenly, near the end, her attention switches to her relationship with Rogers and she talks about how free she feels to talk with Rogers in comparison to her father. How did this occur? I suggest that Gloria was learning at a bodily level all the time she was focusing on other issues. She was experiencing Rogers as accepting. Gradually her body was attuning to this relationship. She was moving towards feeling more open and less defensive, without focusing on that internal openness. Then, suddenly, her attention, now open, shifted—she simultaneously became aware of how open she was feeling with Rogers, and how she did not feel that with her father. Suddenly it 'bubbled up' into awareness. By then a change had already occurred. She'd already made the comparison to her father and was now already different. *Then* her consciously thinking about the difference between her father and Rogers may have *further* led to her articulating this with Rogers and to new learning, but that also happened because she was already in this open, active, receptive organismic state.

Such changes take place at the whole body level. They can take place without the person ever thinking, recognizing, accepting, or any of the other conscious-like activities postulated by writers on therapy coming into play. The change may be a big one, or a subtle adjustment. The person now just is different in how they relate to themselves and the world. I think many changes in therapy are not large. They are fine-tunings, but they lead to more effective functioning.

The bodily state I am describing is one of being 'organismically open' in contrast to a defensive, hyper-alert vigilant state. For a moment the person becomes more open to receiving information both from within and without, exploring, and trying out new ideas or new behaviors. It is like the state of a child who, feeling secure in his relationship with his parents, ventures out to explore. He is exploring the backyard, or the neighborhood, or just exploring in fantasy. His attention is not focused on his openness, but on whatever he is exploring. If he has found a beetle and is looking at it, his attention is on the beetle, not on 'I am now learning about insects.' In so doing he will learn a lot about himself and the world: about small moving objects, insects, his own curiosity, his ability to visually explore. But all this learning will be absorbed organismically and nonconsciously. Later, he may describe his experience and what he learned to his mother, but that will become a new experience of articulating to another what he has observed.

Such states do not only happen through relaxation. The person may instead be highly energized. Experiences of strong emotional activation can also be healing. The key is whether the state, whatever it is, be it relaxed, meditative, hypnotic, or highly activated and emotional, is an open one. Some highly emotional states cloud attention and block creative information processing. These will often be emotional states that are defensive. An example might be getting angry at another driver on the freeway where one is busy justifying one's anger to oneself rather than being open to exploring the situation. In therapy, one can feel strong emotion in a 'safe' atmosphere, which can lead to a dropping of defensiveness and to more fluid information-processing.

Does the body become a better information processor in those moments? That is my thesis. The body adjusts. Could it be neurochemical? It could. Alberto Zucconi (personal communication, August 2007) has postulated that perhaps through receiving empathic responding, a client's mirror neurons—the neurons responsible for empathy—change. Perhaps the therapy environment exerts direct effects on body chemistry such that clients become more physiologically open and information gets processed better.

CHANGE IN OPENNESS AND ATTENTION AND ITS EFFECT ON CREATIVE PROBLEM SOLVING

I am suggesting that the core change is a change from a state of stuckness, helplessness, defensiveness, hypervigilence, or hopelessness into a more activated state of openness and receptivity. Therapy does indeed work by heightening awareness, but not in the usual sense. The typical model of being more aware is that clients become 'more conscious.' What is meant generally by this is that they become more reflective. They are freer to consciously think about things and decide. This may indeed happen, but I think that is a consequence of a change in awareness, not the change in awareness per se.

As I have said, the kind of awareness I am talking about is more like the open attention of a child, who is not necessarily reflecting on him or herself or on his or her learning as he or she plays, explores, or experiences. Rather, he or she is absorbed in the experience of playing or exploring. It is similar to how Carl Rogers describes the highest state on the Process Scale (Walker, Rablen and Rogers, 1960). The person 'becomes' the process of experiencing. Reflection may also be going on, but the body is actively, interactively participating in the experience of the situation.

Clients carry this capacity into everyday life. This does not necessarily mean they are chronically more open. Rather, in problem situations they feel on more solid ground and so are able to be more open in the moment. This allows them to notice new possibilities in the situation, perhaps absorb what is going on and automatically adjust in creative ways, or become aware of new ideas bubbling up. Life, then, provides experiences which lead to new learning and new insights. *Life* is the ultimate therapist. Clients do not necessarily carry new learnings from therapy consciously into problem situations (e.g., 'I can stand up to authority,' 'I do not have to react with anger every time,' 'I am not inferior just because someone puts me down'). The person may simply *find* themselves reacting differently to someone putting them down—more equanimously, less ruffled. The thought 'I'm inferior' may go through their mind but they do not focus on it. Instead they focus on the task at hand and what can be done to deal with that task. They may not even be that aware that they have changed until later when they reflect and say, 'Wow. I just handled that differently!'

It is not the openness *per se* that creates the change. It is the openness *in the context* of experiences that have the potential to be transformed into new learnings. Gloria is an example. In the context of an authority figure, with whom in the person of her father she had problems, her organismically open state now leads her body to notice something new and different, both internally (memories of her father) and externally (her relationship with Rogers). She is now in a position to do some comparing and contrasting, which *in the context of that open state* will lead to new learnings that are meaningful and will 'stick.'

The capacity for new attention may lead the person to try out new behaviors or take new opportunities. These may not always work out, or they may present new problems. But in an organismically open state, the person is better able to explore them and learn from them. And if things do not work out they are better able to adjust.

BUBBLING UP AND EMERGENCE

Carl Rogers frequently talked about things 'bubbling up' inside. An example of bubbling up was Gloria's sudden realization that she could talk with Rogers easily in comparison to her father. Such 'bubblings up' are the stuff of creativity. One cannot make such bubblings up happen. However one can be in a state where the odds of their occurring are higher. They occur as a function of open, fluid attention. The openness state is the state in which individuals are more likely to be creative (Selby, 2004). It is also a state in which intuition is more likely to occur. There is research showing that with complex decisions, often the unconscious makes wiser decisions than conscious calculation (Dijksterhuis and Nordgren, 2006). But one has to be open and receptive to it.

This description of bubbling up suggests that change in therapy is an *emergent* from a complex interaction of factors, as Carl Rogers and Maureen O'Hara (Maureen O'Hara, personal communication, 16th November 2007) believed. It may be theoretically impossible to trace a change back in a simple linear fashion to this or that factor in therapy. Just like one cannot trace water back in a linear fashion to properties of hydrogen and oxygen, it may be a change is a complex emergent arising out of the confluence of factors in therapy and in the person's life. Things 'bubble up' out of the body's complex ability to process information in an open state as new discoveries at a given moment. One can guess at factors that may have contributed. But often these same factors will appear to be present in other cases where no such creative bubbling up has occurred.

WHAT FACTORS PROMOTE THIS KIND OF ORGANISMICALLY OPEN STATE?

In general there are several activities that lead to the kind of organismic openness that promotes change. They include activities that lead to relaxation and letting go, positive and proactive energizing and activating, experiences that 'balance,' experiences that increase a sense of self-efficacy and ableness, and experiences that promote a 'task focus.' A task focus is where the individual focuses attention on the task at hand instead of on his or her adequacy or inadequacy (Bohart and Tallman, 1999; Tallman, 1996).

One implication is that therapy does not only happen in therapy. People may experience such states in everyday life in such a way that change naturally takes place. There are many life experiences that could promote the open learning state. It could be a game of soccer that one gets highly involved in. It could be learning a new musical piece. It could be reading a novel. However the situation must support new learning in a manner similar to what occurs in therapy. What is necessary for therapeutic change to occur is that the situation must promote that open state *and* there be a stimulus present to work on to learn, even if nonconscious. If one is in that open state but there are no problem stimuli present to be worked on and integrated, no change may occur. One may get deeply absorbed in a transcendent experience while hiking in the wild and it may lead to no personality change in deeper issues because one is not 'present to' aspects of the problem (I am not suggesting one ruin a good hike by deliberately thinking about problems).

In everyday life we learn holistically. We learn in any environment as we navigate through it. Therapy is similar. Even if the therapist uses interventions the experience is a holistic learning one. This includes the relationship and interaction with the therapist. It includes the person of the therapist. It includes bringing in or 'crossing' (see Gendlin's idea of crossing, Levin, 1997) situations from outside of therapy with the learning environment in therapy. It is like learning at school. People learn depending on where they are in their lives, things going on in their lives, their classmates, teachers, life plans, and so on. The whole gestalt shifts and changes as new elements are experienced in the context of the gestalt which is current life. When we leave therapy and go into everyday life it is not necessarily that we 'apply' what we have learned to life outside. This is too cognitive. Rather, it is a reciprocal back and forth—everyday life affecting what we have learned in therapy, *which is not static and continually shifts and changes in interaction*, and what we have learned in therapy affecting everyday life in a continual interweaving.

Does this mean that specific interventions never help? Or that change cannot be attributed to specific interventions? No. In some cases it can be. But even then it is those interventions embedded in holistic experience. In particular, many psychotherapeutic activities may promote this ability to be open. Of course the person-centered conditions of empathic understanding, unconditional positive regard, and facilitative congruence are primary. As Rogers said, an authentic meeting of persons can also promote this. If the therapist can be *immediate*, meeting the person in the moment, without facades, being willing to share his or her own experience directly, nondefensively, and engage in a real dialogue, then clients and therapists are *living* the kind of process that Rogers sees as the outcome of therapy. In a sense, clients learn the process of being in process through the living experience of engaging in a meeting of persons with the therapist. This is how therapy can be a by-product of a meeting of persons. Of course this will only happen if the meeting of persons is supportive and genuine, not if it is hostile or otherwise promotes defensiveness.

In addition, activities that give clients something to 'hold on to,' to feel more grounded and balanced, will facilitate this open learning state. This can include engaging in reflective self-exploration that leads clients to feel more self-accepting, more self-understanding, and more like they make sense. In psychodynamic therapy it may include gaining an understanding that leads them to feel more self-accepting. For instance, they may understand that their behavior makes sense based on their childhood experiences.

Activities that promote a sense of mastery also may help. In cognitive-behavioral therapy undergoing exposure may lead clients to feel they are able to handle painful or tumultuous experiences (Goldfried, 1995). They may also learn from the cognitive therapist a new way of thinking that gives them confidence that they can manage their emotions. Learning the new way of thinking may also counter their fears that there is something basically wrong with them. All these learnings do not necessarily transfer to everyday life. But what they can do is give the person a sense of confidence as they face new situations. The person now *feels* that he or she does not have to be on the defensive so much, and becomes more open to new information, new opportunity in the environment, and new and creative thoughts and insights that 'bubble up.'

Internal balance is created by many of these tasks of therapy. Self-exploration in which the person sharpens perceptions of what is bothering him or her may lead to a sense of inner balance and relaxation. Having a 'handle' on that may help when one is confronting a situation in everyday life. One can refer back to the learning, as if to say 'I understand this,' and, being balanced, relax and now notice new opportunities or find some new idea bubbling up. Similarly, learning to challenge dysfunctional cognitions may give one a sense of efficacy. If one begins to feel bad one can say, 'I am catastrophizing here, I can apply my cognitive therapy training and challenge my dysfunctional thinking.'

In conclusion, whatever restores harmony and inner balance and reduces defensiveness, if only momentarily, leads to opportunities for learning and advance *if* the proper conditions are present—new opportunities in the environment, thinking about a prior experience, confronting the person, etc. Change happens *in interaction*. The change need not be a large change. Often the shift in openness/attentiveness is a small one. It may be only momentary. The individual may proceed much like before in most interactions. Perhaps only in the problem situation, if the problem is not so overwhelming that it precipitates new fear and defensiveness, will the person be able to be that balanced and be more open. So the shift may be too subtle and momentary to show up in therapy. In fact, it may not even show up in therapy. My client, who complained over and over, did not show any noticeable shift in therapy. I speculate that the person did 'carry with him' his experience in therapy which allowed him to be more open at key moments in his everyday life and to make the good adjustments and new decisions that he did make.

HOW DOES THIS FIT WITH ROGERIAN THEORY?

What I am proposing is congruent with Rogers' process view of change in psychotherapy (Rogers, 1961). The process conception is about an open way of living. The person moves from being rigid to being more openly a process of change. Openness is a whole body state, not just cognitive openness. The person is described as becoming the process of fluidity and open experiencing. The Process Scale (Walker, Rablen and Rogers, 1960) was developed to measure process changes. A person at the upper end of the Process Scale is what Rogers described as the fully functioning person (Rogers, 1961).

Although the type of openness that Rogers describes on the Process Scale is similar to the kind of openness I am talking about, I think that Rogers' description is 'too large.' By this I mean that Rogers was talking about a change in the whole person of the client, a kind of basic shift in how the person relates to self and world. I think the kinds of changes that happen in therapy are often much smaller. Fundamentally conservative people do not become high on the process scale as a general way of being. They do not become fundamentally fluid, changing, and open. However, in the moment, as they confront a problem situation, they may become more fluid and open, if only momentarily and in the context of that problem. Research using the Process Scale might not pick up such small changes, either in therapy or in life. As an example, my client who endlessly complained showed no movement on the process scale that I could observe in therapy. Yet I believe that he did go home and in key moments was able to feel more grounded, balanced, and open, and notice new things that led to his making creative decisions that moved his life forward.

I also believe that what I am saying is compatible with Gendlin's (1964, 1996) theory of experiencing. I am arguing that much of change is fundamentally noncognitive. Therapy is most basically an experience (Gendlin, 1967, 1968). Change could take place from an experience without there ever being a realization, or an awareness of or an accepting of feelings. The client just now *finds him or herself* different.

Although I think Gendlin is fundamentally right about the nature of experiencing, he has tended to emphasize the *articulation* of experiencing—focusing on feelings, until things 'bubble up,' and there is a felt shift. While I think there is truth in this (it happens), some changes occur without the client ever being aware of a felt shift, although one has taken place. (However, I'm not sure in Gendlin's theory if one can have a felt shift without awareness.) In effect, through the proper experiences, information flows better in the body. In a healing experiential encounter (see also Wyatt, 2007) one's body adjusts to the tenor of the encounter and that information flows up and down in the body. Organismically, new shifts and transformations take place.

CONCLUSION

It is clients who make therapy work through the human capacities for self-healing and self-righting. However, we do not really know how the process works. I suggest that much of the process is nonconscious. It involves moving from a state of defensiveness, hypervigilence, or hopelessness to a state of active, receptive openness. A state of active receptive openness promotes clients' noticing new possibilities both inside and outside of therapy, trying new things out, and having new creative insights and ideas 'bubble up.' Many changes that occur may happen nonconsciously. Any experience that promotes an organismic openness to learning will increase the chances of positive change happening. This is the process involved in client self-healing and self-righting, which is ultimately a part of the actualization process.

REFERENCES

Bohart AC (2007a) Taking steps along a path: Full functioning, openness, and personal creativity. *Person-Centered and Experiential Psychotherapies, 6,* 14–29.

Bohart AC (2007b) The actualizing person. In M Cooper, M O'Hara, PF Schmid, & G Wyatt (Eds) *The Handbook of Person-Centered Psychotherapy and Counseling.* Basingstoke/New York: Palgrave Macmillan, pp. 47–63.

Bohart AC & Tallman K (1999) *How Clients Make Therapy Work: The process of active self-healing.* Washington, DC: American Psychological Association.

Cissna KN & Anderson R (1994) The 1957 Martin Buber–Carl Rogers dialogue, as dialogue. *Journal of Humanistic Psychology, 34* (1), 11–45.

Csikszentmihalyi M (1990) *Flow: The psychology of optimal experience.* New York: Harper & Row.

Dijksterhuis A & Nordgren LF (2006) A theory of unconscious thought. *Perspectives on Psychological Science, 1,* 95–109.

Gendlin ET (1964) A theory of personality change. In P Worchel & D Byrne (Eds) *Personality Change.* New York: Wiley, pp. 102–48.

Gendlin ET (1967) Therapeutic procedures in dealing with schizophrenics. In CR Rogers, ET

Gendlin, DJ Kiesler & CB Truax (Eds) *The Therapeutic Relationship and its Impact*. Madison, WI: University of Wisconsin Press, pp. 369–400.

Gendlin ET (1968) The experiential response. In E Hammer (Ed) *Use of Interpretation in Treatment*. New York: Grune & Stratton, pp. 208–27.

Gendlin ET (1996) *Focusing-Oriented Psychotherapy*. New York: Guilford Press.

Goldfried MR (1995) *From Cognitive-Behavior Therapy to Psychotherapy Integration*. New York: Plenum Press.

Levin DM (1997) (Ed) *Language beyond Postmodernism: Saying and thinking in Gendlin's philosophy*. Evanston, IL: Northwestern University Press.

Rogers CR (1961) The process equation of psychotherapy. *American Journal of Psychotherapy, 15*, 27–45.

Rosenbaum R & Talmon M (2006, September) Implementing single-session approaches in community clinics. One-day workshop for Mental Health Association, State of Victoria, Australia. Bendigo, Australia.

Selby CE (2004) Psychotherapy as creative process: A grounded theory exploration. Unpublished doctoral dissertation, Saybrook Graduate School, San Francisco, CA.

Shostrom EL (Producer) (1965) *Three approaches to psychotherapy: Series one* [Film]. Orange, CA: Psychological Films.

Tallman K (1996) The state of mind theory: Goal orientation concepts applied to clinical psychology. Unpublished Master's thesis, California State University, Dominguez Hills, Carson, CA.

Walker A, Rablen R & Rogers CR (1960) Development of a scale to measure process change in psychotherapy. *Journal of Clinical Psychology, 16*, 79–85.

Wyatt G (2007) Psychological contact. In M Cooper, M O'Hara, PF Schmid & G Wyatt (Eds) *The Handbook of Person-Centred Psychotherapy and Counselling*. Basingstoke, Hants/New York: Palgrave Macmillan, pp. 140–53.

CHAPTER 13

RESILIENCE AND THE SELF-RIGHTING POWER OF DEVELOPMENT: OBSERVATIONS OF IMPOVERISHED BRAZILIAN CHILDREN IN PERSON-CENTERED PLAY THERAPY

Elizabeth Freire, Silvia H. Koller, Aline Piason, Gláuber Gonçalves, Bertrand Freund, Wagner de Lara Machado, Rodrigo de Lima Ávila, Lucas Severo Ache, Florence Beraldin Diedrich, and Maria Cláudia Furtado

Brazil is an industrial power with the world's fifth largest population and the world's eighth largest economy, yet one-fourth of Brazilian children and adolescents live in extreme poverty. About 8% of the population live on less than US $1 a day, and 20% live on less than $2 (Instituto Brasileiro de Geografia e Estatística, 2007). The most common risks faced by youth growing up in poverty are neighborhood violence, father absence, low parental education, family violence, housing difficulties, unemployment, and familial sexual or physical abuse (Hoppe, 1998; Verner and Alda, 2004). Brazilian youths in low-income urban neighborhoods are exposed to heightened developmental risks stemming from violence in their communities, economic deprivation, and family vulnerability (Raffaelli, Koller, Santos and Morais, 2007). Low socioeconomic status and exposure to violence are well-established statistical predictors of subsequent developmental problems among youth (Garmezy, 1993). A recent study with a sample of Brazilian youth in low-income neighborhoods showed that exposure to these risk factors is linked to declines in psychological and behavioral functioning—higher levels of risk are associated with lower levels of adjustment. Exposure within a community to such phenomena as drug trafficking, police raids, assaults, robberies, and shootouts is associated with negative emotionality and elevated substance use. In addition, higher levels of poverty are associated with lower levels of self-esteem and positive emotionality. Higher levels of poverty are also associated with higher levels of negative emotionality, use of licit and illicit substances, and a history of suicide attempts (Raffaelli, Koller, Santos and Morais, 2007). The psychological distress and behavioral dysfunction associated with poverty paints a gloomy picture for youths growing up in the outskirts of large Brazilian cities. Implementing intervention programs aimed at improving this situation is a necessity for these vulnerable young people.

PERSON-CENTERED PLAY THERAPY AS A PROTECTIVE PROCESS

'Risks' and 'assets' currently are seen as important concepts in the field of developmental psychology. Recent research in developmental psychology shows reduction of risks or stressors is not the only effective strategy for intervention with children. The enhancement of 'assets' and the facilitation of protective processes (Masten, 2001) are also important as intervention strategies. Assets, or resources, can counterbalance or compensate for the negative effects of adversity. Therefore, enhancing assets and fostering positive adaptation is an important direction in developing interventions to protect impoverished children from the negative impact of exposure to risks in their unfavorable circumstances (Luthar, Cicchetti and Becker, 2000; Masten and Coatsworth, 1998).

Research in developmental psychology has been exploring the protective factors and mechanisms that enhance resistance to psychosocial adversities and hazards, and enable children to face life's stressors successfully. The evidence supports three sets of protective factors associated with the likelihood of more beneficial outcomes for children and adolescents exposed to psychosocial adversity:

a. personality characteristics, such as autonomy, positive self-esteem, cognitive skills (e.g., competence in communication skills such as language and reading), and a positive social orientation;

b. family cohesion, the presence of a caring adult, and absence of marital discord;

c. presence of external support systems that encourage the youth's coping efforts, e.g., a kind and concerned teacher; a strong maternal substitute; or the presence of a positive or protective institutional structure, such as a caring agency (Garmezy, 1991; Masten and Garmezy, 1985; Rutter, 1993; Werner and Smith, 1992).

Recent studies corroborate the importance of protective processes that promote positive self-esteem and self-efficacy through the availability of secure and supportive personal relationships. At-risk youth with a positive view of themselves are more likely to have the confidence to take active steps to deal with adversity, enhancing their resilience (Masten, 2001; Pesce, Assis, Santos and Oliveira, 2004; Rutter, 1993; Werner and Smith, 2001). A positive sense of self-regard (as opposed to self-derogation) and a sense of self as powerful and empowered (rather than powerless) are strongly associated with resilience in disadvantaged children (Garmezy, 1991).

There is robust evidence that person-centered therapy improves self-concept and promotes increased self-acceptance and increased positive feelings about self (Bozarth, Zimring and Tausch, 2002; Rogers and Dymond, 1954; Rogers, 1959). When working with children, person-centered therapy involves the use of play as a means of mediating the therapeutic relationship. As such, it is named appropriately *play therapy* (Axline, 1969; Dorfman, 1951). According to Moon (2001), person-centered play therapy is a relationship in which the young client experiences acceptance from the therapist, and consequently becomes more self-acceptant and better able to continue forward on her own developmental path in the direction of self-fulfillment. The psychologically nurturing therapy relationship, though often quite limited by time, stimulates 'the inner resources of the child and her innate capacity to find the best way to survive and enjoy her life' (Moon, 2001: 45). As such, person-centered play therapy has the potential to foster a very important protective process in the lives of impoverished and disadvantaged children, promoting their self-empowerment and resilience. Person-centered play therapy thus can be considered a potential protective factor in the lives of children exposed to psychosocial adversity.

PERSON-CENTERED PLAY THERAPY AT THE DELPHOS INSTITUTE

The Delphos Institute is a private, person-centered training institution located in Porto Alegre, the capital of the southernmost state of Brazil. Because of the tremendous potential of person-centered play therapy as a protective process, the staff at Delphos has been developing a program that provides this form of therapy to at-risk youth living in extreme poverty.

The program developed by Delphos Institute has no funding. It depends exclusively on the volunteer efforts of therapists and supervisors. The therapists in this program are undergraduate psychology students participating in their one-year internship in clinical psychology. The program currently is running in two institutions in Porto Alegre. These institutions provide community day programs for impoverished and at-risk children and adolescents from the outskirts of the city. One of the institutions is a public community centre. The other is a private, non-profit Catholic institution. Both provide day programs for children and adolescents from ages 7 to 14 when they are not at school, as public schools in Brazil offer only four hours of class time per day. Programming includes sports, music, handicrafts, educational, and leisure activities. The catholic institution also provides a program for pre-school children (up to 6 years old) and vocational courses for adolescents (14 to 18 years old). Each institution converted one room for use as a play therapy setting. The educational coordinators of the institutions made psychotherapy referrals based on their conversations with teachers and support staff.

This program supports ongoing, naturalistic effectiveness studies, the first results of which are reported elsewhere (Freire, Koller, Piason, Silva and Giacomelli, 2006). Findings indicate that children and adolescents who receive therapy in this program achieve: (a) important and relevant improvement in interpersonal relationships, with more positive attitudes towards others (e.g., peers, family, and teachers); (b) better performance at school; and (c) improvement in mood and emotional functioning, including greater and more stable well-being. The Delphos Institute is currently undertaking a second study, with the use of a quantitative measure, the Strengths and Difficulties Questionnaire (SDQ) (Goodman, 1997, 1999), in addition to qualitative data obtained by interviews with family members and teachers.

Although up to this point the data has been collected only on twelve children, the results are very promising, and will be published shortly. All but one of the children referred for defiant behavior, aggressiveness and hyperactivity were perceived as becoming calmer and more tranquil, with notable improvements in their relationships with peers and teachers. Episodes of aggression and fights with peers have diminished markedly. For two of the children in our study, reported episodes have ceased completely. The children who were referred because of social isolation were perceived as becoming more integrated with peers and more sociable, showing remarkable improvement in their relationships. In addition, three children showed considerable improvement in their academic performance, with increased motivation to learn. The teachers also reported that three children improved noticeably in their communication skills—they became better able to talk about their feelings and needs instead of withdrawing or exploding with anger. The following case histories illustrate some of these outcomes:[1]

Mark

Mark is five years old. He lives with his parents and a six-year-old brother. His mother is unemployed and his father has a very low paid, unskilled job in the construction sector. Mark was referred to psychotherapy for aggressive behavior, hyperactivity and defiant conduct. He became so defiant and restless in the classroom that his teacher would often put him out of class. He became withdrawn and isolated from peers. The educational coordinator believed that his misbehavior was caused by problems at home, since his parents are in the process of separation. Mark attended eight sessions of play therapy, over a period of about three months. Therapy came to an end when his therapist finished his one-year internship in the institution. During his sessions, Mark would play games with his therapist and would tell fantastic stories. For instance, Mark once said that he set fire to the school. He said that he had magic powers, that he could fly, go through walls, and destroy any kind of object. He also said that he used these powers to punish bad people (some of his peers and teachers) and to help people whom he liked (other peers and family members). The therapist did not confront Mark with an 'objective' or shared reality. Instead, he listened to Mark and received these histories with genuine empathy and unconditional positive regard. In the evaluation interviews following therapy, both his teacher and his mother said that the change in Mark's behaviors and attitudes was remarkable. His misbehavior (defiant conduct, aggressiveness and isolation) ceased altogether. He became calm, tranquil and participative in class.

Rachel

Rachel is nine years old and she lives with her mother and three siblings, ages three, seven and seventeen. Her mother works as domestic, and must work shifts on the weekends. Her father is unemployed and he rarely visits the family (once every six months). Rachel self-referred. She met one of the therapists in the courtyard of the institution during a break and asked him if she could come to talk with him in the therapy room. She began the first session asking if she could bring a peer to following sessions. The therapist agreed. In this first session, Rachel talked about her relationship

---

[1]. Identifying information has been disguised in order to preserve client confidentiality.

problems with her peers. She said that she did not like them, she did not like to play with them, and that she had no friends. She also complained about her mother—that she worked too much and did not have time for her. Rachel spent the rest of the first session playing a board game with the therapist. Rachel attended a total of six sessions over a period of three months. Like with Mark, therapy ended when her therapist finished his one-year internship in the institution. Rachel brought a colleague to two of her sessions, and they would play board games with the therapist. Rachel would take the lead in the games, deciding what and how to play and when to stop. The therapist was dedicated to following her lead and to accepting her unconditionally throughout the sessions. In the interviews with her mother and teacher, they confirmed that Rachel had relationship difficulties before therapy. She used to be excluded from the group of peers and would have no friends. Both teacher and mother perceived improvement in her attitudes and behavior after therapy. Rachel became calmer, less aggressive, more engaged in social interactions. She also started to develop friendships.

Lucas
Lucas is eight years old. He lives with his parents and a nine-year-old brother. His mother is unemployed and his father has an informal job making deliveries on a motorbike. Lucas was referred to therapy after being found in the bathroom of the institution making sexual advances towards another boy. His teacher had also complained about his aggressiveness, defiant conduct and hyperactivity. His mother said in her first interview that Lucas had once beaten himself until he bled because he had lost a game. Lucas has attended fifteen sessions over a period of six months, and he remains in therapy. In most of the sessions, Lucas plays soccer with his therapist. In the therapy room Lucas chooses a wall and the door to be the soccer goals. He makes up the rules of the game, and breaks these rules in order to beat the therapist. The therapist does not confront Lucas for 'dishonest' behavior. Rather, she unconditionally accepts his behavior. She makes empathic reflections without judging Lucas' feelings, attitudes or behaviors. The only limits set by the therapist are in regard to the direction Lucas kicks the ball, since there is a risk of breaking the windows due to the forcefulness of his kicks. In the evaluation interview, the teacher reported that Lucas has ceased his defiant and aggressive behavior, and he is now much calmer and tranquil.

PERSON-CENTERED PLAY THERAPY AND THE PROMOTION OF RESILIENCE

The children attending the Delphos program face risk and adversity on a daily basis. They encounter risk not only in their communities (e.g., drug trafficking, police raids, assaults, and shootouts) but also within their own families (e.g., domestic violence, abuse, and neglect). Economic hardship, low levels of parental education, and lack of prospects for the future (due to high rates of unemployment and lack of educational opportunities) are distal risks. These come in addition to proximal risks, such as the enormous psychological distress they already endure within their family lives. Although the experience of person-centered play therapy does not reduce the risk present in their lives, it potentially can reduce some of the negative impact associated with risks. The availability of a secure, acceptant, empathic, and supportive therapeutic relationship, even for a short period, appears in our study to be enough to open an opportunity for the children we observed to develop a new way of relating with others and with themselves. The increased self-esteem and self-efficacy, and the more fulfilling pattern of relating with others that we see as a result of person-centered play therapy reduces the likelihood of these children being caught in the vicious cycle normally generated by their impoverished environments. These newly acquired 'assets' may protect these children from the prospect of school dropout and the subsequent limiting effects on job opportunities that predict failure outcomes across multiple domains of life.

The positive outcomes promoted by person-centered play therapy, despite the significant adversity faced by the children we observed, highlights the power of their growth forces. This points to the remarkable human capacity for developmental recovery, which Masten (2001) called 'the self-righting power of development' (p. 235). Current research on resilience has brought forth a striking positive view of normative human capabilities. Resilience was found to be a common phenomenon that results 'from the operation of basic human adaptational systems. If those systems are protected and in good working order, development is robust even in the face of severe adversity' (Masten, 2001: 227).

Masten (2001) points out that ordinary normative processes account for much of the resilience that is observed across a large range of situations. She concludes that resilience is 'the extraordinary that has revealed the power of the ordinary. Resilience does not come from rare and special qualities, but from the everyday magic of ordinary, normative human resources' (p. 235). While this may be a new finding in the field of developmental psychology, the 'power of the normative human resources' has been recognized by the person-centered approach and acknowledged as its foundation for more than six decades (e.g., Rogers, 1946, 1967) The 'adaptational system' that promotes development even in the face of severe adversity is known in the person-centered theory of personality as the 'actualizing tendency': the trustworthy function of the whole system that drives the organism towards fulfillment, enhancement and actualization (Rogers, 1959).

The brief case histories provided in this paper seem to indicate that the power of change in person-centered play therapy does not reside in the therapist's expertise, knowledge or techniques, since the therapists in this study endeavored to relinquish their power and control in their relationships with the children they saw in therapy. These therapists did not take over the locus of control in the therapeutic relationship; they did not guide the children, did not wield power over them, did not lead them, and did not set the rules. Instead, the therapists followed the children's lead and the children's rules. It seems that for these children the experience of this non-directive relationship with an adult was very empowering with a remarkable, positive effect on their lives.

The case examples provided here, which are a good representation of what we observed more broadly, seem to indicate that the active agent of change in the therapeutic process is ultimately the child's own growth force, i.e., her or his actualizing tendency. Considering the absence of therapist direction or guidance, it is reasonable to conclude that it was the children's own actualizing tendencies that ultimately set the direction for their process of change, moving them towards better relationships and healthier adaptation to their social environments. Consequently, it is the seemingly ordinary, though trustworthy, functioning of their actualizing tendencies which can account for the extraordinary resilience observed in these impoverished children experiencing person-centered play therapy in our program in Brazil.

REFERENCES

Axline V (1969) *Play Therapy*. New York: Ballantine. (Original work published 1947.)

Bozarth JD, Zimring F & Tausch R (2002) Client-centered therapy: Evolution of a revolution. In D Cain & J Seeman (Eds) *Humanistic Psychotherapies: Handbook of research and practice*. Washington DC: American Psychological Association, pp. 147–88.

Dorfman E (1951) Play therapy. In CR Rogers (Ed) *Client-Centered Therapy: Its current practice, implications, and theory*. Boston: Houghton Mifflin, pp. 235–77.

Freire ES, Koller SH, Piason A, Silva RB & Giacomelli D (2006) Person-centered therapy with child and adolescent victims of poverty and social exclusion in Brazil. In G Proctor, M Cooper, P Sanders & B Malcolm (Eds) *Politicizing the Person-Centred Approach: Agenda for social change*. Ross-on-Wye: PCCS Books, pp. 143–55.

Garmezy N (1991) Resiliency and vulnerability to adverse developmental outcomes associated with poverty. *American Behavioral Scientist, 34,* 416–30.

Garmezy N (1993) Children in poverty: Resilience despite risk. *Psychiatry, 56,* 127–36.

Goodman R (1997) The Strengths and Difficulties Questionnaire: A research note. *Journal of Child Psychology and Psychiatry, 38,* 581–6.

Goodman R (1999). The extended version of the Strengths and Difficulties Questionnaire as a guide to child psychiatric caseness and consequent burden. *Journal of Child Psychology and Psychiatry, 40,* 791–801.

Hoppe MW (1998) Redes de Apoio Social e Afetivo de Crianças Expostas a Situações de Risco [Social and Emotional Support Networks of Children Exposed to Risk Situations]. Unpublished Master's thesis, Developmental Psychology, Universidade Federal do Rio Grande do Sul. Porto Alegre, RS.

Instituto Brasileiro de Geografia e Estatística (2007) *Indicadores Sociais*. Retrieved April 6, 2007, from <http://www.ibge.gov.br/home/estatistica/populacao/criancas_adolescentes/>.

Luthar SS, Cicchetti D & Becker B (2000) The construct of resilience: A critical evaluation and guidelines for future work. *Child Development, 71,* 543–62.

Masten AS (2001) Ordinary magic: Resilience processes in development. *American Psychologist, 56,* 227–38.

Masten AS & Garmezy N (1985) Risk, vulnerability, and protective factors in developmental psychopathology. In B Lahey & A Kazdin (Eds) *Advances in Clinical Child Psychology* (Vol. 8). New York: Plenum Press, pp. 1–52.

Masten AS & Coatsworth JD (1998) The development of competence in favorable and unfavorable environments: Lessons from research on successful children. *American Psychologist, 53,* 205–20.

Moon KA (2001). Nondirective client-centered therapy with children. *Person-Centered Journal, 8,* 43–52.

Pesce RP, Assis SG, Santos N & Oliveira RVC (2004) Risco e proteção: Um equilíbrio promotor de resiliência. *Psicologia: Teoria e Pesquisa, 20,* 135–43.

Raffaelli M, Koller SH, Santos EC & Morais NA De (2007) Developmental risks and psychosocial adjustment among low income Brazilian youth. *Development and Psychopathology, 19,* 565–84.

Rogers CR (1946) Significant aspects of client-centered therapy. *The American Psychologist, 1,* 415–22.

Rogers CR (1959) A theory of therapy, personality, and interpersonal relationships as developed in the client-centered framework. In S Koch (Eds) *Psychology: A study of science. Vol. 3: Formulations of the person and the social context.* New York: McGraw-Hill, pp. 184–256.

Rogers CR (1967) *On Becoming a Person: A therapist's view of psychotherapy.* London: Constable.

Rogers CR & Dymond RF (1954) (Eds) *Psychotherapy and Personality Change.* Chicago, IL: University of Chicago Press.

Rutter M (1993) Resilience: Some conceptual considerations. *Journal of Adolescent Health, 14,* 626–31.

Verner D & Alda E (2004) *Youth at Risk, Social Exclusion, and Intergenerational Poverty Dynamics: A new survey instrument with application to Brazil.* World Bank Policy Research Working Paper No. 3296. Retrieved January 6, 2005, from <http://goworldbank.org/U7Z6PLYL10>.

Werner EE & Smith RS (Eds) (1992) *Overcoming the Odds: High risk children from birth to adulthood.* Ithaca, NY: Cornell University Press.

Werner EE & Smith RS (2001) *Journeys from Childhood to Midlife. Risk, resilience and recovery.* Ithaca, NY: Cornell University Press.

CHAPTER 14

PSYCHOTHERAPY AND SEXUAL DIVERSITY: A PERSON-CENTERED APPROACH

JAVIER ARMENTA MEJIA

INTRODUCTION

Historically, the concept of sexual diversity has been understood in many different ways. The most common understandings were those linking homosexual or bisexual conduct to a disease, a moral perversion or a type of mental illness (Ardila, 1998). With the passage of time and the endorsement of the medical model and psychiatry, this pathological interpretation fostered and reflected a society inclined to punish and reject diverse expressions of sexuality. This in turn fomented self-rejection and guilt in those who knew themselves to be different, and behaved and expressed themselves differently than heterosexuals (Castañeda, 1999). We begin with this history, a history plagued with prejudicial labels, psychopathological diagnoses, and societal attitudes of rejection and exclusion. From here, this paper explores a humanist perspective (see Bugental, Schneider and Pierson, 2001; Davis and Neal, 1996, 2000; Lago and Smith, 2003) on sexual diversity that may allow for gradual progress, however tentative, toward more enriching and constructive ways of relating to and experiencing sexuality. In this sense, and taking the person-centered approach as a focal point, some of the following questions may guide us in this exploration: How can we facilitate positive growth in our gay, lesbian, and bisexual clients? Is it possible to speak of sexual diversity while also maintaining confidence in the organism? If the actualizing tendency is one of the fundamental hypotheses of this approach, how can we work in relation to sexual diversity in ways that will reinforce or liberate the actualizing tendency? Can we allow ourselves to accompany another in a 'relational depth,' (Mearns, 1997) even though his or her way of life and experience of sexuality may be different from our own? Can we speak of health, growth, and living fully while also speaking of sexual diversity? (Bower, 2001; Wilkins, 2003).

The author is deeply grateful to Brian Levitt, for his time, patience, and kind support in the publication of this material. This article was originally published in *Revista Mexicana de Psicología Humanista y Desarrollo Humano Prometeo, 39,* (4–8), 2004, and appears here with their kind permission. This paper was translated into English for this book by Brian's father, Dr. Samuel Levitt.

THE ACTUALIZING TENDENCY: OBSTACLES AND BARRIERS

The fundamental hypothesis upon which the person-centered approach rests is that there is a constructive, directional force that exists in every individual and group that propels them toward more creative ways of growth and development. This tendency implies a process directed toward health or functionality (Rogers, 1951; Mearns and Thorne, 1999; Sanders, 2004). While elements of the interpersonal, familial or social environment may have positive and negative influences on the individual, the constructive potential of the actualizing tendency remains a constant. Brodley (2001) maintains that although the actualizing tendency is marked by a constructive directionality we cannot always see its positive impact. Further, as long as the organism is alive, the actualizing tendency cannot be destroyed. As such, when the actualizing tendency is obstructed or blocked temporarily, the individual may feel oppressed or stuck, lacking creativity and having a sense that interpersonal relations are being affected negatively. When this obstruction continues the individual may become self-rejecting and come to experience the 'self' as suppressed, inaccessible, rigid, inadequate, distrustful, alienated, lacking a constructive identity, full of 'shoulds' and presenting a series of social masks or façades (Bower, 2001, 2004). This description, although quite general and perhaps simplistic, highlights the effect on an individual's 'self-concept' when the natural tendency toward growth and health remains blocked or does not function in an integrated or holistic manner.

CONDITIONS OF WORTH

During normal development, the child differentiates a very significant portion from his or her phenomenological field with which they associate various experiences, beliefs and behaviors. This portion of the child's inner world is what we refer to as the 'self,' and it is one of the factors that greatly influences a person's present-moment behaviors. As the 'self' develops, due to certain conditions (e.g., parental or familial rejection and acceptance), it may become divorced or alienated from the child's organismic experience to varying degrees. Very early in his or her development the child may begin distancing their self from their 'organismic experience,' distancing from what they really live, feel or experience. The child may become distanced in some ways from their internal resources and congruence. In some cases this may lead to a 'self-structure' born of introjects that is not really anchored in the individual's lived experiences. For adults this process may manifest itself in obstructed feelings, creating dysfunction, or creating the feeling that one is not fully living the life that he or she wants or hopes for (Bower, 2004).

If we reflect on these process in terms of a way of being (Carrasco and García, 2001; Natiello, 2001) we can see that with the passage of time, and the impact of cultural messages rejecting sexual diversity, an individual may introject these conditions of worth and become dissociated from his or her own feelings, affective desires or expressions by considering them bad, inadequate or repugnant. This is how war against the self begins, with what is perceived as rejected externally being found in one's own lived experience. These are the seeds within the individual of what some have referred to as internalized homophobia (Ardila, 1998; Castañeda, 1999; Davis and Neal, 1996; Isay, 1996; Sanders, 1993). A person facing these external and internal conditions of rejection and disapproval faces an intense and unrelenting struggle, leading to fragmentation and incongruence. Nevertheless, there are underlying constructive resources within the individual that hold the potential for living fully or functioning optimally.

THE THERAPEUTIC PROCESS

In 1957, Carl Rogers put forth what he found, through research, experience, and observations, to be the six necessary and sufficient conditions for constructive personality change. These conditions are stated here as Rogers (1959: 213) presented them in his most fully developed theory statement. We will be considering them in this paper as a framework for facilitating growth with gay, lesbian, and bisexual clients.

1. *Two persons are in contact.* This condition implies that the therapist or facilitator makes a significant difference in the client's perceptual field. The client experiences the facilitator as an 'other' with whom they can connect emotionally. The client may need clarification, understanding, and the perception of an emotional response in a significant other in order to open up and explore a history filled with potentially painful, confusing, or unclear material (Barrett-Lennard, 1998, 2003; Cain, 2002). This implies a receptive attitude or openness in the therapist to any material, verbal or non-verbal, that the client brings to therapy. Some of the obstacles that prevent contact from taking place may be homophobia, heterosexism, the facilitator's own unresolved sexual conflicts, and prejudicial views towards minorities.

Psychological contact requires the facilitator to be comfortable with the client's presence and history, the bond that ties them to the client, and the client's presentation of a way of life and experience that is clearly not heterosexual. As Rafael, a client at the end of a course of therapy, puts it:

> At first I arrived with a lot of fear. I didn't know if the therapist was going to tell me that what I felt was bad, or that they were going to put me in a psychiatric hospital, or that I definitely couldn't be cured. I was afraid he would tell me that I was condemned and that I couldn't be forgiven for feeling what I felt. I didn't know if he could understand me, if he could enter the confusion that I felt and the struggles that seemed to have no end. After several sessions I knew that he understood me, that I was in a safe place, that he wouldn't judge me or laugh at me while telling him everything that I had always kept secret. I can't say exactly, but something in him gave me the confidence to tell my story.

THE CLIENT'S INCONGRUENCE

2. *The first person, whom we shall term the client, is in a state of incongruence, being vulnerable, or anxious.* Generally a person turns to psychotherapy because of suffering or temporary inability to solve a problem, because of a state of incongruence. For gay, lesbian, and bisexual clients, this incongruence may be due in part to social messages that sexual diversity is bad, an illness or a vice—the organism may be fighting against itself, causing fragmentation or leading to unconstructive functioning. It should be remembered that the client's incongruence is not *because* of his or her sexual orientation. Rather, this incongruence comes about because of an environment that is not favorable to a constructive vision of their desires and a positive experience of their own sexuality. The self and the organismic response are experienced as going in totally different directions—they are at odds. This split implies a lack of integration within the individual—the individual's functioning is expressed in defensive responses.

THE FACILITATOR'S CONGRUENCE

3. *The second person, whom we shall term the therapist, is congruent in the relationship.* The congruent facilitator enters the relationship without trying to present a predetermined appearance or image. This implies a certain degree of personal development, which allows the facilitator to be his or her own experience as it unfolds in the moment (Barrett-Lennard, 2003; Rogers, 1961). Congruence can be associated with authenticity, meaning that the experiences lived by the facilitator are within reach of their awareness. The way in which the facilitator interacts with the client is linked with their own organismic experiencing.

Some authors refer to congruence as the process of being oneself, or being that self one truly is (Rogers, 1961). Lietaer (1993) elaborates upon this with the concept of transparency—that which is lived internally is expressed externally. The therapist or facilitator is transparent to the extent that he is able to share or reveal his internal experience in any given moment.

Therapist congruence is crucial in encounters with sexual diversity in others. Growing up in a social environment that rejects sexual diversity, gays, lesbians and bisexuals may develop a feeling of distrust for others—a sense of fearfulness over or vulnerability to their feelings being discovered or exposed. Not wanting to risk this exposure, for fear of rejection and social isolation, is often referred to as staying 'in the closet.' Over time, this continual vigilance to avoid having their 'dangerous secret' exposed can create an 'alienation from experience' (Bass and Kaufman, 1996; Imber-Black, 1993; Isense, 1991). Therapist congruence, or transparency, helps to establish a safer environment for the gay, lesbian, or bisexual client, and a healthier relationship both with the therapist and with the client's own experiences. Being with another person who can be transparent (e.g., a therapist who is not hiding) may lead to clients feeling that they do not have to hide or justify themselves. This may facilitate, step by step, a healing rapprochement for clients with their own organismic experience, which may have been denied or avoided until then because of living in a rejecting, homophobic society.

UNCONDITIONAL POSITIVE REGARD

4. *The therapist is experiencing unconditional positive regard toward the client.* Holding unconditional positive regard implies that the facilitator values every aspect of the gay, lesbian, or bisexual client's lived experiences. Unconditional positive regard for the client is given when the facilitator respects the client's sexual orientation without trying to change it or see it as pathological. The facilitator who holds unconditional positive regard for the client holds an attitude of respect for the unique way of life of each gay, lesbian, or bisexual client, as well as an openness towards the unique expressions of gay, lesbian, and bisexual cultures. The therapist must understand that within or outside of a gay, lesbian, or bisexual community, a plurality of ways of being and acting exist. Therefore, during therapy, the therapist holding unconditional positive regard for an individual client does not adhere to stereotypical visions of the client or their community. The therapist must direct their efforts toward understanding and valuing the individual. Moving beyond facile stereotypes and diagnostic classifications, the work of the facilitator is to accompany the 'emergence of the individual' and their potential path toward wholeness (Davis and Neal, 1996). Unconditional positive regard emerges as an element that allows clients to slowly accept and like themselves and all manifestations of their experience, including aspects of their sexuality that were met previously with rejection and hatred.

EMPATHIC UNDERSTANDING

5. *The therapist is experiencing an empathic understanding of the client's internal frame of reference.* The therapist must use all of his or her resources to achieve an understanding for the client from the client's own frame of reference. According to Rogers (1951: 29) the therapist assumes

> in so far as he is able, the internal frame of reference of the client, to perceive the world as the client sees it, to perceive the client himself as he is seen by himself, to lay aside all perceptions from the external frame of reference while doing so, and to communicate something of this empathic understanding to the client.

Some (e.g., Elliott, Watson, Goldman and Greenberg, 2004) have adapted empathy as a tool to be used within an experiential, emotion-focused approach. Bohart and Greenberg (1997) have described different types of empathy to be 'used' at different moments of therapy. As an attitude, empathic understanding implies entering the client's internal world at the client's pace in order to understand the client's experiences from his or her own perspective.

Gays, lesbians, and bisexuals may encounter a lack of understanding from others as well as from themselves regarding their individual lived experiences. Empathic understanding, understanding others on their own terms, allows individuals to recognize and reorganize their experiences, clarifying some and accepting or reconnecting with parts of their own experience that were formerly disguised, distorted or negated. This re-accommodation enables individuals to regain more complete contact with their own feelings, and not just contact with those feelings judged by themselves or others as all right to have. An expression of the true self emerges, permitting movement beyond the conditional self that was constructed in order to remain hidden and to avoid mockery and rejection from others. In other words, the individual reconnects with his or her organismic valuing process, rather than remaining stuck in rigid or defensive patterns.

THE CLIENT'S PERCEPTION

6. *The client perceives, at least to a minimal degree, conditions 4 and 5, the unconditional positive regard of the therapist for him, and the empathic understanding of the therapist.* The client's perception of unconditional positive regard and empathic understanding, according to person-centered theory (e.g., Davis and Aykroyd, 2002; Mearns and Thorne, 2003; Sanders and Wyatt, 2002), leads to a gradual change and reorganization of the client's experience from a state of incongruence and psychological vulnerability toward ways of functioning that are more creative, constructive and in contact with their organismic experience. Perceiving these core conditions is likely to result in a healing and profoundly constructive experience for many gay, lesbian, and bisexual clients who have lived through a history of rejection and lack of understanding of who they truly are.

FROM OPPRESSION TO FULLY FUNCTIONING

Person-centered theory, as it is applied to psychotherapy, facilitation or accompanying, implies a constructive vision of the human being. It also implies a process in which every human being, inclusive and regardless of sexual diversity issues, can find growth or greater congruence. In this sense, we all become brothers in the search for wholeness, positive change, and a better quality of life. The person-centered facilitator is a companion in this search or pilgrimage who allows clients to fully and freely confront and assume their own existence. Person-centered therapy offers hope for a new beginning and the birth of a better and freer way of being and existing in the world, a way of being that moves beyond alienation and rejection.

REFERENCES

Ardila R (1998) *Homosexualidad y Psicología*. México: El manual moderno.
Barrett-Lennard G (1998) *Carl Rogers' Helping System: Journey and substance*. London: Sage.
Barrett-Lennard G (2003) *Steps on a Mindful Journey: Person-centred expressions*. Ross-on-Wye: PCCS Books.
Bass E & Kaufman K (1996) *Free Your Mind. The book for gay, lesbian and bisexual youth and their allies*. New York: Harper Perennial.

Bohart A & Greenberg L (1997) *Empathy Reconsidered. New directions in psychotherapy.* Washington, DC: APA.
Bower D (Ed) (2001) *The Person-Centered Approach: Applications for living.* San Jose: Writers Club Press.
Bower, D (2004) *Person-Centered/Client-Centered. Discovering the self that one truly is.* San Jose: Writers Club Press.
Brazier D (1993) *Beyond Carl Rogers. Towards a psychotherapy for the 21st century.* London: Constable.
Brodley B (2001) The actualizing tendency concept in client-centered theory. In D Bower (Ed) *The Person-Centered Approach: Applications for living.* San Jose: Writers Club Press, pp. 81–106.
Bugental J, Schneider K & Pierson F (Eds) (2001) *The Handbook of Humanistic Psychology: Leading edges in theory, research and practice.* Thousands Oaks, CA: Sage.
Cain D (Ed) (2002) *Classics in the Person-Centered Approach.* Ross-on-Wye: PCCS Books.
Carrasco M & García A (2001) *Género y psicoterapia.* Madrid, España: Universidad Pontificia de Comillas.
Castañeda M (1999) *La Experiencia Homosexual. Para comprender la homosexualidad desde dentro y desde fuera.* México: Paidos.
Davis D & Neal C (Ed) (1996) *Pink Therapy. A guide for counselors and therapists working with lesbian, gay and bisexual clients.* Buckingham: Open University Press.
Davis D & Neal C (Eds) (2000) *Therapeutic Perspectives on Working with Lesbian, Gay and Bisexual Clients.* Buckingham: Open University Press.
Davis D & Neal C (Eds) (2000) *Issues in Therapy with Lesbian, Gay, Bisexual and Transgender Clients.* Buckingham: Open University Press.
Davis D & Aykroyd M (2002) Sexual orientation and psychological contact. In P Sanders & G Wyatt (Eds) *Rogers' Therapeutic Conditions: Evolution, theory and practice. Vol. 4: Contact and perception.* Ross-on-Wye: PCCS Books, pp. 221–33.
Elliott R, Watson J, Goldman R & Greenberg L (2004) *Learning Emotion-Focused Therapy: The process-experiential approach to change.* Washington, DC: APA.
Imber-Black E (Ed) (1993) *Secrets in Families and Family Therapy.* New York: Norton.
Isay R (1996) *Becoming Gay. The journey to self-acceptance.* New York: Pantheon Books.
Isense R (1991) *Reclaiming Your Life. The gay man's guide to love, self-acceptance, and trust.* Los Angeles, CA: Alyson Books.
Lago C & Smith B (2003) *Anti-discriminatory Counselling Practice.* London: Sage.
Lietaer G (1993) Authenticity, congruence and transparency. In D Brazier (Ed) *Beyond Carl Rogers: Towards a psychotherapy for the 21st century.* London: Constable, pp. 17–46.
Mearns D (1997) *Person-Centred Counselling Training.* London: Sage.
Mearns D & Thorne B (1999) *Person-Centred Counselling in Action.* London: Sage.
Mearns D & Thorne B (2003) *La Terapia Centrada en la Persona Hoy.* España: Desclee de Brouwer.
Natiello P (2001) *The Person-Centred Approach: A passionate presence.* Ross on-Wye: PCCS Books.
Rogers CR (1951) *Client-Centered Therapy.* Boston: Houghton Mifflin.
Rogers CR (1957) The necessary and sufficient conditions of personality change. *Journal of Consulting Psychology, 21,* 95–103.
Rogers CR (1959) A theory of therapy, personality and interpersonal relationships, as developed in the client-centered framework. In S Koch (Ed) *Psychology: A study of a science. Vol. 3: Formulations of the person and the social context.* New York: McGraw-Hill, pp. 184–256.

Rogers CR (1961) *On Becoming a Person*. Boston: Houghton Mifflin.
Sanders G (1993) The love that dare to speak its name: From secrecy to openness in gay and lesbian affiliations. In E Imber-Black (Ed) *Secrets in Families and Family Therapy*. New York: Norton, pp. 215–42.
Sanders P (2004) *The Tribes of the Person-Centred Nation. An introduction to the schools of therapy related to the person-centred approach.* Ross-on-Wye: PCCS Books.
Sanders P & Wyatt G (Eds) (2002) *Rogers' Therapeutic Conditions: Evolution, theory and practice. Vol. 4: Contact and perception.* Ross-on-Wye: PCCS Books.
Wilkins P (2003) *Person-Centred Therapy in Focus*. London: Sage.

CHAPTER 15

AN ESSAY ON CHILDREN, EVIL AND THE ACTUALIZING TENDENCY

KATHRYN A. MOON

Thinking about the actualizing tendency leads me to consider and share my experiences of working with school children. Writing about school children reminds me of my own terrors, losses, mean intentions and evil ways. And so, as I write about the actualizing tendency, I am also writing about children, about myself, and about violence. In the course of this meandering I stumble upon an explanation for the evil in my own nature that relates back to the actualizing tendency as well as back to the essential and ethical value of client-centered constancy in psychotherapy practice.

Rather than ask, 'Why am I evil?' I'm inclined to respond to the question, 'When am I violent?' As postscript to what follows, I suggest that I am violent when the following factors come together: I am hungry for my next meal, I am sad, I am stressed, and I feel interfered with as I am striving for loving relationship, perhaps even struggling to be nurturing. When have I consciously, intentionally acted upon a sadistic urge to inflict suffering on another? I think I can say, 'Never after the age of twelve or thirteen!' Never after realizing I might get myself arrested. But from what did my sadism arise? Odd, my memories from five, seven, and eleven don't tell me. I might guess that my sadism is a contorted self-expression, if you will, a scream of frustration from wanting attention or love, from the hurt of exclusion, and from wanting to be free to be me. But that is only a guess, my current hypothesis.

THE ACTUALIZING TENDENCY: TOO MUCH SCIENCE FOR ME

Client-centered therapists frequently remark upon the power and efficiency of the therapy they practice. We say that the potency of therapy resides in the client. Our work is founded on trust in the client. This trust is theoretically grounded in the hypothesis of the actualizing tendency. This is the idea that the unhindered organism self-maintains and develops according to its individual nature.

I myself have blossomed through being a client in client-centered therapy. I've basked and grown in client-centered consultation, and strived, suffered and thrilled in person-centered groups. Also, I've been enriched from the self-satisfaction that comes with feeling I've been of help to others (Standal, 1954: 46; see also Moon, Rice and

Schneider, 2001: 25). As I watch client after client benefit in the unfettering atmosphere of nonjudgmental 'empathic reception' (Bozarth, 2005: 224; Brodley, 1998: 26), my perspective on the human condition brightens. Perhaps the actualizing tendency hypothesis informs my trust in a free people and so assists me as I move through my day, growing tired, but intending my best with client after client.

But the actualizing tendency hypothesis is not the first premise of my work, and, in fact, I am not fond of its role as first premise justification for client-centered theory. I justify client-centered therapy by its ethical rightness in accepting and sheltering each individual as intrinsically worthy and entitled to self-determination. Consequently, the actualizing tendency itself is relatively unimportant to me, even though it may be that the reason my work is efficacious for clients is because the actualizing tendency motivates them (Rogers, 1951: 195–6, 487–90). I don't know; regardless, it is because client-centered therapy is a perfect fit for the non-directive imperative of my working ethics that I am a client-centered therapist. Yes, I trust the client; but, more importantly, to me, I respect the client. In fact my trust in the client is founded upon my respect for a person's *right* to be free and to self-determine.

I distrust scientific claims made by psychologists, preferring to ground my own approach on philosophical considerations. Rogers straddled the fence between science and philosophy. His work and thought developed out of the tradition of psychology as science. The scientist in him did not fully commit to either free will or determinism. He brought the humility of a phenomenological perspective into the therapy room and brought the words and behaviors of the therapist under close scrutiny, thereby raising the therapist's interpersonal accountability. He realized that 'the general orientation of philosophical phenomenology' would likely further influence the approach he was describing (1959: 250). While the non-directive revolution elevated the patient to the status of person and relegated the therapist to a position of unknowing, Rogers persisted in explaining himself in the terms of science:

> I believe it is obvious that the basic capacity which is hypothesized is of very decided importance in its psychological and philosophical implications. ... Philosophically it means that the individual has the capacity to guide, regulate, and control himself, providing only that certain definable conditions exist. Only in the absence of these conditions, and not in any basic sense, is it necessary to provide external control and regulation of the individual. (p. 221)

His 'philosophical' addressing of the actualizing tendency in the quote above, is, for me, inadequate, not only because he speaks from a hybrid model, but also because I believe it is the wrong way to speak about a person. To me this statement is flawed, not only because Rogers suggests a necessity and hence a right to control and regulate a person, but also because he presumes, as if he were speaking from a stimulus-response model, to predict human behavior as good enough or lacking depending upon certain conditions.

Even were I to agree with Rogers' statement, I find it and the use of the actualizing tendency hypothesis as foundation for practice tainted by a deterministic view, as well as reeking a bit of therapist expertise over a bug under glass. A scientific approach to client-centered therapy seems under-advanced, a vestige from a medical paradigm that potentially pollutes both thought and practice. A slightly later statement by Rogers (1965) only somewhat bridges the significant gap between Rogers' 1959 paragraph above and my own viewpoint. In the later statement, Rogers discussed the 'deep paradox' (1965: 152) of modern awareness. From a scientific perspective, 'man is a complex machine. We are … moving toward a more precise understanding and a more precise control of this objective mechanism … ' (pp. 151–2).

> [I]n another significant dimension of his existence, man is subjectively free; his personal choice and responsibility account for the shape of his life ... A truly crucial part of his existence is the discovery of his own meaningful commitment to life with all of his being. (1965: 152)

Rogers saw man as subjectively free in a determined world.

> If in response to this you say, 'But these views *cannot* both be true,' my answer is, 'This is a deep paradox with which we must learn to live.' (p. 152)

My reading of Rogers' client-centered theory, particularly his notion of congruence in the theories of both personality and therapy, follows his implicit trajectory of a never definable, process view of life and the literal incapacity and lack of right of the therapist to direct, capture, manage or shape the client. Client-centered therapy is the viable version of psychotherapy practice for me precisely because it transcends questions of what is real, what is determined, and what we *perceive* that we know is good or best for the client and, instead, is founded upon respect for the essential person and his or her right to self-create.

When I turn my attention to the idea of an actualizing tendency, I wonder why client-centered therapists bother with what seems to me to be the jargon of science. For me, personal ethical first premises trump the hypotheses of never-conclusive science no matter how authoritatively a scientific assertion appears to be framed or defended, or even how firmly I might believe in this 'fact' at this time. I feel, as Barbara Brodley says:

> Rogers' and other theorists' explanations of personality development, of the genesis of psychological disturbance, or their theories of processes in psychological change are *all irrelevant* to the practice of CCT [client-centered therapy]. For example, even taking Rogers' own theories of the process of change in CCT (Rogers, 1961, 1959) as instructions for what the therapist should focus on undermines the non-directive essence of CCT. (2006: 14)

I think of my own life, where I have been hindered and when I have thrived. I am returned to my ethical conclusion. I must not, only partly because I cannot, presume to know anything about another human being. What I can do, and what I choose to do in my practice of therapy is be a resource, offering empathic acceptance of the person. Whether as client or therapist, I love the rare atmosphere of the therapy room. Forced to work in order to feed, clothe and house myself, I choose to do the work I enjoy where I thrive, aswim in the process of therapeutic relationship.

AN OPINION ON THE HUMAN CONDITION AND THE NATURE OF LIFE

Instead of the actualizing tendency, I think of life. I think of the vitality and force of life, its flow, the moving nature and flicker of life, its vulnerability and its death. It is the energy for perversity, evil and wrongdoing as much as it is the motivation for creativity, self-maintenance, self-development and social cooperation. The force of life is double-edged. Life seeps or springs where it can or must, true or twisted. Each of us is contorted with at least a few quirks. Our thirst for self-maintenance and self-fulfillment carries with it the development of frustrations, anxiety, sadness and loss as well as self-enjoyment.

Reviewing my experiences counseling school children stirred stark reminders of who I am, was, or will be. It leaves me pondering the origins of evil, the sadness inherent in living, my and others' need for attention, and the role of compassion and self-compassion in shared living.

I believe that we cannot live without inflicting harm. We endeavor to raise our children to be strong enough to thrive. But our nurturing binds and preoccupies those we love even though our intention may have been to prepare them for full living. I cannot live and breathe in our shared atmosphere without consuming or destroying limited resources. To walk on the ground is to trample on plants and insects. To obtain is to steal attention. Aware or not, as I assert my will to forward myself, and as I occupy a space, I assign or deny air space, power, free movement, and personal authority to someone else. Conscious or unconscious, aware or not, carnivore or herbivore, living is killing even when it may also be giving.

Thinking of insufficient resources, human fatigue, misguided attempts to help, the failure of society to support parents in their parenting, I had intended to begin this chapter with 'The Old Woman Who Lived in a Shoe'. This rhyme perhaps referred in part to Queen Caroline who bore King George II eight children and in part to her 'white-wigged' husband and his 'children' in Parliament.

> There was an old woman who lived in a shoe,
> She had so many children she didn't know what to do!
> So she gave them some broth without any bread,
> And she whipped them all soundly and sent them to bed!
> (Alchin, nd)

But an older piece, a song that was partially inspired by 'Bloody' Queen Mary who burned three rebellious protestant noblemen at the stake, comes to me even more strongly:

> Three blind mice, three blind mice,
> See how they run, See how they run,
> They all ran after the farmer's wife.
> She cut off their tails with a carving knife.
> Did you ever see such a thing in your life,
> As three blind mice?
> (Alchin, nd)

To me, the dire flight of blind mice is one and the same with the frightened woman's cutting off of their tails. The kinesis of a sense (or perception) of frantic and desperate necessity has been one part of my experience of life and at times has been my predicate for surviving, a desperate striving.

The world's children are ill, orphaned, raped, mutilated, grieved, starving and dying before our eyes on television, by the millions. Village boys string a green lizard up by its tail and use it for target practice for rock-throwing play. The lizard's bright and bloody red wounds make vivid contrast with his green skin. Teeming, pregnant life struggles forth, erupts or implodes. We turn the soil and see discomposed worms, squiggly beetles, and the roots of plants. When I take an early morning hike through the woods and return on the same path an hour later, yellow and red mushrooms have sprouted. Inadvertently, I might step on one. I'm afraid to pick and taste them; they may be poisonous. In one city where I lived as a child, the nose-chained dancing bear had many bare spots on his shaggy hide. It was said that the beggars mutilated their babies because it brought in better alms.

I have little trouble extending my personal understanding of fear, anxiety, yearning and envy into more premeditated destructive, evil, behaviors. As Rogers said of the unhealthy pale and spindly potato sprouts that reached two or three feet '… toward the distant light …' and exhibited '… bizarre, futile growth', and 'desperate expression … Life would not give up, even if it could not flourish' (1980: 118). I burst to live and love.

AUTOBIOGRAPHY, CHILD AND ADULT

Supposedly, I am writing about the actualizing tendency, but that abstract subject leads me to dwell on other subjects closer to my experience, namely suffering and evil. The memories I share here are edited through the lens of my perspective and selected to meet my themes for this chapter. And so I am omitting the interpersonal caring and physical comforts of my childhood, my exuberance at play, the beauty that stays with me from a childhood of family travels. I picture sunned beaches and twinkling light on water, jade, aquamarine, and turquoise waters. I remember avoiding stepping on sea urchin, stingrays, and jellyfish and peeling wet swimsuits off of sticky sandy skin. I was allowed freedom as a child to explore and play in great cities, Munich, Heidelberg, Izmir, San Francisco, Honolulu, and Paris. I picture my handsome father feeding squirrels he'd coaxed upon his shoulder, and remember the closeness I still feel to my mother's breast, her bedtime story reading, and the intellectual explorations she shared with us.

Once, my then two-year-old only child stood for half an hour at the Chicago zoo, mesmerized, gazing quietly between the fence slats at a writhing tumble of piglets scrambling for milk from their huge, reclining mother's teats. Today my many sisters and I laugh with each other at our greedy hunger. We know we are pigs.

My family was not immigrant, but it was migrant. My parents raised a large brood and during the Cold War, with my father working in military intelligence, they moved more than fifty times in forty years. Our migrant life was stress-filled, and even within a loving family with well-intended parents I was buried in a tangle of children—confused, isolated and dissatisfied.

By the age of five, close cousin to Cain and Abel, I felt a degree of hatred in my heart, and sometimes I actively wished to inflict harm, loss or diminishment upon others. By nine, I knew that I was incapable of behaving myself, I was not 'good', and I was doomed to burn in hell.

At six, an American child in Munich, shy and confused in school recess, I imagined myself pirouetting in my ugly hand-me-down dress at the tip-top of the playground climbing equipment. At my request, my mother enrolled me in a ballet class, but the teacher hollered angrily and I was too terrified to return. I stole jewelry from a neighbor and was caught. The neighbor did not tell my parents but exclaimed her surprise: 'Why would I do such a thing?' My silent answer seemed obvious to me: I wanted it for myself.

I was sneaky, dishonest and aroused with sadistic urges. At seven, a friend and I crept up into the attic and pretended to invent a spanking machine. We played at spreading other children across the ironing board platform of a machine with gloved, levered hands that would pound our victims' bodies.

I began my second-grade school year from a house on a forested edge of Heidelberg, away from the American community. I was the same age, seven, as the counseling group of children described later in this chapter. This was the sixth or seventh home of my childhood, and, a few months later, we moved again, this time into the American military community within the city.

My in-school self was anxious, perhaps only semi-conscious or dazed, somewhat preoccupied, alienated within a sense of my wrongness; certainly I had no sense of belonging. And yet, I remember tramping with playmates, down the sidewalk on the way to the candy store, stolen pfennigs in my fist, boisterously chanting, 'We won the war in 1944!'

I admired the girl who sat next to me. She had a pretty name, 'Willomina,' (there had been numerous 'Kathys' in my first-grade class) and she had blond hair and blue eyes. Unlike me, she seemed beautiful and free, like a colt in a meadow, but proper. I was just wrong, wrong in thought, word and deed, and physically wrong, off, dirty and bad. (Hardly the white-communion-dressed child anointed with a garnet cross necklace I see *prancing* in family photos!)

One day that school year I was startled out of my miserable haze. I was told to join a small circle of children at the back of the room. Apparently I was under-pronouncing my 'Rs,' and I needed speech therapy. There I spent some portion of the ensuing year being asked to name, along with the other speech kids, the names of mimeographed pictures. I never managed to hear what was wrong with my 'Rs.' But I wonder if the extra attention of a speech therapy group might have been therapeutic for me.

I didn't realize that I should do homework. My parents came home from a teacher conference and said, 'Kathy, the teacher wonders why you don't study for spelling tests.' I was oddly clueless. Spelling, homework, and assessment had not previously caught my attention. I'm not sure I knew we had spelling tests! Now, explicitly advised to study my spelling words, I gave it a few minutes a week and from then on performed excellently in spelling.

I had a final startling experience that year, one that brought me into an enduring personal haven. On the last day of school, the teacher handed out 'golden book' prizes to children who had done well in school. She announced a special prize for a student who had made the most progress in reading that year. She called my name and handed me a great thick volume of Johanna Spyri's *Heidi*. I was bewildered and stunned, but rushed home, awake and excited and sprawled out on my bed for the remainder of the afternoon barely deciphering but gobbling up my first real book.

I wish I could say that becoming an acknowledged student and an avid reader had once and for all turned me into a good person. But, no, my self-development has proceeded more slowly. Around that same time, I had taken to going out alone into the neighborhood playground looking for a younger child to tease and torment. It was a few years later that I rounded up other children to join me in marauding explorations. At age eleven, I would turn to a friend and say, 'Let's go make trouble.' We would set out to find younger children or old people to taunt, pester and make miserable.

While a teenager, a younger sister and I were preparing dinner for our large family. There was bitter argument in the next room. I felt sad and distraught; also, I was hungry. Dinner is always supposed to be nutritious and aesthetic. It must include a fresh salad with a homemade dressing and be served with silverware and glassware properly laid. Milk must be poured for the children, butter dish and butter knife on the table, and meat, rice and vegetable come to cooking completion at the same time. My sister was arguing with me, not wanting to follow my directions. In my frustration, under stress, feeling a need to seize control, wanting to avoid at all costs escalation of family upset in the next room, I took the first steps of a lunge across the kitchen. My intention was to grab her throat and squeeze out her voice. I stopped in my tracks. It was for only a split second that my body had engaged in action that I did not carry through. I had briefly felt sufficiently circumvented, alarmed, under siege from a rebellious little sister to enter into homicidal motion. I had been stressed while striving to be responsible and to do right, and to attend to my own hunger for dinner.

This same sister and I recently tried to make sense of our somewhat distant relationship. She surprised me by recalling a time in our twenties that I had completely forgotten, a day when I had slapped her face. When she first said I'd done this, I was incredulous; I don't strike people and as an adult I'd never have struck her. But then gradually, in the course of a day she and I spent watching for eagles in the southern Illinois sky, I remembered.

My father had been near death. I was tired from attending to my family, from the burden of experiencing complicated interpersonal as well as physical responsibilities. The emotional stress I felt culminated for me in the moment when I hit my sister. But it was not only that.

She and I were headed home from the hospital on a two-lane highway during a busy commuter hour, probably the same hungry pre-dinner hour in which years earlier I had made my kitchen lunge at her. I was a new and nervous driver and the sun was shining in my eyes. My sister was asserting her opinion about what we should do next. She and I each felt that we had been holding things together, more or less alone. She was giving me directions about what needed to be done next, or who cared for, directions with which I disagreed. I feared that her plan would lead to family upset. Our argument was happening as I drove down the highway. I drew to a stop, waiting to turn left onto our country drive, in fast commuter-hour traffic. My sister's persistent argument was, to me, a din of uncooperative imposition and interference with my best efforts. In the midst of a left turn off of the highway, anxious and wanting to take control, insanely endangering us both, I slapped her face. With hindsight, I realize that in those stressful weeks, we had no time for sadness, and with a smile I realize also, I again must have been hungry. It was nearly three decades later that my sister brought the hurt and chronic domination she felt from me to my attention.

How does that relate to all of *this*? Why does the topic of the actualizing tendency take me to this psychological space of being life-destroying? As young as five and as late as age eleven I felt sadistic; I acted on my wishes to hurt others. I am, at times, a bad person, a distressed and overwhelmed person, a foolish person, and a sad person. I have a capacity for violence. Does the reader not? I ask that not superciliously, but in aloneness.

I feel privileged to be allowed to be a therapist, to have the opportunity to not impede the human life before me, even though I know that inevitably I will err, impede and be impeded. Why, now in my fifties, am I discovering increasing joy as I accept my own sadness? Might I say with a smile, 'My sadness at my badness?' I am human and grateful to be alive. I like myself.

CHILDREN ALONE AND IN GROUPS

The world is a harsh home to its babies! All parents and caregivers were once children fed broth without bread. As parents, no matter how good and well-intended, we suffer stress and inflict some degree of harm even as we love and nurture our children. Woe, then, to the not cherished child of absent or overwhelmed parents.

The first time I attempted to tell the story of one special group of seven-year-olds, it was Thanksgiving morning in Chicago. In a few hours relatives would arrive for the annual feast. I wrote to the international 'cctpca' email network:

> My nine-year-old son is mad at me on this Thanksgiving morning because I'm writing this long message while he wants the computer to play Doom. Doom is apocryphal, dark and violent. Actually, he's mad at me for two reasons. The second is that when I give him the computer in a minute, he wants me to sit with him and watch while he shoots to kill in a simulated struggle for survival. Even though Doom is not my cup of tea … I do sometimes sit with him. But not this morning when I've a Thanksgiving dinner to prepare.

At that time I was working as a counselor in a small school in a city neighborhood of immigrants. There, like the old woman in a shoe, I had many yearning clients and insufficient time to attend to them. Some of the children in this school reminded me of myself in childhood—anxious, shy, angry, confused, envious, delinquent and lost. Most who came to counseling were sustaining a critical level of suffering in one form or another. Many endured physical and verbal abuse, witnessed frequent violence, or had older brothers in gangs or jail. Often the children felt threatened and were already aligned within gang mentality, or sad from discordant, ill or estranged parents. Many had an undocumented immigrant parent who was afraid to assimilate into the community and did not speak English. Young parents struggled in economic hardship. Many of the children, as toddlers, had been temporarily separated from their parents, shipped back home to live with grandparents allowing parents to work overtime to carve out a viable life in the United States.

Again and again there was another child the principal felt must be seen. And, indeed, when I met with the child, I would be astounded that he or she had lasted this long without erupting or imploding in sadness or violence. I attempted to accommodate the many children into the six-hour school day in various ways. I shortened individual sessions, moved the children into groups, enlarged the groups, and shortened group time. I unsuccessfully experimented with seeing children on a rotating basis. I would alert or remind the children of where they were in the rotation. But the children would not leave me alone on their off-week. Even if a child managed to refrain from knocking on my door mid-session, I would hear from the teacher that this child is tearful, or talking about killing himself, please be sure and see him this week even though it is not his turn. My scheduling efforts never met the expressed needs of child, family and school. In desperation, I culled some students from my roster, mainly from a group of kindergartners who after meeting with me for that year when they were only five, appeared to me to be able enough for school and play as they entered the first grade. Generally though, in a client-centered manner, I tried not to 'terminate' a child who was continuing to want counseling. Fortunately, most eighth graders graduated in June, and every September the list began a little shorter than it had ended the previous school year.

I did not want to weed out children by assessing level of need for counseling. There was no right choice as to who should stay or go. The children I did turn away looked at me beseechingly when I came to their room to pick up a classmate. As I walked down the hallway, kids I'd never met called out from the lunch line, 'Miss Kathy, can I come to counseling?' I'd step into a room and, at risk of reprimand from their teacher, children called out, mid-lesson, 'Miss Kathy, I have a problem, I have lots of problems, can I come to counseling?' And the ones who already were lucky counselees called out, 'When will you see us today?' Wanting and need are rampant. There is insufficient time and care wherever we look.

This school was going to be permanently closed at the end of the school year. I was asked to spend a day going to each classroom to facilitate discussion about the final closing. Fortunately for my schedule, teachers of the lower classes declined this opportunity. So I didn't happen to visit the second-grade class of seven-year-olds, the class that contained an entire group of children who were part of the limited number of children I had culled from my roster during their kindergarten year. Later in the current year, the second-grade teacher said her kids seemed upset, and would I come see them after all about the impending school closing. We planned that I would visit her room the very next week. An odd event within this classroom of children intervened, and so, instead of going in the next week to discuss the closing, the principal asked me 'to see' some children from the second grade. Parents were concerned because seven children during a lunch recess had encircled and attacked a classmate. This child had been scratched on his forehead and even bled a little.

I went into this classroom with the principal's list of eight students, seven attackers and one victim. I was privately relieved that the list of perpetrators plus one victim did not include any of the children I'd deemed well-functioning and crossed off my roster two years earlier. I acknowledged the presence and pleading of those now second-grader previous counselees. But I called out the names of only this new group. So I did not call for Walter, who as a kindergartner was an animated conversationalist at home, a gifted student who refused to speak a single word in kindergarten. And I did not take Rose, who when she was five, self-referred and would come talk to me about a family death that had preceded her birth. And I did not call Michael, the youngest of a too-large family, a beautiful boy who used to perform martial ninja dances.

Faced today with the choice to take new children and not attend to my former counselees who I knew wanted my attention, would I do differently? Perhaps I would ask to have a class-wide meeting. Would that have been better for the former kindergartner group members for whom I ached? Maybe better at least for myself. But if I'd made that choice, I suspect my more group-experienced children might have dominated the class-wide group airtime. I don't know. I'll never know. That day I had an understandably pressing mandate from the principal, and it was there that I turned my attention.

The children in this new group were tremendously excited, even though a little scared, as we convened in the vacant music room. As soon as they knew this meeting was not to discipline them, they began to tell me about losing their baby teeth, illnesses, surgeries and going under the anesthesia mask. This usually non-directive therapist uncharacteristically shifted the conversation by mentioning that the principal wanted us to talk about the recess incident when Hector was hurt. The children exclaimed to me that we couldn't talk about it without *Helen*. It had been Helen's idea to make the circle around Hector and she who had scratched his face. Helen's involvement had up until then been unknown to the adults (and for all I know may still be unknown). I announced that I would go get Helen from class. But the children told me that Helen had gotten into trouble for something else and was now exiled and spending the day in a lower-grade classroom. I went and found her in the first-grade classroom. I was struck by her appearance, and perceived her as both waif and sprite. Her demeanor seemed to me to be expressive of life. Perhaps she was sly, maybe sad or wistful; her face was motion. I was entranced with her. She walked silently with me to the music room and sat down quietly in our group, on the edge of her chair. She was small and didn't speak until she was spoken to. When asked, she had plenty to say about how to prevent further episodes of bullying or meanness. We drew up a list of suggestions that we hand-printed in red marker.

This group tackled the work of therapy as though starved for it. We met for forty minutes. When we had a subsequent half-hour meeting the following week, I laid the red marker paper of suggestions on the table as shared property, but it was never referred to by me or any of the children. During the two group meetings, I came to understand that the victim, Hector, came across to several of the children as irritating; he would tag along uninvited, interrupt the conversation of others, and slow down reading-group time. It turned out that he disrupted his reading group because the others read too fast for him to keep up. He also chewed with his mouth open at lunch, and the girls felt rudely imposed upon by his gross table manners. It seemed to me that his hearing was poor, and I made a mental note to suggest to the principal that it be tested. The kids talked quite a bit about the ways others annoyed and angered them. They endeavored to listen politely to each other even while squirming to get in the next word. All nine children seemed able and eager to talk forever. To the best of my knowledge, there were no further reports of second-grade violence in the remainder of that school year.

A week after the follow-up small group session with the notorious nine, I returned to the second-grade classroom to facilitate a school-closing discussion. My three 'terminated' counselees were there. Once silent Walter spoke about how he would miss the school food and the drinking fountain. Rose managed to slip in several statements about how family life is going at home and who from her class she was going to miss. Of my former counselees, I think only my Ninja said nothing. I think that, like me, he was too heart-sore that we no longer had time together.

I was struck then, and I am struck today by the extent of emotional and physical hardship endured by so many. Feelings get hurt every day. We worry. Our wishes go unmet. Near where I live, underclasses of children are born into catastrophic levels of strife-filled existence. Powerless children suffer and struggle to survive and to exist as themselves in the face of chronic insult, fear and injury. The violence, hunger, misery, sadness and hurt that surround us are infinite. There is a cry 'Rapunzel, Rapunzel, let down your golden hair!'

My hair is not golden and I want to be me living my life. But I have a client-centered way of being to offer to my clients. When a client comes to me for therapy, I choose to facilitate rather than deter them from *being* and *becoming* themselves. A client rents time out of my self-preoccupied living and I turn my attention to their intentions, wishes, feelings, thoughts, reactions and meanings. A side benefit of my experiences as a daily witness to the miracle of human growth, renewal and creativity is that I am a pessimistic cynic turned trusting. My cup is more than half full.

Returning to the subjects of evil and the actualizing tendency, I am thinking that violence and evil arise from interference and hindrance in living, being precluded from attending to our attachments and deflected from being who we are and what we want for ourselves and our loved ones. This hypothesis of mine returns me to the ethical base of my working intention and also to the actualizing tendency hypothesis. Beyond the routine, rude requirements of life, in the rare minutes of the therapy hour, client-centered therapy gives me a way to free rather than circumscribe another and to turn my attention to the existence of another. I experience *life-giving* rather than *life-taking*.

REFERENCES

Alchin LK (nd) *Nursery Rhymes—Lyrics and origins!* Retrieved June 28, 2007 from <http://www.rhymes.org.uk>.

Bozarth JD (2005) The art of non-directive 'being' in psychotherapy. In B Levitt (Ed) *Embracing Non-directivity*. Ross-on-Wye: PCCS Books, pp. 203–27. Also published (2001) as 'The art of "being" in psychotherapy'. *The Humanistic Psychologist, Special Triple Issue. The art of psychotherapy, 29,* 1–3.

Brodley BT (1998) Criteria for making empathic responses in client-centered therapy. *The Person-Centered Journal, 5* (1), 20–8.

Brodley BT (2006) A Chicago client-centered therapy: Non-directive and non-experiential. Paper presented at the annual conference of the Association for the Development of the Person-Centered Approach, Fargo, ND.

Moon KA, Rice BA & Schneider C (2001) Stanley W Standal and the need for positive regard. In J Bozarth & P Wilkens, (Eds), *Rogers' Therapeutic Conditions: Evolution, theory and practice. Vol. 3: Unconditional positive regard*. Ross-on-Wye: PCCS Books, pp. 19–34.

Rogers CR (1951) *Client-Centered Therapy: Its current practice, implications, and theory.* Boston: Houghton Mifflin.

Rogers CR (1959) A theory of therapy, personality, and interpersonal relationships, as developed in the client-centered framework. In S Koch (Ed) *Psychology: A study of a science. Vol. 3: Formulations of the person and the social context.* New York: McGraw-Hill, pp. 184–256.

Rogers CR (1961) *On Becoming a Person.* Boston: Houghton Mifflin.

Rogers CR (1965) Freedom and commitment. *Etc., 22* (2), 133–52.

Rogers CR (1980) *A Way of Being.* Boston: Houghton Mifflin.

Standal SW (1954) The need for positive regard: A contribution to client-centered theory. Unpublished doctoral dissertation, University of Chicago.

Chapter 16

CONDITIONS OF WORTH AND AN ARTIST'S JOURNEY

Noel Nera

> Paths cannot be taught,
> they can only be taken.
> Zen Proverb

MUSICAL BEGINNINGS

I grew up in a musical family. Although my parents are not professional musicians, both of them love music. I remember my father enjoying his favorite music on our old record player, enveloping our house in sweet melodies and scintillating rhythms. My mother often sang to me when I was a child. I still remember her favorite tune, a melody so loving and soothing.

I was about three years old when I was 'discovered' giving my first musical performance. One day, my mother inadvertently found me singing and dancing blissfully to the music of Johann Sebastian Bach, popularized in song. I was apparently singing syllables I made up spontaneously that paralleled the rhythm of the lyrics of the song. My mother still reminds me, fondly, of this experience, and I vaguely remember the actual syllables that I used: *toong, epi tai to eng* …. What remains so clear to me was how happy and free I felt, singing and dancing unabashedly to that wonderful tune, thrilled by its beauty and its wondrous rhythm.

Talent in music emerges often in early childhood. Most musicians begin learning their instrument in those tender years. Among pianists, their journey with the piano begins typically at age six or seven. A precocious talent may even begin at the age of two (Mozart began at three). Although I eventually became a pianist, my talent would choose a different instrument as my first: a 12-stringed instrument of Spanish origin commonly played in the Philippines, called *bandurria*. The piano would come later.

I was five when I had my first bandurria, which is played like a mandolin. I found the bandurria to be a very easy instrument to play. Playing it came very naturally to me—my left fingers, playing on the strings, moved with swiftness and precision, while my right hand was adroit in strumming the strings with a pick. I loved playing it. I enjoyed it immensely.

The bandurria is played as a part of a small ensemble of stringed instruments called a *rondalla*, consisting of guitars, bandurrias, and octavinas. The octavina is another

Spanish instrument, tuned an octave lower than the bandurria. A rondalla commonly performs in school functions, as well as in important town events. A music teacher, skilled in conducting such an ensemble, trains and conducts the rondalla. As the best bandurria player in the rondalla, I remember being placed regularly in front of the microphone in our performances. I also remember enjoying private lessons with our teacher, a stern, but caring woman. She gave me my first experience with note reading, and trained me in proper playing techniques.

One of my most memorable experiences with the bandurria involved my father. He wanted to test my skills as a bandurria player, and had a special plan—to hear me play in the dark. Drawing the curtains in my bedroom and turning the lights off, he asked me to play anything I wanted. Without hesitation, I began to play. I remember playing for a long time, playing many different pieces. I also remember playing very well, much to my father's satisfaction. I knew that I made my father proud, and it made me very happy. It was a beautiful moment that we shared, a memory that always makes me smile.

For the next few years, the bandurria would continue to fascinate me. However, my love for it would not last. I was in second grade when I stopped playing. I lost interest in it.

The electronic organ was the next instrument that caught my curiosity. Strangely, the piano was not yet a part of my life. My parents wanted my second eldest brother to learn the electronic organ—it was the craze at that time. To my parents' surprise, I also wanted to learn it, as I was fascinated and excited by the various sounds that it makes. Thus, partly out of curiosity, and partly out of jealousy, I began having organ lessons.

My excitement was short-lived, as the lessons quickly became a nightmare. My organ teacher was a woman of limited patience, whose temper ruled every lesson. Often irritated during lessons, she would hit my hands, either with her hands or with a ruler, every time I made a mistake. The experience was so horrible that I would cry after each lesson. Unfortunately, my parents did not see the seriousness of my predicament. As the lessons progressed, my nightmare continued. I felt helpless; every minute of every lesson became an ordeal.

My brother, whose teacher was different from mine, graduated from his level and finished his lessons successfully. To cap this achievement, he participated in a students' recital, which pleased my parents tremendously. Not surprisingly, I was not included in the recital. I eventually stopped having lessons and failed to finish them, much to my embarrassment.

After my brother's recital, my parents enrolled us in a new school for further organ lessons. Our new organ teacher, the director of the school, was the teacher I had hoped for. A breath of fresh air, this woman was caring, patient and understanding, and knowledgeable of her instrument. Not once did she hit my hands. Not once did she get angry. It was a joy having her as a teacher, and I savored every minute with her. I flourished in the atmosphere she provided, and finally began to enjoy learning the organ. Unfortunately, those sunny days would come to an unexpected end. For some unknown reason, my parents suddenly discontinued our lessons.

ENTER THE PIANO

My talent in piano made a peculiar entrance in my life. As a young teenager, I first began going to a neighborhood piano teacher for beginner lessons. I remember my father, always a part of my music making, taking me to those lessons. However, after only a few lessons, a sudden life event cut my participation short. I became afflicted with a serious illness, curtailing all my activities and schooling. This illness eventually would be a catalyst, I believe, for my piano talent to reveal itself completely.

I was quite ill. I was hospitalized for a month, and missed a year of school as a result. Feeling very weak and suffering from constant bouts of abdominal pain, I was bedridden. It was a mysterious illness, where excruciating pain went unexplained by clinical tests and examinations. The closest diagnosis was pancreatitis. Having lost so much weight, I needed a year before I began a complete recovery. To help with my recovery, my parents bought my first piano, making me very happy. I began to play the piano again, and my father also took me to my first serious piano teacher.

During my recovery, my piano talent exploded with such intensity and momentum that I leapt from one piano training level to the next in a very short time. To my teacher's amazement, I reached the equivalent of university-level playing, performing pieces such as Beethoven's Piano Concerto No. 3, after only one and a half years of training. Those dramatic jumps felt effortless. Nothing seemed to be difficult; everything felt right.

Piano competitions played a significant role in my life at this time. Competing with pianists who began learning the piano ten or more years ahead of me, I won every competition that I entered. One competition awarded me a special prize, in addition to the first prize, in recognition of my rapid achievement in piano. Although I had only been playing for a year and a half, it never occurred to me that I was competing against students who had been playing much longer. I did not see my late start as a hindrance at that time. It only became a factor when I was older, becoming a personal demon I had to face and overcome.

CONFLICTS AND DIVERSIONS

As a young person about to enter university, I was excited by the possibility of pursuing a career in music, particularly as a concert artist. I had dreams of studying in one of the most prestigious music schools in the United States. However, my desire to be a musician was met with strong opposition from my parents. They portrayed the difficult life of a musician and the lack of money associated with the profession as a frightening reality. My parents' view of music as a career, while honest and rooted in practicality, was a major blow to me. Although I understood and respected their concerns, I felt unrecognized as an artist, with a talent to be valued, nurtured, and protected. To my impressionable mind, their opposition meant that what I do and who I am had questionable value and eventually defined my sense of self-worth. The concept that music is not valuable, and that money is more important than art, became a central issue in my future struggles as a musician, a faulty concept that would haunt me for years.

Faced with parental objections over a music career, I abandoned my dreams of becoming a professional musician. It was one of the saddest decisions in my life. With a career in music out of the picture, I was confused as to what to study in university. Adding to the confusion was my parents' concern about the toll of university work on my health. Unsure of what to do, and seeing my father and oldest brother as accountants, I enrolled as a business student in university. Luckily, I realized my mistake quickly. I transferred to the Zoology program as a pre-med student the following year. As a high school student, I loved science, and I was good at it. Aside from becoming a musician, I dreamed of becoming a medical doctor. Choosing to be a pre-med student reawakened that dream, a decision that pleased my parents.

While a pre-med student, I continued to follow my passion for the piano by enrolling as a part-time student in a nearby music conservatory. There I met one of the few extraordinary piano professors who would shape my future as a pianist. She was a very fine pianist and an outstanding pedagogue, possessing a remarkable combination of knowledge, experience, intuition, and charm. She had a natural ability to bring out the best in her students, while respecting each student's individuality. When it came to interpreting music, she trusted my instincts and allowed my artistic expression to emerge naturally. She would give suggestions in interpretation, but would not force them upon me, or tell me that I was wrong. She believed in my ability as a pianist, and regarded me as an artist from the beginning.

I still feel privileged to have been so lovingly mentored by such a remarkable musician and artist. Although I already possessed a good technique when I met her, she gave me my most complete training in piano technique. I owe my technical proficiency at the piano to her. She was thorough in her approach to technique, and had a clear method on how to teach and acquire it. Always generous and kind as a person, she was unstinting with her time—it was not unusual to meet with her two or three times a week for lessons that could last for hours. Under her artistic guidance, I grew tremendously as a pianist and as a musician.

Graduating magna cum laude in Zoology, I was accepted into medical school. My life would become more complicated, as I began the challenging path of a medical student. Although being a medical student was exciting, I knew immediately that medicine was not the right path. My studies did not interest me. I was unhappy and troubled—my music suffered tremendously from neglect. After a year, I took a temporary leave from medical studies. I never returned, much to my parents' consternation. I continued to be confused as to which career path to follow, as pursuing music did not feel like a viable option. Still interested in the sciences, I decided to pursue post-baccalaureate studies in physical therapy.

I was miserable. The physical therapy program was extremely demanding. Continuing to learn something so entirely different from music, and neglecting my music at the same time, caused me severe stress and even more confusion. Despite the rigors of the program, I continued to find opportunities for piano performances. One of my physical therapy professors heard one of those performances. His spontaneous response to my performance was, 'why are you in physical therapy and not in music?'

The honesty of his remark struck me. I knew he was right. It was inevitable that I would leave the program. Coincidentally, in the midst of this trying and confusing time, a ray of hope entered my life—I met my future partner-in-life. Our first meeting was revealing—I introduced myself as a classical pianist. Describing myself as a physical therapy student never occurred.

Choosing to leave physical therapy training was a turning point in my life—it represented an honest and courageous acknowledgment that music, despite my parents' objection, is my life and my path. The decision echoed what my mentor in the conservatory mentioned poignantly to me years before: that my mind may be in medicine, but my heart will always be in music. She was absolutely right—music is my life, it is my calling. Deep soul-searching gave me enough courage to correct a wrong path and return to music, and music patiently awaited my return. Parental pressures and expectations, as well as some personal delusions, made it more difficult to be brave. Leaving the physical therapy program, I was forced to acknowledge who I really am—a musician. I then became a full-time music student in university. For the first time in a long time, I was happy.

UNDERGRADUATE STUDIES IN MUSIC

Music schools are interesting institutions, providing very specialized, professional training. However, they unintentionally, though invariably, create a pernicious social order. This 'caste system' is based on perceived talent, dividing music students into groups of those who 'can' and 'cannot' play. I once asked a fellow pianist how another student plays, and he swiftly described her as 'sweet.' The implication was that she belonged to the 'cannot' play group, and therefore was not a good pianist. This hierarchy of talent fosters discrimination and dysfunctional behaviors. The 'can play' camp basks in an atmosphere of inflated and misplaced egos, while the 'cannot play' group cowers under harsh and unreasonable judgments.

For music students, competition is a way of life. Students compare themselves to each other with severity. Cut-throat at times, competitions can be cruel and devastating to some. Others seem to feed on them. When it is cruel, competition can sap one's spirit and create intense fear. When I first performed in front of my peers, I remember feeling disconnected from myself, feeling so intimidated. I was so nervous, my fingers were shaking, and I could not understand why. All I knew was this particular performance was very important—this was my first foray into the competitive environment of music school.

Playing in front of fellow students is often uncomfortable, as judgment can be expressed ruthlessly. Fear can easily enter into one's playing if one does not already feel secure as a pianist. Artistic vision can be compromised and extinguished. While I was seen as belonging to the 'can play' group, the fear of judgment always loomed.

Age bias in relation to music and talent is another phenomenon reinforced in music schools—younger students are valued more highly and seen as more special. The general public appears also to support this belief—eager to be dazzled by child geniuses and showering talented young children with praise. As an older student, I had to grapple with this phenomenon. I was never concerned about my age as a pianist until I was in university. Although I played well, knowing that some of my peers were younger made me feel insecure and uncomfortable at times. A fellow pianist once made a point of telling me that he was seven years younger, triggering a cascade of insecurities in me. At that time, I did not understand that producing 'good' or 'valuable' art has nothing to do with age. For many years, beginning with my university experience, I was under the illusion that because I was a late starter, I could never become the artist I wanted to be. I believed that I could never compete with younger pianists. Sadly, that illusion would continue to feed my self-doubts, and remain a struggle in my often fragile development as an artist for years.

University piano professors wield perhaps the most powerful influence on piano students hoping to become artists. They exert influence that can either build or destroy talent. I had teachers who were very fine pianists, but they were terrible teachers. Most of them were tied to working within the framework of the 50- to 60-minute weekly private lesson, and did nothing beyond that. They had no clear idea how to nurture a student properly through the difficult stages of artistic development. In the middle of a lesson, my piano professor compared me unfavorably with another student whose skills, according to this teacher's assessment, were better than mine. For a student, whose ego as an artist was still developing, and who faced intense daily competition from his peers, a comparison like this was demoralizing. Moreover, it was unnecessary. I felt devastated. Looking back I can see that this teacher did not genuinely care to see me for who I was. Though I could not put words to it then, his comments were insensitive and irresponsible—they also revealed a lack of understanding of how talent should be guided and protected.

After being in the undergraduate music program for two years, it became clear to me that I needed a different environment that would support my growth as an artist better. I realized that removing myself from the undergraduate environment and pursuing graduate level training was a necessary next step in my developmental process as an artist. I needed to grow differently, and I understood that undergraduate training was holding me back. My piano professor, not surprisingly, expressed reluctance and did not believe that I was ready for graduate school. I prepared myself for graduate school piano auditions without my professor's full support. Without a bachelor's degree in music, I was accepted with scholarship to one of the premier music schools in the United States.

GRADUATE STUDIES IN MUSIC

The highly competitive graduate-level environment within a well-known school pushed my ability as a musician and as a pianist to a level I had previously thought of as unattainable. Surrounded by many highly accomplished pianists, I was challenged to improve tremendously in a very short time. Unfortunately, my experience with piano teachers who lacked the ability or interest to nurture talent continued.

My first teacher, a world-class pianist and a well-known artist, was a prize winner in major international piano competitions. However, he was a poor teacher. When there were technical difficulties in a piece that I could not solve, he was not interested in solving them. His solution was to give abstract finger exercises that had nothing to do with the actual problems with a particular passage of a piece. When questions about musical interpretation arose, he would typically say, 'show me the goods.' I found this frustrating and unhelpful, as it communicated his lack of interest in working with me, unless I brought a finished product—it did nothing to guide me properly in solving problems with musical interpretation.

My next professor, also a fantastic pianist, was a dedicated teacher—many of her students adored her. However, I found her ego could get in the way of allowing my artistry and individuality to emerge. While working on the second movement of Robert Schumann's Fantasy in C major, Op.17, she was insistent on a certain tempo, an approach that went contrary to my natural pulse for the music. As she was the professor and responsible for grading my work, I denied my musical instincts and followed her prescribed tempo. I did not play the piece well. Her insistence on her tempo showed complete disregard for my natural response to the music. Her artistic vision and experience took precedence over my own.

FINDING MY OWN PATH

After graduate school, I began to question seriously the role of universities in training artists. The accepted wisdom is that university training is important, if not essential, to development as a musician. My experiences caused me to think otherwise. All of my university piano professors were unable to provide an environment that carefully molded artistic talent. Moreover, none of my university teachers provided a supportive and secure environment to foster my growth as an artist.

It is a common belief among music students that advanced university music training, particularly a doctoral program in music, refines artistry. Blinded by this idea for a long time, I erroneously believed I needed a doctorate to reach the highest levels of artistry. Complicating that struggle was the power of 'image.' The idea of being a 'doctor' was so attractive, as a doctorate in music seems to bestow a certain 'status,' a seal of approval that one is a 'finished' artist. I grappled with this 'image' many times. Ultimately, I came to realize that it is an illusion. A doctorate in music does not make an artist.

Foregoing further schooling, I sought additional training through apprenticeship. Since the time of Bach, apprenticeship with a master was the common path for an aspiring artist. Seeking people who would support me in furthering my artistic development, I was fortunate to find two outstanding artists and pedagogues who had an enormous impact on my development. The first was an Israeli-American concert pianist. His belief in my talent was so strong, and expressed in such a genuine and caring manner, that it made me realize I have something unique and special to offer. The second was a well-respected Canadian pedagogue, whose novel approach to rhythm inherent in music opened my mind, body, and spirit to a whole new world of music making, suffused with vitality and energy.

Developing as an artist is a complex process, requiring honesty, courage, passion, determination, perseverance, and dedication. To understand and develop my artistry to the highest level, I have learned to take my talent into my own hands. I am finding that I must travel this path alone, without help from anyone. Although I remain fearful of this journey, especially after having teachers for years, I know it is the next step in finding my self and my unique voice as an artist.

The resolution to work alone has not come without struggle. I have been plagued by constant self-doubts and an unceasing need for approbation. I have had to fight the yearning to always have a teacher beside me. It requires courage and resolve to find the confidence that I need to work alone. As challenging as this period is, it is also bringing a priceless reward: freedom. So essential to an artist, the freedom to create breathes life into every work of art. This period I find myself in now is marked by free exploration, sustained by constant self-study.

It has become an exciting adventure to understand and live with composers who 'speak' to me the most. I continue to peruse the major piano literature relentlessly, studying the lives and works of such geniuses as Bach, Mozart, Beethoven, Schubert, Liszt, Chopin, and Schumann, and immersing myself in countless recordings of their works. Alongside my thirst for music literature is a constant desire to understand what constitutes great piano playing. In my practice studio, Vladimir Horowitz, Claudio Arrau, Artur Schnabel, Alfred Cortot, Friedrich Gulda, and other great pianists of the twentieth century have become my constant companions in analyzing great piano playing. Through studying audio and video recordings of them, I am deepening my understanding of the essence of architecture, rhythmic propulsion, tonal nuances, piano technique, color, poetry and drama in interpreting and communicating music effectively.

The mechanics of piano playing are also an ongoing fascination and an integral part of my development as an artist. Probing like a scientist, I apply myself repeatedly as a test subject in understanding the various and oftentimes conflicting ideas on piano technique. I read and reread books on the subject to have a clearer understanding of the elements involved in technique as elucidated by different authors. Through these studies, I continue to discover and appreciate the piano as a complicated instrument to master, and endlessly fascinating to play.

I find myself now in the midst of a lengthy and satisfying period of self-study, producing what I need most: a deeper understanding of myself as a person and as an artist. This solitary path is yielding a mature love for myself, giving me the essential nurturance many of my teachers failed to provide, and helping me understand and gain the courage to face the demons that have haunted me for years. A necessary step in artistic development, my deeper self-awareness is allowing me to communicate more effectively as an artist, creating my unique musical voice in the process. I am becoming more secure and certain in developing this unique voice, essential in the expression of my being. Finally, I am learning to realize and appreciate the value of what I do. Whether or not I experience the approbation of others, I am finding my value as an artist in society. Applause or no applause, I continue to follow this path.

CHAPTER 17

THE ACTUALIZATION OF THE EXISTENTIAL SELF IN HUMAN DYING

GARRY PROUTY

IN MEMORIAM
EUGENE SOUTHWELL, PhD
1928–2005

This essay in philosophical psychology is an exploration of the actualizing process in the existential self as it occurs in human dying. The following three observations are drawn from the dying process of the psychotherapist Eugene Southwell. He was dying of cancer. Through these observations we hope to draw some conclusions about self-actualization in the face of death.

OBSERVATION I
(EUGENE'S WIFE)

Courage? What can I say? He lived courageously from the first time he was diagnosed with cancer until his death. Each day he lived as he chose.

When we went to Dr. Devine's office, he was told he had three to six weeks, but could do more radiation. He told Tom (Dr. Devine) he did not wish to continue any more treatments. We cried a bit. After office staff left, Gene and I talked. We cried together, and I told him how empty life would be without him and how much I would miss him. I know he didn't want to leave me, but he knew I didn't want him to suffer. All he wanted was to be with us with as little pain as possible. We promised that. The next day we made end of life decisions: Cremation, burial, mausoleum? Monies? Donations? The lawyer and the funeral director came, and we finished discussing these issues. *Then miraculously he began his journey to the unknown, and so he was free.*

He was free to live as if he would live forever, doing the usual and daily things he always did. He worked on his computer each and every day. He worked on the genealogy of his two family lines. He worked on the money and checked the retirement funds. He

---

Author's note: I wish to thank Mrs. Helen Southwell and Ms. Kimberly Schultz for their permission to publish this chapter, and also for their personal heartfelt writings. I wish also to thank Thomas Devine, M.D., for his effective pain management, which reduced Eugene's stress and enabled these psychological processes to occur.

This paper is dedicated to Helen Southwell, who died suddenly of cancer as this paper was being written.

shopped for new pants as he lost weight—I think at least six pairs of them. He shopped with Kimberly (our granddaughter) for shoes, knowing he would probably wear them only a few times. He bought shoe trees for each pair as he always did. Except for the physical things he needed to keep going, he lived a normal life. He usually knew when it was time to clean his trachea. He lived his life as he had always done, he lived 'in charge', and that was the way I wanted it to be for him to the end.

The Saturday before final hospice, he allowed everyone to come to see him. He was kind and thoughtful and loving. *He told everyone he loved that he loved her or him.* I didn't know how much impact he had had on people's lives and on my friends as well. This man had done so much in his life for others (and for himself). Gene had that kind of love in him and tried sometimes to hide it. I may not remember this as we speak, but before he went to the hospice, people just kept calling or wanting to visit him, and he never said no, never. He gave of himself and told them goodbye, and those he loved he told them that—especially those who needed to know someone loved them. If it got to be too much, I would limit the time, but he saw everyone who came. I know I gave up some of my time with him to have this done, but we had to do it his way.

The time he spent with me and friends was *golden*. It came to the point of facing death, and he did it. The thing he showed and taught us was that we, too, did not have to fear dying. I miss him, but the memories and joy of living together are making sadness more palatable. He was a force.

OBSERVATION II
(EUGENE'S GRANDDAUGHTER)

What I found most surprising about Papoo as he was dying was how little fear he showed. He never felt sorry for himself and did not ask the questions 'Why me?' and 'Why did this happen to me?' When we were told his cancer had returned and that there was little the doctors could do as far as treatment went, he cried for a little bit, but then he became really practical. He wanted to know what steps needed to be taken next and how we could minimize his pain during the course of the illness. The doctors were unable to tell us how long he would live, and I think this bothered everyone except him. I don't think he spent his time dreading his impending death. He accepted it in a way I never thought possible. I felt he coped with his death in such a dignified way when the rest of us were falling to pieces emotionally. I know that he was sad he was going to pass away, but I don't think he ever expressed that. His main concern was that we would all be able to deal with what was happening to him and that we would all be able to live happy lives ourselves. I remember once when I was particularly depressed about the circumstances, he confronted me by wanting to know what the hell I was so depressed about. He wanted me to stop feeling sorry for myself and for him. I feel that he wanted us to be able to accept his death in the way that he did. His attitude was more matter-of-fact than anything else. Interestingly, until his last day he continued to live as if he was never going to die. He continued to read and write and stimulate his mind. He loved his

Chicago Cubs and his evening news. Although most people lose interest in world events as they are passing away, he never exhibited this. As he lived, he died: that is, he lived and died on his own terms. When he wanted something, he asked for it (sometimes demanded it), which I felt was consistent with his lifelong behavior. Not only that, he did not withdraw from people, either friends or relatives. He wanted to continue talking to people and giving advice to them. It was important to him to give everyone who loved him some sense of closure with his passing. All the phone calls that were needed to deliver the news, he did himself. I don't think that it was extremely difficult for him to share this news with everyone in his life, but he also never complained about having to do that. He knew his limitations, and when it became emotionally overwhelming, he would stop making phone calls for the day. That was really impressive to me because had I been in his place, I think I would have been frantic or felt a sense of urgency in finishing what needed to be done. He, on the other hand, finished his business in a sort of regimented and paced manner.

OBSERVATION III
(MY OBSERVATIONS AS EUGENE'S FRIEND)

Originally, I had known Eugene in the context of an employer–employee relationship in a private psychotherapy clinic for a number of years. Gradually, over this time, we became more collegial. Ultimately, the relationship became increasingly friendly and intimate.

In spring 2005, Eugene was diagnosed with cancer and hospitalized for surgery. At that time, work done on his tongue made his speech blurred and awkward. I noticed that his attitude was accepting, lacked depression, and was very oriented toward the task of speech therapy. I remember thinking he was better adjusted than I could be.

During the summer, he seemed to have recuperated and again seemed positive—showing humor at a birthday party. At this point, I lost major concern and thought he had survived cancer, as had another friend.

Suddenly, there was a new expansion of the cancer to his lungs, and a terminal diagnosis. I was shocked and went into denial: he would be all right because of the excellent medical care he was receiving—I would not believe in his death. Eugene came home, but then another hospitalization followed. Ever so slowly, I began the process of acceptance by visiting him at the hospital. At the hospital, he was comatose, and they expected him to die. The next day, he was conscious, not speaking and seeming very weak. Contact with him was limited to hand squeezing. The nurses asked me if he had enough contact so as not to turn off the life support systems. I honestly thought he was still relating through the hand squeezing. Validation of this thought came through humor. One of the nurses was very officious, so when I left him for the day, I turned and did a Charlie Chaplin as Adolf Hitler imitation of the nurse. He immediately burst into a smile, showing that he understood the whole situation. He survived, went through a rehab facility, and returned home not knowing if or when he would die.

When Eugene returned home, I was no longer in denial. I decided to visit his home more frequently. My last visit was the most memorable. When we arrived, he was making plans for his mausoleum with his wife and a cemetery representative. After their meeting was complete, he came into the living room to talk with me. I commented on his directness and clarity about his last wishes. He replied, *'Death doesn't frighten me',* which made his previous stability, humor, and non-pathological states understandable.

He was not disintegrating from fear. He had faced his ultimate destiny with *courage*. The conversation drifted for a while: we talked about the TV program playing in the background, but I was struggling with the realization that I lacked such courage. He then said there was something he wanted to tell me. He said simply that he *loved* me. I then realized that this dying man was expressing from his depths the courage and love in his being. In other words, he was self-actualizing even as he faced death. He finished by asking if my wife and I would have a last meal together with him and his wife—to celebrate our relationship. It did not happen, for he died a few days later. Eugene had no religious convictions, and there were no institutional expressions in his final service, yet I felt powerfully moved on my ultimate existential levels. He taught me how to die.

THE COURAGE NOT TO BE

Eugene Southwell self-actualized through his love, freedom, autonomy and most importantly through his courage. Hopefully, through our observations, we have provided an accurate portrait of an existential self emerging during the dying process. The vignettes all portray a courageous facing of death. Through these vignettes, three issues emerge. First, is the issue of death itself. In existential phenomenological terms death is a terrifying nothingness involving a dissolution of self into a forever. The second issue is self-actualization in the face of death. How can we speak of self-actualization in the face of death? Is this not a contradiction, or worse yet, meaningless? Rogers (1963) proposed that the actualizing tendency exists as long as the organism is alive. In facing death, the organism is still alive. So long as there is life, the potential for making meaning is always present—the actualizing tendency, as organismic, remains relevant to the end. There is no contradiction when speaking of self-actualization in the face of death. The third issue is courage. Tillich (1952) explored existential courage—the courage to be. What is the courage *not to be*, and is it possible? We learn by Eugene Southwell's example that *it is only when we have courage in the face of eternal nothingness that we affirm the existence of the self.* This courage is a manifestation of the self. It is the ultimate 'I am.' Self-actualization is seen in the courageous act of affirming the self in the face of death.

REFERENCES

Rogers CR (1963) The actualizing tendency in relation to motives and consciousness. In *Nebraska Symposium on Motivation*. Lincoln, NE: University of Nebraska Press, pp. 1–24.
Tillich P (1952) *The Courage to Be*. New Haven: Yale University Press.

CHAPTER 18

BEYOND FIEFDOMS

Brian E. Levitt

> Imagine there's no countries,
> It isn't hard to do.
> John Lennon

When I hear people talking about positive psychology, what I hear most often is that it is naïve and limited. When I hear people talking about the person-centered approach I hear that it is passive, 'just supportive,' and, of course, it is about repeating what clients say. Like positive psychology it is also, apparently, naïve and limited. When I read the steady stream of literature produced in these movements, there are numerous attempts to define and reify them from within. Yet the reality is that each movement is made of myriad, and often changing, voices. These voices converge and diverge in many ways between and within each movement.

Often there is enough convergence within a movement that we can pull back and recognize ourselves within it, a part of a greater whole with which we can somehow identify. Sometimes we can convince ourselves that we have found truth, reinforced by the comfort of seemingly sharing it with others. Yet most reasonable people would agree that none of us has a monopoly on the truth of a movement. I certainly have my own ideas and understanding of what I think the person-centered approach is, and more specifically what it means to be non-directive, or what the actualizing tendency means. But I am just one voice in a sea of many.

I think it is still worth asking such questions as, 'What does it mean when I say I am person-centered or non-directive?' 'Does it mean the same thing as when any of the other authors in this book describe themselves with the same language?' 'Is it the same thing as when the reader describes himself, herself or others with these terms?' There is perhaps comfort to be gained in finding other voices that seem to be expressing the same thing we would wish to express. It is all too easy to live within such comfort and together create a fiefdom outside of which we do not venture. All we need is within our fiefdom. We are home. We have no need for bridges. We already have truth. Yet when we take the time to explore other communities, other movements, as more than just a casual tourist, new worlds and new depths open up. The facile stereotypes are recognized more readily for what they are, and the full beauty of diversity has the chance to emerge.

At the same time, we likely share some common values or similar beliefs when we use the same words or labels to define ourselves. And there is value, to be sure, in defining a movement such as the person-centered approach or positive psychology that then has the potential to challenge mindsets, inform values, and further humanize the work we do with others. These two movements support core ideas that can push us beyond limited and limiting conceptions of ourselves and others. The person-centered approach points beyond diagnosis and objectification. As an organismic, holistic approach, it points beyond dualism and the confines of the biomedical model. Positive psychology points beyond a focus limited to illness and pathology to a more full and complete view of human experience. These approaches challenge the mainstream. They challenge existing power structures, and can wake us up to new realities that lie *beyond* fiefdoms—ours and those of others. The person-centered approach and positive psychology bring awareness to the overemphasis on illness and the negative in mainstream psychology. Positive psychology does so by putting the focus on the other side of the dualism, the positive. The person-centered approach does so by resolving the dualism, by facing and embracing the whole. Both movements seem to hold and foster similar hopes—empowerment, freeing human potential, a good life.

Barbara Held's brave voice in the *Journal of Theoretical and Philosophical Psychology* (2005) has made me rethink not only positive psychology, but also the person-centered approach. Held explores the notion of voices in positive psychology—dominant voices and otherwise, challenging the idea that one person speaks for an entire movement or captures all of its potential and diversity. Here I became intrigued, as I have long been witnessing a similar scenario of dominant and non-dominant voices in the person-centered community. Carl Rogers' work in the person-centered approach holds within it the seeds for vastly different voices. Kathy Moon (2003) has pointed this out as a split between the scientific and the ethical. Barry Grant (1990) has described it as a difference between instrumental and principled non-directivity. Indeed, Rogers' 1963 paper on the actualizing tendency, reprinted in this book, is a prime example of voices within his own writing that are never reconciled—this tension continues to play out within the person-centered community. The beauty of an edited volume such as *Reflections on Human Potential*, or its companion volume, *Embracing Non-directivity*, is that it becomes evident that we each have an individual voice, a unique perspective. Embracing this reality may lead us out of our fiefdoms and provide us with important bridges to others.

Within this book each author's voice is a bridge that can challenge us to venture beyond the comfort of our personal and professional fiefdoms. Joseph and Patterson point out that positive psychology challenges mainstream psychology to broaden its focus, as it has been focused on distress and dysfunction at the expense of inquiry into well-being and optimal functioning. They suggest that the person-centered approach has long been an alternative to the biomedical approach that mainstream psychology has followed. They argue further that this model is a good fit for positive psychology, which aims to look beyond the biomedical model of illness. The person-centered approach has always adopted a holistic view—it is an organismic approach as opposed to an illness model. Distress and dysfunction are not viewed as illnesses, but as expressions of what the person-centered approach frames as a tendency to actualize, encompassing so-called positive and negative aspects of human experience.

There is a resurgence in the notion of the human tendency towards actualization, a basic human potential, now being seen in self-determination theory. Joseph and Patterson look at trends in Self-Determination Theory with an eye towards how this neatly dovetails with the non-directive ideology and trust in human potential implicit in the person-centered approach. In a sense, what is old (actualizing tendency theory) is made new (self-determination theory)—as we now see a research base in self-determination theory that supports one of the key theoretical formulations of the person-centered approach (the actualizing tendency). Interestingly, without much dialogue between the person-centered approach and self-determination theory, we see the parallel development of two fiefdoms with much in common that is mutually enriching. There is much potential in opening our gates to what lies beyond—to grow from the opportunity of exchanges with other vibrant communities.

Rogers' 1963 paper on the actualizing tendency in relation to motives is a seminal paper, building a strong case for an organismic perspective in understanding human being. Rogers' understanding of an organismic tendency to actualize reinforced his exploration of the importance of the therapeutic relationship as opposed to techniques or orientation or ability to classify and describe personality characteristics of others. An important value underlying the therapy relationships given support by this organismic model is that of unconditional positive regard. If there is only one motivating force or direction of the organism, and it is toward actualization of the organism's potentials, then all aspects of it are a part of this direction and are to be trusted equally and unconditionally. No aspect of the client is to be regarded conditionally, as that aspect is always an expression of the potential of the whole and trustworthy organism.

Rogers' view is radical—that there is nothing gained by classifying and objectifying the other through diagnosis, conceptualizations, or judgments. There are clear values implications of his conceptualization of an organismic tendency to actualize, and these ought to be considered by therapists in relation to clients. Rogers is arguing here that it is not meaningful to classify what is happening in the other—that life is holistic, organismic, directional, and in process—human potential always defies static concepts such as diagnostic and formulaic abstractions. Rogers argues that there is danger for both the individual and the therapist when classifying as opposed to being. It is essential to break free of our own personal fiefdoms to recognize the fullness of the other whom we face in therapy. This not only shows respect for the individual, but shows a recognition that we cannot make people something other than what they are—that this is folly.

Merry sheds further light on person-centered theory as organismic by exploring what it means that the tendency to actualize underlies all aspects of the organism. In other words, underlying everything expressed by the individual is a single, constructive, positive thrust. He explores what on the surface appear to be some logical inconsistencies in person-centered theory (such as how person-centered theory would explain self-defeating or sabotaging behaviors), and resolves them with the awareness that the theory is ultimately holistic and organismic. There is always an underlying trustworthy direction. Human potential is always present in all expressions of the organism.

Bozarth and Brodley explore the concept of the actualizing tendency and describe it as a functional concept or premise, which guides the work of the therapist. This understanding is firmly rooted in the notion that our theories guide our values and behaviors. In addressing the notion of the fully functioning person, which positive psychology naturally would be friendly towards, they reinforce the idea that the actualizing tendency of the organism operates most effectively and fully when we have trust in the organism—trust in the person. This returns us to a foundational principle in the person-centered approach—trust in the entire person, the other we meet in therapy. The relationship is emphasized as the key to enhancing the other's tendency to actualize, as opposed to techniques and orientations. Again, there is no need to classify, reify, or theorize the other—there is movement beyond the fiefdom of personality theory, as first suggested in Rogers' 1963 paper. A further implication of trusting the other and not theorizing about them is that the ultimate authority for the other rests in that person. This is what Bozarth and Brodley refer to as an extreme focus on 'self-authority' of the client. It is a radical movement beyond the fiefdom of the therapist, and whatever fiefdoms we drag with us into the therapy room.

In my paper on the myth of the actualizing tendency, I attempt to pull away from the fiefdoms of psychological theories by drawing attention to our tendency to reify theory rather than recognize it as a guiding story that has the potential to shape our values and behaviors. The value in any theory lies in what we do with it. This is an argument that seems to underlie both person-centered and positive psychology literature—that mainstream theories may bias us towards not focusing on the fullness of human experience. As it is framed in positive psychology, the mainstream is focusing almost exclusively on illness and distress. The person-centered approach asserts that the mainstream is focusing on theories and spinning constructs at the expense of the person. My stance is one that brings ethical issues more sharply into focus, as primary over scientific ones. The value of person-centered theory is in the way it guides us to think of others, the way it guides us to think of the personhood of the client. Person-centered theory reinforces the idea that the potential for cure, healing and growth are all located in the individual client and are best brought forth in the context of a relationship, not through the application of techniques by an expert.

Seeing the actualizing tendency as a guiding story reminds us that human potential is always present in every aspect and expression of the other. Our trust in the other necessitates a stance of unconditional positive regard for whatever our clients are and present to us. It is a stance that challenges us beyond our most personal fiefdom—the fiefdom of our own views, our own self—to be more fully aware of an entirely distinct world of the other. Simply put, we cannot build bridges to others by re-visioning and reshaping them in our own image. There is great challenge in realizing that we live in a world filled with individuals all distinct from ourselves. In facing this challenge I fall short often.

Tudor examines the way that language creates mindsets that easily can go unquestioned. Whereas I suggest that our theories are stories that guide us, Tudor points out that the very words we use frame our thinking and change our perceptions. He raises awareness of the implications of the actualizing tendency as a noun, which has no temporality. There is potential for reification and objectification, much like diagnostic categories. This is in stark contrast to our human existence, which is temporal, in process. Diagnosis is bound to the past. There is no movement in it. It makes a significant difference to think in terms of people tending to actualize, rather than having an actualizing tendency—the emphasis is placed on a continuous process.

Tudor, in his second chapter in this book, cautions against the reduction of the person to a symptom or diagnosis, concluding that it is ultimately anti-human. He reminds us that Rogers was one of the first psychologists to value health and functioning as well as pathology and dysfunctional behavior. Tudor also emphasizes the social domain and the interdependence of the individual and the environment. He advocates a full acknowledging of the other, declaring that the task of the therapist is dis-alienation, an obligation to go beyond our own limited fiefdom and build bridges to the other. Indeed, he promotes the idea that building bridges, dis-alienation, is healthy.

Schmid explores the relational aspect of the actualizing tendency by exploring a relational understanding of the person. He argues that the tendency to actualize is not just within the person, but also finds expression and meaning within the context of relationship. There is no actualization without relationship. He points to the need to move beyond the person of the therapist in understanding the other. He finds that to embrace the other truly is to embrace relationship. In other words, he may be promoting movement beyond fiefdoms of self-ishness, self-centeredness and self-absorption to interconnectedness, as human potential is ultimately relational. He points to the idea of the relationship itself as therapy, which moves beyond mainstream notions of therapies as techniques or manualized approaches. He also recognizes the importance of moving beyond the fiefdom of theory to look at what theory points to and how it shapes and reflects our values.

Bozarth and Wang point out how Rogers' work moves beyond the fiefdom of expertism in trusting the client's tendency to actualize. They look at the core concept of congruence within person-centered theory and recognize it as an expression of the actualizing tendency. It is an organismic expression of actualization that expresses wholeness or unity. They emphasize the use of the term 'unitary actualizing tendency' as a way of appreciating the integral connections of the therapist's attitudes to the actualizing tendency. This stance pushes for a clearer vision of the whole, breaking down barriers.

Cornelius-White and Kriz also highlight Roger's holistic thinking in their exploration of the formative tendency. They explore systems theory and recognize the need to move beyond the old paradigm of the mechanistic, behaviorist biomedical model of being human in understanding self-directed, organized change. The concept of the formative tendency implies a need to build bridges beyond the individual as an isolated system. Bridges are always necessary. Cornelius-White and Kriz remind us that the person-centered approach is about building bridges to the unique other, the individual client, to fully appreciate their personhood and their inherent worth and potential. Their focus on systems theory and the formative tendency concept serves to remind us to consider and appreciate the infinite bridges that exist.

Zucconi highlights the revolutionary aspect of Rogers' work by examining the paradigm shift that it assumes. The person-centered approach offers a movement from a mechanistic and reductionistic framework to a systemic, organismic framework. Even now mainstream psychology seems to be clinging to reductionistic manualized treatments, diagnoses, and a mechanistic view of the individual. The person-centered approach is really a movement beyond this way of thinking. Moving well beyond the old paradigm that diminishes the personhood of the individual. Though it may seem a minor point to some, the shift from patient to client signals an important change in mindset—a greater respect for and trust in the individual and their role as decision-makers and choice-makers in directing their own lives. It is a critical bridge to human potential.

Zucconi also reminds us that every approach to health presumes a set of values and a view of human nature. What we adhere to and what we do reflects our values, and this may go easily unexamined. There is a political aspect to our actions, and thus a political aspect to the approach upon which we base our actions. The person-centered approach is a political movement away from control of the other, and this is a significant departure from other approaches that are rooted in a mechanistic or bio-medical frame. The question, politically, is 'who has the control?' or 'who has the power?' Mainstream practice takes that control away from the client, and in so doing may undermine a sense of individual responsibility, leading us to feel as if we are not in control of our own lives and health. The person-centered approach and positive psychology recognize the role of the therapist as a facilitator of the client's direction, with an emphasis on the client being capable of self-direction.

Wolter-Gustafson voices some of the same themes as Zucconi, particularly in noting the obsolescence of dualistic models of health and psychology. She argues that the non-directive, organismic person-centered approach is a non-dualist model that marks a significant paradigm shift. Whether a movement truly moves beyond the negative psychology described by the positive psychology movement is a worthwhile question— as Wolter-Gustafson states, 'Regardless of a psychology's stated positive and progressive goals or its theories of health, happiness or wholeness, if the processes proceed from a positivist epistemology, it represents no change at all' (p. 150).

Wolter-Gustafson applies the core conditions in their fullest sense to all aspects of the person. She encourages us to break down dualities of health and illness and to recognize the value of a process that is inclusive and does not separate parts of the person off as not good enough because they do not meet certain standards of 'health.' Wolter-Gustafson argues for a person-centered theory of organismic actualization and health. She argues for the breakdown of the fiefdoms of mind and body, building bridges to see mind and body as organismic and not distinct entities from each other. This is an important departure from thinking that is rooted in the Cartesian mind–body split.

The concept of unconditional positive regard that is integral to the person-centered approach, as Wolter-Gustafson helps us further to appreciate, is a non-dualist construct in that multiple realties are embraced. All is included and nothing is split off or categorized. If we look at movements as containing multiple voices and realities that are all to be embraced as expressions of the whole, we can see a greater whole. The person-centered approach and positive psychology are not things that can be defined by any one voice. In this sense, I believe there are no tribes in the person-centered approach (a metaphor that holds popular acceptance). Rather than tribes, I see a multitude of individual voices. This is an important perspective to consider if we are to try to find bridges within and between our communities. This idea is also reflected in the contents of this book—that a fuller picture of an idea or movement can emerge from the collection of a multitude of voices. Wholeness can emerge from embracing the worth of all parts. This idea is very consistent with the person-centered approach.

Bohart carries this theme of the emergent—that therapeutic change is a by-product of the meeting of two persons, and not the product of conscious efforts by either the therapist or the client. He also asserts that people are active self-healers who bring their innate resources to bear as clients within the context of the therapy relationship. Yet people also carry this potential in everyday life outside of any professional intervention. This is a humbling perspective in many ways, and reflecting on this may help therapists move beyond the confines of self-importance that theory and professional training can reinforce. It is a perspective that respects the power of the person.

The issue of power is, indeed, often at the heart of person-centered discourse. Freire and her co-authors remind us of the significance of an adult yielding power and providing an environment where a child can flourish. They illuminate the power of a child's growth force, even a severely disadvantaged child. They also show us a bridge between the person-centered approach and positive psychology by framing resilience as a function of the actualizing tendency. They remind us that for decades the person-centered approach has recognized human potential in this way. They also assert that person-centered play-therapy—non-directive therapy—works in large part because of the potential for growth that each child has, which is always present and can always be trusted. This potential exists in all children regardless of their circumstances, and we are reminded again that psychotherapy is a political act.

Mejia also reminds us that psychotherapy is a political act. He points out that the person-centered approach offers hope for moving beyond alienation and rejection—moving beyond pathologizing to embrace our clients as they are and for who they are. The person-centered approach recognizes the fullness of human existence and experience as something to be embraced and promoted. Unfortunately, to some it may still seem radical that a facilitator would value *every* aspect of a queer person's lived experience. But in the person-centered approach there is no search for pathology. The person-centered approach, in this sense, is also a framework for healing the impact of prejudice, which remains an open wound in our world. When the therapist is able to move beyond prejudice, clients, too, can confront their own prejudices and can heal themselves. This impact of the person-centered approach is often unacknowledged, though the ripple effects continue to be felt throughout society. This political piece is another bridge that might find its way to the positive psychology movement, with its stance of understanding and developing the positive.

A common theme taken up by the person-centered approach is that the personal is political. The three papers that conclude this book inform us directly and indirectly that the theoretical is also political by reminding us that the personal is essential. Not all person-centered practitioners and thinkers see the actualizing tendency as essential to their work (e.g., see Moon's and Levitt's chapters in this book), departing from scientific theory as foundational to their therapeutic work and preferring to begin with ethical considerations. Moon goes beyond the abstraction of scientific theory, revealing the personal to be immediate and profound. She moves beyond the grand fiefdom of science. Her paper is very brave and quintessentially person-centered. She explores the theme of trust in the client, reminding us that we must have enough comfort with ourselves to face the other. Moon's voice encourages us to leave our own personal fiefdom and the safety of a larger fiefdom such as science to truly face the other. She does so through beautiful reflections on self-acceptance and her acceptance of others.

The person-centered approach holds that theory is located best in the individual, in the client, and not in the therapist. When we come to see theory from this perspective, new worlds open up to us with amazing fullness. The potential for building bridges to these worlds is always present. Nera's paper offers us a unique perspective, as it presents an entirely personal theory in reflecting on his own path as an artist. We are welcomed into his world and his experiences in coming to understand himself. What emerges is a very human story of the inevitable unfolding of human potential and the impact of external and internal pressures—or as Rogers might have it, conditions of worth. His chapter stands as a reminder of the importance of an individual's personal theory. It is direct and powerful in its immediacy, and it is a reminder that the personal is indeed political. Like Moon's chapter before it, it is quintessentially person-centered.

Prouty's exploration allows us to consider the potential in someone's dying days and in their death. He invites us into the lives of those who experienced another person in his dying, and in doing so helps us to see that human potential reaches beyond death. He shows us how those around a man facing his own death faced their own mortality and now carry the impact of his inspiration on them beyond his death. He also explores how a dying man continued to actualize in relationship to those around him. This brings us full circle to one of Rogers' assertions with regard to the actualizing tendency—as long as there is life, there is potential.

If we take an honest look and recognize each individual reality as meaningful and valuable (which for me is a cornerstone of person-centered thinking) we can recognize that the very thing we try not to do to our clients we may be doing to ourselves. By labeling our views, identifying with those labels, and deciding what box we fit in best we may be diagnosing ourselves. Perhaps there is some safety in belonging and defining ourselves as a part of a movement, and in trying to further define that movement within which we find a home. It becomes a familiar place populated by like-minded others. How often we seek out others looking for agreement, others who reinforce our sense of rightness. How much harder to break free of this and truly encounter someone who might challenge our feelings of rightness and comfort.

This book and the companion volume that preceded it reflect a broader notion, that we are really a collection of unique voices and perspectives. While I can feel at home in the person-centered community, these days I prefer being a global nomad. I can find various points of agreement and disagreement with the authors in this volume and in its companion, but all that really matters to me is the moment of encounter with another person. In such moments I am open unconditionally to another person's world, without imposing theory or my own frame of reference. I am trusting fully the other and their process. Whatever the label placed on me for working in this way, I see this as the essence of non-directivity, the essence of the person-centered approach. Rogers once asked a simple yet profound question, 'Do we see each person as having worth and dignity in his own right?' (1951: 20). If you find this question meaningful, perhaps we share some unspoken bridges that allow us to travel beyond our own tiny fiefdoms, beyond the need to define ourselves or others, in service of the human potential and value in each person we encounter.

REFERENCES

Grant B (1990) Principled and instrumental nondirectiveness in person-centered and client-centered therapy. *Person-Centered Review,* 5 (1), 77–88.

Held B (2005) The 'virtues' of positive psychology. *Journal of Theoretical and Philosophical Psychology,* 25 (1), 1–34.

Levitt BE (Ed) (2005) *Embracing Non-directivity: Reassessing person-centered theory and practice in the 21st century.* Ross-on-Wye: PCCS Books.

Moon K (26 October 2003) Email posted to the CCTPCA listserve.

Rogers CR (1951) *Client-Centered Therapy: Its current practice, implications, and theory.* Boston: Houghton Mifflin.

CONTRIBUTORS

THE EDITOR
Brian E. Levitt, PsyD, CPsych, is a senior psychologist with Kaplan and Kaplan Psychologists in Hamilton, Ontario, where he has a practice in rehabilitation psychology. Prior to immigrating to Canada, Brian was a clinical psychologist in the United States. While there, he trained for three years at the Chicago Counseling and Psychotherapy Center, the center that grew from Carl Rogers' work at the University of Chicago. After his studies at the Center, which included a post-doctoral fellowship, he joined the staff as a therapist and trainer. He also trained for two years at the Pre-Therapy Institute in Chicago, under the tutelage of Garry Prouty, earning certification in the practice of Pre-Therapy. Brian is the editor of two books published by PCCS Books, *Embracing Non-directivity* and *Reflections on Human Potential*.

THE CONTRIBUTORS
Arthur C. Bohart, PhD, is currently affiliated with Saybrook Graduate School and Research Center and is also professor emeritus at California State University, Dominguez Hills. Art is the author of a number of articles and chapters on person-centered psychotherapy, empathy, and the client as active self-healer, including *How Clients Make Therapy Work: The process of active self-healing* (co-author, Karen Tallman, APA, 1999).

Jerold D. Bozarth, PhD, is Professor and Director, Person-Centered Studies Project in the Department of Counseling and Human Development Services, University of Georgia.

Barbara Temaner Brodley, PhD (1932–2007) received her doctorate in clinical psychology at the University of Chicago, where she was on the staff of the Counseling Center founded by Carl Rogers. For 50 years she was a psychotherapist, educator, and writer with an unwavering dedication to non-directive (client-centered) psychotherapy. As a writer and educator she had a profound influence on many of the leading thinkers in the person-centered approach. Often noted for her clarity of thought, her numerous papers remain a potent force in understanding non-directive (client-centered) psychotherapy as an effective form of psychotherapy.

Jeffrey H.D. Cornelius-White, PsyD, LPC, is Dean's Fellow for Teaching and Learning, Associate Professor of Counseling, and former Director of School Counseling at Missouri State University and Adjunct Assistant Professor for the Cooperative EdD Program in Educational Leadership and Policy Analysis University of Missouri-Columbia, (USA), Co-Editor of *The Person-Centered Journal*, Content Editor of the *Journal of Border Educational Research*, and a World Association for Person-Centered and Experiential Psychotherapy and Counseling board member.

Elizabeth Freire, PhD, is a Brazilian psychologist, person-centred therapist and supervisor. She has published a book in Portuguese about the theory and practice of person-centred therapy and has several articles and chapters published in English. Beth had been the director of a post-graduate person-centred course in clinical psychology in Brazil until 2004, when she came to Glasgow. She is currently working as tutor and researcher in the Counselling Unit of the University of Strathclyde.

Gláuber Gonçalves, Bertrand Freund, Wagner de Lara Machado, Rodrigo de Lima Ávila, Lucas Severo Ache, Florence Beraldin Diedrich, and **Maria Cláudia Furtado** are Brazilian undergraduate psychology students who have been working as therapists and researchers in the program that provides person-centred play therapy to children victims of poverty and social exclusion described in the chapter.

Stephen Joseph, PhD, is Professor of Psychology, Health and Social Care at the University of Nottingham where he is co-director of the Centre for Trauma, Resilience, and Growth, and an Honorary Consultant Psychologist in Psychotherapy in Nottinghamshire HealthCare NHS Trust.

Silvia H. Koller, PhD, is Brazilian, Professor at the Federal University of RS, Brazil, Chair of the Center for Studies on At Risk Children, President of the Brazilian Association for Research and Graduate Studies in Psychology, and Ad Hoc Representative of Latin America at International Society for Studies in Behavioral Development (ISSBD). Her research focuses on developmental and positive psychology, and has been granted by Kellogg Foundation, World Childhood Foundation, World Bank and Brazilian agencies. Currently, she is the Editor of the *Interamerican Journal of Psychology* and Associate Editor of the *IJBB* (ISSBD).

Jürgen Kriz, PhD, Professor of Psychotherapy and Clinical Psychology at the University of Osnabrück; person-centered psychotherapist, guest-professor at several universities, honorary member of various therapeutic associations, author of 20 books and 250 articles, 'Grand Viktor Frankl Award of the City of Vienna', 2004, for his 'life work which has won international acclaim in the field.'

Javier Armenta Mejia is a clinical psychologist in Tijuana, Mexico. He works currently at Xochicalco University's School of Psychology. E-mail: <armentaxavier@hotmail.com>.

Tony Merry (1948–2004) was Reader in Psychology at the University of East London. He contributed to person-centred events in nine European countries including several with Carl Rogers in England, Ireland and Hungary. He was the author of several books and articles on counselling and psychotherapy including *Learning and Being in Person-Centred Counselling* and *Invitation to Person-Centred Psychology* (both PCCS Books). He co-founded the British Association for the Person-Centred Approach (BAPCA) in 1989 and edited its journal *Person-Centred Practice* from 1993–2004.

Kathryn A. Moon is a psychotherapist in private practice in Chicago. She is an adjunct faculty member at Argosy University, Chicago Campus. She trained at the Chicago Counseling and Psychotherapy Center, was a staff member there, and also served on its Training Committee. She is the author of several articles and book chapters about client-centered theory and practice.

Noel Nera is a Filipino-Canadian classical pianist. He has given solo and chamber music performances in the US, Canada, and Asia. He is currently working on the complete Mozart sonatas for performance and recording in 2009. Other plans include a complete traversal of Beethoven's 32 piano sonatas, as well as Schubert's piano sonatas. Noel's formal training includes two Master of Music degrees in piano performance. Further training includes studies with Natan Brand, Donald Walker, and Philip Cohen. He resides in Oakville, Ontario, with his partner, Brian Levitt, two cats, and a dog. When he is not developing his art, he enjoys creating gardens and taking long strolls in his neighbourhood and the local ravine trails.

Tom Patterson is a Clinical Psychologist at Coventry and Warwickshire Partnership Trust, UK, working across Adult and Older People's Services. His interests include the non-medicalised evaluation of therapeutic outcome, and the relevance of the person-centred paradigm to clinical psychology.

Aline Piason is a Brazilian psychologist, person-centred therapist, supervisor, and one of the Directors of Delphos Institute. She has been working as supervisor and researcher in the program that provides person-centred play therapy to child victims of poverty and social exclusion described in the chapter.

CONTRIBUTORS

Garry Prouty, PhD, was trained in Person-Centered/Experiential Psychotherapy by Eugene Gendlin of the University of Chicago. He developed his own therapeutic approach at clinics and hospitals dealing with psychotic and retarded clients. He is the founder of the Pre-Therapy International Network, a European organization for working with psychotic persons. Currently, he is a Fellow of the Chicago Counseling, Psychotherapy and Research Center. He is author and co-author of numerous books and articles on Pre-Therapy.

Carl Rogers (1902–1987) is considered by many to be the most influential American psychologist of the twentieth century. He was a leading figure in Humanistic Psychology and a driving force in the human potential movement that first took hold in the 1960s. His approach to psychotherapy, which he initially called 'Nondirective Therapy,' grew in scope and influence well beyond the confines of the therapy room. With a significant impact on the realms of conflict resolution, education, and business, he relabeled it the 'Person-Centered Approach' to reflect its broader applications. His classic texts include *On Becoming a Person* and *A Way of Being*.

Peter F. Schmid, Univ.Doz. HSProf. Mag. Dr., founder of person-centered training in Austria, works at the Institute for Person-Centered Studies (IPS of APG) and is Chair of the Department for Person-Centered Psychotherapy Science at the Sigmund Freud University in Vienna and part-time faculty member of Saybrook Graduate School in San Francisco. He is author and co-editor of 14 books and numerous publications in German and English, and co-editor of the international journals *Person-Centered and Experiential Psychotherapies* and *PERSON*.

Keith Tudor is a qualified and registered psychotherapist with a private/independent practice in Sheffield offering therapy, supervision and consultancy. He is a Director of Temenos (<www.temenos.ac.uk>) and its MSc course in Person-Centred Psychotherapy and Counselling. He is a widely published author on positive mental health, and in the field of psychotherapy and counselling, including five books on the person-centred approach.

Chun-Chuan Wang obtained a PhD from the University of Virginia in the United States and is an Associate Professor of the Department of Counseling Psychology at the National Hualien University of Education in Taiwan. Her current research interests are in the fields of classical client-centered theory and bereavement. Being the only person who teaches classical client-centered therapy in Taiwan, she hopes that a better understanding of classical client-centered theory will be possible through her efforts.

Carol Wolter-Gustafson, EdD, Boston University. My experience was shaped by work with Carl Rogers, 25 years of facilitating graduate learning and maintaining a private practice in Boston. My work is about integrating theory and practice and cultivating pathways out of the 'us-versus-them' gender territory that fuels violence locally and globally. I am writing and creating programs that facilitate organismic integration.

Alberto Zucconi is a clinical psychologist, president and cofounder with Carl Rogers and Charles Devonshire of the Person-Centered Approach Institute (IACP), and teaches client-centered therapy in the Faculty of Medicine of the University of Siena, Italy. With Robert Elliott, he has created the International Research Project on the Effectiveness of Psychotherapy and Psychotherapy Training (<www.IPEPPT.net>).

INDEX

A
academic performance 190
Ackerman SJ 12, 13
actualisation 11
    as dialectical process 88, 98
    as encounter process 88, 98
    and the environment 52
    and the expression of potential 49
    flexibility of 52
    human way of 96
    and therapeutic principles 106
actualising tendency 2, 3, 6, 17, 18, 19, 20, 21, 22, 27, 29, 30, 31, 33, 34, 35, 38, 43, 46, 50, 54, 104
    and autonomy 36, 73, 77, 103, 105
    in client-centred therapy 38
    as creativity 95
    definition 105
    as directional process 35
    and environment 20
    implications of 34
    as motivational construction 75
    myth of 56, 61, 62, 63, 65, 66, 230
    obstacles to 196
    and philosophy 204
    Rogers' concept of 35, 87, 104 (see also CR Rogers)
adjectives 68, 74
Adler A 79
adolescents 187
    vocational courses for 189
Alchin LK 206, 214
Alda E 187, 194
alienation 58, 63, 64, 65, 172, 231, 233
    from experience 198
    in relationships 172
Allport GW 78, 81
anchorage 168
Anderson AL 128, 129
Anderson R 79, 81, 176, 185
Anderson SR 152, 159
Angyal, A 18, 33, 34, 71, 73, 75, 79, 81, 103, 118, 122, 127, 129, 161, 169, 171, 172
anxiety 25, 48, 50, 113, 177
Anzenbacher A 89, 98
Aquinas St Thomas 89, 91, 98
Ardila R 195, 197, 200
Aristotle 71, 73, 74, 77, 78, 89, 90, 93, 94, 96, 98, 162, 164

    theory of causality 91
Arndt J 7, 16
Arrau C 222
Assis SG 188, 194
Association for Humanistic Psychology Practitioners 72, 81
Assor A 9, 10, 13
Atwood G 80, 83
authenticity 86, 131, 166, 167, 172
autonomous functioning 8
autonomy 2, 7, 8, 9, 18, 36, 73, 75, 77, 85, 97, 98, 103, 117, 161, 165, 166, 170, 169, 188
awareness, edge of 48
Axline V 188, 193
Aykroyd M 200, 201

B
Bach JS 215, 221, 222
Barrett-Lennard GT 6, 8, 12, 13, 25, 32, 86, 98, 129, 197, 198, 200
Bass E 198, 200
Beach FA 21, 32
becoming 77, 78, 80, 89
Beethoven L van 217, 222
behaviour 22
    of a congruent individual 168
    destructive 37
    extensional 106
    goal-directed 46
behavioral direction of all organisms 103
behaviorism 123, 163
    classical 116
being 77
    a person, dialectical meaning of 85
    in process 164
    verbal 80
belonging 77, 79
Benjamin LS 12, 13
Berger PL 136, 144
Bergin AE 33, 45, 157, 159
Bergson H 95, 98
Berlyne, DE 19, 32
Bernieri F 8, 15
Bertalanffy L 18, 19, 32, 34, 45, 134, 144
Beutler LE 12, 13
Bible 57, 59
Biblical myth 58
binary
    -based intellectual theories 148
    reasoning 147

INDEX

biological disease processes 59
biomedical
    model 140, 228, 231
        terminology 142
    paradigm 139
biopsychosocial
    model 137, 138, 140
    systems 139
bisexual 136, 195
Bloom BS 168, 172
body chemistry 180
body-being/ness 150, 151
Bohart AC ii, 79, 81, 86, 87, 91, 95, 97, 98, 175, 182, 185, 199, 201, 233
Bohm D 162, 172
Boniwell I 1, 15
Bower D 195, 196, 201
Boxer J 164, 173
Boyle M 60, 61, 66
Bozarth JD i, 8, 12, 13, 14, 40, 45, 61, 66, 73, 74, 75, 76, 81, 88, 99, 104, 106, 109, 114, 129, 154, 158, 188, 193, 204, 214, 230, 231
brain as a 'supersystem of systems' 147
Brandchaft B 80, 83
Brazier D 201
Brendel DH 144
Brodley BT i, 73, 74, 75, 76, 81, 87, 88, 94, 99, 104, 114, 196, 201, 204, 205, 214, 230
Bronfenbrenner U 127, 129
Brown M 71, 81
Brunswik E 71, 83
'bubbling up' 181–2
Buber M 79, 86, 96, 99, 163, 168, 172
Bugental J 195, 201
Bulhan HA 172
C
Cain D 13, 197, 201
Campbell J 56, 66
Capra F 134, 144
Carrasco M 196, 201
Cartesian mind–body split 232
Cartwright DS 39, 45
case history 102, 190
Castañeda M 195, 197, 201
change 22, 23, 176
    model 178
    locus of responsibility for 131
    process view of 184
    unconscious 176, 185
child/'s
    inner world 196
    organismic experience 196
children 187, 210, 203
    and adolescents, at-risk 189
    disadvantaged 189
    in group therapy ii, 210
    and poverty ii, 188
    pre-school 189
    resilience in disadvantaged 188
Cicchetti D 188, 193
Cissna KN 79, 81, 176, 185
Clarkson P 170, 172
client
    as therapist 86
    congruence 106, 113
    frame of reference 39
    incongruence 113, 198
    likability 26
    perception 24, 200
    respect for 204
    self-authority of 40
    and self-healing 175
    trust in 38
client-centered
    model of health 148
    therapy 33, 34
        aim of 3
clinical psychology 148
Coatsworth JD 188, 193
cognitive behavioral theory 148, 175, 176, 183
Colgrave S 152, 158
Columbus, C 69
communication
    accurate flow of 153
    disturbed 153
    and meta-messages 144
    skills 190
conditional regard
    experiences of 9
    parental 9
conditions
    and actualising tendency 48
    core 86, 232 (see also necessary and sufficient conditions)
    necessary for therapy 25
    of worth 3, 5, 9, 27, 48, 151, 196
        and introjection 5, 9
        and psychological well-being 10
congruence i, 4, 8, 12, 24, 25, 33, 39, 43, 44, 64, 106, 108, 141, 167, 168, 198, 205
    client 103, 113
    as manifestation of the actualizing tendency 110, 111
    of the therapist 24, 106
Cook, J 132
Cooper DA 70, 81

Cooper M 51, 52, 55, 67, 84, 86, 99, 154, 158
Cooper R 137, 144
Cornelius-White CF 130
Cornelius-White, JHD i, 12, 13, 88, 93, 99, 116, 120, 126, 127, 128, 129, 130, 231
Cortot, A 222
Coulson WR 144, 145
Cowan M 135, 144
Crandall R 75, 82
creativity 96, 97, 180, 181
Csikszentmihalyi M 1, 73, 81, 179, 185
cultural
    conditioning 120, 128
    'creatives' 152
    factors 4, 134, 135, 136, 196
    narcissistic 169
    reality 142
cultures 142
Cunningham-Burley S 72, 82

D

Damasio A 147, 151, 158
Davis, D 195, 197, 199, 200, 201
death/dying 223, 224, 226, 234
Deci, EL 6, 7, 9, 10, 11, 12, 13, 14, 15
defensive/ness 8, 9, 23, 77
    coping strategies 9
    opposite of 8
Delphos Institute 189, 191
Dember WN 19, 32
Descartes R 147, 148, 149, 158, 162, 163
    The Western Intellectual Tradition 148–50
diagnosis/es 60, 61, 79, 231, 234
    of affective disorders 59
    mental illness 63
Diagnostic and Statistical Manual of Mental Disorders (DSM) 59, 60, 61, 153
    diagnostic constructs in 59
    and homosexuality 60
dialectical interface 6
dialogical model 88
Dijksterhuis A 181, 185
dimensional model 4
directional tendency 103
disease 153, 156
    -based paradigm 140
    process, complex 153
dissociation 26, 29, 30, 31, 150
doctors, status of 143
Dorfman E 188, 193
Driesch HAE 19, 95, 99
drug use 10
dual/ism/istic ii, 147, 148, 162, 228
    attributions, female/male 147

biases 150
Cartesian 162
    descriptions of reality 149
    language 150
    model of reality 147
    model of health and psychology 154, 232
    and non-dualistic paradigms 150–3
Duncan N 9, 14
Dymond RF 12, 15, 166, 174, 188, 194
dysfunction/al 49, 153
    attitudes 136
    behaviour 136, 153, 165

E

Earl RW 19, 32
Eckert J 99
ecological balance 126–8
ecology 138
    total 134
educational functioning 168
Egan G 135, 144
ego-involvement experiments 10
Einstein, A 133
    Theory of Relativity 133
Eliot TS 169, 172
Elliot AJ 7, 10, 15, 16
Elliott R 144, 199, 201
emergence 181–2
emotional distress 59, 60, 65
empathic understanding 33, 39, 63, 64, 102, 106, 108, 112, 154, 199
empathy 4, 11, 12, 23, 25, 44, 72, 86, 108, 190
    Rogers' definition 108
encounter 84, 85, 98
Engelhart MD 172
entelechy 93, 94
environment/al 4, 50, 53, 168, 169
    circumstances, destructive 34
    conditions 54
    field 171
    inadequate 40
    supportive 169
epistemology of Carl Rogers 141
Ermarth ED 147, 158
ethical
    base 213
    considerations 234
    rightness 204
    value 203
Evans RI 163, 172
evil 203, 207, 213
evolution 151
evolutionary
    psychology 71

tendency 123
existential/ism 78, 120, 163
    living 38
    psychology 163
    self in human dying 223
    theologians 163
    therapy 176
exosystem 135
experience/ing 8, 38, 67, 155, 176, 181
extensionality 106, 168

F
Fairhurst I 154, 158
family cohesion 188
Farson R 131, 145
fear 64, 219, 226
felt shift 185
Fichte JH 92, 99
field theory 171
Finke J 72, 81, 88, 94, 99
First, MB 59, 60, 61, 66
Ford JG 3, 14, 45, 46
formative tendency 34, 94, 116, 118, 119
    development of 116
Fox, E 57, 67
Frances A 59, 60, 61, 66
Freire ES ii, 189, 193, 233
Freud, S 19, 32, 134, 140
Fromm, E 33
fully functioning person 2, 10, 33, 37, 38, 44, 78, 87, 93, 95, 105, 109, 111, 155, 165, 200, 230
Furst EJ 172

G
Galileo, G 21, 133
García A 196, 201
Garmezy N 187, 188, 193
Gaylin NL 96, 99
Gendlin ET 88, 99, 145, 149, 150, 158, 182, 184, 185, 186
    idea of crossing 182
General System Theory 133–5
genes 22
Gergen KJ 144, 145
gestalt psychology 80, 117, 119
Giesekus U 171, 172
Gilson, E 78, 82
Gloria 179, 181
God 57, 58, 70, 149
Goldfried MR 183, 186
Goldman R 199, 201
Goldstein, K 18, 20, 32, 33, 34, 71, 82, 103, 105, 114, 117, 118, 129
Goodman P 75, 82, 173
Goodman R 189, 193

Goodyear RK 34, 45, 157, 159
Graham H 162, 172
Grant B 228, 235
Greenberg L 199, 201
Grummon DL 166, 168, 172
Gulda, F 222
Guthrie Ford J 55
Guzman R 81
Gyoergyi S 118

H
Halkides G 25, 32
Hall C 71, 82
Harbaugh AP 126, 129
Harlow HF 19, 32
harmful iatrogenic outcomes 144
Haugh S 154, 159
health/y ii, 147, 154, 156, 158, 161, 162, 164, 171, 232
    concept of 136, 150
    and happiness 162
    and holism 162
    and homonomy 170
    as an individualistic concept 168
    philosophy and 162
    policies and practices 169
    processes 141, 161
    promotion 137, 138, 142, 191
        developing strategies for 138
    relationships 171
    sciences 137
        paradigm change in 137
    systemic approach to 139
    understanding of 161
healthcare
    professionals 137, 143
    Western model of 153
Hefferline RF 75, 82, 173
Heidegger M 120
Heisenberg W 134
    principle 134, 144
Held B 228, 235
Henderson V 156, 159
Heron J 93, 99
heteronomy 2, 18, 36, 73, 103, 169
heterosexuals 195
Hillman J 169, 173
Hirschberger J 89, 94, 99
Hitler A 225
Hodgins HS 8, 9, 14
holistic-systemic paradigm 140, 170
Holland R 168, 173
Holt K 8, 15
homonomy 73, 75, 77, 79, 161, 169–70

homophobia 197
homosexual/ity 60, 195
    as a mental illness in *DSM* 60
    pathological status of 60
Hoppe MW 187, 193
Horney K 33
Horowitz V 222
hospice 224
Houser-Marko L 7, 16
Howel P 143, 146
human
    being
        and social nature 37
        as structures-in-process 95
        as a unified organism 140
        without other humans 92
    condition 206
    development, process theory of 54
    functioning, continuum of 4
    motivation, organismic theory of 6
    nature, theory of 72
    organism 77, 171
    potential 65, 71, 126, 229, 230, 231
        movement 72
        and positive psychology 68
humanism and Rogers i 72
humanistic
    personality and developmental theory 85
    psychology 72, 124, 161
    psychotherapy 161
Humphrey A 81
hypnotic states 179

I
idealism 78
Illich I 143, 145
illness ii, 140, 141, 161, 164, 165, 168, 172, 232
    ideology 4
Imber-Black E 198, 201
incongruence 3, 26, 49, 109, 111, 113, 198, 200
    development of 47
individualism/istic 163, 169
    approach to psychology 168
Instituto Brasileiro de Geografia e Estatística 187, 193
Interdisciplinary Systems Theory 118, 119, 120, 121
intervention strategies 188
introjections 9, 125
Isay R 197, 201
Isense R 198, 201
Islam 78

J
Jacob 57–8, 65, 66
Jahoda M 72, 82, 164, 173
James W 72

Jefferson T 149, 163
Jews 149
John ES 166, 172
Johnson R 129
Jones A 75, 82
Joseph S i, 1, 4, 7, 11, 14, 15, 61, 67, 228, 229
Joubert N 164, 169, 173

K
Kant E 163
Kantor JR 71, 82
Kasser T 9, 10, 11, 14, 16
Kaufman K 198, 200
Keen S 69, 82, 171, 173
Keller EF 147, 154, 159
Keyes CLM 73, 82, 165, 170, 173
Kierkegaard S 92, 99, 163,
Kiesler DJ 145, 186
King M 121, 129
Kirk SA 144, 145
Kirschenbaum, H 78, 82, 102, 104, 114, 156, 159, 163, 173
Knee CR 8, 9, 14
Koch S 155
Koestner R 7, 8, 9, 14, 15
Koller SH 187, 189, 193, 194
Kriz J i, 71, 82, 88, 94, 99, 116, 117, 118, 119, 120, 121, 122, 123, 124, 126, 127, 129, 130, 231
Krupnick JL 131, 145
Kuhn TS 132, 133, 145
Kutchins H 144, 145

L
labels/ling 144, 150
Lachman L 151, 159
Lago C 195, 201
Lambert MJ 33, 45, 157, 159
Land D 96, 99
language 68, 70, 75, 76, 78, 81, 147
Lasch C 169, 173
Layard R 73, 82
Leary DE 76, 82
Leibnitz G 163
LeShan L 151, 152, 159
Levant R 159
Levin DM 182, 186
Levinas E 92, 99
LeVine RA 169, 173
Levine S 151, 152, 159
Levitt BE 62, 67, 106, 114, 234, 235
Lewin K 171, 173
Liccione J 25, 32
Liebeskind E 9, 14
Lietaer G 198, 201
Lindzey G 71, 82

Index

Linley PA 1, 4, 11, 15, 61, 67
Lloyd G 148, 149, 159
Locke, J 163
locus of evaluation 78
Lodge HS 153, 159
Lopez SJ 4, 11, 15, 61, 67
Luckmann T 136, 144
Lukács, G 79, 82
Lukas E 173
Luthar SS 188, 193

M

macrosystems 135
Maddux JE 4, 5, 11, 15, 61, 67
Magallanes M 81
Malchow H 130
Marx K 172, 173
Marxism 78, 79
Maslow AH 2, 15, 18, 33, 34, 38, 45, 70, 72, 73, 78, 79, 82, 95, 103, 104, 105, 106, 114, 118, 152, 159
Masten AS 188, 192, 193
Masten R 151, 159
Masters H 72, 82
Mathews F 69, 82
Matthies M 124, 130
May R 72, 163, 173
McCulloch GF 164, 173
McNamee S 144, 145
Mearns, D 48, 52, 53, 54, 55, 80, 83, 84, 86, 88, 99, 101, 195, 196, 200, 201
mechanistic science 116
medical
    model 11, 58, 60, 153, 162, 195
    profession, control of 143
medicine
    allopathic 141
    Chinese 141
    Western 140
Mejia JA ii, 233
mental health 73, 137, 140, 161, 169
    and positive psychology 164
    promotion 165
    research 166
    six categories of concepts of 164–5
mental illness 58, 60, 63, 164, 165
    myth of 58, 59, 60, 61, 66
Mente, A 171, 172
Merry, T i, 74, 76, 82, 87, 101, 229
mesosystem 135
metaphors 70
microsystem 135
mind–body connection 140, 147
Mir M 81, 82

Mitchell KM 12, 16
MMPI scales 25
Money M 170, 173
Moon KA ii, 188, 189, 194, 214, 228, 234, 235
Morais N De 187, 194
Moreno ZT 95, 100
Morrison J 67
motivation/al 10, 11, 20, 21, 31, 34, 38, 40, 46, 47, 63, 68, 70, 72, 87, 102, 229
    and the behavior of organisms 18
    interviewing (MI) 12
    person-centred theory of 70
    for personal growth and change 46
    principle 35
    tendency 35, 107
    unitary and holistic theory of 68, 70
Murphy G 71, 82
Murray H 79
myth of Jacob in the desert 57–8

N

Napier MB 154, 159
narcissistic culture 169
Natiello P 154, 159, 196, 201
National Institute of Mental Health (NIMH) 132, 147
natural science systems theory 122
Neal, C 195, 197, 199, 201
necessary and sufficient conditions 3, 12, 61, 108, 112, 197 (see also core conditions)
Neimeyer RA 144, 145
Nera N ii, 234
neurology 71
neuropsychiatry 71
neuroscience 71
neurosis 27
Newton, I 133
    science 133, 134, 140
Nobles WW 169, 173
non-defensive 167, 168
non-directive/ity i, 44, 62, 63, 75, 97, 104, 121, 157, 158, 228, 232, 233, 235
non-dualistic model of health 154
non-judgemental attitude 72, 152
Norcross, J 131, 145
Nordgren, LF 181, 185
nouns 70, 78, 80, 231

O

O'Hara, M 99, 116, 126, 128, 130, 154, 159, 176, 179, 182
organism/ic 6, 20, 50, 71, 74, 103, 109, 152, 167, 169
    conception of health 147
    being directional 18, 75, 155
    and its environment 168

experience 27, 47, 109
    child's 196
  growth 103, 153
  health 153
    and integrity 152, 154, 155, 156
  openness 180, 181, 182
  as an organized whole 6, 155
  philosophy and psychology 71, 78
  processes 30
  theory of human motivation 6
  valuing 3, 5, 7
    process (OVP) 2, 7, 9, 10, 11, 200
Ornish D 139, 145
Ornstein R 149, 159
Other, the 85, 91, 98

P

paradigm shift 132, 134, 137, 140, 144, 232
  Rogers' revolutionary i, 140, 144, 154, 232
Paradise, N 19, 32
parental warmth, absence of 9
patient 143, 144
  invalidation of 143
  Rogers and labelling 144
  synonyms of the word 143
Patterson TG i, 1, 7, 11, 15, 228, 229
Patterson, CH 34, 45, 75, 82, 157, 159
Pavis S 72, 82
Pelletier KR 139, 145
Perls FS 75, 82, 171, 173
personality
  and behavior, theory of 18, 155
  change 26
  disorder 162
  Rogers' theory of 104, 155
person-centred
  anthropology 84, 85
  approach
    as empirically based 13
    is political 232
    and research 12
  image of the human being 84
  literature i
  model of health 150, 154–5
  personality theory 2, 11
  play therapy 188, 189, 191, 192
  psychology 165
    and health 166
  psychotherapist 144
  psychotherapy 161
  Systems Approach 127
  theory 5, 7, 8, 9, 11, 12, 47
    and positive psychology 11
  training courses 167

persons, meeting of 176, 179
Pert CB 147, 159
Pesce RP 188, 194
Pestana M 164, 173
pesticides 139
Peters H 80, 83
pharmacotherapy 131
phenomenology 163
Phillips A 161, 170, 173
philosophical terms, critique Rogers' use of 76
Piason A 189, 193
Pierson F 195, 201
Pincus HA 59, 60, 61, 66
placebo responses 131
Planck M 133
Plato 93
play therapy 188, 189, 191, 192
Polanyi M 25, 32
politics/al
  aspect to the approach 232
  implications of the PCA ii
  is personal 233
  of psychotherapy 141, 144
positive psychology 1, 4, 72, 161, 164, 227, 228, 230
  and medical model 4
  and person-centred theory 1
  roots of 72
positive regard 12, 23, 25, 107, 110 (see also
    unconditional positive regard)
positivist epistemology 150
potato sprouts 36, 95, 103, 207
poverty 187
presence 86, 92
process
  of becoming 81
  Scale, the 184
  of therapy 178
Proctor G 66, 67, 154, 159
Protagoras 90
protective
  factors 188
  process 188, 189
Prouty G ii, 234
psychiatric model 140
psychiatrists, scientific authority of 58
psychoanalysis 148
psychobiology 71
psychodynamic therapy 175, 176
psychological
  adjustment 106, 167
  and biological research 20
  change 24, 205
  climate 34, 167

Index

created by the therapist 23
contact 197
distress 4, 47, 49, 59, 60, 192
functioning, healthy 8
health 73, 157
science 140
psychology 232
  abnormal 153
  American 150
  developmental 71, 188
  and health, role between 154, 161ff
  and psychotherapy, history of 165
psychopathology 4, 165
psychosis 27, 157
psychosomatics 71
psychotherapeutic change 12
  processes of 11
psychotherapy
  is dialogue 98
  individual 66, 87, 169
  paradigm shift in 140–1
  is political 142, 144, 233
  rationale for 34
  research 11, 33 (see also research)
  Rogers' process scale of 91
  role of actualisation in 41
psychotic process 64
PsycINFO 116

Q
Q-sort adjustment score 25
Quantum Mechanics 133

R
Rablen R 181, 184, 186
Raeburn J 164, 169, 173
Raffaelli M 187, 194
Raskin JD 144, 145
Raskin N 144, 145
Rawsthorne LJ 10, 15
Ray PH 152, 159
reality 155
  is constructed socially 144
  consensual 168
  mechanistic model of 156
reasoning 147
reductionism 137, 139, 232
reductionistic manualized treatments 232
relational depth 86, 195
relationship/s
  between client(s) and therapist 84
  deep 10
  with the Divine 151
  genes and behavior 22
  Inventory 25

is therapy 86
research 12, 31, 34, 46, 61, 86, 97, 131, 142, 157, 181
  and client-centered approach 33
  in developmental psychology 188
  effectiveness studies 189
  empirical studies 12, 157
  findings from Self-Determination Theory 11
  into mental health 166
  meta-analysis of 7
  on personal adjustment in children 165
  qualitative data 189
  quantitative
    measure 189
    studies 157
  on resilience 192
  Self-Determination Theory (SDT) 10, 12
  studies 25
  -supported model of psychotherapy 33, 157
resilience 192
  in disadvantaged children 188
resistance to psychosocial adversities 188
Rice BA 203, 214
Ricken F 89, 100
Rigney M 169, 173
Rogers CR i, 2, 3, 8, 10, 12, 17, 33, 45, 71, 72, 73, 102, 155, 159, 204–5, 229
  views on actualisation 34–7, 46–7, 51, 53, 61, 68, 74–5, 87–8, 94, 104–6, 117, 121
Rogers DE 145
Rosenbaum R 177, 186
Rosenberg M 25, 32
Roth G 9, 10, 13
Roy DE 80, 83
Russell D 160
Rutter M 188, 194
Ryan RM 6, 7, 9, 10, 11, 12, 14, 15
Ryan W 151, 160

S
sadism 203, 208
Sameroff AJ 9, 14
Sanders G 197, 202
Sanders P 5, 15, 61, 67, 196, 200, 202
Sanford R 35
sanity 161
Santos EC 187, 188, 194
Sartre JP 88
schizophrenia 59
schizophrenic
  group 25
  individuals 25
Schmid PF i, 80, 83, 84, 85, 86, 87, 91, 92, 96, 97, 98, 99, 100, 127, 130, 154, 160, 167, 174, 231

Saint Paul 149
Schnabe A 222
Schneider C 204, 214
Schneider K 195, 201
Schwartz W 9, 14
science
    mechanistic 116
    normal 133
    Western 120, 123, 126
scientific claims psychologists 204
Seeman J 13, 116, 126, 130, 153, 156, 157, 160, 165, 174
Selby CE 181, 186
self 69, 72, 196
    -actualisation 2, 3, 8, 10, 11, 12, 36, 46, 104, 169
        and Kurt Goldstein 117
        and unitary actualisation 102
    -awareness 36
    -concept 2, 46, 103, 109, 169
        freedom of choice of the 88
        plurality of 51
    configurations of 52
    -criticism 177
    -defence 49
    -Determination Theory (SDT) 5, 6, 8, 7, 9, 10, 11, 12, 229
    -directed behavior 103
    -disclosure 177
    -esteem 164, 188
        lower levels of 187
    -experience 109
    -fulfilling prophecies 141
    -healing 152, 175, 178, 233
    -limiting factors 52
    -maintenance 49
    -organization 116
    as psychological construct 117
    -psychology 80
    -regard 188
        conditional 9, 107
        unconditional positive 109
    -regulation 141
    -righting power of development 192
    -structure 47, 48
    -understanding 103
Seligman MEP 1, 7, 15, 73, 74, 83
sensory deprivation 19
sexism 120
sexual
    diversity ii, 195, 196
    gratification 53
    urges 29
Shapiro A 74, 82

Shapiro DA 33, 45, 157, 159
Sheldon KM 7, 11, 12, 15, 16
Shlien J 61, 67, 159
Shorter E 145
Shostrom EL 179, 186
Siegel DJ 80, 83
Skinner BF 134
sleep disorders 59
Smith B 195, 201
Smith RS 188, 194
Snyder CR 4, 11, 15, 61, 67
social
    behaviour, constructive 37
    construction of reality 136, 144
    constructionists 151
    and cultural factors 4
    -environmental
        conditions 5
        factors and 10
        relationship conditions 12
    forces 120
    functioning 165, 168
    isolation 190
    nature of human beings 79
    well-being 73
    and physical reality 165
societal pressures creating conditions of worth 153
societies, Western 161
Southwell E 223–226
spirituality 151
Spotts JE 25, 32
Standal SW 109, 115, 203, 214
stem cells 46
Stevens JO 80, 83
stimulation, absence of 19
Stoler N 26, 32
Stolorow RD 80, 83
Strengths and Difficulties Questionnaire 189
suicide 157, 187
Sullivan HS 165
Summers G 80, 83
systems
    science 119
    theory i, 133–5, 156
Szasz T 58, 61, 67

T

Taft J 76, 83, 169
Tallman K 86, 91, 97, 99, 175, 182, 185, 186
Talmon M 177, 186
Tausch R 8, 12, 13, 188, 193
Teilhard de Chardin P 96, 101
television consumption 10
Tengland P-A 164, 174

Index

theological exegesis 149
therapeutic
    alliance 131
    attitudes 39
    change 8
    conditions 76, 106
    process 197
    relationship 85, 168
        dialogical nature of 84, 85
    nature of 72
therapist/s
    attitudinal qualities of 35
    briefly trained 73
    and client congruence i
    congruence of 24, 25, 102, 106, 198
        begets client congruence 113
    empathy and 23, 40
    role of the 5, 38
    regard, unconditionality of 23
therapy
    aims of 72
    co-creating 86
    de-centering 126
    observations in 102
    as personalization 97
    relationship 84, 86, 169
    theory of 85
Thorne B 48, 52, 53, 54, 55, 86, 88, 99, 196, 200, 201
Thou–I relationship 85
thought, Eastern 152
Tillich P 163, 226
Timothy 149
Tolman EC 71, 83
Torah, the 57
total ecology model 134
Truax CB 12, 16, 25, 32, 145
trust 40, 121, 126, 230
    in the client 33, 39, 41, 42, 103, 203, 204
    in the client's tendency to grow 38, 40, 103, 105, 152, 156, 229, 231
    in his (or her) organism 28, 30, 38, 64, 78
Tudor K i, ii, 69, 71, 73, 74, 75, 76, 78, 80, 83, 87, 88, 94, 101, 164, 165, 169, 174, 230

U

unconditional positive regard (UPR) 4, 33, 39, 40, 44, 62, 63, 79, 102, 106, 107, 190, 199, 229, 230, 232
unitary actualizing tendency 102, 105, 110, 112, 231
United States
    Declaration of Independence 149
    Joint Commission on Mental Illness 164

V

values 2, 5, 142
Van Belle HA 35, 45, 78, 83, 113, 115, 163, 174
Van Werde D 168, 174
Vansteenkiste M 6, 12, 14, 16
vascular dementia 59
Ventura M 169, 173
verbs 77, 78, 80
Verner D 187, 194
victim, blame the 151, 152
violence 203, 213
Vitz P 168, 174

W

Wakefield JC 144, 145
Walker A 181, 184, 186
Wallach L 66, 67
Wallach MA 66, 67
Wang C-C i, 61, 66, 231
Wann TW 163, 174
Watson J 199, 201
Weischedel W 89, 101
Werner EE 71, 188, 194
Werner H 83
Western Intellectual Tradition 148–50, 151
Wheeler RH 71, 83
White RW 20, 32
Whitehead AN 71, 74, 78, 79, 83, 170, 174
Whitney NJ 169, 174
wholeness 152
Whyte LL 28, 29, 30, 32
Wilkins P 87, 101, 154, 160, 195, 202
Winnicott 161, 164
Wolter-Gustafson C ii, 155, 160, 232
Wood JK 130
working alliance 142
World Health Organisation 138, 145
    manifesto on health promotion (Ottawa Charter) 132
Worrall M 69, 71, 74, 75, 76, 78, 80, 83, 88, 94, 101, 174
Worsley R 4, 14
Wyatt G 99, 116, 130, 185, 186, 200, 202

Y

Yahweh (YWHW) 58, 65

Z

Zax M 9, 14
Zimring FM 8, 12, 13, 188, 193
Zucconi A i, 143, 144, 146, 180, 232
Zuckerman M 8, 9, 14